Rothstei

Rick Steves®

BEST OF
IRELAND

Rick Steves & Pat O'Connor

Contents

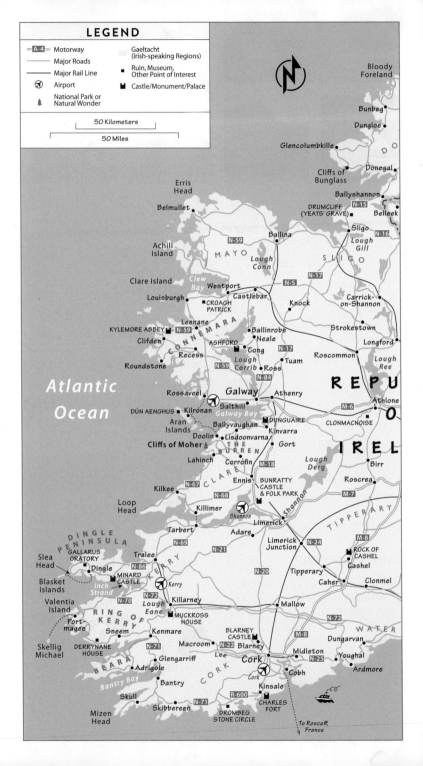

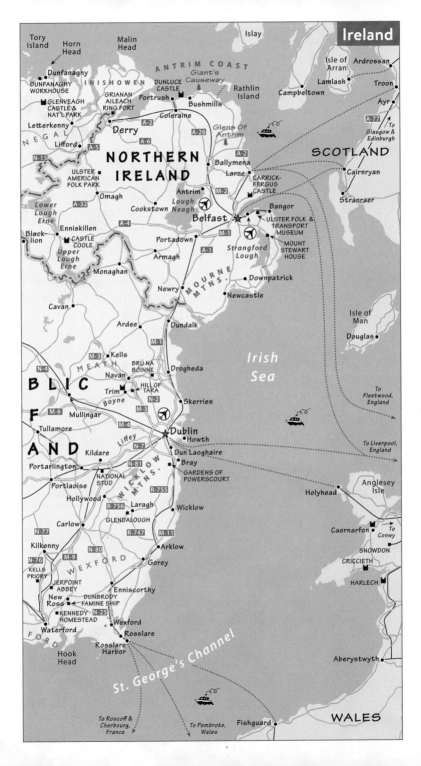

Introduction

Flung onto the foggy fringe of the Atlantic pond like a mossy millstone, Ireland drips with mystery, drawing you in for a closer look. You won't find the proverbial pot of gold, but you will treasure the engaging and feisty Irish people. Irish culture—with its unique language, intricate art, and mesmerizing music—is as intoxicating as the famous Irish brew, Guinness.

The Irish revere their past and love their proverbs (such as "When God made time, he made a lot of it"). Ireland is dusted with prehistoric stone circles, beehive huts, and standing stones—some older than the pyramids. While much of Europe has buried older cultures under new, Ireland still reveals its cultural bedrock.

Today's Ireland is vibrant, cosmopolitan, and complex. The small island (about the size of Maine) holds two distinctly different Irelands: the Republic of Ireland (an independent nation that's mainly Catholic) and Northern Ireland (part of the United Kingdom, roughly half Protestant and half Catholic). No visit is complete without a look at both.

Want to really get to know Ireland? Belly up to the bar in a neighborhood pub and engage a local in conversation. The Irish have a worldwide reputation as talkative, musical, moody romantics with a quick laugh and a ready smile. Come join them.

THE BEST OF IRELAND

In this selective book, I recommend Ireland's top destinations—a mix of lively cities, cozy towns, and natural wonders—along with the best sights and experiences they have to offer.

The biggie on everyone's list is Dublin, the energetic, friendly capital of the Republic of Ireland. But there's so much more to see. The island is dotted with Celtic and Christian ruins, cliffside fortresses, and prehistoric sites. Brú na Bóinne's burial mounds are older than Stonehenge. There's the proud town of Kilkenny, the historic Rock of Cashel, colorful Kinsale, and two peninsula loops: the famous Ring of Kerry and the more intimate Dingle Peninsula. Youthful Galway is a good launch pad for dramatic scenery: the sheer Cliffs of Moher (in County Clare) and craggy Aran Islands.

In Northern Island, historic Belfast sheds light on the political Troubles that once bitterly divided this country. The lush Antrim Coast delights visitors, with fun-loving Portrush serving as a handy home base.

Beyond the major destinations, I'll briefly cover the Best of the Rest—great destinations that don't quite make my top cut, but are worth seeing if you have more time or specific interests: Wicklow

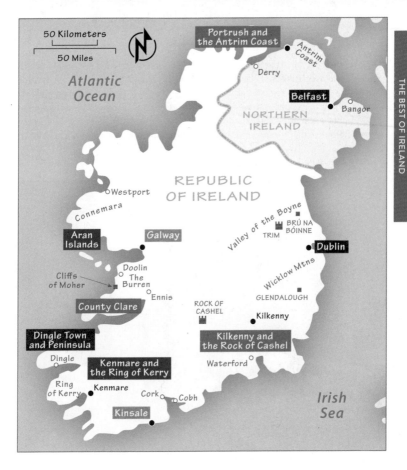

50 Kilometers

50 Miles

N

Atlantic
Ocean

Portrush and
the Antrim Coast

Antrim
Coast

Derry

Belfast

Bangor

NORTHERN
IRELAND

REPUBLIC
OF IRELAND

Westport

Connemara

Valley of the Boyne

BRÚ NA
BÓINNE
TRIM

**Aran
Islands**

Galway

Dublin

Doolin
The
Burren

Cliffs
of Moher

Ennis

Wicklow Mtns

GLENDALOUGH

County Clare

ROCK OF
CASHEL

Kilkenny

**Dingle Town
and Peninsula**

**Kilkenny and
the Rock of Cashel**

Dingle

**Kenmare and
the Ring of Kerry**

Waterford

Ring
of Kerry

Kenmare

Cork

Cobh

Kinsale

Irish
Sea

Mountains, the region of Connemara, and
the town of Derry.

To help you link the top sights, I've
designed a two-week itinerary (on page
24), with tips to help you tailor it to your
interests and time.

THE BEST OF DUBLIN

The bustling capital of the Republic of Ireland is a fascinating concoction of treasured Dark Age gospels, Celtic artifacts, and rambunctious pubs. It shows its heart in its sights—from the Kilmainham Gaol (jail where the English imprisoned Irish activists) to the Guinness Storehouse, which deifies the national beer. Its musical tradition and a writers' heritage fuel trad and literary pub crawls. While its greatest sight is the medieval Book of Kells, the best thing about Dublin is its people.

❶ *Christ Church Cathedral* sits atop Norman crypts and anchors the historic heart of Dublin.

❷ The friendly pulse of this vibrant city is best felt in its many **traditional pubs.**

❸ The **Ha' Penny Bridge,** just beyond the inn, replaced ferries and charged locals a half-penny toll.

❹ *Dublin Castle* was the center of dominant English control in Ireland for almost eight centuries.

❺ The popular **Musical Pub Crawl** introduces Irish traditional sessions to tune-loving travelers.

❻ Monastic scribes copying scriptures painstakingly created the **Book of Kells** during the Dark Ages.

❼ *Grafton Street* is a pedestrian shopping mecca, inviting for a stroll on a sunny day.

THE BEST OF KILKENNY AND THE ROCK OF CASHEL

Two fine stops between Dublin and Dingle are medieval Kilkenny and the massive Rock of Cashel. Kilkenny is a sturdy, hardworking town, with a castle, cathedral, and atmospheric pubs featuring live traditional folk music. The evocative Rock of Cashel has majestic hill-topping ruins that you can explore and ponder. South of Kilkenny, you can make excursions to an old abbey, a replica of a famine ship, and the birthplace of Waterford crystal.

❶ *The ruins of the* **Rock of Cashel** *are the most evocative sight in Ireland's interior.*

❷ **Waterford's crystal craftsmanship** *draws enthusiastic visitors from around the world.*

❸ *Colorful shop fronts and unpretentious pubs line the medieval streets of* **Kilkenny.**

THE BEST OF KINSALE

Quaint Kinsale has served as a port since prehistoric times. Stroll the pedestrian-friendly medieval quarter and take the excellent walking tour that makes the town's history come alive. The squat Charles Fort on the harbor offers great bay views and an engrossing museum that covers rugged British military life. Kinsale is also Ireland's gourmet capital; try to fit in three meals. Nearby, the historic town of Cobh has a special appeal for visitors with Irish roots.

❶ Kinsale, long a historic port, has a fun, fresh look.

❷ Cobh's docks once creaked with Titanic passengers and US-bound emigrants.

❸ Walking tours transform Kinsale's back lanes with tales of former maritime glory.

THE BEST OF KENMARE AND THE RING OF KERRY

The colorful town of Kenmare, known for tidiness and lacework, is a good base for side-stepping the throngs flocking to Ireland's famous scenic loop. Allow a full day to tour the 120-mile Ring of Kerry, exploring ancient ring forts, peaceful towns with names like Sneem and Portmagee, and dramatic islands. Time it right and drive clockwise around the peninsula to avoid the parade of tour buses going in the opposite direction.

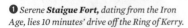

❶ *Serene **Staigue Fort,** dating from the Iron Age, lies 10 minutes' drive off the Ring of Kerry.*

❷ *Visitors to **sheep ranches** can observe shearing and shepherd-dog training.*

❸ ***Muckross House** hosted Queen Elizabeth I and attracts garden lovers today.*

❹ ***Kenmare** offers a respite from crowds and a base for exploring the Ring of Kerry.*

THE BEST OF DINGLE TOWN AND PENINSULA

My favorite Gaelic village—Dingle—welcomes you to my favorite Irish peninsula. Wander the town's charming lanes, check out the stained-glass windows in the chapel, look for the resident dolphin in the harbor, and sound out the Gaelic signs. You're in a Gaeltacht, a region where the traditional Irish language and ways are prized. The 30-mile loop around the peninsula is awash with beehive huts, prehistoric stone pillars, and ancient ring forts. Look up to see the rugged hills; look down to see the surging waves. And slow down...to take it all in.

❶ *A* bodhrán *drum, sold at Dingle's music shops, helps keep the beat in* **traditional Irish music.**

❷ *The cute, colorful* **town of Dingle** *delights travelers.*

❸ **Fungi the dolphin** *is a playful ambassador for boat tours around Dingle harbor.*

❹ *Early Christians gathered on the peninsula at holy places like* **Gallarus Oratory.**

❺ *Art Nouveau stained-glass artistry adorns Dingle's convent* **chapel of Díseart.**

THE BEST OF COUNTY CLARE

This county on the rugged western coast offers the thrilling Cliffs of Moher, prehistoric structures in the wildflower wonderland of the Burren, and several musical towns. Little Doolin attracts music lovers with a trio of trad pubs, while Kinvarra hosts a medieval banquet for the lord or lady in you.

❶ The 650-foot-high **Cliffs of Moher** drop dramatically into the Atlantic.

❷ **Dunguaire Castle,** standing sentry beside Galway Bay, offers memorable castle banquets.

❸ The little crossroads of **Doolin** sports lively **trad music sessions** in three steamy pubs.

❹ In **the Burren,** the **Poulnabrone Dolmen** was a tomb built 5,000 years ago.

THE BEST OF GALWAY

Galway is a youthful university town with a great street scene and lively nightlife, punctuated by pubs and street musicians. It's also a springboard to the Cliffs of Moher and the Burren to the south, the Aran Islands offshore, and the region of Connemara to the north.

❶ *Banners for the original 14 Norman founding "tribes" of Galway grace* **Eyre Square.**

❷ *The* **Spanish Arch** *slices through the town's medieval wall.*

❸ *A youthful international college population energizes Galway's* **pedestrian corridor.**

❹ *Proud Irish step dancing is fun to watch in Galway's* **music pubs.**

THE BEST OF THE ARAN ISLANDS

The windswept Aran Islands have a stark and rugged beauty. From Galway, make a memorable crossing to Inishmore. The island has simple towns, hiking trails, and a slew of early churches, but all roads lead to Dún Aenghus, an Iron Age fort at the edge of a high cliff. The smaller island of Inisheer, with a hilltop castle, church ruins, and an evocative shipwreck, makes a fine excursion from Doolin.

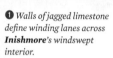

❶ Walls of jagged limestone define winding lanes across **Inishmore**'s windswept interior.

❷ Islander-owned minivans greet travelers at the dock and scoot them efficiently around Inishmore.

❸ A thousand years ago, devoted pilgrims flocked to Inishmore and rest now near the **Seven Churches.**

❹ The small isle of **Inisheer** sees fewer visitors and offers peaceful solitude to modern hermits.

THE BEST OF BELFAST

Once the center of the Troubles, the no-nonsense capital of Northern Ireland has come a long way. Political murals depict its fractured past, but today's Belfast has a hopeful future, with bustling pedestrian zones, a cosmopolitan restaurant scene, and a bold, shiny *Titanic* museum that draws crowds.

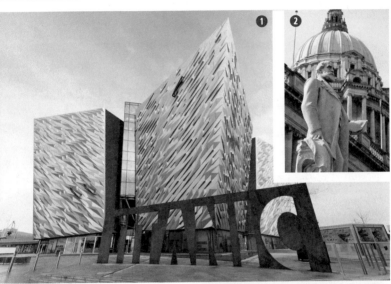

❶ *The high-tech* **Titanic exhibition** *tells one of history's most famous stories.*

❷ *The stately* **Victorian grandeur** *of City Hall hints at former Industrial Revolution wealth.*

❸ *Rural craftsmanship is kept alive in simple village dwellings at* **Cultra Folk Park.**

❹ *The historic* **Crown Liquor Saloon** *offers private snugs in which to enjoy your mellow pint.*

THE BEST OF PORTRUSH AND THE ANTRIM COAST

With old-time amusement arcades and waterfront dining, the small-town beach resort of Portrush is the gateway to the wonders of the lovely Antrim Coast. Explore the stunning basalt Giant's Causeway, stroll the ruins of Dunluce Castle, and test your nerve crossing the Carrick-a-Rede Rope Bridge, suspended high over a watery channel below.

❶ *Unpretentious* **Portrush** *thrives on summer crowds exploring the scenic Antrim Coast.*

❷ *Hikers and birdwatchers thrill to the lofty* **Carrick-a-Rede Rope Bridge.**

❸ **Dunluce Castle** *perches on a sea stack accessed by a strategic bridge.*

THE BEST OF THE REST

With extra time or interest, splice any of the following destinations into your trip. Glendalough takes you back in time to a monastic settlement dating from the 10th to the 12th century. The region of Connemara has abbey ruins, a lakeside mansion, a pilgrimage mountain, and the genteel town of Westport. Derry is a revitalized Northern Ireland town that's come to terms with the Troubles.

❶ *St. Kevin's leafy monastery at **Glendalough** nestles in the **Wicklow Mountains.***

❷ ***Derry** has stout town walls, an excellent history museum, and passionate murals.*

❸ ***Connemara**'s rugged vistas attract painters, naturalists, hikers, and photographers.*

❹ *Prim **Westport** makes a good stop or a home base when exploring Connemara.*

TRAVEL SMART

Approach Ireland like a veteran traveler, even if it's your first trip. Design your itinerary, get a handle on your budget, line up your documents, and follow my travel strategies on the road.

Designing an Itinerary

Choose your top destinations. My itinerary (on page 24) gives you an idea of how much you can reasonably see in 14 days, but you can adapt it to fit your own interests and time frame. Rollicking Dublin is a must. Seekers of nonstop beauty visit the Republic's rugged west coast—the Dingle Peninsula, Ring of Kerry, Cliffs of Moher, and Aran Islands—and Northern Ireland's Antrim Coast. Historians can choose among sights prehistoric (such as Boyne Valley and the Burren), medieval (Rock of Cashel and Glendalough), and recent (Belfast for the Troubles). Music

lovers follow their ear to pubs playing live traditional music. The top musical towns are—in this order—Dingle, Doolin, Galway, Westport, and Dublin. Photographers want to go just about everywhere.

Decide when to go. Peak season, July and August, offers long days, the best weather, and a busy schedule of tourist fun. Shoulder-season travelers (May, early June, Sept, and early Oct) experience smaller crowds, decent weather, and all the sights and fun. Off-season, November through April, prices drop, but activities are fewer and sights have limited hours or are closed entirely. Plan for rain no matter when you go. Ireland is as far north as central Canada.

Connect the dots. Link your destinations into a logical route. Determine which cities in Europe you'll fly into and out of (begin your search for flights at Kayak. com). All direct flights from the US to Ireland land in Dublin, Shannon, or Belfast; cautious drivers may find Shannon Airport to be a less stressful entry or exit point into or out of Ireland than Dublin.

Decide if you'll be traveling by car, public transportation, or a combination. A car is particularly helpful for exploring the interior and peninsulas (where public transportation can be sparse), but is useless in cities (park it). If relying on public transportation, these destinations are easiest—Dublin, Dingle, Galway, Aran Islands, and Belfast—using a combination of trains, buses, taxis, and minibus tours, plus a flight or boat to the islands. Trains don't cover the entire island, and bus travel is slow due to multiple connections and/or frequent stops (carefully check route options and schedules online).

If your trip extends beyond Ireland, look into budget flights rather than automatically going with a ferry-and-train combination (check Skyscanner.com for cheap flights within Europe).

Fine-tune your itinerary. Figure out how many destinations you can comfortably fit in the time you have. Don't overdo

Rick Steves Audio Europe

My free Rick Steves Audio Europe app makes it easy to download audio content to enhance your trip. This includes my audio tours of many of Europe's top destinations, as well as a far-reaching library of insightful travel interviews from my public radio show with experts from around the globe—including many of the places in this book. The app and all of its content are entirely free. You can download Rick Steves Audio Europe via Apple's App Store, Google Play, or the Amazon Appstore. For more information, see www.ricksteves.com/audioeurope.

Average Daily Expenses Per Person: $155

Cost	Category	Notes
$50	Meals	$20 for lunch and $30 for dinner
$65	Lodging	Based on two people splitting the cost of a $130 double room that includes breakfast (solo travelers pay about $100 per room)
$35	Sights and Entertainment	Figure $10-15 per major sight, $5 for minor ones, and $50-75 for splurges
$5	City Transit	Buses or metro
$155	**Total**	(Allow more for Dublin)

it—few travelers wish they'd hurried more. Allow enough days per destination. Check if any holidays or festivals will fall during your trip—these attract crowds and can close sights (for the latest, visit Ireland's website, www.ireland.com).

Even if you're flying into Dublin Airport, you don't need to start your trip in Dublin. You could pick up a car at the airport and drive to Trim for a gentler small-town start, and let Dublin be the finale (after you've returned the car back at the airport), when you're rested and ready to tackle the big city.

If you have time for only one idyllic peninsula on your trip, choose the Dingle Peninsula over the famous Ring of Kerry. If you want to include both, this book will help you do it efficiently and enjoyably.

For detailed suggestions on how to

THE BEST OF IRELAND IN 2 WEEKS

This unforgettable trip will show you the very best Ireland has to offer.

DAY	PLAN	SLEEP IN
	Arrive in Dublin	Dublin
1	Sightsee Dublin	Dublin
2	Dublin	Dublin
3	Rent a car, drive to Kilkenny for lunch, visit the Rock of Cashel, and end in Kinsale	Kinsale
4	Kinsale	Kinsale
5	Drive to Kenmare for lunch, then visit sheep farm and Muckross House, and end in Dingle Town	Dingle
6	Dingle Town	Dingle
7	Drive the Dingle Peninsula loop	Dingle
8	Drive to the Cliffs of Moher, then through the Burren, ending in Galway	Galway
9	Day-trip by plane or boat to Inishmore (Aran Islands)	Galway
10	Drive to Portrush, stopping en route at either the Connemara sights or town of Derry	Portrush
11	Antrim Coast	Portrush
12	Drive to Belfast	Belfast
13	Belfast	Belfast
14	Drive to Valley of the Boyne and visit Brú na Bóinne	Trim
	Return car and fly home	

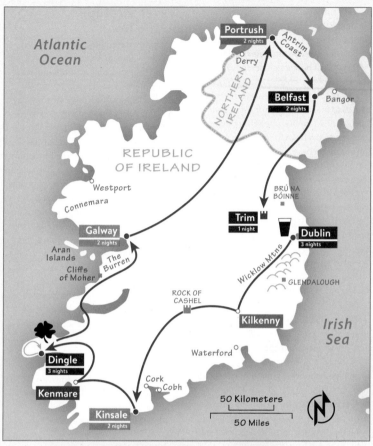

Atlantic Ocean

Portrush
2 nights

Antrim Coast

Derry

NORTHERN IRELAND

Belfast
2 nights

Bangor

REPUBLIC OF IRELAND

Westport

Connemara

BRÚ NA BÓINNE

Trim
1 night

Dublin
3 nights

Galway
2 nights

Aran Islands

Cliffs of Moher

The Burren

Wicklow Mtns

GLENDALOUGH

ROCK OF CASHEL

Kilkenny

Irish Sea

Waterford

Dingle
3 nights

Kenmare

Cork

Cobh

Kinsale
2 nights

50 Kilometers

50 Miles

spend your time, I've included day plans for destinations in the chapters that follow.

Balance intense and relaxed days. After a day of hectic sightseeing, plan for some downtime. Follow up big cities with laid-back towns. Minimize one-night stands to maximize rootedness; it's worth taking a drive (or bus ride) after dinner to get settled in a town for two nights. Staying in a home base (like Galway) and making day trips can be more time-efficient than changing locations and hotels.

Give yourself some slack. Every trip—and every traveler—needs slack time (laundry, picnics, people-watching, and so on). Many travelers greatly underestimate this. You can't see it all, so pace yourself. Assume you will return.

Ready, set... You've designed the perfect itinerary for the trip of a lifetime.

Trip Costs per Person

Run a reality check on your dream trip. You'll have major transportation costs in addition to daily expenses.

Flight: A round-trip flight from the US to Dublin costs about $1,200-1,600.

Car Rental: Figure on a minimum of $300 per week, not including tolls, gas, parking, and insurance. Rentals are cheapest if arranged from the US.

Public Transportation: For a two-week trip, allow $200 per person. You will generally save money by buying train and bus tickets in Ireland rather than using a rail pass (for more, see page 355).

Budget Tips: It's easy to cut your daily costs (to about $100/day), particularly outside of Dublin. Cultivate the art of picnicking, stay in hostels or basic hotels, and see only the sights you most want to see. When you splurge, choose a special experience you'll always remember (such as a flight to the Aran Islands or the medieval banquet in Kinvarra). Minimize souvenir shopping—how will you get it all home? Focus instead on collecting lifelong and wonderful memories.

Travel Strategies on the Road

Be your own tour guide. As you travel, get up-to-date info on sights, reserve tickets and tours, reconfirm hotels and travel arrangements, and check transit connections. Upon arrival in a new town, lay the groundwork for a smooth departure; confirm the train, bus, or road you'll take when you leave. You can find out the latest by checking with tourist-information offices (TIs) and your hoteliers, and doing research on your own by phone or online.

Take advantage of deals. You'll find deals throughout Ireland (and mentioned in this book). For example, early-bird dinners at nice restaurants are often a great value. City transit passes (for multiple rides or all-day usage) lessen your cost per ride. To take the financial bite out of sightseeing, consider combo-tickets and sightseeing passes that cover multiple museums. Some accommodations give a discount for payment in cash and/or longer stays.

For an inexpensive, genuinely Irish night out, find the pubs in town and follow your ear; live traditional music is a joy to experience for the price of a beer.

Plan for rain. No matter when you go, the weather can change several times in a day. Bring a jacket and dress in layers. Just keep traveling and take full advantage of "bright spells." A spell of rain is the perfect excuse to go into a pub and meet a new friend.

Outsmart thieves. Although theft isn't a major problem outside of Dublin, it's still smart to wear a money belt. Tuck it under your clothes, and keep your cash, credit cards, and passport secure inside it. Carry only a day's spending money in your front pocket. In case of loss or theft, see page 338.

Be proactive to minimize the effects of potential loss: Keep your expensive gear to a minimum. Bring photocopies of important documents (passport and cards) to aid in replacement if they're lost

Before You Go

☐ **Make sure your passport is valid**. If it's due to expire within six months of your ticketed date of return, renew it. Allow up to six weeks to get or renew a passport (www.travel.state.gov).

☐ **Book rooms well in advance,** especially if your trip falls during peak season or any major holidays or festivals. For tips on making hotel reservations, see page 346.

☐ **Consider travel insurance.** Compare the cost of the insurance to the cost of your potential loss. Check whether your existing insurance (health, homeowners, or renters) covers you and your possessions overseas. For tips, see www.ricksteves.com/insurance.

☐ **Call your bank.** Alert your bank that you'll be using your debit and credit cards in Europe; also ask about transaction fees, and get the PIN number for your credit card (see page 339). You won't need to bring along euros or pounds for your trip—instead, withdraw currency from cash machines in Europe.

☐ **Bringing your phone?** Consider an international plan to reduce the cost of calls, texts, and data (or rely on Wi-Fi). See page 351 for different ways to stay connected in Europe.

☐ **Download apps** to your mobile device to use on the road, such as maps, transit schedules, and my free *Rick Steves Audio Europe* app.

☐ **Watt's up?** Bring an electrical adapter with three rectangular prongs (sold at travel stores in the US) to plug into Ireland's outlets. You won't need a convertor because newer electronics—such as tablets, laptops, and battery chargers—are dual voltage and convert automatically to Europe's 220-volt system. Don't bring an old hair dryer or curler; buy a cheapie in Europe.

☐ **Drivers,** there are age restrictions for younger and older drivers; see page 360. Bring your driver's license.

☐ **Pack light.** You'll walk with your luggage far more than you think (see packing list on page 368).

☐ **Refer to the Practicalities chapter,** where you'll find everything you need to know to travel smoothly in Ireland.

☐ **Get updates** to this book at www.ricksteves.com/update.

or stolen. While traveling, back up your digital photos and files frequently.

Guard your time, energy, and trip. Taking a taxi can be a good value if it saves you a long wait for a cheap bus or an exhausting walk across town. To avoid long lines, take advantage of the crowd-beating tips in this book (such as visiting sights early or late). When problems arise (bad food, a late bus, or rainy days), keep things in perspective. You're on vacation...and you're in Ireland!

Connect with the culture. Enjoy the friendliness of the Irish people; most interactions come with an ample side-helping of fun banter. Ask questions—many locals are as interested in you as you are in them. Slow down, step out of your comfort zone, and be open to unexpected experiences. When an interesting opportunity pops up, say "yes."

Rick Steves' Travel Philosophy

Travel is intensified living—maximum thrills per minute and one of the last great sources of legal adventure. Travel is freedom. It's recess, and we need it.

Affording travel is a matter of priorities. (Make do with the old car.) You can eat and sleep—simply, safely, and enjoyably—anywhere in Europe for $100 a day plus transportation costs. In many ways, spending more money only builds a thicker wall between you and what you traveled so far to see. Europe is a cultural carnival, and time after time, you'll find that its best acts are free and the best seats are the cheap ones.

A tight budget forces you to travel close to the ground, meeting and communicating with the people. Never sacrifice sleep, nutrition, safety, or cleanliness to save money. Simply enjoy the local-style alternatives to expensive hotels and restaurants.

Connecting with people carbonates your experience. Extroverts have more fun. If your trip is low on magic moments, kick yourself and make things happen. If you don't enjoy a place, maybe you don't know enough about it. Seek the truth. Recognize tourist traps. Give a culture the benefit of your open mind. See things as different, but not better or worse. Any culture has plenty to share.

Of course, travel, like the world, is a series of hills and valleys. Be fanatically positive and militantly optimistic. If something's not to your liking, change your liking.

Travel can make you a happier American, as well as a citizen of the world. Our Earth is home to seven billion equally precious people. It's humbling to travel and find that other people don't have the "American Dream"—they have their own dreams. Europeans like us, but with all due respect, they wouldn't trade passports.

Thoughtful travel engages us with the world. It reminds us what is truly important. By broadening perspectives, travel teaches new ways to measure quality of life.

Globetrotting destroys ethnocentricity, helping us understand and appreciate other cultures. Rather than fear the diversity on this planet, celebrate it. Among your most prized souvenirs will be the strands of different cultures you choose to knit into your own character. The world is a cultural yarn shop, and we're weaving the ultimate tapestry.

Happy travels! *Taisteal sásta!*

Rick Steves

Key to This Book

Updates

This book is updated regularly—but things change. Once you pin it down, Ireland wiggles. For the latest, visit www.ricksteves.com/update.

Abbreviations and Times

I use the following symbols and abbreviations in this book:

Sights are rated:

▲▲▲ Don't miss

▲▲ Try hard to see

▲ Worthwhile if you can make it

No rating Worth knowing about

Tourist information offices are abbreviated as **TI,** and bathrooms are **WC**s. To categorize accommodations, I use a **Sleep Code** (described on page 344).

Like Europe, this book uses the **24-hour clock.** It's the same through 12:00 noon, and then keeps going: 13:00, 14:00, and so on. For anything over 12, subtract 12 and add p.m. (14:00 is 2:00 p.m.).

When giving **opening times,** I include both peak season and off-season hours if they differ. So, if a museum is listed as "May-Oct daily 9:00-16:00," it should be open from 9 a.m. until 4 p.m. from the first day of May until the last day of October (but expect exceptions).

For **transit** or **tour departures,** I first list the frequency, then the duration. So, a train connection listed as "2/hour, 1.5 hours" departs twice each hour, and the journey lasts an hour and a half.

Map Legend

⅄ Viewpoint	✈ Airport	Tunnel
↑ Entrance	Ⓣ Taxi Stand	Pedestrian Zone
⊕ Tourist Info	▮ Tram Stop	Railway
WC Restroom	Ⓑ Bus Stop	Ferry/Boat Route
⚑ Castle	▼ Pub	Tram
⌂ Church	Ⓟ Parking	Stairs
▪ Statue/Point of Interest	)(Mtn. Pass	Walk/Tour Route
⊠ Elevator	Park	Trail

Republic

The modern Irish state has existed since 1922, but its inhabitants proudly claim their nation to be the only contemporary independent state to sprout from purely Celtic roots (sprinkled with a few Vikings and shipwrecked Spanish Armada sailors for good measure). The Romans never bothered to come over and organize the wild Irish. Through the persuasive and culturally enlightened approach of early missionaries such as St. Patrick, Ireland is one of the very few countries to have initially converted to Christianity without much bloodshed. The religious carnage came a thousand years later, with the Reformation. Irish culture absorbed the influences of Viking raiders and Norman soldiers of fortune, eventually enduring the 750-year shadow of English domination.

Just a few decades ago, Ireland was an isolated, agricultural economic backwater that had largely missed out on the Industrial Revolution. Things began to turn around when Ireland joined the European Community (precursor to the EU) in 1973. The Irish government instituted farsighted tax laws, including a corporate tax rate of only 12.5 percent (compared to 35 percent in the US) to entice foreign corporations to set up shop here. It proved so successful in attracting US business that America has now invested more in Ireland than in Brazil, India, Russia, and China combined.

# of Ireland

Today, the Republic of Ireland attracts expatriates return-ing to their homeland and new foreign investment. As the only officially English-speaking country to have adopted the euro currency (Britain uses the pound), Ireland makes an efficient base from which to access the European marketplace. Nearly 35 percent of the Irish population is under 25 years old, leading many high-tech and pharmaceutical firms to locate here, taking advantage of this young, well-educated labor force. And during the Celtic Tiger economic boom, Ireland became a destination for immigrants—mostly from the Third World and the newer EU nations. Eastern Europeans (especially Poles) came in search of higher pay...a reversal from the days when many Irish fled to start new lives abroad.

As time passes, relations between Ireland and her former colonial master Britain are starting to heal. In May 2011, Queen Elizabeth II became the first British monarch to visit the Repub-lic of Ireland since Ireland's 1922 split from the United Kingdom, which occurred during her grandfather's reign. Her four-night visit unexpectedly charmed the Irish people and did much to repair old wounds between the two countries, which are now, in the words of the Queen, "equal partners and good neighbors."

Republic of Ireland Almanac

Official Name: The Republic of Ireland (a.k.a. just "Ireland" or, in Irish, Éire).

Population: Ireland's 4.6 million people (same as Louisiana) are of Celtic stock. They speak English, though Irish Gaelic is spoken in pockets along the country's west coast. Nearly nine in 10 are nominally Catholic, though only one in three attends church.

Latitude and Longitude: 53°N and 8°W. The latitude is equivalent to Alberta, Canada.

Area: With 27,000 square miles—half the size of New York State—it occupies the southern 80 percent of the island of Ireland. The country is small enough that radio broadcasts manage to cover traffic snarls nationwide.

Geography: The isle is mostly flat, ringed by a hilly coastline. The climate is moderate, with cloudy skies about every other day.

Biggest Cities: The capital of Dublin (1.1 million) is the only big city; more than one in four Irish live in the greater Dublin area. Cork has 190,000 people, while Limerick has about 91,000 and Galway about 76,000.

Economy: The Gross Domestic Product is $225 billion, and the GDP per capita is $46,800—one of Europe's highest and nearly 10 percent more than Britain's. Major moneymakers include tourism and exports (especially to the US and UK) of machines, medicine, Guinness, glassware, crystal ware, and software. Traditional agriculture (potatoes and other root vegetables) is fading fast, but dairy still does well.

Government: The elected president, Michael Higgins, appoints the Taoiseach (TEE-shock) or prime minister (currently Enda Kenny), who is nominated by Parliament. The Parliament consists of the 60-seat Senate, chosen by an electoral college, and the House of Representatives, with 166 seats apportioned after the people vote for a party. Major parties include Fianna Fáil, Fine Gael, and Sinn Fein, the political arm of the (fading) Irish Republican Army. Ireland is divided into 28 administrative counties—including Kerry, Clare, Cork, Limerick, and so on.

The Average Irish: A typical Irish person is 5'7", 35 years old, has two kids, and will live to be 80. An Irish citizen consumes nearly five pounds of tea per year and spends $5 on alcohol each day.

The flag of the Republic of Ireland

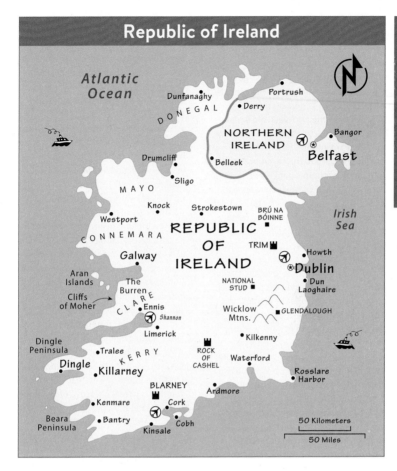

Republic of Ireland

Atlantic Ocean

Dunfanaghy

Portrush

Derry

DONEGAL

NORTHERN IRELAND

Bangor

Drumcliff

Belleek

Belfast

Sligo

MAYO

Knock

Strokestown

BRÚ NA BÓINNE

Irish Sea

Westport

REPUBLIC

CONNEMARA

OF

TRIM

Howth

Galway

IRELAND

Dublin

Aran Islands

The Burren

NATIONAL STUD

Dun Laoghaire

Cliffs of Moher

CLARE

Ennis

Wicklow Mtns.

GLENDALOUGH

Shannon

Limerick

Kilkenny

Dingle Peninsula

Tralee

KERRY

ROCK OF CASHEL

Waterford

Dingle

Killarney

BLARNEY

Rosslare Harbor

Kenmare

Ardmore

Beara Peninsula

Bantry

Cork

Cobh

Kinsale

50 Kilometers

50 Miles

Just a couple of days after the Queen's visit, Barack Obama dropped in for a brief 12-hour stop, guided by former American ambassador to Ireland (and Pittsburgh Steelers owner) Dan Rooney. Being one-sixteenth Irish, O'Bama made sure to helicopter into his ancestral home village of Moneygall in County Offaly and have a pint with Henry, his cousin eight times removed, whom he nicknamed "Henry VIII." Later that day, he delivered a speech to a huge crowd packed into Dublin's College Green, drawing cheers when he dusted off his Irish Gaelic and proclaimed, "Is féidir linn." ("Yes we can.")

Don't worry if your Irish Gaelic is rustier than the president's—the vast majority of Irish people speak English, though you'll still encounter Irish Gaelic if you venture to the western fringe of the country. The Irish love of conversation shines through wherever you go. All that conversation is helped along by the nebulous concept of Irish time, which never seems to be in short supply. Small shops post their hours as "9:00ish until 5:00ish." The local bus usually makes a stop at "10:30ish." A healthy disdain for being a slave to the clock seems to be part of being Ir-"ish." And the warm welcome you'll receive has its roots in ancient Celtic laws of hospitality toward stranded strangers. You'll see

"Céad míle fáilte" in tourism brochures and postcards throughout Ireland— it translates as "a hundred thousand welcomes."

Time marches on for the Irish government as well. In 2013, the Irish people voted (by a thin 52 percent majority) not to abolish their 90-year-old Senate (Seanad; SHAN-ud), the upper house of the Irish Parliament. The Irish government itself had proposed this revolutionary solution to economic hard times, saying that it would have saved taxpayers €20 million per year. But opponents of the referendum said the Senate was necessary as a watchdog to hold cabinet ministers accountable.

The resilient Irish character was born of dark humor, historical reverence, and a scrappy, "we'll get 'em next time" rebel spirit. The influence of the Catholic Church is less apparent these days, as 30 percent of Irish weddings are now civil ceremonies. But the Church still plays a part in Irish life. The average Irish family spends almost €500 on celebrations for each of their children's first communions. And the national radio and TV station, RTE, pauses for 30 seconds at noon and at 18:00 to broadcast the chimes of the Angelus bells—signaling the start of Catholic devotional prayers. The Irish say that if you're phoning heaven, it's a long-distance call from the rest of the world, but a local call from Ireland.

RTE: The Voice of Ireland

Many a long drive or rainy evening has been saved by the engaging programs I've happened upon on RTE: Raidió Teilifís Éireann. What the BBC is to Britain, RTE is to Ireland: This government-owned company and national public broadcaster produces and broadcasts a wide range of programs on television, radio, and online. Look for it as you travel (via RTE's smartphone apps, on the radio in your car, or on TV at your B&B).

First hitting the airwaves on New Year's Eve 1961, today's RTE TV broadcasts are all digital and in the English language on RTE channels one and two. But don't shy away from channel four (TG4), with Irish language TV shows subtitled in English—it's a great way to get a feel for the sound of the language. You couldn't find a richer or more accessible introduction to Irish culture.

Got a serious appetite for all things Irish? Online at www.rte.ie/archives, you'll find a treasure trove of fascinating archived RTE programs—everything from coverage of JFK's 1963 visit, to elderly recollections of the 1916 Uprising, to the poetry of Seamus Heaney, to Gaelic sports.

Dublin's Leinster House, seat of Irish government

RTE broadcaster

Dingle Peninsula

Dublin

With its stirring history and rich culture, Ireland's capital holds its own in arts, entertainment, food, and fun. This fair city will have you humming, "Cockles and mussels, alive, alive-O."

Dublin, the seat of English rule in Ireland for 750 years, was the heart of a "civilized" Anglo-Irish area known as "the Pale." Anything "beyond the Pale" was considered uncultured and almost barbaric...purely Irish. During the 18th century, the British Empire was in its glory days, and Dublin was right there with it, becoming an elegant capital. Squares and boulevards built in the Neoclassical, Georgian style gave the city an air of grandeur. The National Museum, the National Gallery, and many government buildings are in the Georgian section of town. Few buildings (notably Christ Church and St. Patrick's cathedrals) survive from before this period.

But nationalism—and a realization of the importance of human rights—would forever change Dublin. Throughout the 19th century, as Ireland endured the Great Potato Famine and saw the beginnings of the modern struggle for independence, Dublin was treated more like a British colony than a partner. The tension culminated in the Easter Uprising of 1916, followed by a successful guerilla war for independence and a tragic civil war. With many of its grand streets in ruins, Dublin emerged as the capital of the British Empire's only former colony in Europe.

While bullet-pocked buildings and dramatic statues keep memories of Ireland's struggle alive, the city looks toward a brighter future. Dubliners are energetic and helpful, while visitors enjoy a big-town cultural scene wrapped in a small-

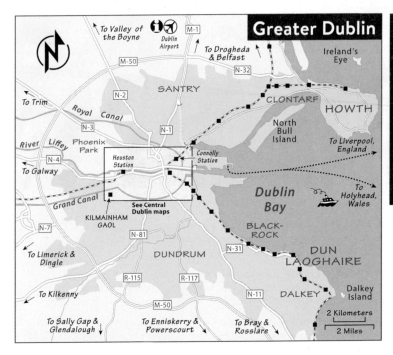

Greater Dublin

DUBLIN IN 2 DAYS

Sprawling, bustling Dublin has a compact core containing most of the sights, making it easy to enjoy. This city is a must for travelers interested in Celtic/Viking artifacts, Irish literature, or rebel history. If that's not you, head for the charm of smaller towns. For most people, Dublin deserves three nights and two days. You can connect many of the sights with a hop-on, hop-off sightseeing bus tour (see page 44).

Day 1: Visit the Book of Kells and Trinity Old Library when it opens at 9:00, hopefully ahead of midmorning cruise-ship crowds. Then take the Trinity College guided walk. Browse Grafton Street and have lunch. Head to the National Museum's Archaeology branch (closed Mon). See Number Twenty-Nine Georgian House (reserve guided tour ahead of time, closed Sun-Mon). Nearby parks for exploring or relaxing are Merrion Square and St. Stephen's Green.

On any evening: Have an early-bird special at a nice restaurant. Go for an evening guided pub tour (musical or literary). Drop in on Irish music in the rowdy Temple Bar area. Catch a concert or play, or try the storytelling dinner at The Brazen Head.

Day 2: Take the Dublin Castle tour, followed by a visit to Christ Church Cathedral. Grab a pub lunch, then continue on to the Guinness Storehouse and Kilmainham Gaol.

With extra time: Choose among my Dublin Walk (along O'Connell Street), National Gallery, writers' sights (Chester Beatty Library, Dublin Writers Museum), the *Jeanie Johnston* Tall Ship and Famine Museum, and more.

ORIENTATION

Greater Dublin sprawls with 1.1 million people—almost a quarter of the country's population. But the center of tourist interest is a tight triangle between O'Connell Bridge, St. Stephen's Green, and Christ

DUBLIN AT A GLANCE

▲▲▲**Traditional Irish Musical Pub Crawl** A fascinating, practical, and enjoyable primer on traditional Irish music. **Hours:** April-Oct daily at 19:30, Nov-March Thu-Sat only. See page 44.

▲▲▲**National Museum: Archaeology** Interesting collection of Irish treasures from the Stone Age to today. **Hours:** Tue-Sat 10:00-17:00, Sun 14:00-17:00, closed Mon. See page 55.

▲▲▲**Kilmainham Gaol** Historic jail used by the British as a political prison—today a museum that tells a moving story of the suffering of the Irish people. **Hours:** Mon-Sat 9:30-16:30, Sun 10:00-16:30. See page 75.

▲▲**Historical Walking Tour** Your best introduction to Dublin. **Hours:** May-Sept daily at 11:00 and 15:00, April and Oct daily at 11:00, Nov-March Fri-Sun only at 11:00. See page 44.

▲▲**O'Connell Street** Dublin's grandest promenade and main drag, packed with history and ideal for a stroll. **Hours:** Always open. See page 45.

▲▲**O'Connell Bridge** Landmark bridge spanning the River Liffey at the center of Dublin. **Hours:** Always open. See page 45.

▲▲**Trinity College Tour** Ireland's most famous school, best visited with a 30-minute tour led by one of its students. **Hours:** Departs every 30 minutes May-Sept daily 10:15-15:40, Feb-April and Oct-Nov Sat-Sun only, no tours Dec-Jan; weather permitting. See page 51.

▲▲**Book of Kells in the Trinity Old Library** An exquisite illuminated manuscript, the most important piece of art from the Dark Ages. **Hours:** June-Sept Mon-Sat 9:00-18:00, Sun 9:30-18:00; Oct-May Mon-Sat 9:30-17:00, Sun 12:00-16:30. See page 51.

▲▲**Grafton Street** The city's liveliest pedestrian shopping mall. **Hours:** Always open. See page 60.

▲▲**Dublin Castle** The city's historic 700-year-old castle, featuring ornate English state apartments, must be toured with a guide. **Hours:** Mon-Sat 9:45-16:45, Sun 12:00-16:45. See page 61.

▲▲**Chester Beatty Library** American expatriate's eclectic yet sumptuous collection of literary and religious treasures from Islam, the Orient, and medieval Europe. **Hours:** Mon-Fri 10:00-17:00, Sat 11:00-17:00, Sun 13:00-17:00; closed Mon Oct-April. See page 62.

▲▲**Temple Bar** Dublin's rowdiest neighborhood, with shops, cafés, theaters, galleries, pubs, and restaurants—a great spot for live traditional music. **Hours:** Always open. See page 67.

▲**National Gallery** Fine collection of top Irish painters and European masters. **Hours:** Mon-Sat 9:30-17:30, Thu until 20:30, Sun 11:00-17:30. See page 59.

▲**Merrion Square** Enjoyable and inviting park with a fun statue of Oscar Wilde. **Hours:** Always open. See page 60.

▲**Number Twenty-Nine Georgian House** Restored 18th-century house; tours provide an intimate glimpse of middle-class Georgian life. **Hours:** Tue-Sat 10:00-17:00, closed Sun-Mon, closed mid-Dec-mid-Feb. See page 60.

▲**St. Stephen's Green** Relaxing park surrounded by fine Georgian buildings. **Hours:** Always open. See page 61.

▲**Dublinia** A fun, kid-friendly look at Dublin's Viking and medieval past with a side order of archaeology and a cool town model. **Hours:** Daily March-Sept 10:00-17:00, Oct-Feb 11:00-16:30. See page 66.

▲**Dublin Writers Museum** Modest collection of authorial bric-a-brac. **Hours:** June-Aug Mon-Fri 10:00-18:00, Sat 10:00-17:00; Sept-May Mon-Sat 10:00-17:00; Sun 11:00-17:00 year-round. See page 69.

▲**Hugh Lane Gallery** Modern and contemporary art, starring Monet, Bacon, and Irish artists. **Hours:** Tue-Thu 10:00-18:00, Fri-Sat 10:00-17:00, Sun 11:00-17:00, closed Mon. See page 72.

▲**Guinness Storehouse** The home of Ireland's national beer, with a museum of beer-making, a gallery of clever ads, and Gravity Bar with panoramic city views. **Hours:** Daily 9:30-17:00, July-Aug until 19:00. See page 75.

▲**National Museum: Decorative Arts and History** Shows off Irish dress, furniture, silver, and weaponry with a special focus on the 1916 rebellion, fight for independence, and civil war. **Hours:** Tue-Sat 10:00-17:00, Sun 14:00-17:00, closed Mon. See page 77.

▲**Gaelic Athletic Association Museum** High-tech museum of traditional Gaelic sports such as hurling and Irish football. **Hours:** Mon-Sat 9:30-17:00, Sun 10:30-17:00. On game Sundays, it's open to ticket holders only. See page 77.

Jeanie Johnston **Tall Ship and Famine Museum** This replica sailing ship tells the story of the transatlantic crossings that carried more than 2,500 Irish emigrants to new lives after the Great Potato Famine. **Hours:** Daily April-Oct 10:00-16:00, Nov-March 11:00-16:00. See page 73.

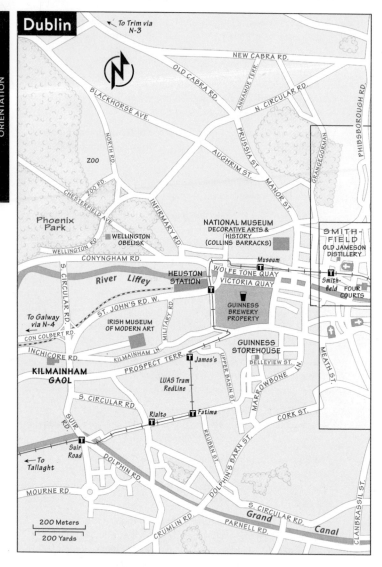

Dublin

To Trim via N-3

NEW CABRA RD.

OLD CABRA RD.

BLACKHORSE AVE.

ANNAMOE TERR.

N. CIRCULAR RD.

PRUSSIA ST.

AUGHRIM ST.

MANOR ST.

GRANGEGORMAN

PHIBSBOROUGH RD.

NORTH RD.

ZOO

ZOO RD.

CHESTERFIELD AVE.

Phoenix Park

WELLINGTON OBELISK

WELLINGTON RD.

CONYNGHAM RD.

INFIRMARY RD.

NATIONAL MUSEUM
DECORATIVE ARTS &
HISTORY
(COLLINS BARRACKS)

Museum

SMITH-
FIELD
OLD JAMESON
DISTILLERY

River   Liffey

HEUSTON
STATION

WOLFE TONE QUAY

VICTORIA QUAY

Smith-
field

FOUR
COURTS

S. CIRCULAR RD.

To Galway
via N-4

ST. JOHN'S RD. W.

MILITARY RD.

CON COLBERT RD.

IRISH MUSEUM
OF MODERN ART

GUINNESS
BREWERY
PROPERTY

INCHICORE RD.

KILMAINHAM LN.

PROSPECT TERR.

GUINNESS
STOREHOUSE

MEATH ST.

KILMAINHAM
GAOL

James's

UPPER BASIN ST.

BELLEVIEW ST.

MARROWBONE LN.

LUAS Tram
RedLine

S. CIRCULAR RD.

Rialto

Fatima

REUBEN ST.

DOLPHIN'S BARN ST.

CORK ST.

SUIR RD.

Suir
Road

DOLPHIN RD.

To
Tallaght

MOURNE RD.

DOLPHIN RD.

S. CIRCULAR RD.

Grand   Canal

CLANBRASSIL ST.

CRUMLIN RD.

PARNELL RD.

200 Meters

200 Yards

Church Cathedral. Within or near this triangle, you'll find Trinity College (Book of Kells), a cluster of major museums (including the top choice, the National Museum: Archaeology branch), Grafton Street (top pedestrian shopping zone), Temple Bar (trendy and touristy nightlife center), Dublin Castle, and the hub of most city tours and buses. The only major

sights outside this easy-to-walk triangle are the Kilmainham Gaol, the Guinness Storehouse, and the National Museum: Decorative Arts and History branch at Collins Barracks (all west of the center).

The River Liffey cuts the town in two. Focus on the southern half, where most of your sightseeing will take place. Dublin's wide main drag, O'Connell Street,

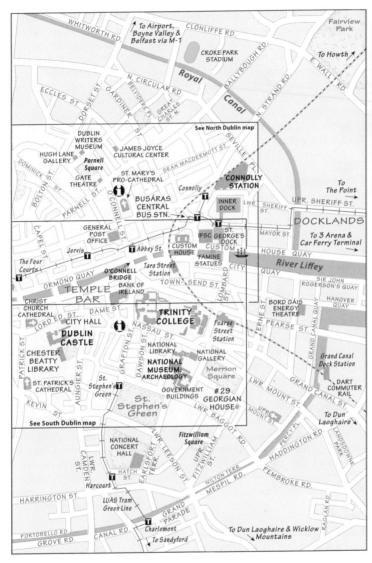

starts north of the river at the Parnell Monument and runs south, down to the central O'Connell Bridge. After crossing the bridge, this major city axis changes its name to Westmoreland and continues south, past Trinity College and through pedestrian-only Grafton Street to St. Stephen's Green.

Many long Dublin streets change their names every few blocks. A prime example of this: the numerously named quays (pronounced "keys") that run east-west along the River Liffey.

Tourist Information

Dublin's **main TI** is a thriving hub, with staffers doling out the lowdown on the city. You can buy tickets to events here and browse brochures for destinations throughout Ireland (June-Sept Mon-Sat 9:00-17:30, Oct-May Mon-Sat 9:30-17:30, Sun 10:30-15:00 year-round, a block off Grafton Street at 25 Suffolk Street, tel. 01/884-7700 or 01/605-7700, www.visitdublin.com). A smaller satellite TI is halfway down the east side of **O'Connell Street** (Mon-Sat 9:00-17:00, closed Sun). Another TI is at the **airport** (daily 8:00-20:00, Terminal 1).

Sightseeing Pass

The **Dublin Pass** saves some time that would be spent waiting in line, but is a good deal only if you like to visit lots of sights quickly (€39/1 day, €61/2 days, €71/3 days, €105/6 days, sold at TIs, www.dublinpass.ie). The pass covers 33 museums, churches, literature-related sights, and expensive stops such as the Guinness Storehouse (€18) and the Old Jameson Distillery (€15), plus the Aircoach airport bus (€7, one-way from the airport to the city only; doesn't cover Airlink buses). If you took the Aircoach from the airport and visited both the Guinness Storehouse and the Old Jameson Distillery that same day, you'd only save €1 with the pass. The pass doesn't include the Book of Kells at Trinity College and gives only minor discounts on some bus tours and walking tours. Most travelers won't get their money's worth, especially those with no interest in Guinness or Old Jameson.

Tours

The Historical Walking Tour of Dublin, rated ▲▲, is a superb introduction to the city. The guides are hardworking history graduates adept at enlivening Dublin's basic historic strip (€12, free for kids under 14, allow 2 hours, May-Sept daily at 11:00 and 15:00, April and Oct daily at 11:00, Nov-March Fri-Sun only at 11:00, depart from front gate of Trinity College, private tours available, mobile 087-688-9412 or 087-830-3523, www.historical insights.ie).

The **Traditional Irish Musical Pub Crawl,** rated ▲▲▲, includes entertaining visits to three pubs, where you'll listen to musicians talk about, play, and sing traditional Irish music. While having only two musicians makes the music a bit thin (aficionados will say you're better off finding a good session), it's an education in traditional Irish music. In summer, it often sells out; reserve ahead online. There is a maximum of 50 people per tour. To get a discount, use voucher code "RSIRISH" (€12, beer extra, allow 2.5 hours, April-Oct daily at 19:30, Nov-March Thu-Sat only, meet upstairs at Gogarty's Pub at the corner of Fleet and Anglesea in the Temple Bar area, tel. 01/475-3313, www.musical pubcrawl.com).

Dublin City Bike Tours visit 20 points of interest north and south of the River Liffey, covering more ground (five miles) than walking tours. "Get your *craic* on a saddle." Designed for riders of average fitness, they set a casual pace, and rarely let a little rain stop them (€24 includes bike, helmet, snack, and water; €4 discount with this book—show when you pay, cash only, reserve in advance, 2.5 hours, March-Nov daily at 10:00, additional tours Fri and Sat at 14:00, custom tours available for groups of 8 or more, departs Isaac's Hostel a half-block west of Busáras Central Bus Station at 2-5 Frenchman's Lane, mobile 087-134-1866, www.dublincitybiketours.com).

City Sightseeing Dublin offers a hop-on, hop-off tour on red double-decker buses with live running commentary, following 1.5-hour circuits (choose the red route over the blue). Get on or off at your choice of about 20 stops, including the far-flung Kilmainham Gaol and Guinness Storehouse. The 48-hour ticket only costs €3 more than the 24-hour ticket and is worth it for the extra freedom it creates in your itinerary. Their map, free with your ticket, details various discounts for sights in Dublin (€22 from driver for 48-hour ticket, 15 percent discount if booked online, 4/hour, daily 9:00-17:30, www.citysightseeingdublin.ie).

Dublin Bus Tours offers a similar service for a similar price, though it doesn't stop right at Kilmainham Gaol, but 200 yards away (green buses, tel. 01/703-3028, www.dublinsightseeing.ie).

The **City of a Thousand Welcomes** offers a free service that brings together volunteers and first-time visitors for an informal orientation to the city over a cup of tea or a pint. Sign up online in advance, pick an available time slot, and meet your Dublin ambassador at the Little Museum of Dublin on St. Stephen's Green before heading for a nearby tearoom or pub (free, must be at least 21, 15 St. Stephen's Green, tel. 01/661-1000, mobile 087-131-7129, www.cityofathousandwelcomes.com).

Audio Tours App offered by the Dublin TI puts good-quality "Dublin Discovery Trails" audio tours on your smartphone (download via Apple's App Store or Goggle Play).

Helpful Hints

Theft and Safety: Irish destinations, especially Dublin, are not immune to **pickpockets.** Wear a money belt or risk spending a couple of days on the phone canceling credit cards and at the embassy waiting for a replacement passport. Wasting vacation time this way is like paying to wait in line at the DMV.

Festivals: Book ahead during festivals and for any weekend. **St. Patrick's Day** is a four-day March extravaganza in Dublin (www.stpatricksday.ie). June 16 is **Bloomsday,** dedicated to the Irish author James Joyce and featuring the Messenger Bike Rally (www.jamesjoyce.ie). Hotels raise their prices and are packed on rugby weekends (about four per year), during the all-Ireland Gaelic football and hurling finals (Sundays in September), and during summer rock concerts.

Internet Access: Internet cafés are plentiful. All of these places are open daily, generally from about 10:00 to 20:00

(shorter Sat-Sun hours): **Viva Internet** (Lord Edward Street near City Hall and Christ Church Cathedral, tel. 01/672-4725); **Central Internet Café** (6 Grafton Street, easy-to-miss door is directly opposite AIB Bank, tel. 01/677-8298, www.centralinternetcafe.com); and **Global Internet Café** (north of the River Liffey, 8 O'Connell Street Lower, tel. 01/878-0295).

Maps: The best free city map can be found at the Kilkenny Shop at 6 Nassau Street (bordering the south side of the Trinity College campus). At any TI, you can pick up *The Guide*, which includes a decent city map (free), along with a minimal schedule of happenings in town. The excellent *Collins Illustrated Discovering Dublin Map* is the ultimate city map (€7 at TIs and newsstands).

DUBLIN WALK

This self-guided walk, worth ▲▲, follows grand, historic **O'Connell Street** through the heart of north Dublin. Since the 1740s, it has been a 45-yard-wide promenade. In 1794, the first O'Connell Bridge connected it to the Trinity side of town. These days, the street is pedestrian-friendly.

Ⓞ Self-Guided Walk

• *Start your tour on the...*

❶ **O'Connell Bridge:** This bridge, worth ▲▲, spans the River Liffey, which historically has divided the wealthy, cultivated south side of town from the working-class north side. While there's plenty

O'Connell Bridge

Dublin Walk

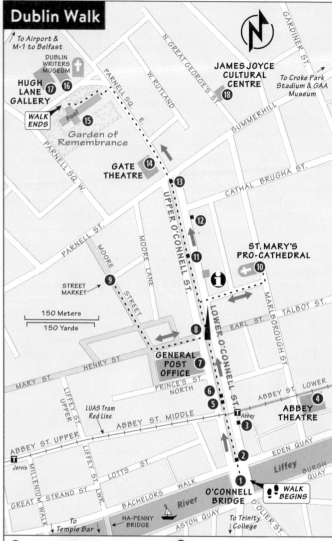

N

To Airport &
M-1 to Belfast

DUBLIN
WRITERS
MUSEUM

HUGH
LANE
GALLERY

WALK
ENDS

Pool

Garden of
Remembrance

GATE
THEATRE

STREET
MARKET

150 Meters

150 Yards

PARNELL SQ. W.

PARNELL SQ. E.

PARNELL SQ. N.

N. GREAT GEORGE'S ST.

W. RUTLAND

GARDINER ST.

JAMES JOYCE
CULTURAL
CENTRE

To Croke Park
Stadium & GAA
Museum

SUMMERHILL

CATHAL BRUGHA ST.

UPPER O'CONNELL ST.

LOWER O'CONNELL ST.

ST. MARY'S
PRO-CATHEDRAL

MOORE ST.

PARNELL ST.

MOORE LANE

STREET

HENRY ST.

MARY ST.

LIFFEY ST. UPPER

GENERAL
POST
OFFICE

PRINCE'S ST.
NORTH

EARL ST.

TALBOT ST.

MARLBOROUGH ST.

ABBEY ST. LOWER

ABBEY
THEATRE

LUAS Tram
Red Line

ABBEY ST. MIDDLE

Abbey

ABBEY ST. UPPER

Jervis

MILLENNIUM WALK

GREAT STRAND ST.

LIFFEY ST. LWR.

LOTTS ST.

BACHELORS WALK

River

HA-PENNY
BRIDGE

ASTON QUAY

To
Temple Bar

O'CONNELL
BRIDGE

WALK
BEGINS

D'OLIER ST.

EDEN QUAY

Liffey

BURGH
QUAY

To Trinity
College

---

1. O'Connell Bridge
2. Daniel O'Connell Statue
3. William Smith O'Brien Statue
4. Abbey Theatre
5. Sir John Gray Statue
6. James Larkin Statue
7. General Post Office
8. Millennium Spire
9. Moore Street Market

10. St. Mary's Pro-Cathedral
11. Father Matthew Statue
12. Gresham Hotel
13. Charles Stewart Parnell Monument
14. Gate Theatre
15. Garden of Remembrance
16. Dublin Writers Museum
17. Hugh Lane Gallery & Francis Bacon Studio
18. James Joyce Cultural Centre

of culture above the river, even today the suburbs (a couple of miles north of the Liffey) are considered rougher and less safe. Dubliners joke that north-side residents are known as "the accused," while residents on the south side are addressed as "your honor."

From the bridge, look upriver (west) as far upstream as you can. On the left in the distance, the **big concrete building**—nicknamed "the bunker" and considered an eyesore by locals—houses the city planning commission. Ironically, it's in charge of the still-buried precious artifacts of the first Viking settlement, established in Dublin in the ninth century. Archaeologists were given minimal time to study the dig before officials paved paradise and put up a parking lot (actually the Dublin City Council offices).

Across the river from that stands the (still distant) green dome of the **Four Courts**—the Supreme Court building. It was shelled and burned in 1922 during the tragic civil war that followed Irish independence. The national archives office burned, and irreplaceable birth records were lost,

making it more difficult today for those with Irish roots to trace their ancestry.

The closest bridge upstream—the elegant iron **Ha' Penny Bridge**—leads into the Temple Bar nightlife district. Just beyond that old-fashioned, 19th-century bridge is Dublin's pedestrian **Millennium Bridge,** inaugurated in 2000. (Note that buses leave from O'Connell Bridge—specifically Aston Quay—for the Guinness Storehouse and Kilmainham Gaol.)

Turn 180 degrees and look east downstream to see the tall **Liberty Hall** union headquarters (16 stories tall, some say in honor of the 1916 Easter Uprising). Modern Dublin is developing downstream. During the Celtic Tiger boom, the Irish (always clever tax fiddlers) subsidized and revitalized this formerly dreary quarter. A short walk downstream along the north bank leads to a powerful series of gaunt statues memorializing the Great Potato Famine of 1845-1849. Beyond, you'll see the masts of the *Jeanie Johnston*, a replica transport ship (see page 73).

• Now start north up O'Connell Street, walking on the wide, tree-lined median strip between the lanes of traffic.

Busy O'Connell Street

Statues and Monuments: The median is dotted with statues celebrating great figures from Ireland's past—particularly the century (c. 1830-1930) when Ireland rediscovered its roots and won its independence. At the base of the street stands the man for whom Dublin's main street is named—❷ **Daniel O'Connell** (1775-1847). He was known as the "Liberator" for founding the Catholic Association and demanding Irish Catholic rights in the British Parliament. He organized thousands of nonviolent protestors into so-called "monster meetings," whose sheer size intimidated the British authorities.

Farther along is ❸ **William Smith O'Brien,** O'Connell's contemporary and leader of the Young Ireland Movement, who was more willing to use force to reach his goals. After a failed uprising in Tipperary, he was imprisoned and exiled to Australia. At Abbey Street, a block detour east leads to the famous ❹ **Abbey Theatre,** where turn-of-the-century nationalists (including the poet-playwright W. B. Yeats) staged Irish-themed plays. The original building suffered a fire and was rebuilt into a nondescript, modern building, but it's still the much-loved home of the Irish National Theatre.

• *Continue up O'Connell Street.*

Look for the statue of ❺ **Sir John Gray,** who, as a newspaperman and politician, was able to help O'Connell's cause. The statue of ❻ **James Larkin,** arms outstretched, honors the founder of the Irish Transport Workers Union.

• *On your left is the...*

❼ **General Post Office:** This is not just any P.O. It was from here that Patrick Pearse read the Proclamation of Irish Independence in 1916, kicking off the Easter Uprising. The building itself—a kind of Irish Alamo—was the rebel headquarters and scene of a bloody five-day siege that followed the proclamation. The post office was particularly strategic because it housed the telegraph nerve center for the entire country. Its pillars are still pockmarked with bullet holes (open for business and sightseers Mon-Sat 8:00-20:00, closed Sun). You may want to visit the "GPO: Witness History" **exhibition,** which opened in 2016 for the Easter Uprising centenary (daily 9:30-17:30, www. gpowitnesshistory.ie). The small **An Post Museum,** which stamp collectors and Irish rebels at heart will enjoy, is on the ground floor (€2, Mon-Sat 10:00-17:00, closed Sun, on the right as you enter, www.anpost.ie/historyandheritage).

• *Stand at the intersection of O'Connell and Henry Streets, at the base of the can't-miss-it...*

❽ **Spire:** There used to be a monument here that didn't wave an Irish flag—a tall column crowned by a statue of the British hero of Trafalgar, Admiral Horatio Nelson. It was blown up in 1966—the IRA's contribution to the local celebration of the Easter Uprising's 50th anniversary. The spot is now occupied by the Spire: 398 feet of stainless steel. While it trumpets rejuvenation on its side of the river, it's a memorial to nothing and has no real meaning. Dubious Dubliners call it the tallest waste of €5 million in all of Europe. Its nickname? Take your pick: the Stiletto in the Ghetto, the Stiffy on the Liffey, the Pole in the Hole, the Poker near the Croker (after nearby Croke Park), or the Spike in the Dike.

• *Detour west (left) down people-filled Henry Street (Dubliners' favorite shopping lane), then wander to the right into the nearby...*

❾ **Moore Street Market:** Many merchants here have staffed the same stalls for decades. Start a conversation. It's a great workaday scene. You'll see lots of mums with strollers—a reminder that Ireland is one of Europe's youngest countries, with more than 35 percent of the population under the age of 25. At the end of the 1916 Easter Uprising, the rebel leaders retreated from the burning post office to the market, where they finally surrendered to British troops (Mon-Sat 8:00-18:00, closed Sun).

• *Return to O'Connell Street. A block east (right) of O'Connell, down Cathedral Street, detour to...*

⑩ St. Mary's Pro-Cathedral: Although this is Dublin's leading Catholic church, it rather curiously isn't a "cathedral." The pope declared Christ Church to be a cathedral in the 12th century—and later, gave St. Patrick's the same designation. (The Vatican has chosen to stubbornly ignore the fact that Christ Church and St. Patrick's haven't been Catholic for centuries.) Completed in 1821, this Neoclassical church is in the style of a Greek temple.

• *Back on O'Connell Street, head up the street (north) until you find the statue of...*

⑪ Father Matthew: A leader of the temperance movement of the 1830s, Father Matthew was responsible, some historians claim, for enough Irish peasants staying sober to enable Daniel O'Connell to organize them into a political force. (Perhaps studying this example, the USSR was careful to keep the price of vodka affordable.)

Nearby, the fancy **⑫ Gresham Hotel** is a good place for an elegant tea or beer. In an earlier era, the beautiful people alighted here during visits to Dublin. In the 1960s, Richard Burton and Liz Taylor stayed at the hotel while he was filming *The Spy Who Came in from the Cold*. (In those days, parts of Dublin were drab enough to pass for an Eastern Bloc city.)

• *Standing boldly at the top of O'Connell Street is a monument to...*

⑬ Charles Stewart Parnell: Ringing the monument are the names of the four ancient provinces of Ireland and all 32 Irish counties (including North and South, since this was erected before Irish partition). It's meant to honor Charles Stewart Parnell (1846-1891), the member of Parliament who nearly won Home Rule for Ireland in the late 1800s (and who served time at Kilmainham Gaol). A Cambridge-educated Protestant of

Ⓐ *General Post Office*

Ⓑ *The Spire*

Ⓒ *Moore Street Market*

Ⓓ *Statue of Charles Stewart Parnell*

landed-gentry stock, Parnell envisioned a modern, free Irish nation of Catholics—but not set up as a religious state. The Irish people, who remembered their grandparents' harsh evictions during the famine, came to love Parnell (despite his privileged birth) for his tireless work to secure fair rents and land tenure. Momentum seemed to be on his side. With the British prime minister of the time, William Gladstone, favoring a similar form of Home Rule, it looked as if Ireland was on its way toward independence as a Commonwealth nation, similar to Canada or Australia. Then a sex scandal broke around Parnell and his mistress, the wife of another Parliament member. The press, egged on by the powerful Catholic bishops (who didn't want a secular, free Irish state), battered away at the scandal until finally Parnell was driven from office. Sadly, after that, Ireland became mired in the Troubles of the 20th century: an awkward independence (1921) resulting in a divided island, a bloody civil war, and sectarian violence for decades afterward. Wracked with exhaustion and only in his mid-40s, Parnell is thought to have died of a broken heart.

• *Continue straight up Parnell Square East. At the ⑭ Gate Theatre (on the left), actors Orson Welles, Geraldine Fitzgerald, and James Mason had their professional stage debuts. One block up, on the left, is the...*

⑮ **Garden of Remembrance:** Honoring the victims of the 1916 Uprising, this spot was where the rebel leaders were held before being transferred to Kilmainham Gaol. The park was dedicated in 1966 on the 50th anniversary of the revolt that ultimately led to Irish independence. There were patriotic commemorations here during the 2016 centennial. The bottom of the cross-shaped pool is a mosaic of Celtic weapons, symbolic of how the early Irish proclaimed peace by breaking their weapons and throwing them into a lake or river. The Irish flag flies above the park: green for Catholics, orange for Protestants, and white for the hope that they can live together in peace (free, daily 8:30-18:00).

One of modern Ireland's most stirring moments occurred here in May of 2011, when Queen Elizabeth II made this the first stop on her historic visit to Ireland.

Garden of Remembrance

She laid a wreath at the *Children of Lir* sculpture under this flag and bowed her head in silence out of respect for the Irish rebels who had fought and died trying to gain freedom from her United Kingdom. This was a hugely cathartic moment for both nations. Until this visit, no British monarch had set foot in the Irish state since its founding 90 years earlier.

• *Your walk is over. Two excellent museums are nearby, standing side-by-side: the* 🏛 **Dublin Writers Museum** *(in a splendidly restored Georgian mansion, see page 69) and the art-filled* 🏛 **Hugh Lane Gallery** *(page 72). Here at the north end of town, it's also convenient to visit the* 🏛 **James Joyce Cultural Centre** *(a short walk away, see page 71) or the* **Gaelic Athletic Association Museum** *at Croke Park Stadium (described on page 77, a 20-minute walk or short taxi ride away). Otherwise, hop on your skateboard and zip back to the river.*

SIGHTS

South of the River Liffey

▲▲TRINITY COLLEGE TOUR

Founded in 1592 by Queen Elizabeth I to establish a Protestant way of thinking about God, Trinity has long been Ireland's most prestigious college. Originally, the student body was limited to rich Protestant men. Women were admitted in 1903, and Catholics—though allowed entrance by the school much earlier—were only given formal permission by the Catholic Church to study at Trinity in the 1970s. Today, half of Trinity's 12,500 students are women, and 70 percent are culturally Catholic (although only about 20 percent of Irish youth are churchgoing).

Trinity students organize and lead 30-minute **tours** of their campus. You'll get a rundown of the mostly Georgian architecture; a peek at student life past and present; and the enjoyable company of your guide, a witty Irish college kid.

Cost and Hours: €5, €13 with entry to see Book of Kells (where the tour leaves

you), May-Sept daily 10:15-15:40, Feb-April and Oct-Nov Sat-Sun only, no tours Dec-Jan, departs roughly every 30 minutes, weather permitting; look just inside the gate for posted departure times and a ticket seller on a stool.

▲▲BOOK OF KELLS IN THE TRINITY OLD LIBRARY

The Book of Kells—a 1,200-year-old version of the gospels of the Bible—was elaborately inked and meticulously illustrated by faithful monks. Combining Christian symbols and pagan styles, it's a snapshot of medieval Ireland in transition. Arguably the finest piece of art from what is generally called the Dark Ages, the Book of Kells shows that monastic life in this far fringe of Europe was far from dark.

Rick's Tip: *Lines are longest at midday (roughly 11:00-14:30). Ideally,* **buy tickets in advance** *or* **queue up before the library opens** *to have the Book of Kells to yourself.*

Cost and Hours: €10, €13 "fast-track" ticket skips the line—buy in advance

Tour at Trinity College

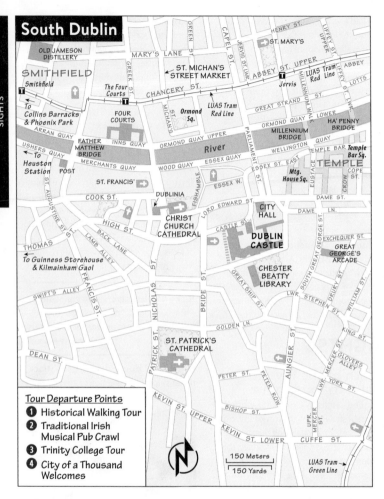

South Dublin

OLD JAMESON
DISTILLERY

MARY'S LANE

ST. MARY'S

HENRY ST.

LIFFEY ST. UPPER

SMITHFIELD

Smithfield

ABBEY ST. UPPER

LUAS Tram
Red Line

ABBEY

ST. MICHAN'S
STREET MARKET

Jervis

LOTTS

To
Collins Barracks
& Phoenix Park

The Four
Courts

CHANCERY ST.

GREAT STRAND

FOUR
COURTS

LUAS Tram
Red Line

Ormond
Sq.

ORMOND QUAY LOWER

HA' PENNY
BRIDGE

ARRAN QUAY

FATHER
MATTHEW
BRIDGE

INNS QUAY

ORMOND QUAY UPPER

MILLENNIUM
BRIDGE

QUAY

USHERS QUAY

River

WELLINGTON

TEMPLE BAR

Temple
Bar Sq.

To
Heuston
Station

MERCHANTS QUAY

WOOD QUAY

ESSEX QUAY

ESSEX ST. EAST

TEMPLE

POST

ST. FRANCIS'

ESSEX W.

Mtg.
House Sq.

EUSTACE

COPE
ST.

COOK ST.

DUBLINIA

FISHAMBLE

LORD EDWARD ST.

CITY
HALL

DAME ST.

DAME

LN.

CHRIST
CHURCH
CATHEDRAL

CASTLE ST.

DUBLIN
CASTLE

EXCHEQUER ST.

HIGH ST.

THOMAS

To Guinness Storehouse
& Kilmainham Gaol

LAMB ALLEY

BACK LANE

CHESTER
BEATTY
LIBRARY

GREAT SHIP ST.

GREAT
GEORGE'S
ARCADE

SWIFT'S ALLEY

FRANCIS ST.

NICHOLAS ST.

BRIDE ST.

GOLDEN LN.

LWR. STEPHEN

DRURY ST.

WILLIAM ST.

KING ST.

DEAN ST.

ST. PATRICK'S
CATHEDRAL

PATRICK ST.

PETER ST.

PETER ROW

AUNGIER ST.

MERCER ST.

GLOVERS
ALLEY

KEVIN ST. UPPER

BISHOP ST.

LWR. YORK ST.

KEVIN ST. LOWER

CUFFE ST.

UPR.
MERCER
ST.

Tour Departure Points

1 Historical Walking Tour

2 Traditional Irish
Musical Pub Crawl

3 Trinity College Tour

4 City of a Thousand
Welcomes

N

150 Meters
150 Yards

LUAS Tram
Green Line

online, €13 regular entry with Trinity College tour admission; extra Audi O'Guide commentary-€5; June-Sept Mon-Sat 9:00-18:00, Sun 9:30-18:00; Oct-May Mon-Sat 9:30-17:00, Sun 12:00-16:30; tel. 01/896-2320, www.tcd.ie/library/bookofkells.

➡ SELF-GUIDED TOUR

Your visit has three stages: 1) an exhibit on the making of the Book of Kells, including two brief videos, old manuscripts, and poster-sized reproductions of its pages (your best look at the book's detail); 2) the Treasury, the darkened room containing the Book of Kells itself and other, less-ornate contemporaneous volumes; and 3) the Old Library's main chamber (called the Long Room), featuring historical objects.

Background: The Book of Kells was a labor of love created by dedicated Irish monks cloistered on the remote Scottish island of Iona. They slaughtered 185 calves, soaked the skins in lime, scraped off the hair, and dried the skins into a cream-colored writing surface called vellum. Only then could the tonsured monks pick up their swan-quill pens and get to work.

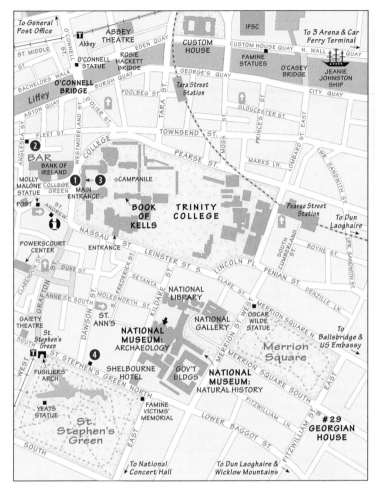

The project may have been underway in 806 when Vikings savagely pillaged and burned Iona, killing 68 monks. The survivors fled to the Abbey of Kells (near Dublin). Scholars debate exactly where the book was produced: It could have been made entirely at Iona or at Kells, or started in Iona and finished at Kells.

For eight centuries, the glorious gospel sat regally atop the high altar of the monastery church at Kells, where the priest would read from it during special Masses. In 1654, as Cromwell's ravaging armies approached, the book was smuggled to

Dublin for safety. Here at Trinity College, it was first displayed to the public in the mid-1800s. In 1953, the book got its current covers and was bound into four separate volumes. The 1,200-year journey of the Book of Kells reached its culmination in 2012, when it came out as an iPad app.

The Exhibit: The first-class "Turning Darkness into Light" exhibit, with a one-way route, puts the illuminated manuscript in its historical and cultural context, preparing you to see the original book and other precious manuscripts in the treasury. Make a point to spend time in the exhibit (before reaching the actual Book of Kells). Especially interesting are the five-minute video clips showing the exacting care that went into transcribing the monk-uscripts and the ancient art of bookbinding. Two small TV screens (on opposite walls of the exhibition room) run continuously, silently demonstrating the monks' work.

The Book: The Book of Kells contains the four gospels of the Bible. It's 680 pages long (or 340 "folios," the equivalent of one sheet, front and back). The Latin calligraphy—all in capital letters—follows ruled lines, forming neat horizontal bars across the page. Sentences end with a "period" of three dots. The black-brown ink was made from the galls of oak trees. Scholars have found a number of spelling errors that were never corrected, apparently because the look was more important than accuracy.

The text is elaborately decorated—of the 680 pages, only two are without decoration. Each gospel begins with a full-page illustration of the Evangelists and their symbols: Matthew (angel), Mark (lion), Luke (ox), and John (eagle)—you'll see these in the exhibit. These portraits are not realistic; the apostles pose stiffly, like Byzantine-style icons, with almond-shaped eyes and symmetrically creased robes. The true beauty lies in the intricate designs that surround the figures.

The colorful book employs blue, purple, red, pink, green, and yellow pigments (all imported)—but no gold leaf. Letters and borders are braided together. On most pages, the initial letters are big and flowery, like in a children's fairytale book. The entire Chi-Rho page is dedicated to just the letters "XP" (the first two letters of Christ's name in Greek), made into an elaborate maze of interlacing lines.

Elsewhere, the playful monks might cross a "t" with a fish, form an "h" from a spindly-legged man, or make an "e" out of a coiled snake. Animals crouch between sentences. It's a jungle of intricate designs, inhabited by tiny creatures, both real and fanciful, with no two the same—humans, angels, gargoyles, dragons, wolves, calves, and winged lions.

Stylistically, the monks mixed Christian symbols (the cross, fish, peacock, snake) with pagan motifs (spirals, key patterns, knotwork; some swirls are similar to those seen on the carved stones at Newgrange—see page 96). The designs are also reminiscent of the jewelry of the day, with its ornate filigree patterns studded with knobs (like the Tara Brooch, described on page 58).

Scholars think three main artists created the book: the "goldsmith" (who did the filigree-style designs), the "illustrator" (who specialized in animals and grotesques), and the "portrait painter" (who did the Evangelists and Mary). Some of the detail work is unbelievably minute—akin to drawing a Persian carpet on the tiny face of a single die. Did the monks use

Book of Kells

Old Library, Trinity College

a magnifying glass? There's no evidence they had such strong lenses.

The Old Library: The Long Room, the 200-foot-long main chamber of the Old Library (from 1732), is stacked to its towering ceiling with 200,000 books. Among the displays here, you'll find one of a dozen surviving original copies of the **Proclamation of the Irish Republic.** Patrick Pearse read out its words at Dublin's General Post Office on April 24, 1916, starting the Easter Uprising that led to Irish independence. Notice the inclusive opening phrase ("Irishmen and Irishwomen") and the seven signatories (each of whom was executed).

Another national icon is nearby: the oldest surviving Irish **harp,** from the 15th century (sometimes called the Brian Boru harp). The brass pins on its oak and willow frame once held 29 strings. These weren't mellifluous catgut strings, like those on a modern harp, but wire strings that made a twangy sound when plucked. In Celtic days, poets—the equal of kings and Druid priests—wandered the land, uniting the people with songs and stories. The harp's inspirational effect on Gaelic culture was so strong that Queen Elizabeth I (1558-1603) ordered Irish harpists to be hung and their instruments smashed. Even today, the love of music is so intense that Ireland is the only country with a musical instrument as its national symbol. You'll see this harp's likeness everywhere, including on the back of Irish euro coins, on government documents, and on every pint of Guinness.

▲▲▲NATIONAL MUSEUM: ARCHAEOLOGY

Showing off the treasures of Ireland from the Stone Age to modern times, this branch of the National Museum is itself a national treasure. The soggy marshes and peat bogs of Ireland have proven perfect for preserving old objects. You'll see 4,000-year-old gold jewelry, 2,000-year-old bog mummies, Viking swords, and the collection's superstar—the exquisitely wrought Tara Brooch. Visit here to get an introduction to the rest of Ireland's historic attractions: You'll find a reconstructed passage tomb like Newgrange, Celtic art like the Book of Kells, Viking objects from Dublin, a model of the Hill of Tara, and a sacred cross from the Cong Abbey. Hit the highlights of my tour, then browse at will, aided by good posted information. For background information on Irish art, see page 332.

Cost and Hours: Free, Tue-Sat 10:00-17:00, Sun 14:00-17:00, closed Mon, guided tours offered sporadically (€3, mostly weekends, call in morning or check website), €3 audioguide covers only Treasury room, good café, between Trinity College and St. Stephen's Green on Kildare Street, tel. 01/677-7444, www.museum.ie.

◑ SELF-GUIDED TOUR

On the ground floor, enter the main hall. In the center (down four steps) are displays of prehistoric gold jewelry. To the left are the bog bodies, to the right is the Treasury, and upstairs is the Viking world. We'll start at Ireland's beginning.

❶ **Stone Age Tools:** Glass cases hold flint and stone axeheads and arrowheads (7000 B.C.). Ireland's first inhabitants—hunters and fishers who came from Scotland—used these tools. These early people also left behind standing stones (dolmens) and passage tombs.

❷ **Reconstructed Passage Tomb:** At the corner of the room, you'll see a typical tomb circa 3000 B.C.—a mound-shaped, heavy stone structure, covered with smaller rocks, with a passage leading into a central burial chamber where the deceased's ashes were interred. This is a modest tomb; the vast passage tombs at Newgrange and Knowth are many times bigger (see pages 96 and 97).

❸ **The Hill of Tara:** The famous passage-tomb burial site at Tara, known as the Mound of the Hostages, was used for more than 1,500 years as a place to inter human remains. The cases in this side

National Museum: Archaeology

Not to Scale

To St. Stephen's Green

WC   WC

VIKINGS VIDEO (UPSTAIRS)

8

4 METALWORKING

M E T A L W O R K I N G

HEAD ▪

HORN ▪

HOARD

T R E A S U R Y

▪ BELT

7

5 IRELAND'S GOLD

BROOCH

▪ CHALICE

KINGSHIP & SACRIFICE

6

2

1

VIKING ART

BELL ▪

CONG ▪

ARM ▪

3

MUSEUM SHOP

CAFE

FADDAN ▪ MORE

ENTER HERE OFF KILDARE STREET

KILDARE STREET

ENTRANCE

FENCE

Courtyard

To Trinity College

1 Stone Age Tools
2 Reconstructed Passage Tomb
3 Hill of Tara
4 Metalworking

5 Ireland's Gold
6 Bog Bodies
7 Treasury
8 Up to First Floor (Vikings)

gallery display some of the many exceptional Neolithic and Bronze Age finds uncovered at the site.

Over the millennia, the Mound became the very symbol of Irish heritage. This is where Ireland's kings claimed their power, where St. Patrick preached his deal-clinching sermon, and where, in 1843, Daniel O'Connell rallied Irish patriots to

demand their independence from Britain.

❹ The Evolution of Metalworking: Around 2500 B.C., Ireland discovered how to make metal—mining ore, smelting it in furnaces, and casting or hammering it into shapes. The rest is prehistory. You'll travel through the Bronze Age (axeheads from 2000 B.C.) and Iron Age (500 B.C.) as you examine assorted spears, shields, swords, and war horns. The cauldrons made for everyday cooking were also used ceremonially to prepare elaborate ritual feasts for friends and symbolic offerings for the gods. The most impressive metal objects are in the center of the hall.

❺ Ireland's Gold: Ireland had modest gold deposits, mainly gathered by prehistoric people panning for small nuggets and dust in the rivers. But the jewelry they left, some of it more than 4,000 years old, is exquisite. The earliest fashion choice was a broad necklace hammered flat (a *lunula*, so called for its crescent-moon shape). This might be worn with accompanying earrings and sun-disc brooches. The Gleninsheen Collar (c. 700 B.C.) was found by a farmer in a crevice of the exposed bedrock of the Burren. It's thought that this valuable status symbol was hidden there during a time of conflict, then forgotten—if it had been meant as an offering to a pagan god it more likely would have been left in a body of water (the portal to the underworld). Later Bronze Age jewelry was cast from clay molds into bracelets and unique "dress fasteners" that you'd slip into buttonholes to secure a cloak. Some of these gold objects may have been gifts to fertility gods, offered by burying them in marshy bogs.

❻ Bog Bodies: When the Celts arrived in Ireland (c. 500 B.C.-A.D. 500), they brought with them a mysterious practice: They brutally murdered sacrificial slaves or prisoners and buried them in bogs. Several bodies—shriveled and leathery, but remarkably preserved—have been dug up from around the Celtic world (in the British Isles and Northern Europe).

Clonycavan Man is from Ireland. One summer day around 200 B.C., this twenty-something man was hacked to death with an axe and disemboweled. In his time, he stood 5'9" tall and had a Mohawk-style haircut, poofed up with pine-resin hair product imported from France. Today you can still see traces of his hair. Only his upper body survived; the lower part may have been lost in the threshing machine that unearthed him in 2003.

Why were these people killed? It appears to have been a form of ritual human sacrifice of high-status people. Some may have been enemy chiefs or political rivals, but regardless, their deaths were offerings to the gods to ensure rich harvests and good luck. Other items (now on display) were buried along with them—gold bracelets, royal cloaks, and finely wrought cauldrons.

❼ Treasury: Irish metalworking is legendary, and this room holds 1,500 years of superb examples. Working from one end of the long room to the other, you'll journey from the world of the pagan Celts to the coming of Christianity, explore the stylistic impact of the Viking invasions (9th-12th century), and consider the resurgence of ecclesiastical metalworking (11th-12th century).

Pagan Era Art: A mysterious pagan god greets you in a **carved stone head** from circa A.D. 100. The god's three faces express the different aspects of his stony personality. This abstract style—typical of Celtic art—would be at home in a modern art museum. A **bronze horn** (first century B.C.) is the kind of curved war trumpet that the Celts blasted to freak out the Roman legions. The fine objects of the **Broighter Hoard** (first century B.C.) include a king's golden collar, decorated in textbook Celtic style, with interlaced vines inhabited by stylized faces. The tiny

Bog mummy

boat was an offering to the sea god. The coconut-shell-shaped bowl symbolized a cauldron. By custom, the cauldron held food as a constant offering to Danu, the Celtic mother goddess, whose mythical palace was at Bru na Bóinne.

Early Christian Objects: Christianity officially entered Ireland in the fifth century (when St. Patrick converted the pagan king), but Celtic legends and art continued well into the Christian era. You'll see various crosses, shrines (portable reliquaries containing holy relics), and chalices decorated with Celtic motifs. The **Belt Shrine**—a circular metal casing that held a saint's leather belt—was thought to have magical properties. When placed around someone's waist, it could heal the wearer or force him or her to tell the truth.

The **Chalice of Ardagh** and the nearby **Silver Paten** were used during Communion to hold blessed wine and bread. Get close to admire the fine workmanship. The main bowl of the chalice is gilded bronze, with a contrasting band of intricately patterned gold filigree. It's studded with colorful glass, amber, and enamels. Mirrors below the display case show that even the underside of the chalice was decorated. When the priest grabbed the chalice by its two handles and tipped it to his lips, the base could be admired by God.

Tara Brooch: A rich eighth-century Celtic man fastened his cloak at the shoulder with this elaborate ring-shaped brooch, its seven-inch stick-pin tilted rakishly upward. Made of cast and gilded silver, it's ornamented with exquisitely filigreed gold panels and studded with amber, enamel, and colored glass. The motifs include Celtic spirals, snakes, and stylized faces, but the symbolism is neither overtly pagan nor Christian—it's art for art's sake. Despite its fanciful name, the brooch probably has no actual connection to the Hill of Tara. In display cases nearby, you'll see other similar (but less impressive) brooches from the same period—some iron, some bronze, and one

in pure gold.

Viking Art Styles: When Vikings invaded Dublin around A.D. 800, they raped and pillaged. But they also opened Ireland to a vast and cosmopolitan trading empire, from which they imported hoards of silver (see the display case of ingots). Viking influence shows up in the decorative style of reliquaries like the **Lismore Crozier** (in the shape of a bishop's ceremonial shepherd's crook) and the **Shrine of St. Lochter's Arm** (raised in an Irish-power salute). The impressive **Bell of St. Patrick** was supposedly owned by Ireland's patron saint. After his death, it was encased within a beautifully worked shrine (displayed alongside) and kept safe by a single family, who passed it down from generation to generation for 800 years.

Cross of Cong: "By this cross is covered the cross on which the Creator of the world suffered." Running along the sides of the cross, this Latin inscription tells us that it once held a sacred relic, a tiny splinter of the True Cross on which Jesus was crucified. That piece of wood (now lost) had been given in 1123 to the Irish high king, who commissioned this reliquary to preserve the splinter (it would have been placed right in the center, visible through the large piece of rock crystal).

Cross of Cong

Every Christmas and Easter, the cross was fitted onto a staff and paraded through the abbey at Cong, then placed on the altar for High Mass. The extraordinarily detailed decoration features gold filigree interspersed with colored glass, enamel, and (now missing) precious stones. Though fully Christian, the cross has Celtic-style filigree patterning and Viking-style animal heads (notice how they grip the cross in their jaws).

Before leaving the Treasury and heading upstairs, check out the **Faddan More Psalter**—a (pretty beat-up) manuscript of the Book of Psalms from the same era as the Book of Kells.

❽ **Viking Ireland** (c. 800-1150, on first floor): Dublin was born as a Viking town. Sometime after 795, Scandinavian warriors rowed their long ships up the River Liffey and made camp on the south bank, around the location of today's Dublin Castle and Christ Church. Over the next two centuries, they built "Dubh linn" into an important trading post, slave market, metalworking center, and the first true city in Ireland. (See a model of Dublin showing a recently excavated area near Kilmainham Gaol.)

The state-of-the-art Viking boats ("Viking" means seafarer) worked equally well in the open ocean and shallow rivers, and were perfect for stealth invasions and far-ranging trading. Soon, provincial Dublin was connected with the wider world—Scotland, England, Northern Europe, even Asia. The museum's displays of swords and spears make it clear that, yes, the Vikings were fierce warriors. But you'll also see that they were respected merchants (standardized weights and coins), herders and craftsmen (leather shoes and bags), fashion-conscious (bone combs and jewelry), fun-loving (board games), and literate (runic alphabet). What you won't see are horned helmets, which, despite the stereotype, were not common. By 1000, the pagan Vikings had intermarried with the locals, become Christian, and were

subjects of the Irish king.

The Rest of the Museum: Part of the first floor is dedicated to medieval Ireland—daily life (ploughs, cauldrons), trade (coins, pottery), and religion (crucifixes and saints). Up one more flight, the Egyptian room has coffins, shabtis, and canopic jars—but no mummies. Also upstairs, check out the informative video on the Viking influence on Irish culture (25 minutes, in the triangular room in the corner of the building, above the Treasury).

▲ NATIONAL GALLERY

This gallery, adjacent to the archaeology branch, is not as extensive as national galleries in London or Paris, but its collections are well worth your time. The museum boasts an impressive range of works by European masters, and also displays the works of top Irish painters, including Jack B. Yeats (the brother of the famous poet).

Cost and Hours: Free, Mon-Sat 9:30-17:30, Thu until 20:30, Sun 11:00-17:30, Merrion Square West, tel. 01/661-5133, www.nationalgallery.ie.

Tours: The museum offers a free audioguide (donations accepted) as well as free 45-minute guided tours (Sat at 12:30; Sun at 12:30 and 13:30).

Visiting the Museum: Study the floor-plan flier and take advantage of the free audioguide. Be sure to walk the series of rooms on the ground floor devoted to Irish painting and get to know artists you

Caravaggio, The Taking of Christ

may not have heard of before. Visit the National Portrait Gallery on the mezzanine level for an insight into the great personalities of Ireland. You'll find European masterworks on the top floor, including a rare Vermeer (one of only 30-some known works by the Dutch artist), a classic Caravaggio (master of chiaroscuro and dramatic lighting), a Monet riverscape, and an early Cubist Picasso still life.

Try not to miss the wonderfully romantic *Meeting on the Turret Stairs*—Ireland's favorite painting (as voted by readers of the *Irish Times*)—by Frederic Burton. Because this vividly painted watercolor is vulnerable to fading, it's on view for only two hours per week (Mon and Wed 11:30-12:30).

Perhaps the most iconic of all the Irish art in this museum is the melodramatic depiction of the *Marriage of Strongbow and Aiofe* by Daniel Maclise. It captures the chaotic union of Norman and Irish interests that signaled the start of English domination of Ireland 850 years ago. Notice how the defeated Irish writhe and lament in the bright light of the foreground, while the scheming Norman warlords skulk in the dimly lit middle ground. The ruins of conquered Waterford smolder at the back.

Merrion Square and Nearby
▲MERRION SQUARE

Laid out in 1762, this square is ringed by elegant Georgian houses decorated with fine doors—a Dublin trademark. (If you're inspired by the ornate knobs and knockers, there's a shop by that name on nearby Nassau Street.) The park, once the exclusive domain of the residents, is now a delightful public escape and ideal for a picnic. To learn what "snogging" is, walk through the park on a sunny day, when it's full of smooching lovers. Oscar Wilde, lounging wittily on a boulder on the corner nearest the town center and surrounded by his clever quotes, provides a fun photo op.

▲NUMBER TWENTY-NINE GEORGIAN HOUSE

The carefully restored house at Number 29 Lower Fitzwilliam Street gives an intimate glimpse of middle-class Georgian life (which seems pretty high-class). Before entering, notice how many of the windows in the Georgian building across the street had once been bricked up to cut tax bills (back in the days when glass was a taxable luxury). From the sidewalk, descend the stairs to the basement-level entrance (corner of Lower Fitzwilliam and Lower Mount Streets, opposite southern corner of Merrion Square). Start with an interesting 15-minute video before exploring this 1790 Dublin home. As you climb its five floors, you'll find storyboards in each room explaining the everyday lives lived here.

Cost and Hours: €6, Tue-Sat 10:00-17:00, closed Sun-Mon, closed mid-Dec-mid-Feb, tours at 15:00, tel. 01/702-6165, www.esb.ie/no29.

Grafton Street and St. Stephen's Green Area
▲▲GRAFTON STREET

Once filled with noisy traffic, today's Grafton Street is Dublin's liveliest pedestrian shopping drag and people-watching paradise. A decade ago, when the Celtic Tiger economy was in mid-roar, this street had the fifth-most expensive retail rents in the world, behind Tokyo, London, New York, and Moscow (rents have since declined). A 10-minute stroll past street musicians takes you from Trinity College to St. Stephen's Green (and makes you wonder why some American merchants are so terrified of a car-free street).

Walking south from Trinity College, you'll pass two venerable department stores: the Irish Brown Thomas and the English Marks & Spencer. Johnson's Court alley leads to the Powerscourt Townhouse Shopping Centre, which tastefully fills a converted Georgian mansion. The huge, glass-covered St. Stephen's Green Shopping Centre and the peaceful green itself mark the top of Grafton Street. For fun, gather a pile of coins and walk the street, setting each human statue into action with a donation.

▲ST. STEPHEN'S GREEN

This city park was originally a medieval commons, complete with gory public executions. It was enclosed in 1664 and gradually surrounded with fine Georgian buildings. Today, it provides 22 acres of grassy refuge for Dubliners. At the northwest corner (near the end of Grafton Street) you'll be confronted by a looming marble arch erected to honor British officers killed during the Boer War. Locals nicknamed it "Traitor's Arch," as most Irish sympathized with the underdog Boers.

During the 1916 Easter Uprising, a group of rebels (who had read about WWI trench warfare in Flanders) dug up the park to hunker down in it, believing they would have a fortified position. Passionate as they were, these rebels were a mishmash of romantic poets, teachers, aristocratic ladies, and slum dwellers. They

St. Stephen's Green

hadn't figured on veteran British troops easily trumping their move by placing snipers atop the Shelbourne Hotel (with a bird's-eye view into the trenches). During the battle, there were surreal daily truces when both sides held their fire so that the park's keeper could safely feed his flock of ducks. The rebels eventually abandoned their positions in the park for better cover inside the College of Surgeons, at the west end of St. Stephen's Green.

On a sunny afternoon, this open space is a wonderful world apart from the big city. When marveling at the stateliness of Georgian Dublin, remember that during the Georgian period, Dublin was the second-most important city in the British Empire. Area big shots knew that any money wrung from the local populace not spent in Dublin would end up in London. Since it was "use it or lose it," they used it—with gusto—to beautify their city.

Dublin Castle and Nearby
▲▲DUBLIN CASTLE

Built on the spot of the first Viking fortress, this castle was the seat of English rule in Ireland for 700 years. Located where the Poddle and Liffey rivers came together, making a black pool (*dubh linn* in Irish), Dublin Castle was the official residence of the viceroy who implemented the will of the British royalty. In this stirring setting, the Brits handed power over to Michael Collins and the Irish in 1922. Today, it's used for fancy state and charity functions (which may sporadically close it to the public).

Standing in the courtyard, you can imagine the ugliness of the British-Irish situation. Notice the statue of justice above the gate—pointedly without her blindfold and admiring her sword. As Dubliners say, "There she stands, above her station, with her face to the palace and her arse to the nation." The fancy interior is viewable on a 45-minute tour, which offers a fairly boring room-by-room walk through the lavish state apartments of this most English of Irish palaces. (You can also tour on your own using the provided information.) The tour finishes with a look at the foundations of the Norman tower and the best remaining chunk of the 13th-century town wall.

Cost and Hours: €8.50 for one-hour guided tour, €6.50 to visit on your own, tickets sold in courtyard under portico opposite clock tower, tours depart hourly, Mon-Sat 9:45-16:45, Sun 12:00-16:45, tel. 01/645-8813, www.dublincastle.ie.

▲▲CHESTER BEATTY LIBRARY

This priceless, delightfully displayed collection of constantly rotating artifacts includes rare ancient manuscripts and beautifully illustrated books from around the world, plus a few odd curios. Start on the ground floor with the short film about Beatty (1875-1968), a rich American mining magnate who traveled widely, collected 66,000 objects assiduously, and retired to Ireland. Then head upstairs to see the treasures he bequeathed to his adopted country.

Cost and Hours: Free, Mon-Fri 10:00-17:00, Sat 11:00-17:00, Sun 13:00-17:00, closed Mon Oct-April, coffee shop, tel.

Dublin Castle

01/407-0750, www.cbl.ie. You'll find the library in the gardens of Dublin Castle (follow the signs).

◒ SELF-GUIDED TOUR

Start on the second floor. Note that exhibits may rotate, so they may not always be on display in the order outlined here.

Sacred Traditions Gallery: This space is dedicated to sacred texts, illuminated manuscripts, and miniature paintings from around the world. The doors swing open, and you're greeted by a video highlighting a diverse array of religious rites—a Christian wedding, Muslims kneeling for prayer, whirling dervishes, and so on.
• *Tour the floor clockwise, starting with Christian texts on the left side of the room. There you'll find several glass cases containing...*

Ancient Bible Fragments: In the 1930s, Beatty acquired (possibly through the black market) these 1,800-year-old manuscripts, which had recently been unearthed in Egypt. The Indiana Jones-like discovery instantly bumped scholars' knowledge of the early Bible up a notch. There were Old Testament books (Genesis, Deuteronomy), New Testament books (Gospels, Acts, Revelation), and—rarest of all—the Letters of Paul. Written in Greek on papyrus more than a century before previously known documents, these are some of the oldest versions of these texts in existence. Unlike most early Christian texts, the manuscripts were not rolled up in a scroll but bound in a book form called a "codex." On display (the collection changes) you may see pages from a third-century Gospel of Luke or the Gospel of John (c. A.D. 150-200). Jesus died around A.D. 33, and his words weren't recorded until decades later. Most early manuscripts date from the fourth century, so these pages are about as close to the source as you can get.

Letters (Epistles) of Paul: The Beatty has 112 pages of Saint Paul's collected letters (A.D. 180-200). Paul, a Roman citizen

(c. A.D. 5-67; see Albrecht Dürer's engraving of the saint), was the apostle most responsible for spreading Christianity beyond Palestine. Originally, Paul reviled Christians. But after a mystical experience, he went on to travel the known world, preaching the Good News in sophisticated Athens and the greatest city in the world, Rome, where he died a martyr to the cause. Along the way, he kept in touch with Christian congregations in cities like Corinth, Ephesus, and Rome with these letters. It's thanks to Paul that we have sayings such as "The love of money is the root of all evil"; "Love is patient, love is kind"; "Whatever a man sows, so shall he reap"; and "Fight the good fight."

Continuing up the left side of the room, you'll find gloriously illustrated **medieval Bibles** and **prayer books,** including an intricate, colorful, gold-speckled Book of Hours (1408).

• *Turn the corner into the center of the room, to find the sacred texts of...*

Islam: The angel Gabriel visited Muhammad (c. 570-632), instructing him to write down his heavenly visions in a book—the Quran. You'll see Qurans with exquisite calligraphy, such as one made in Baghdad in 1001. Nearby are other sacred Islamic texts, some beautifully illustrated, where you may find the rare illuminated manuscript of the "Life of the Prophet" (c. 1595), produced in Istanbul for an Ottoman sultan.

• *On the right side of the room, you enter the world of...*

East Asian Religions: Statues of Gautama Buddha (c. 563-483 B.C.) and Chinese Buddhist scrolls attest to the pervasive influence of this wise man. Buddha was born in India, but his philosophy spread to China, Japan, and Tibet (see the mandalas). Continuing clockwise, you will reach the writings from India, the land of a million gods—and the cradle of Buddhism, Hinduism, Sikhism, and Jainism.

• *Your visit continues downstairs on the first floor, in the gallery devoted to the...*

Arts of the Book: The focus here is on the many forms a "book" can take—from the earliest clay tablets and papyrus scrolls, to parchment scrolls and bound codexes, to medieval monks' wondrous illustrations, to the advent of printing and bookbinding, to the dawn of the 21st century and the digital age.

• *Tour the floor clockwise. Immediately to the left, find a glass case containing...*

Egyptian and Other Ancient Writings: A hieroglyph-covered papyrus scroll from the Book of the Dead (c. 300 B.C.) depicts a pharaoh on his throne (left) presiding over a soul's judgment in the afterlife. The jackal-headed god Anubis (center-right) holds a scale, weighing the heart of a dead woman to see if it's light enough for her to level up to the next phase of eternity. The Beatty also has a large selection of ancient Egyptian love songs (including, I believe, the number one hit of 1160 B.C., "I Love You, Mummy Dearest"). Nearby (in a freestanding glass case, near the bottom), if you look hard, you could find a few small cuneiform tablets and cylinder seals from as far back as 2700 B.C. These objects from ancient Sumeria (modern-day Iraq)

Islamic manuscript painting, Chester Beatty Library

Modern Ireland's Turbulent Birth

Imagine if our American patriot ancestors had fought both our Revolutionary War and our Civil War over seven chaotic years...and then appreciate the resilience of the Irish people. Here's a summary of what happened when.

1916: A nationalist militia called the Volunteers (led by **Patrick Pearse**) and the socialist Irish Citizen Army (led by **James Connolly**) join forces in the **Easter Uprising,** but they fail to end 750 years of British rule. The uprising is unpopular with most Irish, who are unhappy with the destruction in Dublin and preoccupied with World War I. But when 16 rebel leaders (including Pearse and Connolly) are executed, sympathy grows for the martyrs and the cause of Irish Independence.

Two important rebel leaders escape execution. Brooklyn-born **Eamon de Valera** is spared because of his American passport (the British don't want to anger their potential ally in World War I). **Michael Collins,** a low-ranking rebel officer refines urban guerrilla-warfare strategies in prison. After his release, he becomes the rebels' military and intelligence leader.

1918: World War I ends and a general election is held in Ireland. Outside of Ulster, the nationalist **Sinn Fein** party wins 73 out of 79 seats in Parliament. Only 4 out of 32 counties vote to maintain the Union with Britain (all 4 are in Ulster, part of which would become Northern Ireland). Rather than take their seats in London, Sinn Fein representatives abstain from participating in a government they see as foreign occupiers.

1919: On January 19, the abstaining Sinn Fein members set up a rebel government in Dublin called Dáil Éireann. On the same day, the first shots of the **Irish War of Independence** are fired as rebels begin ambushing police barracks. De Valera is elected by the Dáil to lead the rebels, with Collins as his deputy. Col-

are older than the pyramids and represent the very birth of writing.

• *Continue up the left side of the room, perusing displays on...*

Printing, Illustrating, and Bookbinding: The printing press with movable type was perfected by Johannes Gutenberg in Germany sometime in the early 1450s. The printed sheets were folded, sewn together, and wrapped in a cover. With the engraving process, beautiful illustrations could also be reproduced on a mass scale. Until the 20th century, it was common for a book buyer to acquire the printed sheets and then select a lavish custom-made cover.

• *Turn the corner to the center of the room.*

Islamic World: These are secular books—science textbooks and poetry— many from the rich Persian culture (modern-day Iran). Some are richly illustrated with elaborate calligraphy. It's often noted that Islam forbids visual art, strictly following the Bible's dictum against "graven" images. But, as you can see, that restriction doesn't apply to nonreligious texts.

• *Continue to the right side of the room.*

Far East: Besides albums and scrolls, you might see eye-catching Japanese woodblock prints, ornate Chinese snuff bottles, rhino-horn cups, and the silk dragon robes of Chinese emperors of the Qing dynasty (1644-1911). The Qianlong Emperor (r. 1736-1795)—a poet and arts patron—welcomed European Jesuits to his court and commissioned a huge collins' web of spies infiltrates British intelligence at Dublin Castle. The Volunteers rename themselves the **Irish Republican Army;** meanwhile the British beef up their military presence in Ireland by sending in WWI vets, the Black and Tans. A bloody war ensues.

1921: Tired of bloodshed, the British begin negotiations with the rebels. De Valera leads rebel negotiations, but then entrusts them to Collins (a clever politician, de Valera sees that whoever signs a treaty will be blamed for its compromises). Understanding the tricky position he's been placed in, Collins signs the **Anglo-Irish Treaty** in December, lamenting that in doing so he has signed his "own death warrant."

The Dáil narrowly ratifies the treaty (64 to 57), but Collins' followers are unable to convince de Valera's supporters that the compromises are a stepping stone to later full independence. De Valera and his anti-treaty disciples resign in protest. **Arthur Griffith,** founder of Sinn Fein, assumes the presidential post.

In June, the anti-treaty forces, holed up in the Four Courts building, are fired upon by Collins and his pro-treaty forces—thus igniting the **Irish Civil War.** The British want the treaty to stand and even supply Collins with cannons, meanwhile threatening to reenter Ireland if the anti-treaty forces aren't put down.

1922: In August, Griffith dies of stress-induced illness, and Collins is assassinated 10 days later. The pro-treaty forces prevail, backed by popular opinion and British-supplied military equipment.

1923: In April, the remaining IRA forces disarm, ending the civil war...but many of their bitter vets vow to carry on the fight. De Valera distances himself from the IRA and becomes the dominant Irish political leader for the next 40 years.

lection of books, including some carved from jade. A graceful Sumatran book, written on tree-bark pages, is bound so that it unfolds like an accordion—yet another example of great ingenuity in presenting the written word.

DUBLIN CITY HALL
The first Georgian building in this very Georgian city stands proudly overlooking Dame Street, in front of the gate to Dublin Castle. Built in 1779 as the Royal Exchange, it introduced the Georgian style (then very popular in Britain) to Ireland. Step inside (it's free) to feel the prosperity and confidence of Dublin in her 18th-century glory days. In 1852, this building became the City Hall. Under the

grand rotunda, a cycle of heroic paintings tells the city's history. (The mosaics on the floor convey such homilies as "Obedience makes the happiest citizenry.")

Pay your respects to the 18-foot-tall statue of Daniel O'Connell, the great

Dublin City Hall

orator and liberator who, in 1829, won emancipation for Catholics in Ireland from the much-despised Protestants over in London. The body of modern Irish rebel leader Michael Collins lay in state here after his assassination in 1922. The greeter at the information desk is eager to give you more information. Downstairs is the excellent *Story of the Capital* exhibition (€4), which has storyboards and video clips of Dublin's history.

Cost and Hours: free to enter, €4 exhibit includes audioguide, Mon-Sat 10:00-16:00, closed Sun, coffee shop, tel. 01/222-2204.

Dublin's Cathedrals Area

Because of Dublin's English past (particularly Henry VIII's Reformation, which led to the dissolution of the Catholic monasteries in both Ireland and England in 1539), neither of its top two churches is Catholic. Christ Church Cathedral and nearby St. Patrick's Cathedral are both Church of Ireland (Anglican). In the late 19th century, the cathedrals underwent extensive restoration. The rich Guinness brewery family forked out the dough to try to make St. Patrick's Cathedral outshine Christ Church—whose patrons were the equally rich, rival Jameson family of distillery fame. However, in Catholic Ireland, these Anglican sights feel hollow, and they're more famous than visit-worthy.

CHRIST CHURCH CATHEDRAL

Occupying the same site as the first wooden church built on this spot by King Sitric in late Viking times (c. 1030), the present structure is a mix of periods: Norman and Gothic, but mostly Victorian Neo-Gothic (1870s restoration work). Inside you'll find the reputed tomb of the Norman warlord Strongbow, who led the thin edge of the English military wedge that eventually dominated Ireland for centuries. This oldest building in Dublin has an unusually large underground crypt, containing stocks, statues, the cathedral's

silver, and an atmospheric café.

Cost and Hours: €6 includes downstairs crypt silver exhibition, €13.25 combo-ticket includes Dublinia (described next); Mon-Sat 9:00-18:00, Sun 12:30-14:30; €4 guided tours Mon-Fri at 11:00, 12:00, 14:00, and 15:00; tel. 01/677-8099, www.christchurchdublin.ie.

Evensong: A 45-minute evensong service is sung Thu at 18:00, Sun at 15:30.

▲DUBLINIA

This exhibit, which highlights Dublin's Viking and medieval past, is a hit with youngsters. The exhibits are laid out on three floors. The ground floor focuses on Viking Dublin, explaining life aboard a Viking ship and inside a Viking house. Viking traders introduced urban life and commerce to Ireland—but kids will be most interested in gawking at their gory weaponry.

The next floor up reveals Dublin's day-to-day life in medieval times, from chivalrous knights and damsels in town fairs to

Christ Church Cathedral

the brutal ravages of the Plague. Like the rest of Europe at that time (1347-1349), Ireland lost one-third of its population to the Black Death. The huge scale model of medieval Dublin is especially well done. The top floor's "History Hunters" section is devoted to how the puzzles of modern archaeology and science shed light on Dublin's history. From this floor, you can climb a couple of flights of stairs into the tower for so-so views of Dublin, or exit across an enclosed stone bridge to adjacent Christ Church Cathedral.

Cost and Hours: €8.50, €13.25 combo-ticket includes Christ Church Cathedral, daily March-Sept 10:00-17:00, Oct-Feb 11:00-16:30, last entry 45 minutes before closing, top-floor coffee shop open in summer, across from Christ Church Cathedral, tel. 01/679-4611, www.dublinia.ie.

ST. PATRICK'S CATHEDRAL
The first church here was built on the site where St. Patrick baptized local pagan

converts. The core of the Gothic structure you see today was built in the 13th century. After the Reformation, it passed into the hands of the Anglican Church. A century later, Oliver Cromwell's puritanical Calvinist troops—who considered the Anglicans to be little more than Catholics without a pope—stabled their horses here as a sign of disrespect.

Jonathan Swift (author of *Gulliver's Travels*) was dean of the Cathedral for 32 years in the 18th century. His grave is located near the front door (on the right side of the nave), where his cutting, self-penned epitaph reads: "He lies where furious indignation can no longer rend his heart." Check out the large wooden Door of Reconciliation hanging in the north transept, with the rough hole in the middle. This was the Chapter House door through which two feuding, sword-bearing 15th-century nobles shook hands..."chancing their arms" and giving the Irish that expression of trust.

Cost and Hours: €6 donation to church, Mon-Fri 9:00-17:00, Sat 9:00-18:00, Sun 12:30-14:30 & 16:30-18:00, last entry one hour before closing.

Evensong: You'll get chills listening to the local "choir of angels" Mon-Fri at 17:45 and Sun at 15:15.

▲▲ *Temple Bar*
This much-promoted area—with trendy shops, cafés, theaters, galleries, pubs with live music, and restaurants—feels like the heart of the city. It's Dublin's touristy "Left Bank," and as in Paris, it's on the south shore of the river, filling the cobbled streets between Dame Street and the River Liffey.

Three hundred years ago, this was the city waterfront, where tall sailing ships offloaded their goods (a "bar" was a loading dock along the river, and the Temples were a dominant merchant family). Eventually, the city grew eastward, filling in tidal mudflats, to create the docklands of modern Dublin. Once a bustling

St. Patrick's Cathedral interior

Georgian center of craftsmen and merchants, this neighborhood fell on hard times in the 20th century. Ensuing low rents attracted students and artists, giving the area a bohemian flair. With government tax incentives and lots of development money, the Temple Bar district has now become a thriving cultural (and beer-drinking) hot spot.

Temple Bar can be an absolute spectacle in the evening, when it bursts with revelers. The noise, pushy crowds, and inflated prices have driven most Dubliners away. But even if you're just gawking, don't miss the opportunity to wander through this human circus. It can be a real zoo on summer weekend nights, holidays, and nights after big sporting events let out. Women in funky hats, part of loud "hen" (bachelorette) parties, promenade down the main drag as drunken dudes shout from pub doorways to get their attention. Be aware that a pint of beer here is at least €1 more than at less glitzy pubs just a couple of blocks away (north of the River Liffey or south of Dame Street).

Temple Bar Square, just off Temple Bar Street (near Ha' Penny Bridge), is the epicenter of activity. It hosts free street theater and a Saturday book market, and has handy ATMs. On busy weekends, people-watching here is a contact sport. You're bound to meet some characters.

Irish music fans find great CDs at humble **Claddagh Records.** Unlike big, glitzy chain stores, this is a little hole-in-the-wall shop staffed by informed folks who love turning visitors on to Irish tunes. Grab a couple of CDs for your drive through the Irish countryside (Mon-Sat 11:00-17:30, closed Sun, Cecilia Street, just around the corner from Luigi Malone's, tel. 01/677-0262). Farther west and somewhat hidden is **Meeting House Square,** with a lively organic-produce market (Sat 10:00-18:00). Bordering the square is the **Irish Film Institute,** which shows a variety of art-house flicks. A bohemian crowd relaxes in its bar/café, awaiting the next film (6 Eustace Street, main entry on Eustace Street, box office daily 13:30-21:00, tel. 01/679-5744, www.irishfilm.ie).

Rather than follow particular pub or restaurant recommendations (though mine are listed on page 81), venture down a few side lanes off the main drag to see what looks good.

If the rowdy Temple Bar scene gets to

Temple Bar

be too much, cross the River Liffey on the **Millennium Pedestrian Bridge,** where you'll find a mellower, more cosmopolitan choice of restaurants with outdoor seating in the Millennium Walk district (the best two-block stretch is Millennium Walk itself; enter at the end of the bridge). The next bridge east is the pedestrian-only **Ha' Penny Bridge,** named for the halfpence toll people used to pay to cross it. Two recommended restaurants—the cheap Epicurean Food Hall and the trendy The Church—are nearby (see page 82).

North of the River Liffey

The main attraction north of the river—O'Connell Street—is covered by the self-guided walk on page 45. After you're oriented with the walk, consider the following sights.

▲DUBLIN WRITERS MUSEUM

No other country so small has produced such a wealth of literature. As interesting to those who are fans of Irish literature as it is boring to those who aren't, this three-room museum features the lives and works of Dublin's great writers. It's a low-tech museum, where you read informative plaques while perusing display cases with minor memorabilia—a document signed by Jonathan Swift, a photo of Oscar Wilde reclining thoughtfully, an early edition of Bram Stoker's *Dracula,* a George Bernard Shaw playbill, a not-so-famous author's tuxedo, or a newspaper from Easter 1916 announcing "Two More Executions To-day." If unassuming attractions like that stir your blood—or if you simply want a manageable introduction to Irish lit—it's worth a visit.

Cost and Hours: €7.50, includes helpful audioguide; June-Aug Mon-Fri 10:00-18:00, Sat 10:00-17:00; Sept-May Mon-Sat 10:00-17:00; Sun 11:00-17:00 year-round; coffee shop, 18 Parnell Square North, tel. 01/872-2077, www.writers museum.com.

Background: The museum isn't exclusive about "Irish" writers. Born here? Lived here? Wrote about Ireland, wrote in Irish, or were sympathetic to the cause of Irish nationalism? You're in. Some of the writers featured by the museum were born in Ireland, but that's about it—they lived elsewhere, wrote in English, and gained fame for non-Irish works. One trait they all seem to share is a stubborn streak of personal independence, perhaps related to Ireland's national struggle to assert its cultural identity. The museum is housed in a Georgian home, making for an elegant setting to appreciate these pioneering writers. (For an overview of Irish literature, see page 72.)

Visiting the Museum: The collection is chronological. **Room 1** starts with Irish literature's deep roots in the roving, harp-playing **bards** of medieval times. By telling stories in the native language, they helped unify the island's culture. But "literature" came only with the arrival of the English language. **Jonathan Swift** (1667-1745)—Ireland's first great writer—was born in Dublin and served as dean of St. Patrick's Cathedral, though he spent much of his life in London. His stinging

Oscar Wilde

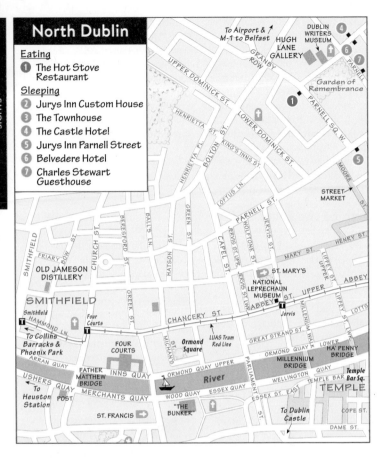

North Dublin

Eating
1. The Hot Stove Restaurant

Sleeping
2. Jurys Inn Custom House
3. The Townhouse
4. The Castle Hotel
5. Jurys Inn Parnell Street
6. Belvedere Hotel
7. Charles Stewart Guesthouse

(Map labels) DUBLIN WRITERS MUSEUM · HUGH LANE GALLERY · To Airport & M-1 to Belfast · GRANBY ROW · UPPER DOMINICK ST. · Garden of Remembrance · PARNELL SQ. W. · HENRIETTA ST. · LOWER DOMINICK ST. · KING'S INNS ST. · BOLTON ST. · LOFTUS LN. · MOORE ST. · STREET MARKET · PARNELL ST. · GREEN ST. · JERVIS ST. · MARY ST. · HENRY ST. · WOLFTONE ST. · CAPEL ST. · JERVIS ST. UPPER · LIFFEY ST. UPPER · ABBEY ST. UPPER · SMITHFIELD · FRIARY · BOW ST. · CHURCH ST. · BERESFORD ST. · BALL'S LN. · HATSON ST. · OLD JAMESON DISTILLERY · ST. MARY'S · NATIONAL LEPRECHAUN MUSEUM · GREEK ST. · Jervis · MILLENNIUM WALK · LOTTS · Smithfield · HAMMOND LN. · Four Courts · CHANCERY ST. · GREAT STRAND ST. · LIFFEY ST. LWR. · To Collins Barracks & Phoenix Park · FOUR COURTS · MICHAN'S ST. · Ormond Square · LUAS Tram Red Line · ORMOND QUAY UPPER · ORMOND QUAY LOWER · HA' PENNY BRIDGE · ARRAN QUAY · FATHER MATTHEW BRIDGE · INNS QUAY · MILLENNIUM BRIDGE · PARLIAMENT ST. · WELLINGTON QUAY · Temple Bar Sq. · USHERS QUAY · MERCHANTS QUAY · River · WOOD QUAY · ESSEX QUAY · ESSEX ST. EAST · TEMPLE BAR · To Heuston Station · POST · ST. FRANCIS · "THE BUNKER" · To Dublin Castle · COPE ST. · DAME ST.

satire of societal hypocrisy set the tone of rebellion found in much Irish literature. The **theater** has been another long-standing Irish specialty, starting with the 18th-century playwright Oliver Goldsmith. In the **1890s,** sophisticated Dublin (and Trinity College) was a cradle for great writers who ultimately found their fortunes in England: the playwright/poet/wit Oscar Wilde, Bram Stoker (who married Wilde's girlfriend), and the big-idea playwright George Bernard Shaw. Poet **W. B. Yeats** stayed home, cultivating Irish folklore at soirees (hosted by the literary patron Lady Augusta Gregory) and inspired by his unrequited muse, the feminist Irish revolutionary Maude Gonne (see her portrait).

Room 2 continues with Yeats' **Abbey Theatre,** the scene of premieres by great Irish playwrights (including Yeats, Shaw, and Wilde), and a source of political unrest during the 1916 Easter Uprising. Dublin was also a breeding ground for bold new ideas, producing Modernist writers Samuel (*Waiting for Godot*) Beckett and James Joyce (his Cultural Centre is described next). As the 20th century progressed, playwrights such as Sean O'Casey, Brendan Behan, and Brian Friel kept Dublin at the forefront of modern theater. You can read a long letter by terrorist/bad boy Brendan Behan from Hollywood about schmoozing with Groucho, Harpo, and Sinatra.

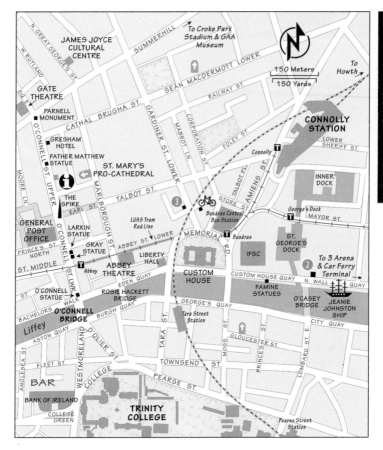

Finish your visit by going **upstairs** to see a refined Georgian library, then peruse the busts and portraits in the Gallery of Writers.

JAMES JOYCE CULTURAL CENTRE

Aficionados of James Joyce's work (but few others) will want to visit this micro-museum.

Cost and Hours: €5, Mon-Sat 10:00-17:00, Sun 12:00-17:00, closed Mon Oct-March, two blocks east of the Dublin Writers Museum at 35 North Great George's Street, tel. 01/878-8547, www.jamesjoyce.ie.

Background: James Joyce (1882-1941) was born and raised in Dublin, wrote in great detail about his hometown, and mined the local dialect for his pitch-perfect dialogue. His best-known work, *Ulysses*, chronicles one day in the life of the fictional Leopold Bloom (June 16, 1904) as he wanders through the underside of Dublin. In his own life, Joyce left Dublin (on June 17, 1904) to live in Paris. He never took up the cause of Irish nationalism and rarely delved into Irish mythology. His focus was the Modernist question of how to find one's place in a post-religious world without traditional guidelines. His stream-of-consciousness writing style (which, truthfully, can be hard to follow and often boring) is meant to mimic the multiple strains of thought running through a person's mind at any

Dublin's Literary Life

Dublin in the 1700s, grown rich from a lucrative cloth trade, was one of Europe's most cultured and sophisticated cities. The buildings were decorated in the Georgian style still visible today, and the city's Protestant elite shuttled between here and London, bridging the Anglo-Irish cultural gap. Jonathan Swift (1667-1745) was the era's greatest Anglo-Irish writer—a brilliant satirist and author of *Gulliver's Travels*. He was also dean of St. Patrick's Cathedral (1713-1745) and one of the city's eminent citizens.

Around the turn of the 20th century, Dublin produced some of the world's great modern writers. Bram Stoker (1847-1912) was creator of *Dracula*. Oscar Wilde (1854-1900) penned *The Picture of Dorian Gray* and a clutch of fine plays. George Bernard Shaw (1856-1950) wrote *Pygmalion*, *Major Barbara*, *Man and Superman*, and a host of other dramas. William Butler Yeats (1865-1939) was a prolific poet and playwright on Irish themes. And James Joyce (1882-1941) whipped up a masterpiece called *Ulysses*.

one moment. Joyce's frank depictions of sexuality helped employ two generations of censors in Ireland and America.

Visiting the Centre: Your visit begins (top floor) with videos on Joyce's life and his enormous influence on subsequent writers. Next, a touchscreen display traces Bloom's Dublin Odyssey. Photos of Joyce and quotes from his books decorate the walls. A re-creation of a messy, cramped study evokes Joyce's struggles through poverty and criticism as he forged his own

path. Down one flight, see portraits of Joyce and his wife and muse, Nora Barnacle. (The first time they, um, went on a date was June 16, 1904.) On the ground floor, a film version of one of Joyce's short stories, *The Dead*, plays eternally. In a tiny back courtyard, you can see the original door from 7 Eccles Street, the address of Leopold Bloom.

▲HUGH LANE GALLERY

This collection of mostly modern and contemporary art has a sampling of Impressionist masterpieces that come from the gallery's founding collection, once owned by Sir Hugh Lane. Genteel and bite-sized, the museum is particularly worth a visit for a well-known Monet painting, an exhibit on modern artist Francis Bacon, and a few select paintings by Irish artists.

Cost and Hours: Free, Tue-Thu 10:00-18:00, Fri-Sat 10:00-17:00, Sun 11:00-17:00, closed Mon, Parnell Square North, tel. 01/222-5550, www.hughlane.ie.

Visiting the Gallery: Head to **Room 1,** where you'll find **Monet's *Waterloo Bridge*** (1900). On a visit to London, the once-bohemian, now-famous Impressionist Claude Monet checked into Room 618 of the Savoy Hotel and set to work painting Waterloo Bridge at different times of day and in various weather conditions. This painting is the best known of 41 versions of the scene. Monet—the master of capturing hazy, filtered light—loved London for its fog. With the Thames in the foreground, the bridge in the middle, and belching smokestacks in the distance, Monet had three different layers of atmospheric depth to explore.

Also in Room 1 is *Portrait of Hugh Lane* by the American society portraitist John Singer Sargent. In 1905, the dapper Sir Hugh, an art dealer, bought Monet's *Waterloo Bridge* as part of his mission to bring modern art to provincial Dublin (see a Degas painting nearby). Unfortunately, Sir Hugh went down on the *Lusitania* in 1915 and didn't see this gallery open.

Room 3 is devoted to Jack B. Yeats—the famous poet's little brother—who had a long career as a magazine illustrator, novelist, set designer for the Abbey Theatre, painter, and even Ireland's first Olympic medalist (for art). Yeats helped establish the modern movement in Ireland, and he encouraged Hugh Lane to patronize Irish artists. In his own paintings, Yeats turned to the Irish countryside and common laborers for subjects. Over time, his style evolved from realistic rural scenes to thickly painted, swirling works at the edge of abstraction. In **Room 4,** check out the next generation of Irish artists Yeats influenced—abstract and Pop Art of the 1970s and 1980s.

Francis Bacon Studio: Although he spent most of his life in London, Francis Bacon (1909-1992) was born in Dublin and raised in nearby Naas. After his death, his entire London studio was reconstructed here, just as the artist had left it.

After a wandering youth of odd jobs and petty crime, Bacon took up painting in his late thirties. He jumped onto the art stage in 1945 with his bleak canvases of twisted, deformed, screaming-mouthed men caged in barren landscapes—which hauntingly captured the mood of post-WWII Europe. He would become Britain's premier painter, but he continued to live simply. He stayed in his small, cramped flat with an even smaller studio (this one) for his entire life. Here he painted his famous series of "Heads"—portraits of his friends, especially of his life partner, George Dyer.

The place is a mess—empty paint cans, slashed canvases, books, photos, and newspapers everywhere—leaving only enough space for Bacon to set up his canvas in the middle of it all and paint. (If I were caged here, I'd scream.) As trashed as the studio is, it reflects Bacon's belief that "chaos breeds energy."

Spend 10 minutes with the 1985 filmed interview of Bacon, which was conducted in the studio. He speaks articulately about his work and reminisces about his down-and-out days. In nearby rooms are touchscreen terminals, photos of Bacon, a few unfinished works, and display cases of personal items, such as his coffee-table book on Velázquez, the Old Master who inspired Bacon's famous portrait of a screaming pope.

JEANIE JOHNSTON TALL SHIP AND FAMINE MUSEUM

Docked on the River Liffey, this seagoing sailing ship is a replica of a legendary Irish "famine ship." The original *Jeanie Johnston* embarked on 16 six- to eight-week transatlantic crossings, carrying more than 2,500 Irish emigrants to their new lives in America and Canada in the decade after the Great Potato Famine. While many barely seaworthy hulks were known as "coffin ships," the people who boarded the *Jeanie Johnston* were lucky: With a humanitarian captain and even a doctor, not one life was lost. Your tour guide will introduce you to the ship's main characters and help illuminate day-to-day life aboard a cramped tall ship 160 years ago.

Monet, Waterloo Bridge

Jeanie Johnston *tall ship*

From Famine to Revolution

After the Great Potato Famine (1845-1849), destitute rural Irish moved to the city in droves, seeking work and causing a housing shortage. Unscrupulous landlords subdivided the city's once-grand mansions, vacated when gentry moved to London after the 1801 Act of Union, so the tiny rooms could then be crammed with poor renters. Dublin became one of the most densely populated cities in Europe—one of every three Dubliners lived in a slum. According to the 1911 census, one district counted 835 people living in 15 houses (many with a single outhouse in back or a communal chamber pot in the room). Tuberculosis was rampant, and infant mortality skyrocketed.

Those who could get work clung tenaciously to their jobs. Terrible working conditions prompted many to join trade unions. A 1913 strike and employer lock-out, known as the "Dublin Lockout," lasted for seven months. The picket lines were brutally put down by police in the pocket of rich businessmen, led by newspaper owner and hotel magnate William Murphy. In response, James Larkin and James Connolly formed the Irish Citizen Army, a socialist militia to protect the poor trade unionists.

Murphy eventually broke the unions. Larkin headed for the US to organize workers there. During World War I, he praised the rise of the Soviet Union and later was persecuted during the postwar "Red Scare" (even doing time in Sing Sing prison for advocating "unlawful means" to overthrow the US government). Meanwhile, Connolly stayed in Ireland and brought the Irish Citizen Army into the 1916 Easter Uprising as an integral part of the rebel forces. During the uprising, he slyly had a rebel flag flown over Murphy's prized hotel on O'Connell Street. The uninformed British artillery battalions took the bait and pulverized it.

Connolly was the last of the rebel leaders executed in Dublin in 1916. Unable to stand in front of the firing squad in Kilmainham Gaol (his ankle was shattered by a bullet while he was defending the General Post Office), Connolly was tied to a chair and shot sitting down. Of the 16 rebel executions, his was the one most credited with turning Irish public opinion in favor of the rebel martyrs.

Today you'll find heroic Dublin statues to honor them both. James Larkin, arms outstretched, is in front of the post office on O'Connell Street. James Connolly is on Beresford Place, behind the Customs House.

Because this ship makes goodwill voyages to Atlantic ports, it may be away during your visit.

Cost and Hours: €9, visits by 45-minute tour only, tours depart hourly, daily April-Oct 10:00-16:00, Nov-March 11:00-16:00, on the north bank of the Liffey just east of Sean O'Casey Bridge, tel. 01/473-0111, www.jeaniejohnston.ie.

Outer Dublin

The Kilmainham Gaol and the Guinness Storehouse are located west of the old center and can be combined in one visit, linked by a 20-minute walk; the hop-on, hop-off City Sightseeing Dublin tour bus (see page 44); a five-minute taxi ride; or public bus #40. (To ride the bus from the jail to the Guinness Storehouse, leave the prison and take three rights—crossing no streets—to reach the bus stop.)

▲▲▲KILMAINHAM GAOL (JAIL)

Opened in 1796 as Dublin's county jail and a debtors' prison, Kilmainham was considered a model in its day. In reality, this jail was frequently used by the British as a political prison. Many of those who fought for Irish independence were held or executed here, including leaders of the rebellions of 1798, 1803, 1848, 1867, and 1916. National heroes Robert Emmett and Charles Stewart Parnell each did time here. The last prisoner to be held in the jail was Eamon de Valera, who later became president of Ireland. He was released on July 16, 1924, the day Kilmainham was finally shut down. The buildings, virtually in ruins, were restored in the 1960s. Today, it's a shrine to the Nathan Hales of Ireland.

Cost and Hours: €7, Mon-Sat 9:30-16:30, Sun 10:00-16:30, last entry one hour before closing; bus #69 or #70 from Aston Quay or #13 or #40 from O'Connell Street or College Green—confirm with driver; tel. 01/453-5984. The humble upstairs café serves sandwiches and coffee.

Visiting the Jail: Start your visit with a one-hour guided **tour** (2/hour, includes 15-minute prison-history slide show in the prison chapel—spend waiting time in museum). It's touching to tour the cells and places of execution—hearing tales of oppressive colonialism and heroic patriotism—alongside Irish schoolkids who know these names well. The museum has an excellent exhibit on Victorian prison life and Ireland's fight for independence. Don't miss the museum's dimly lit Last Words 1916 hall upstairs, which displays the stirring final letters that patriots sent to loved ones hours before facing the firing squad.

▲GUINNESS STOREHOUSE

A visit to the Guinness Storehouse is, for many, a devout pilgrimage. But some visitors are surprised to find the vibe to be more like a Disneyland for beer lovers. Don't look for conveyor belts of beer bottles being stamped with bottle caps. Instead, you'll find huge crowds, high decibel music, and wall-sized, dreamy TV beer ads.

Kilmainham Gaol

The Record-Breaking Records Book

Look up "beer" in the *Guinness World Records*, and you'll discover that the strongest brew ever sold had an alcohol volume of 55 percent (a Scottish brew called *The End of History*), and that the record for removing beer bottle caps with one's teeth is 68 in one minute. But aside from listing records for such amazing—or amazingly stupid—feats, the famous record book has a more subtle connection with beer.

In 1951, while hunting in Ireland's County Wexford, Sir Hugh Beaver, then the managing director at Guinness Breweries, debated with his companions over which was the fastest game bird in Europe: the golden plover or the red grouse. That night at his estate, after scouring countless reference books, they were disappointed not to find a definitive answer.

Beaver realized that similar questions were likely being debated nightly across pubs in Ireland and Britain. So he hired twins Norris and Ross McWhirter, who ran a fact-finding agency in London, to compile a book of answers to various questions. They began assembling the first edition of the book by contacting experts, such as astrophysicists, etymologists, virologists, and volcanologists. In 1955, the *Guinness Book of Records* (later renamed *Guinness World Records*) was published. By Christmas, it topped the British best-seller list.

In the beginning, entries mostly focused on natural phenomena and animal oddities, but grew to include a wide variety of extreme human achievements. After more than a half-century of noting record-breaking traditions around the globe, the volume continues to provide answers to burning questions, identifying the wealthiest cat in the world, the largest burrito ever made, and the record time for peeling 50 pounds of onions (an event that likely caused a lot of tears).

The iconic books are now available in more than 100 countries and 26 languages, with more than 3.5 million copies sold annually. As the best-selling copyrighted book of all time, it even earns a record-breaking entry within its own pages.

Arthur Guinness began brewing the renowned stout here in 1759, and by 1868 it was the biggest brewery in the world. Today, the sprawling brewery complex fills several city blocks, but the Storehouse occupies just one of them.

Cost and Hours: €18, includes a €5 pint; €1 off with your hop-on, hop-off bus ticket or 10 percent discount if you book online; daily 9:30-17:00, July-Aug until 19:00; enter on Bellevue Street, bus #123 from Dame Street and O'Connell Street; tel. 01/408-4800, www.guinness-store house.com.

Visiting the Brewery: Around the world, Guinness brews more than 10 million pints a day. Although the home of Ireland's national beer welcomes visitors with a sprawling modern museum, there are no tours of an actual working brewery here.

The museum fills the old fermentation plant used from 1902 through 1988, which reopened in 2000 as a huge shrine to the tradition. Step into the middle of the ground floor and look up. A tall, beer-glass-shaped glass atrium—14 million pints big—soars upward past four floors of exhibitions and cafés to the skylight. Then look down at Arthur's original 9,000-year lease, enshrined under Plexiglas in the floor...and you realize that at £45 per year, it was quite a bargain. (The brewery eventually purchased the land, so the lease is no longer valid.)

The actual exhibit makes brewing seem more grandiose than it is and presents Arthur as if he were the god of human happiness. His pints contain only 200 calories, but they pack a 4.2 percent alcohol content. Highlights are the cooperage (with 1954 film clips showing the master keg-makers plying their now virtually extinct trade), a display of the brewery's clever ads, and a small exhibit about the beer's connection to the *Guinness World Records* (see sidebar).

The tasting rooms provide a 10-minute detour. In the "white room" you're introduced to using your five senses to appreciate the perfect porter. Then in the "black room" you're told how to taste it from a leprechaun-sized beer glass.

Atop the building, the **Gravity Bar** provides visitors with a commanding 360-degree view of Dublin—with vistas all the way to the sea—and an included beer.

▲NATIONAL MUSEUM: DECORATIVE ARTS AND HISTORY

This branch of the National Museum, which occupies the huge, 18th-century stone Collins Barracks in west Dublin, displays Irish dress, furniture, weapons, silver, and other domestic baubles from the past 700 years. History buffs will linger longest in the "Soldiers & Chiefs" exhibit, which covers the Irish at war both at home and abroad since 1500 (including the American Civil War). The sober finale is the "Understanding 1916" room, offering Ireland's best coverage of the painful birth of this nation, an event known as the "Terrible Beauty." Guns, personal letters, and death masks help illustrate the 1916 Easter Uprising, the War of Independence against Britain, and Ireland's civil war. Croppies Acre, the large park between the museum and the river, was the site of Dublin's largest soup kitchen during the Great Potato Famine in 1845-1849.

Cost and Hours: Free, Tue-Sat 10:00-17:00, Sun 14:00-17:00, closed Mon, good café; on north side of the River Liffey in Collins Barracks on Benburb Street, roughly across the river from Guinness Storehouse, easy to reach by the LUAS red line—get off at Museum stop; tel. 01/677-7444, www.museum.ie. Call ahead for sporadic tour times.

▲GAELIC ATHLETIC ASSOCIATION MUSEUM

The GAA was founded in 1884 as an expression of an Irish cultural awakening. It was created to foster the development of Gaelic sports, specifically Gaelic football and hurling, and to exclude English sports such as cricket and rugby. The GAA played an important part in the fight for independence. This museum, at 82,000-seat Croke Park Stadium in east Dublin, offers a high-tech, interactive introduction to Ireland's favorite games. Relive the greatest moments in hurling and Irish-football history. Then get involved: Pick up a stick and try hurling, kick a football, and test your speed and balance. A

The Gaelic Athletic Association

The GAA has long been a powerhouse in Ireland. Ireland's national pastimes of Gaelic football and hurling pack stadiums all over the country. When you consider that 80,000 people—paying at least €20 to €30 each—stuff Dublin's Croke Park Stadium and that all the athletes are strictly amateur, you might wonder, "Where does all the money go?"

Ireland has a long tradition of using the revenue generated by these huge events to promote Gaelic athletics and Gaelic cultural events throughout the country. So, while the players participate only for the glory of their various counties, the money generated is funding children's leagues, school coaches, small-town athletic facilities, and traditional arts, music, and dance—as well as the building and maintenance of giant stadiums such as Croke Park (which claims to be the third-largest stadium in Europe).

Gaelic sports are a heartfelt expression of Irish identity. There was a time when the Irish were not allowed to be members of the GAA if they also belonged to a cricket club (a British game). In 1921, during the War of Independence, Michael Collins (leader of the early IRA) orchestrated the simultaneous assassination of a dozen British intelligence agents around Dublin in a single morning. The same day, the Black and Tans retaliated. These grizzled British WWI veterans, clad in black police coats and tan surplus army pants, had been sent to Ireland to stamp out the rebels. Knowing Croke Park would be full of Irish Nationalists, they entered the packed stadium during a Gaelic football match and fired into the stands, killing 13 spectators as well as a Tipperary player. It was Ireland's first Bloody Sunday, a tragedy that would be repeated 51 years later in Derry.

Today Croke Park's "Hill 16" grandstands are built on rubble dumped here after the 1916 Uprising; it's literally sacred ground. And the Hogan stands are named after the murdered player from Tipperary. Queen Elizabeth II visited the stadium during her historic visit in 2011. Her warm interest in the stadium and in the institution of the GAA did much to heal old wounds.

15-minute film (played on request) gives you a "Sunday at the stadium" experience.

Cost and Hours: €6, Mon-Sat 9:30-17:00, Sun 10:30-17:00, on game Sundays the museum is open to ticket holders only, café, located under the stands at Croke Park Stadium, a 20-minute walk northeast of Parnell Square—enter from St. Joseph's Avenue off Clonliffe Road, tel. 01/819-2323, www.crokepark.ie/gaa-museum.

Tours: There are two tours. The €12.50 stadium tour is worth it only for rabid fans who want a glimpse of the huge stadium and yearn to know which locker room is considered the unlucky one. On the €20 "Etihad Skyline" rooftop tour, you'll see views from lofty catwalks 17 stories above the field (tours include museum and are offered 4-6 times a day—see website or call for times).

EXPERIENCES

Shopping

Shops are open roughly Monday-Saturday 9:00-18:00 and until 20:00 on Thursday. Hours are shorter on Sunday (if shops are open at all). Good shopping areas include:

• **Grafton Street,** with its neighboring streets and arcades (such as the fun Great George's Arcade between Great George's and Drury Streets), and nearby shopping centers (Powerscourt Townhouse and St. Stephen's Green). Francis Street creaks with antiques.

• **Henry Street,** home to Dublin's top department stores (pedestrian-only, off O'Connell Street).

• **Nassau Street,** lining Trinity College, with the popular Kilkenny department store, the Irish Music store, and lots of touristy shops.

• **Temple Bar,** worth a browse any day for its art, jewelry, New Age paraphernalia, gift shops, books, and music (try Claddagh Records for Irish music, Mon-Sat 11:00-17:30, closed Sun, Cecilia Street). On Saturdays at Temple Bar's Meeting House Square, vendors sell food in the morning (from 9:00) and books in the afternoon (until 18:00).

• **Millennium Walk,** a trendy lane stretching two blocks north from the River Liffey to Abbey Street. It's filled with hip restaurants, shops, and coffee bars. It's easy to miss—look for the south entry at the pedestrian Millennium Bridge, or the north entry at Jervis Street LUAS stop.

• **Street markets,** such as Moore Street, with produce, noise, and lots of local color (Mon-Sat 8:00-18:00, closed Sun, near General Post Office), and St. Michan Street, with fish (Tue-Sat 7:00-15:00, closed Sun-Mon, behind Four Courts building).

Theater

Abbey Theatre is Ireland's national theater, founded by W. B. Yeats in 1904 to preserve Irish culture during British rule (€15-40, generally nightly at 19:30, Sat matinees at 14:00, 26 Lower Abbey Street, tel. 01/878-7222, www.abbeytheatre.ie). **Gate Theatre** does foreign plays as well as Irish classics (Cavendish Row, tel. 01/874-4045, www.gatetheatre.ie). The **Gaiety Theatre** offers a wide range of quality productions (King Street South, toll tel. 0818-719-388, www.gaietytheatre.ie). The **Bord Gáis Energy Theatre** is the newest and spiffiest venue (Grand Canal Square, tel. 01/677-7999, www.bordgaisenergy theatre.ie). Street theater takes the stage in Temple Bar on summer evenings. Browse the listings and fliers at the TI.

Concerts

The **Steeple Sessions** are traditional Irish music concerts that attract Ireland's best trad musicians for 1.5-hour sessions. Their location—in the Unitarian Church at the southwest corner of St. Stephen's Green—may change; check their website (€15, June-Aug Tue and Thu at 20:00, tel. 01/678-8470, 112 St. Stephen's Green

Enjoying Dublin's shopping streets

Dublin lights up at night.

West, www.steeplesessions.com).

The **3 Arena,** once a railway terminus (easy LUAS access), is now sponsored by a hip phone company. Residents call it by its geographic nickname: The Point. It's considered one of the country's top live-music venues (East Link Bridge, toll tel. 0818-719-300, www.3arena.ie).

At the **National Concert Hall,** the National Symphony Orchestra performs most Friday evenings (€20-40, off St. Stephen's Green at Earlsfort Terrace, tel. 01/417-0000, www.nch.ie).

Pub Action

Folk music fills Dublin's pubs, and street entertainers ply their trade in the midst of the party people in Temple Bar and among shoppers on Grafton Street. The Temple Bar area in particular thrives with music—traditional, jazz, and pop. Although it's pricier than the rest of Dublin, it really is the best place for tourists and locals (who come here to watch the tourists). For locations, see the "Dublin Restaurants" map on page 84.

Gogarty's Pub has foot-tapping sessions downstairs daily at 14:00 and upstairs nightly from 21:00. Use this pub as a kickoff for your Temple Bar evening (at corner of Fleet and Anglesea, tel. 01/671-1822). It's also where the Traditional Irish Musical Pub Crawl starts (see page 44).

A 10-minute hike up the river west of Temple Bar takes you to a twosome with a local and less-touristy ambience. **The Brazen Head,** which lays claim to being the oldest pub in Dublin, is a hit for an early dinner and late live music (nightly from 21:30), with atmospheric rooms and a courtyard perfect for balmy evenings. They also host great "Food, Folk, and Fairies" storytelling dinner evenings (see page 81). **O'Shea's Merchant Pub,** just across the street, is filled with locals and encrusted in memories of County Kerry football heroes. The front half is a restaurant, but the magic is in the back half. There's live traditional music nightly at 21:30 (enter on Bridge Street, tel. 01/679-3797, www.themerchanttemplebar.com).

The **Palace Bar** is a well-preserved gin joint, with almost 135 years of history. It attracted Dublin's literary greats from the start, and contrasts sharply (and refreshingly) with the prefab offerings down the street in the Temple Bar mayhem (east end of Temple Bar, where Fleet Street hits Westmoreland Street at 21 Fleet Street, tel. 01/671-7388, www.thepalacebar dublin.com).

Porterhouse has an inviting and varied menu, Dublin's best selection of microbrews, and live music. You won't find Guinness here, just tasty homebrews. Try one of their fun sampler trays. You can check their music schedule online (€12-15 entrées, corner of Essex Street East and Parliament Street, tel. 01/671-5715, www. porterhousebrewco.com).

Most trad sessions include a fiddle.

Dublin nightlife

EATING

It's easy to find fine, creative eateries all over town. While you can get decent pub grub for €15 on just about any corner, consider saving that for the countryside. There's no reason to eat Irish in cosmopolitan Dublin—going local these days is the same as going ethnic. The city's good restaurants are packed from 20:00 on, especially on weekends. Many restaurants serve free jugs of ice water with a smile.

Rick's Tip: *Eating an early dinner saves time and money, as many better restaurants offer an* **early-bird special** *(17:30-19:00).*

Afternoon Tea

The **Shelbourne Hotel** has been a Dublin landmark since 1824, built to attract genteel patrons and Dublin's upper-crust socialites (not to mention British Army snipers during the 1916 Easter Uprising). But schlubs like us can dip our toes in the aristocratic fantasy by enjoying the tradition of afternoon tea (no shorts, tank tops, or Molly Hatchet T-shirts). The menu is a swirl of finger sandwiches, buttermilk scones, clotted cream, strawberry jam, ginger loaf, and fine coffee...as well as 22 varieties of tea. You'll find it in the ground floor Lord Mayor's Lounge (reservations smart; €39.95 Mon-Fri, €42.95 Sat-Sun, €14 champagne; seatings Mon-Thu at 12:30, 14:45, and 17:00; Fri-Sun at 11:45, 14:00, 16:15, and 18:30; 27 St. Stephen's Green, tel. 01/663-4500).

Dinner with Entertainment

The Brazen Head hosts "Food, Folk, and Fairies" evenings, which are more culturally highbrow than the title might suggest, while still remaining fun. Even at €46, the evening is a great value and gives your mind as much to chew on as your mouth. You get a hearty, four-course meal that's punctuated between courses by soulful Irish history and fascinating Irish mythology, delivered by an engaging local folklorist (reservations smart; March-Dec daily 19:00-22:00, Jan-Feb Thu and Sat only; by south end of Father Matthew Bridge, 2 blocks west of Christ Church Cathedral at 20 Bridge Street; pub tel. 01/677-9549, show tel. 01/218-8555, www.irishfolktours. com).

Further down the intellectual food chain are the **Parliament** and **Arlington Hotel Pubs.** These two locations host "Celtic Nights," featuring dinner shows with Irish music and dance. At either place, you'll be entertained by an Irish Rovers-type band singing ballads and a dance troupe scuffing up the floorboards to the delight of tour groups. The Arlington Hotel is north of the River Liffey (23 Bachelors Walk, near the north end of O'Connell Bridge, tel. 01/804-9100). The Parliament Hotel is south of the river (at the corner of Lord Edward Street and Exchange Street Upper, roughly opposite City Hall, tel. 01/670-8777). Be sure you know at which location you're booking reservations (€34, shows nightly at 20:00, dinner reservations required, www. arlingtonhoteltemplebar.com).

Quick and Easy near Grafton Street

Cornucopia is a small, earth-mama-with-class, proudly vegetarian, self-serve place two blocks off Grafton. It's friendly and youthful (hearty €12 lunches, €17 dinner specials, Mon-Wed 8:30-21:00, Thu-Sat 8:30-22:00, Sun 12:00-21:00, 19 Wicklow Street, tel. 01/677-7583).

The Farm, Dublin's healthiest dining option, shuns processed food and features fresh, organic, and free-range fare that's affordable and pretty darn tasty (€15-25 main courses, €22 two-course and €25 three-course early-bird specials before 19:00, daily 11:00-22:00, a half-block south of Trinity College at 3 Dawson

Street, tel. 01/671-8654).

The Hairy Lemon has a weird name (like a lot of Dublin pubs do), but its friendly staff, central location, and above-average menu keep me coming back. Hearty eaters will love their famous stew-like Dublin Coddle (daily 11:30-22:00, 41 Lower Stephen Street, tel. 01/697-2568).

O'Neill's Pub is a venerable, dark, and tangled retreat offering good grub, including dependable €12-15 carvery lunches. It's very central, located near the main TI (daily 12:00-22:00, Suffolk Street, tel. 01/679-3656).

Avoca Café is a good-value eatery on two levels. The upstairs, on the second floor above the Avoca department store, has simple yet satisfying meals (€9-17 lunches, Mon-Sat 9:30-17:30, Sun 11:00-17:30, close to the TI at 11-13 Suffolk Street, tel. 01/672-6019). The **Avoca Sandwich Counter** is a cramped basement dweller brightened by whitewashed walls. It whips up portable €7-9 sandwiches that you can enjoy on the run (daily generally 10:00-17:00).

The Duke and **Davy Burns**—two pubs on Duke Street—serve reliable pub lunches. (The nearby Cathach Rare Books shop, at 10 Duke Street, displays a rare edition of *Ulysses* inscribed by James Joyce, among other treasures, in its window.)

Wagamama Noodle Bar, like its popular sisters in Britain, is a pan-Asian slurp-a-thon with great and healthy noodle and rice dishes served at long communal tables by energetic waiters. There's often a line, but it moves quickly (€12-19, daily 12:00-22:00, South King Street underneath St. Stephen's Green Shopping Centre, tel. 01/417-1878).

Yamamori is a plain, mellow, and modern Japanese place serving seas of sushi and noodles (€10-15 lunches, €16-20 dinners, daily lunch 12:00-17:30 & dinner 17:30-23:00, 71 South Great George's Street, tel. 01/475-5001).

Supermarkets: **Dunnes,** on South Great George's Street, is your one-stop shop for assembling a picnic meal (Mon-Sat 8:30-19:00, Thu-Fri until 20:00, Sun 11:00-19:00, across from Yamamori). They have another outlet in the basement of St. Stephen's Green Shopping Centre. **Marks & Spencer** department store has a fancy grocery store in the basement, with fine takeaway sandwiches and salads (Mon-Fri 8:00-21:00, Thu until 22:00, Sat 8:00-20:00, Sun 10:00-19:00, Grafton Street).

Hip and Fun in North Dublin

The Church is a trendy café/bar/restaurant/nightclub/beer garden housed in the former St. Mary's Church. In its former life as a church, it hosted the baptism of Irish rebel Wolfe Tone and the marriage of brewing legend Arthur Guinness. The choir balcony has a huge pipe organ and a refined menu; the ground floor nave is dominated by a long bar and pub grub; and a disco thumps like hell in the bunker-like basement. On warm summer nights, the outdoor terrace is packed. Eating here is as much about the scene as the cuisine (€25 three-course early-bird special before 18:00, balcony restaurant open daily 17:00-22:30, pub grub daily 12:00-21:00, reservations smart Fri and Sat nights, corner of St. Mary's and Jervis Streets, tel. 01/828-0102, www.thechurch.ie).

The Hot Stove is an elegant and serene little basement operation serving locally sourced dishes created by chef Joy Beattie (€28 two-course and €32 three-course early-bird specials before 18:30; Tue-Fri 12:00-14:30 & 17:30-21:30, Sat 17:30-22:00, closed Sun-Mon; behind the Garden of Remembrance at 38 Parnell Square West, see map on page 70, tel. 01/874-7778, www.thehotstove.ie).

The Epicurean Food Hall offers a fun selection of food stalls with big and split-table portions. Choices include Greek, Mexican, Chinese, Thai, Turkish, Italian,

Brazilian, and good old Irish fish-and-chips. It's a hit with locals—and visitors—seeking cheap eats (daily 9:00-19:00, Thu-Sat until 20:00, 100 yards north of the Ha' Penny Bridge on Lower Liffey Street).

Fast and Cheap near Christ Church Cathedral

Many of Dublin's late-night grocery stores sell cheap salads, microwaved meat pies, and made-to-order sandwiches (such as **Spar** and **Centra** markets, open 24 hours a day in the city, spread all over Dublin). A €12 picnic dinner brought back to the hotel might be a good option after a busy day of sightseeing.

Queen of Tarts, with some outdoor seating, does yummy breakfasts, fruit salads, sandwiches, and wonderful pastries. Get yours to go, and enjoy a picnic with a Georgian view in one of Dublin's grassy squares (€9-12 breakfasts, €12-18 lunches, Mon-Fri 8:00-19:00, Sat 9:00-19:00, Sun 9:00-18:00, hidden beside Kinlay House on Cow's Lane, tel. 01/670-7499).

Chorus Café is a friendly little hole-in-the-wall diner, perfect for breakfast or lunch with a newspaper (€9 breakfasts, €12 lunches, Mon-Fri 8:30-17:30, Sat 9:30-17:30, closed Sun, Fishamble Street, tel. 01/616-7088). A bit of trivia: next door is the site of the first performance of Handel's *Messiah.*

Classy Restaurants and Cafés

These stylish restaurants offer well-presented food at fair prices. They're located within a block of each other, just south of Temple Bar and Dame Street, near the main TI. And just 50 yards down the street from the TI (in front of the old church), you'll pass a statue of "sweet" Molly Malone (which Dubliners irreverently call "the Tart with the Cart").

Trocadero serves beefy European cuisine to Dubliners interested in a slow, romantic meal. The dressy, red-velvet interior is draped with photos of local actors. The three-course pre-theater special is a fine value at €25 (17:00-19:00, leave by 19:45). Come early or make a reservation—it's a favorite with theatergoers (€18-29 meals, Mon-Sat 17:00-24:00, closed Sun, 4 St. Andrew Street, tel. 01/677-5545, www.trocadero.ie).

Boulevard Café is mod, trendy, and likeable, dishing up Mediterranean cuisine that's heavy on the Italian. Their salads, pasta, and sandwiches cost roughly €12-17, and two-course lunch specials are €19 (Mon-Sat 10:00-18:00). It's smart to reserve for dinner (€17-25 dinner, Mon-Sat 12:00-24:00, closed Sun, 27 Exchequer Street, tel. 01/679-2131, www.boulevardcafe.ie).

In Temple Bar

Il Baccaro, a cozy Italian wine tavern with an arched brick ceiling, is tucked in a quiet corner of Meeting House Square (€15-20 pasta dinners, daily 17:30-22:30, lunches Sat 12:00-16:00 only, closed Sun, tel. 01/671-4597).

Gallagher's Boxty House is touristy and traditional—a good, basic value with creaky floorboards and old Dublin ambience. Its specialty is the boxty, the generally bland-tasting Irish potato pancake filled and rolled with various meats, veggies, and sauces. Their Gaelic Boxty is the liveliest, but they also serve stews and corned beef (€16-23, daily 11:00-22:30, reservations wise, 20 Temple Bar, tel. 01/677-2762, www.boxtyhouse.ie).

Rick's Tip: *Restaurants and lodging are* **more expensive** *the closer you get to the* **touristy Temple Bar district.** *In a Temple Bar pub, a pint of beer costs €5—a sobering thought.*

Luigi Malone's, with its fun atmosphere and varied menu of pizza, ribs, pasta, sandwiches, and fajitas, is just

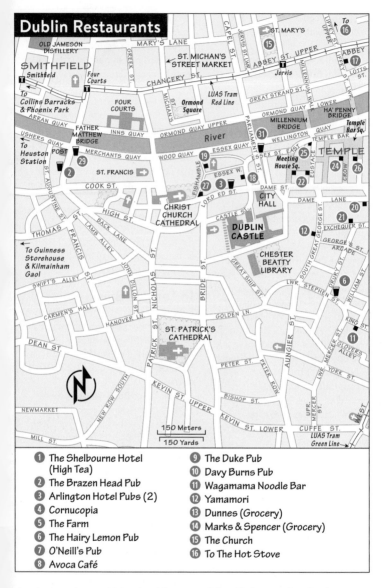

Dublin Restaurants

1. The Shelbourne Hotel (High Tea)
2. The Brazen Head Pub
3. Arlington Hotel Pubs (2)
4. Cornucopia
5. The Farm
6. The Hairy Lemon Pub
7. O'Neill's Pub
8. Avoca Café
9. The Duke Pub
10. Davy Burns Pub
11. Wagamama Noodle Bar
12. Yamamori
13. Dunnes (Grocery)
14. Marks & Spencer (Grocery)
15. The Church
16. To The Hot Stove

the place to take your high-school date (€15-25 meals, Mon-Sat 12:00-22:00, Sun 13:00-21:30, corner of Cecilia and Fownes streets, tel. 01/679-2723).

The Shack, while a bit touristy, has a reputation for good quality. It serves traditional Irish chicken, seafood, and steak dishes (€16-27 entrées, €19 three-course early-bird special offered 17:00-19:00, open daily 12:00-22:00, in the center of Temple Bar, 24 East Essex Street, tel. 01/679-0043).

The Bad Ass Café, where Sinéad O'Connor once waitressed, has been

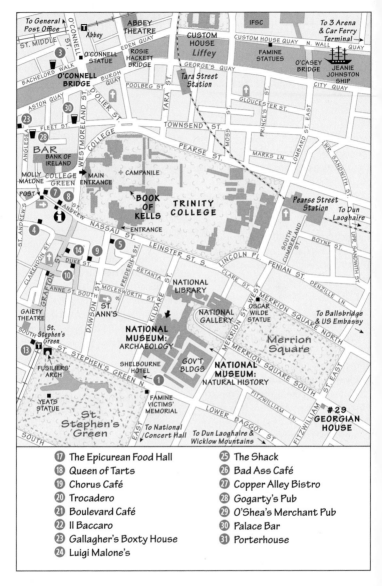

The following legend entries appear on the map:

- ⑰ The Epicurean Food Hall
- ⑱ Queen of Tarts
- ⑲ Chorus Café
- ⑳ Trocadero
- ㉑ Boulevard Café
- ㉒ Il Baccaro
- ㉓ Gallagher's Boxty House
- ㉔ Luigi Malone's
- ㉕ The Shack
- ㉖ Bad Ass Café
- ㉗ Copper Alley Bistro
- ㉘ Gogarty's Pub
- ㉙ O'Shea's Merchant Pub
- ㉚ Palace Bar
- ㉛ Porterhouse

spiffed up since her tenure. The fare is uncomplicated pizza, pasta, burgers, and salads that are cheap by Temple Bar standards. There's even a fun kids' menu, and live music or comedy most Fri and Sat evenings (€14-19 meals, daily 12:00-22:00, 9 Crown Alley, tel. 01/675-3005).

Copper Alley Bistro, a bit farther from the Temple Bar chaos and more reasonably priced, serves comfort-food lunches and dinners (daily 12:00-21:30, corner of Fishamble and Lord Edward streets, just opposite Christ Church Cathedral, tel. 01/679-6500).

SLEEPING

Dublin is popular, loud, and expensive. Rooms can be tight. Book ahead for weekends, particularly in summer and during rugby season. On Sundays in September, fans converge on Dublin for the all-Ireland finals in Gaelic football and hurling. Prices are often discounted on weeknights (Mon-Thu) and from November through February. Many hotels use dynamic pricing (adjusting depending on demand); check for the latest prices and specials on hotel websites. Book directly with the hotel for the best deals.

Big and practical places (both cheap and moderate) are most central near Christ Church Cathedral, on the edge of Temple Bar. For classy, older accommodations, stay a bit farther out (southeast of St. Stephen's Green).

South of the River Liffey
Near Christ Church Cathedral

These hotels cluster near Christ Church Cathedral, a 5-minute walk from the rowdy evening scene (at Temple Bar), and 10 minutes from the sightseeing center (Trinity College and Grafton Street). The cheap hostels in this neighborhood have some double rooms. Full Irish breakfasts, which cost €8-10 at the hotels, are cheaper at the many small cafés nearby; try the **Queen of Tarts** or **Chorus Café** (see listings under "Eating," earlier).

$$ Jurys Inn Christ Church, one of three Jurys Inns in downtown Dublin, is central and offers business-class comfort in 182 identical rooms. This no-nonsense, American-style hotel chain has a winning keep-it-simple-and-affordable formula. If "ye olde" is getting old—and you don't mind big tour groups—this is a good option. Request a room far from the noisy elevator (Db-€99-159 Sun-Thu, €119-189 Fri-Sat, breakfast-€10, book long in advance for weekends, check website for discounts, parking-€15/day, Christ Church Place, tel. 01/454-0000, US tel. 800-423-

6953, www.jurysinns.com, jurysinnchristchurch@jurysinns.com). The other Jurys Inns, described later, are near Connolly Station and Parnell Square.

$$ Harding Hotel is a hardworking, traditional red-brick place with 52 earth-tone rooms that get stuffy on rare hot days (Sb-€55-99; Db-€70-109 Sun-Thu, €109-169 Fri-Sat; extra bed-€25, breakfast-€9; ask for Rick Steves discount if booking by email or online using the code "REG52014"; on weekends, request a quiet upper-floor room away from the fun-but-noisy ground-floor pub; on Fishamble Street across the street from Christ Church Cathedral, tel. 01/679-6500, www.hardinghotel.ie, info@hardinghotel.ie).

$ Kinlay House, around the corner from Harding Hotel, is the backpackers' choice for its cheap beds, central location, and all-ages-welcome atmosphere. This huge, red-brick, 19th-century Victorian building has 200 metal beds in spartan rooms—a mix of singles, doubles, small coed dorms (4-6 beds, good for families), and a few giant dorms. It fills up most days—call well in advance, especially for singles, doubles, and summer weekends (S-€40, Sb-€50, D-€60, Db-€70, dorm beds-€18, includes small breakfast, kitchen access, launderette, luggage storage, lockers, lots of stairs, Christ Church, 2 Lord Edward Street, tel. 01/679-6644, www.kinlaydublin.ie, info@kinlaydublin.ie).

$ Four Courts Hostel is a 234-bed hostel within a five-minute walk of Christ Church Cathedral and Temple Bar. Bare and institutional (as hostels typically are), it's also spacious and well-run, with a focus on security and efficiency (dorm beds-€18, S-€48, Sb-€50, bunk D-€52, bunk Db-€55, includes small breakfast, elevator, laundry service, some parking-€10/day, luggage storage, 15 Merchant's Quay, from Connolly Station or Busáras Central Bus Station take LUAS to Four Courts stop and cross river via Father Matthew Bridge, tel. 01/672-5839, www.fourcourtshostel.com, info@fourcourtshostel.com).

Trinity College Area

You can't get more central than Trinity College; these listings offer a good value for the money.

$$$ Trinity Lodge offers fine, quiet lodging in 26 rooms split between two Georgian townhouses on either side of Frederick Street South, just south of Trinity College (Sb-€99-179, Db-€165-209, Tb-€199-259, 12 South Frederick Street, tel. 01/617-0900, www.trinitylodge.com, trinitylodge@eircom.net).

$$ Trinity College turns its 800 student-housing dorm rooms on campus into no-frills, affordable accommodations in the city center each summer. Look for the easy-to-miss Accommodations Office (open Mon-Fri 8:00-18:00) inside the huge courtyard, 50 yards down the wall on the left from the main entry arch (late-May-early-Sept, S-€72, Sb-€74, D-€118, Db-€120, includes continental breakfast, cooked breakfast-€4 extra, tel. 01/896-1177, www.tcd.ie/accommodation/visitors, reservations@tcd.ie).

Near St. Stephen's Green

Dublin is filled with worn-yet-comfy townhouses. Albany House and Fitzwilliam Townhouse are dependable, basic lodgings, while Brooks and Buswells are cushier.

$$$ Brooks Hotel is a fine choice for great service, tending 98 plush rooms in an ideal central location. This splurge rarely disappoints (Db-€145-199, Tb-€210-270, higher rates during big events, Drury Street, tel. 01/670-4000, www.brookshotel.ie, reservations@brookshotel.ie).

$$$ Buswells Hotel, one of the city's oldest, is a pleasant Georgian-style haven with 67 rooms in the heart of the city (Sb-€119-159, Db-€129-199, Tb-€149-209, breakfast-€12.50, between Trinity College and St. Stephen's Green at 23 Molesworth Street, tel. 01/614-6500, www.buswells.ie, info@buswells.ie).

$$ Albany House's 50 restful rooms come with high ceilings, Georgian ambience, and some stairs (Sb-€70-120, Db-€120-160, Tb-€120-180, one block south of St. Stephen's Green at 84 Harcourt Street, tel. 01/475-1092, www.albanyhousedublin.com, info@albanyhousedublin.com).

$$ Fitzwilliam Townhouse rents 14 plain rooms in a Georgian townhouse near St. Stephen's Green (Sb-€69-89, Db-€79-149, Tb-€109-179, Qb-€129-189, breakfast-€10, 41 Upper Fitzwilliam Street, tel. 01/662-5155, www.fitzwilliamtownhouse.com, info@fitzwilliamtownhouse.com).

$ Avalon House Hostel, near Grafton Street, rents 282 simple, clean backpacker beds (dorm beds-€22, S-€30, Sb-€35, twin D-€60, twin Db-€70, includes small breakfast, elevator, launderette, kitchen, lockers, a few minutes off Grafton Street at 55 Aungier Street, tel. 01/475-0001, www.avalon-house.ie, info@avalon-house.ie).

Away from the Center

The listings that follow—all southeast of St. Stephen's Green—are unique places (except for the business-class Mespil Hotel), and they charge accordingly. If you're going to break the bank, do it here.

$$$ Number 31 is a hidden gem reached via gritty little Leeson Close (a lane off Lower Leeson Street). Its

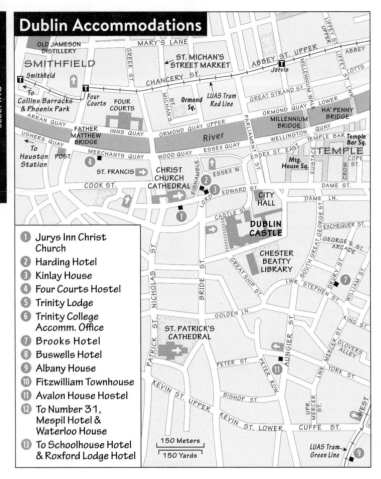

Dublin Accommodations

1. Jurys Inn Christ Church
2. Harding Hotel
3. Kinlay House
4. Four Courts Hostel
5. Trinity Lodge
6. Trinity College Accomm. Office
7. Brooks Hotel
8. Buswells Hotel
9. Albany House
10. Fitzwilliam Townhouse
11. Avalon House Hostel
12. To Number 31, Mespil Hotel & Waterloo House
13. To Schoolhouse Hotel & Roxford Lodge Hotel

understated elegance is top-notch, with 6 rooms in a former coach house and 15 rooms in an adjacent Georgian house; the two buildings are connected by a quiet little garden. Guests appreciate the special touches, such as the sunken living room and tasty breakfasts served in a classy glass atrium (Sb-€110-180, Db-€150-220, Tb-€190-280, Qb-€230-340, free parking, 31 Leeson Close, tel. 01/676-5011, www.number31.ie, info@number31.ie).

$$$ The Schoolhouse Hotel taught as many as 300 students in its heyday (1861-1969) and was in the middle of the street-fight that was the 1916 Easter Uprising.

Now it's a serene hideout with 31 pristine rooms and a fine restaurant (Sb-€99-169, Db-€119-199, book early, 2 Northumberland Road, tel. 01/667-5014, www.schoolhousehotel.com, reservations@schoolhousehotel.com).

$$$ Mespil Hotel is a huge, modern, business-class hotel renting 254 identical three-star rooms (most with a double and single bed) at a good price with all the comforts. This place is a cut above Jurys Inn (Sb, Db, or Tb-€79-195, breakfast-€12, elevator; small first-come, first-served free parking; 10-minute walk southeast of St. Stephen's Green or take

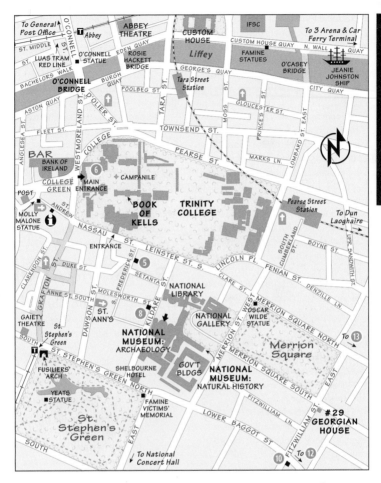

bus #37, #38, or #39, 50 Mespil Road; tel. 01/488-4600, www.mespilhotel.com, mespil@leehotels.com).

$$ Roxford Lodge Hotel is well managed and a great value. In a quiet residential neighborhood a 25-minute walk from Trinity College, it has 24 tastefully decorated rooms awash with Jacuzzis and saunas. The €150-200 executive suite is honeymoon-worthy (prices swing high and low—Sb-€75-110, Db-€85-165, Tb-€115-189, Qb-€125-210, breakfast-€12, parking, 46 Northumberland Road, tel. 01/668-8572, www.roxfordlodge.ie, reservations@roxfordlodge.ie).

$$ Waterloo House sits proudly Georgian on a quiet residential street with 19 comfortable and relaxing rooms and a pleasant back garden (Sb-€69-99, Db-€89-140, Tb-€119-195, Qb-€130-195, parking, 8 Waterloo Road, tel. 01/660-1888, www.waterloohouse.ie, info@waterloohouse.ie).

North of the River Liffey
Near Connolly Station
This once-tattered neighborhood (like much of the north side) is gradually being rejuvenated. To locate these hotels, see the map on page 70.

$$ Jurys Inn Custom House, on Custom House Quay, offers the same value as the other Jurys Inns in Dublin, but it's less central. Its 239 rooms border the financial district, a 10-minute riverside hike from O'Connell Bridge. Of the three Jurys Inns in the city center, this one is most likely to have rooms available (Db-€99-159 Sun-Thu, €119-189 Fri-Sat, breakfast-€10.50, parking-€15/day, tel. 01/854-1500, US tel. 800-423-6953, www.jurysinns.com, jurys inncustomhouse@jurysinns.com).

$$ The Townhouse, with 81 small, stylish rooms (some with views into a central garden courtyard), hides behind a brick Georgian facade one block north of the Customs House (Sb-€69-99, Db-€89-149, Tb-€99-169, limited parking-€10/day—reserve ahead of time, 47 Lower Gardiner Street, tel. 01/878-8808, www.townhouseofdublin.com, info@townhouseofdublin.com).

Near Parnell Square

A swanky neighborhood 250 years ago, this is now workaday Dublin with a steady urban hum. To locate these hotels, see the map on page 70.

$$ The Castle Hotel is a formerly grand but still comfortable Georgian establishment embedded in the urban canyons of North Dublin. A half-block east of the Garden of Remembrance, it's a good value with pleasant rooms and the friendly Castle Vaults pub in its basement (Sb-€69-139, Db-€89-189, Tb-€149-239, discount with 2-night stay, Great Denmark Street, tel. 01/874-6949, www.castle-hotel.ie, info@castle-hotel.ie).

$$ Jurys Inn Parnell Street has 253 predictably soulless but good-value rooms. It's a block from the north end of O'Connell Street and the cluster of museums on Parnell Square (Db-€99-149 Sun-Thu, €129-199 Fri-Sat, breakfast-€10, tel. 01/878-4900, www.jurysinns.com, jurysinn parnellst@jurysinns.com).

$$ Belvedere Hotel has 92 plain-vanilla rooms that are short on character but long on dependable, modern comforts (Db-€99-149 Sun-Thu, €109-169 Fri-Sat, cheaper if you book on their website, Great Denmark Street, tel. 01/873-7700, www.belvederehotel.ie, reservations@belvederehotel.ie).

$$ Charles Stewart Guesthouse, big and basic, offers 60 forgettable rooms for a fair price in a good location (Sb-€59-89, Db-€89-159, Tb-€109-169, Qb-€129-199, breakfast-€7, frequent midweek discounts, ask for a quieter room in the back, just beyond top end of O'Connell Street at 5 Parnell Square East, tel. 01/878-0350, www.charlesstewart.ie, info@charlesstewart.ie).

TRANSPORTATION

Getting Around Dublin

Public transportation is readily available and user-friendly. Sightseers can make good use of a hop-on, hop-off bus ticket to link the best sights (see page 44, and the Freedom Pass, on next page).

By Bus

Cheap public buses cover the city thoroughly. Most lines start at the four quays, or piers, that are nearest O'Connell Bridge. If you're away from the center, nearly any bus takes you back downtown. Some bus stops are "request only" stops: Be alert to the bus numbers (above the windshield) of approaching buses. When you see your bus coming, hold your arm out from your side with your palm extended into the street to flag it down. Tell the driver where you're going, and he'll ask for €1.95-3.30 depending on the number of stops. Bring change or lose any excess. **Bus #90** connects the bus and train stations.

The **bus office** has free bus-route maps and sells two different city-bus passes (Mon 8:30-17:30, Tue-Fri 9:00-17:30, Sat 9:00-14:00, Sun 9:30-14:00, 59 O'Connell Street Upper, tel. 01/873-

4222, www.dublinbus.ie). The five-day **Rambler pass** is handy for a longer stay, costing €29.50 and covering the Airlink airport bus (but not Aircoach buses). The three-day **Freedom Pass** for €33 covers city buses, Airlink, and the hop-on, hop-off Dublin Bus Tour. Passes are also sold at TIs, newsstands, and markets citywide (mostly Centra, Mace, Spar, and Londis).

By Light Rail (LUAS)
The city's light-rail system has two main lines (red and green) that serve inland suburbs. The more useful line for tourists is the **red line**, with an east-west section connecting the Heuston and Connolly train stations (a 15-minute ride apart) at opposite edges of the Central 1 Zone. In between, the Busáras Central Bus Station, Smithfield, and Museum stops can be handy (€1.80, 6/hour, runs 5:30-24:45, tel. 1-800-300-604, www.luas.ie). Check the 15-foot-high pillars at each boarding platform that display the time and destination of the next LUAS train. Make sure you're on the right platform for the direction you want to go.

By Taxi
Taxis are everywhere and easy to hail (cheaper for 3-4 people). Cabbies are generally honest, friendly, and good sources of information (€4.10 daytime minimum 8:00-20:00, €4.45 nighttime minimum 20:00-8:00, €1/each additional adult, figure about €12 for most crosstown rides, €40/hour for guided joyride).

Arriving and Departing
By Train
Dublin has two train stations. **Heuston Station,** on the west end of town, serves west and southwest Ireland (45-minute walk from O'Connell Bridge; take the LUAS light rail or bus #90). **Connolly Station,** which serves the north, northwest, and Rosslare, is closer to the center (15-minute walk from O'Connell Bridge).

Each station has ATMs, but no lockers.

The two train stations are connected by the red line of the LUAS light-rail system and by bus. **Bus #90** runs along the river, linking the train stations, bus station, and city center (€1.90, 6/hour).

To reach Heuston Station from the city center, catch bus #90 on the south side of the river; to get to Connolly Station and the Busáras Central Bus Station from the city center, catch #90 on the north side of the river.

TRAIN CONNECTIONS
Note that trains (and buses) generally run less frequently on Sundays. Irish Rail train info: toll tel. 1850-366-222, www. irishrail.ie.

From Dublin's Heuston Station to: Tralee, near Dingle (every 2 hours, 6/day on Sun, most change in Mallow), **Ennis** (10/day, 3.5-4 hours, change in Limerick, Limerick Junction, or Athenry), **Galway** (8/day, 2.5-3 hours).

From Dublin's Connolly Station to: Waterford (8/day, 2.5 hours), **Portrush** (7/day, 2/day Sun, 5 hours, transfer in Belfast or Coleraine). The **Dublin-Belfast train** connects the two Irish capitals in two hours at 90 mph on one continuous, welded rail (8/day Mon-Sat, 5/day Sun, about €40 for "day return" ticket). Northern Ireland train info: tel. 048/9089-9400, www.translink.co.uk.

By Bus
Bus Éireann, Ireland's national bus company, uses the **Busáras Central Bus Station** (pronounced bu-SAUR-us...like a dinosaur). Located next to Connolly Station, it's a 15-minute walk or a short ride on bus #90 to the city center. Buses run less often on Sundays. Bus info: tel. 01/836-6111, www.buseireann.ie.

From Dublin by Bus to: Belfast (hourly, most via Dublin Airport, 3 hours), **Trim** (almost hourly, 1 hour), **Ennis** (almost hourly, 4-5.5 hours), **Galway** (hourly, 3.5 hours; faster on CityLink—

hourly, 2.5 hours, tel. 091/564-164, www.
citylink.ie), **Limerick** (hourly, 3-3.5 hours),
Dingle (4/day, 8-9 hours, transfer at Limerick and Tralee).

By Plane

Dublin Airport, seven miles from Dublin, has two terminals. Terminal 2 serves American carriers (Delta, United, and American), plus most Aer Lingus flights. Terminal 1 serves Ryanair, Aer Arann, Air Canada, Aer Lingus (some regional flights), and most European carriers, including British Airways, SAS, Lufthansa, Air France, Swiss, and Iberia (airport code: DUB, tel. 01/814-1111, www.dublin airport.ie).

Both terminals, located an easily walkable 150 yards apart, have ATMs, exchange bureaus, cafés, Wi-Fi, and luggage storage. At Terminal 1, the left-luggage office (daily 6:00-23:00) is across the street in the Short-Term Car Park Atrium, along with a small supermarket. Terminal 1 also has a TI (daily 8:00-20:00), pharmacy, bus-and-rail info desk, and car-rental agencies (on ground/arrivals level).

Getting Downtown by Bus: You have two main choices—Airlink (double-decker green bus) or Aircoach (single-deck blue bus). Both pick up on the street directly in front of airport arrivals, at ground level at both terminals.

If taking the Airlink bus, consider getting a **Rambler** city-bus pass or **Freedom Pass,** both of which cover the journey (no pass covers the Aircoach); for pass info, see page 91 . Read the following description first to make sure Airlink is the best choice for your trip.

Airlink: Airlink bus #747 stops at both airport terminals, linking the airport to the city center along a strip a few blocks north and south of the river. This bus generally runs an east-west route that parallels the Liffey River, and includes the Busáras Central Bus Station, Connolly Station, O'Connell Street, Trinity College, Christ Church, and Heuston Station. Ask the driver which stop is closest to your hotel (€6, pay driver, 3/hour, 35-45 minutes, tel. 01/873-4222, www.dublinbus.ie).

Aircoach: This bus generally runs a north-south route that follows the O'Connell and Grafton streets axis. To reach recommended hotels near St. Stephen's Green (south of the city center), the Aircoach bus is best (€7, covered by Dublin Pass, 3/hour, runs 5:00-23:30, pay driver and confirm best stop for your hotel, tel. 01/844-7118, www.aircoach.ie).

City Bus: The cheapest (and slowest) way from the airport to downtown Dublin is by city bus; buses marked #16A, #41, #41A, and #41B go to O'Connell Street (€2.50, exact change required, no change given, 4/hour, 55 minutes, tel. 01/873-4222, www.dublinbus.ie).

Taking a Taxi: Taxis from the airport into Dublin cost about €30.

Sleeping at the Airport: A safe bet is **$$ Radisson Blu Dublin Airport** (Db-€89-129, book online direct for best prices, tel. 01/844-6000, www.radisson blu.ie).

To and from London: If you're connecting Dublin and London directly, flying is your best bet. There's no need to waste a valuable day going by slower surface transportation. **Ryanair** dominates the discount airline market, but note it uses London airports—Luton and Stansted—that are a significant distance from the city center (1.5 hours, Irish tel. 1520/444-004, www.ryanair.com). Options to Heathrow include **British Airways** (Irish tel. 1-890-626-747, US tel. 800-247-9297, www.ba.com) and **Aer Lingus** (tel. 081-836-5000, www.aerlingus.com). To get the lowest fares, ask about round-trip ticket prices and book months in advance (though Ryanair offers nearly constant deals).

By Car

Trust me: You don't want to drive in downtown Dublin. Cars are unnecessary for sightseeing in town, parking is expensive (about €25/day), and traffic will get your fighting Irish up. If you have a car, ask your hotelier about the best places to park. See Dublin by taxi, bus, or on foot, and save your car-rental days for cross-country travel between smaller towns.

Car Rental: Consider renting a car as you leave Dublin for other points in Ireland. If you rent a car at Dublin Airport, you can bypass the worst of the big-city traffic by taking the M-50 ring road south or west.

Agencies with locations in Dublin and at the airport include **Avis** (35 Old Kilmainham Road, tel. 021/428-1111, airport tel. 01/605-7500, www.avis.ie), **Hertz** (151 South Circular Road, tel. 01/676-7476, airport tel. 01/844-5466, www.hertz.ie), **Budget** (151 Lower Drumcondra Road, tel. 01/837-9611, central reservations tel. 09066/27711, airport tel. 01/844-5150, www.budget.ie), and **Europcar** (2 Haddington Road, tel. 01/614-2888, airport tel. 01/812-0410, www.europcar.ie).

Toll Roads: The M-50 uses an automatic tolling system called eFlow. Your rented car should come with an eFlow tag installed; confirm this when you pick up your car at the airport. The €3.10 toll per trip is automatically debited from the credit card that you used to rent the car (for pass details, see www.eflow.ie).

Your rental car's eFlow tag will work automatically only for the M-50 ring road that circles urban Dublin. On any other Irish toll roads, you'll have to pay with cash (under €3). These roads mostly run outward from Dublin toward Waterford, Cork, Limerick, and Galway (roads farther west are free). Toll motorways are usually blue on maps and are shown with the letter "M" followed by the route number (toll info and map: www.nra.ie/tolling-information).

By Ferry

There are seven daily crossings between Dublin Port (two miles east of O'Connell Bridge) and Holyhead, Wales. The two-hour crossing (€39) costs only a bit more than the slower 3.5-hour sailing (€35). You must board at least 30 minutes before the scheduled sailing time or risk being denied boarding. Since these boats can fill up in advance on summer weekends, try to book at least a week ahead during this peak period. Your choices are **Irish Ferries** (4 crossings/day, Dublin tel. 0818-300-400, UK tel. 08705-329-129, www.irishferries.com) and **Stena Line** (3/day, Dublin tel. 01/204-7777, UK tel. 08447-707-070, www.stenaline.com).

NEAR DUBLIN

Not far from urban Dublin, the stony skeletons of evocative ruins sprout from the lush Irish countryside. The story of Irish history is told by ancient burial mounds, early Christian monastic settlements, huge Norman castles, and pampered estate gardens.

These sights are separated into two regions:

North of Dublin, the interesting Valley of the Boyne features the ancient Brú na Bóinne burial site and the medieval town of Trim. It's on my two-week itinerary.

South of Dublin, the Wicklow Mountains have the Glendalough monastic settlement, set amid woods and lakes, and the manicured Gardens of Powerscourt. The Wicklow Mountains qualify as a Best of the Rest destination—enjoyable if you have extra time or interest.

VALLEY OF THE BOYNE

The peaceful, green Valley of the Boyne, 30 miles north of Dublin, is worth a visit for the prehistoric and spiritual sights at Brú na Bóinne. The town of Trim makes

Valley of the Boyne

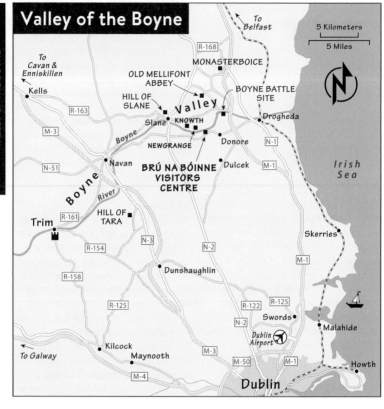

To Belfast

5 Kilometers

5 Miles

R-168

To Cavan & Enniskillen

MONASTERBOICE

OLD MELLIFONT ABBEY

Kells

BOYNE BATTLE SITE

HILL OF SLANE

Valley

R-163

Drogheda

M-3

Slane

KNOWTH

Boyne

NEWGRANGE

Donore

N-1

N-51

Navan

BRÚ NA BÓINNE VISITORS CENTRE

Dulcek

M-1

Irish Sea

Boyne

River

HILL OF TARA

Trim

R-161

N-3

Skerries

R-154

N-2

M-1

R-158

Dunshaughlin

R-125

R-125

R-122

Swords

N-2

Malahide

To Galway

Kilcock

Maynooth

Dublin Airport

M-3

M-50

M-1

Howth

M-4

Dublin

an easy overnight stop for drivers (on the first or last night of your trip), and boasts a 13th-century castle—Ireland's biggest.

Brú na Bóinne

Mysterious and thought-provoking, the burial mounds at Brú na Bóinne ("dwelling place of the Boyne") are older than the Egyptian pyramids. This archaeological site is also commonly called "Newgrange," after its star attraction. Here you can visit two 5,000-year-old passage tombs—Newgrange and Knowth (rhymes with "south"). These are massive grass-covered burial mounds built atop separate hills, with a chamber inside reached by a narrow stone passage.

Planning Your Visit

There are three sights at Brú na Bóinne:

Newgrange, Knowth, and the state-of-the-art visitors center with its excellent museum. Start at the visitors center—no one is allowed to visit the tombs on their own. From here, buy your ticket and catch the next available shuttle bus to the tombs, where a guide gives a 30-minute tour.

Each tomb site takes about 1.5 hours to visit (30-minute round-trip bus ride plus 30-minute guided tour plus 30 minutes of free time). The museum at the visitors center is well worth an additional 30-60 minutes. If you add in waiting time for the next available shuttle bus, you're looking at a minimum of 2.5 hours to do one of the tombs (along with the museum), or 4 hours to do both tombs (and museum).

Which tomb is best? If you can't see both, pick Newgrange because it's more famous and allows you inside. (On the other hand, wait times for the Newgrange shuttle bus can be longer.) Knowth is bigger and flanked by small mounds, but you can't access its narrow passages. Each site is worthwhile, but for many, seeing one is enough.

Rick's Tip: *You might* **pick your tomb** *according to whichever shuttle bus is leaving next.*

Orientation

Cost: Newgrange–€6, Knowth–€5; the museum is included in both tomb prices.

Hours: May-Sept daily 9:00-18:30, slightly shorter hours off-season. The last entry to the visitors center is 45 minutes before closing; the last bus to the tombs leaves 1.75 hours before closing. Newgrange is open year-round, while Knowth is open Easter to mid-Oct only.

Crowd-Beating Tips: Arrive early—ideally before 10:00 in peak season—to avoid the big midday bus-tour crowds from Dublin. Visits are limited, and on busy summer days those arriving in the afternoon may not get a spot on a shuttle bus. No reservations are possible.

Getting There: By **car,** drive 45 minutes north from Dublin on N-1 to Drogheda, where signs direct you to the visitors center. If you're using a GPS, input "Brú na Bóinne" rather than "Newgrange" to get to the visitors center, where you must check in.

The 15-seat **Newgrange shuttle bus** runs daily from Dublin to the visitors center. It departs Dublin at 8:45 and 11:15 from Gresham Hotel on Upper O'Connell Street, and at 9:00 and 11:30 from the Dublin TI on Suffolk Street. Return trips depart Brú na Bóinne at 13:30 and 16:30. Seat reservations are essential; it fills up in summer (and may not run every day in winter). Depending on your departure time, you'll have 3.5 to 6.5 hours for sightseeing. It's logistically tricky (though not

impossible) to see both tombs in 3.5 hours (€17 round-trip, 45 minutes each way, must book in advance, run by Over the Top Tours, tel. 01/838-6128 or Ireland toll-free 1-800-424-252, www.overthetop tours.com).

Information: Tel. 041/988-0300, www.heritageireland.ie.

Tours from Dublin: Mary Gibbon's tours visit Brú na Bóinne (including inside the Newgrange tomb), and additional sights—the Hill of Tara and Hill of Slane—in a seven-hour trip (€35, Mon-Fri, 9:30 pickup at Mespil Hotel at 50-60 Mespil Road, plus stops at St. Stephen's Green, Upper O'Connell Street, and more—see website for times, home by 16:30; Sat-Sun Mespil Hotel 7:50, plus other stops, home by 15:30; book directly with tour company instead of TI, mobile 086-355-1355, www.newgrangetours.com, info@newgrange tours.com).

Sights

BRÚ NA BÓINNE VISITORS CENTRE AND MUSEUM

Buy your ticket (to one or both tombs), find out when the next shuttle bus leaves, then spend your waiting time in the terrific museum, grabbing lunch in the cheery downstairs cafeteria, and using the WCs (there are no WCs at the tomb sites).

The museum introduces you to the Boyne River Valley and its tombs. No one knows who built the 40 burial mounds found in the surrounding hills. Exhibits re-create what these pre-Celtic people might have been like—simple farmers and hunters living in huts, fishing in the Boyne, equipped with crude tools of stone, bone, or wood.

Then around 3200 B.C., someone had a bold idea. They constructed a chamber of large stones, with a long stone-lined passage leading up to it. They covered it with a huge mound of dirt and rocks in successive layers. Sailing down the Boyne to the sea, they beached at Clogherhead (12.5 miles from here), where they found hundreds of five-ton stones, weathered smooth by the tides. Somehow they transported them back up the Boyne, possibly by tying a raft to the top of the stone so it was lifted free by a high tide. They then hauled these stones up the hill by rolling them atop logs and up dirt ramps, and laid them around the perimeter of the burial mound to hold everything in place. It would have taken anywhere from five years to a generation to construct a single large tomb.

Why build these vast structures? Presumably, it was to bury VIPs. A dead king might be carried up the hill to be cremated on a pyre. Then they'd bring his ashes into the tomb, parading by torchlight down the passage to the central chamber. The remains were placed in a ceremonial basin, mingled with those of illustrious ancestors.

The museum displays replicas of tools and objects found at the sites, including the ceremonial basin stone and a head made out of flint, which may have been carried atop a pole during the funeral procession. Marvel at the craftsmanship of the perfectly spherical stones (and the phallic one), and wonder at their purpose.

The tombs may also have served an astronomical purpose; they're precisely aligned to the movements of the sun, as displays and a video illustrate. You can request a short tour and winter solstice light-show demo at a full-size replica of the Newgrange passage and interior chamber.

Since the tombs are aligned with the heavens, it begs the question: Were these structures sacred places where primal Homo sapiens gathered to ponder the deepest mysteries of existence?

▲▲▲NEWGRANGE

This grassy mound atop a hill is 250 feet across and 40 feet high. Dating from 3200 B.C., it's 500 years older than the pyramids at Giza. The base of the mound is ringed by dozens of "kerbstones," each about nine feet long and weighing five tons.

The entrance facade is a mosaic of white quartz and dark granite. This reconstruction dates to the 1970s; not every archaeologist agrees it originally looked like this. Above the doorway is a square window called the roofbox, which played a key role (as we'll see). In front of the doorway lies the most famous of the kerbstones, the 10- by 4-foot entrance stone.

The Newgrange burial tomb predates the Egyptian pyramids.

Its left half is carved with three mysterious spirals, which have become a kind of poster child for prehistoric art.

Most of Newgrange's kerbstones have designs carved into them. This was done with super-hard flint tools; the Neolithic ("New Stone Age") people had not mastered metal. The stones feature common Neolithic motifs: not people or animals, but geometric shapes—spirals, cross-hatches, bull's-eyes, and chevrons.

Entering the tomb, you walk down a narrow 60-foot passage lined with big boulders. Occasionally you have to duck or turn sideways to squeeze through. The passage opens up into a central room—a cross-shaped central chamber with three alcoves, topped by a 20-foot-high igloo-type stone dome. Bones and ashes were placed here in a ceremonial stone basin, under 200,000 tons of stone and dirt.

While we know nothing of Newgrange's builders, it most certainly was a sacred spot—for a cult of the dead, a cult of the sun, or both. The tomb is aligned precisely east-west. As the sun rises on the shortest day of the year (winter solstice, Dec 21), a ray of light enters through the roofbox and creeps slowly down the passageway. For 17 minutes, it lights the center of the sacred chamber (your guide will demonstrate this). Perhaps this was the moment when the souls of the dead were transported to the afterlife, via that ray of life-giving and life-taking light. Then the light passes on, and, for the next 364 days, the tomb sits again in total darkness.

▲▲▲KNOWTH

This site is an impressive necropolis, with one grand hill-topping mound (similar to Newgrange) surrounded by several smaller satellite tombs. The central mound is 220 feet wide, 40 feet high, and covers 1.5 acres.

You'll see plenty of mysteriously carved kerbstones and new-feeling grassy mounds that you can look down on from atop the grand tomb.

Knowth's big tomb has two passages: one entering from the east, and one from the west. Like Newgrange, it's likely aligned so the rising and setting sun shone down the passageways to light the two interior chambers. Neither passage is open to the public, but you can visit a room carved into the mound by archaeologists, where a cutaway lets you see the layers of dirt and rock used to build the mound. You also get a glimpse down one of the passages.

The Knowth site thrived from 3000 to 2000 B.C. The central tomb dates from about 2000 B.C. It was likely used for burial rituals and sun-tracking ceremonies to please the gods and ensure the regular progression of seasons for crops. The site then evolved into the domain of fairies and myths for the next 2,000 years, and became an Iron Age fortress in the early centuries after Christ. Around A.D. 1000, it was an all-Ireland political center, and later, a Norman fortress was built atop the mound. Now, 4,000 years after prehistoric people built these strange tombs, you can stand atop the hill at Knowth, look out over the surrounding countryside, and contemplate.

Trim

The sleepy, workaday town of Trim, straddling the River Boyne, is marked by the towering ruins of Trim Castle, which seem to say, "This little town was big-time...800 years ago." Trim makes a great landing pad into—or launching pad out of—Ireland. If you're flying into or out of Dublin Airport and don't want to deal with big-city Dublin, this is a perfect alternative—an easy 45-minute, 30-mile drive away. You can rent a car at the airport and make Trim your first overnight base, or spend your last night here before returning your car at the airport. Compared to Dublin, accommodations in Trim are inexpensive.

Orientation

Trim's main square is a traffic roundabout, and everything's within a block or two.

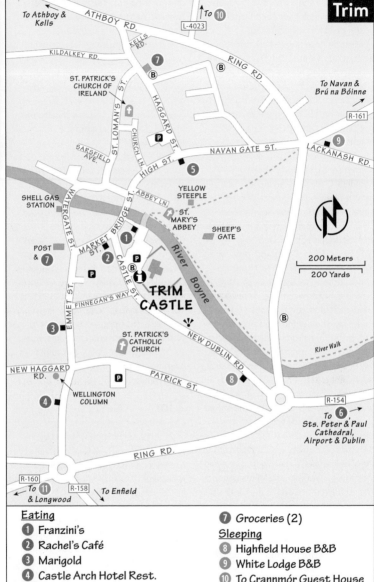

Trim

Eating
1. Franzini's
2. Rachel's Café
3. Marigold
4. Castle Arch Hotel Rest.
5. James Griffin Pub
6. To Marcie Regan's Pub
7. Groceries (2)

Sleeping
8. Highfield House B&B
9. White Lodge B&B
10. To Crannmór Guest House
11. To Tigh Catháin B&B

Most of the shops and eateries are on or near Market Street, along with banks and a supermarket.

Getting There: Buses run from Dublin's Busáras Central Bus Station to Trim nearly hourly, dropping off at the bus shelter next to Trim's TI and the castle entrance on Castle Street (1-hour trip, bus info: tel. 01/836-6111, www.buseireann.ie). Trim has no train station.

Day-tripping drivers can park on the street or in a public lot. Use the pay-and-display parking system; buy a ticket at one of the machines spaced along the street, and display it on your dashboard (€1/hour, 2-hour maximum, Mon-Sat 9:00-18:00, free Sun). If you're overnighting, park at your B&B.

Tourist Information: The TI is right next to the castle and has a handy coffee shop (June-Aug Mon-Fri 9:30-17:30, Sat-Sun 11:30-17:30, shorter hours Sept-May, Castle Street, tel. 046/943-7227).

Tours: The TI organizes sporadic one-hour **Trim Living History Tours** (€5, tours depart from TI, call ahead to reserve, tel. 046/943-7227). **Medieval Trim Tours** are led by Cynthia Simonet (€2.50, 45 minutes, tours depart from castle parking lot in front of Franzini's restaurant, call ahead to reserve, mobile 086-370-7522).

Taxi: DKs Taxi can give you a lift to nearby Boyne sites (mobile 085-132-3005).

Sights

▲▲ TRIM CASTLE

This is the biggest Norman castle in Ireland. Set in a grassy riverside park at the edge of this sleepy town, its mighty keep towers above a very ruined outer wall. It replaced a wooden fortification that was destroyed in 1173 by Irish High King Rory O'Connor, who led a raid against the invading Normans. The current castle was completed in the 1220s and served as a powerful Norman statement to the restless Irish natives.

Today the castle remains a remarkable sight—so remarkable that it was used in the 1994 filming of *Braveheart* (which was actually about Scotland's—not Ireland's—fight for freedom). The best-preserved walls ring the castle's southern perimeter and sport a barbican gate that contained two drawbridges. The massive 70-foot-high central keep, which is mostly a hollow shell, has 20 sides. This experimental design was not implemented elsewhere because it increased the number of defenders needed to cover all the angles.

Trim's huge Norman castle surveys the Boyne River.

Make time to take a 15-minute walk outside, circling the castle walls.

Cost and Hours: €4 for castle grounds, €4 for entrance to keep and required tour; mid-March-Oct daily 10:00-18:00; Nov-mid-March Sat-Sun 10:00-17:00, closed Mon-Fri; last entry one hour before closing, 45-minute tours run 2/hour but spots are limited and can fill up—so arrive early in peak season, tel. 046/943-8619, www.heritageireland.ie.

Eating

The restaurants and cafés along Market Street are friendly, wholesome, and unassuming.

Franzini's is the only place in town with a fun dinner menu and enough business to make it work. They serve pasta, steak, fish, and good salads in a modern, candlelit ambience. Nothing's Irish except the waiters (€17-25 dishes, €20 two-course or €25 three-course early-bird dinners before 19:30, Mon-Sat 17:00-22:00, Sun 13:00-21:00, on French's Lane across from the castle parking lot, tel. 046/943-1002).

Rachel's Café is a good bet along Market Street (€8-10 salads, sandwiches, and meat pies, daily 8:30-17:30, mobile 086-275-1768).

Marigold fits the bill if you're in the mood for Chinese food (daily 17:00-23:00 except Sun from 16:00, Emmett Street, tel. 046/943-8788).

The **Castle Arch Hotel,** popular with locals, serves hearty pub grub at reasonable prices in its bistro (€12-15 meals, daily 12:30-21:30, tel. 046/943-1516).

For a fun pub experience, check out Trim's two best watering holes. The **James Griffin** (on High Street) is full of local characters with traditional Irish music sessions on Monday, Wednesday, and Thursday nights. Tiny, low-ceilinged **Marcie Regan's** is a fun, unpretentious pub next to the old Norman bridge over the River Boyne, a half-mile stroll north of town.

Spar Market has everything you need for a picnic (daily 8:00-21:00, Emmett Street), as does **Super Valu,** a larger store that's a bit farther from the town center (daily 8:00-22:00, Haggard Street).

Sleeping

$ Highfield House B&B, across the street from the castle and a five-minute walk from town, is a stately 190-year-old former maternity hospital, with hardwood floors and 10 spacious, high-ceilinged rooms (Sb-€50-60, Db-€78-86, Tb-€99-110, Qb-€140, family-friendly; overlooks roundabout where Dublin Road hits Trim, just before castle at Castle Street; tel. 046/943-6386, mobile 086-857-7115, www.highfieldguesthouse.com, info@highfieldguesthouse.com, Geraldine and Edward Duignan).

$ White Lodge B&B, a 10-minute walk northeast of the castle, has six comfortable rooms with an oak-and-granite lounge. They also offer a family-friendly self-catering house next door. A handy 300-yard trail leads from across the street to the castle—enter next to the modern sculptures (Sb-€45, Db-€72, Tb-€84, Qb-€94, 10 percent discount for active-duty members of the US and Canadian armed forces with this book, parking, New Road, tel. 046/943-6549, www.whitelodge.ie, info@whitelodge.ie, Todd O'Loughlin).

These two B&Bs are in the quiet countryside about a mile outside Trim (phone ahead for driving directions). **$ Crannmór Guest House** has five rooms with cheery color schemes (Sb-€45-55, Db-€76-80, Tb-€90-110, Qb-€110, north of the Ring Road on Dunderry Road L-4023, tel. 046/943-1635, mobile 087-288-7390, www.crannmor.com, cranmor@eircom.net). **$ Tigh Catháin B&B,** southwest of town, has four large, bright, lacy rooms with a comfy, rural feel and organically grown produce at breakfast (Db-€70-80, Tb-€90-110, cash only, on R-160/Longwood Road, tel. 046/943-1996, mobile 086-257-7313, www.tighcathain-bnb.com, tighcathain.bnb@gmail.com).

BEST OF THE REST

WICKLOW MOUNTAINS

The Wicklow Mountains, while only 15 miles south of Dublin, feel remote—enough so to have provided a handy refuge for opponents to English rule. Rebels who took part in the 1798 Irish uprising hid out here for years. The area only became more accessible in 1800, when the frustrated British built a military road. Today, this same road—now R-115—takes you through the Wicklow area, with the Gardens of Powerscourt on the north end and the monastic settlement of Glendalough at the south end.

Getting There

By car or tour, it's easy. It's not worth the trouble on public transport.

By Car: Take N-11 south from Dublin toward Bray, then R-117 to Enniskerry, the gateway to the Wicklow Mountains. Signs direct you to the Gardens of Powerscourt and on to Glendalough. From Glendalough, if you're heading west, you can leave the valley (and pick up the highway to the west) over the famous but dull mountain pass called the Wicklow Gap.

By Tour from Dublin: Wild Wicklow Tours covers the region via tight but comfortable buses (€28, daily year-round, 8:50 pickup at Shelbourne Hotel at 27 St. Stephen's Green—northern edge, 9:20 pickup at Gresham Hotel at 23 Upper O'Connell Street, return to Dublin by 17:30, advance booking required, tel. 01/280-1899, www.wildwicklow.ie).

Over the Top Tours bypasses mansions and gardens to focus on scenery, with a stop at Glendalough (€28, 9:20 pickup at Gresham Hotel at 23 Upper O'Connell Street, 9:45 pickup at Dublin TI on Suffolk Street, return by 17:30, tel. 1-800-424-252, Dublin tel. 01/860-0404, mobile 087-259-3467, www.overthetoptours.com).

Sights

▲▲GARDENS OF POWERSCOURT
A mile above the village of Enniskerry, the Gardens of Powerscourt cover 47 acres

Powerscourt mansion is surrounded by Italian Renaissance–style gardens.

within the 700-acre estate. While the mansion isn't much, its aristocratic gardens (1858-1875) are Ireland's best.

Upon entry, you'll get a flier laying out 40-minute and one-hour walks. The "one-hour" walk takes 30 minutes at a relaxed amble, with the Great Sugar Loaf Mountain as a backdrop, and a fine Japanese garden, Italian garden, and goofy pet cemetery along the way.

Cost and Hours: €8.50, daily March-Oct 9:30-17:30, Nov-Feb 9:30-dusk, last entry at 17:00, great cafeteria, tel. 01/204-6000, www.powerscourt.ie.

▲▲GLENDALOUGH

The steep wooded slopes of Glendalough (GLEN-da-lock, "Valley of the Two Lakes"), at the south end of Wicklow's military road, hide Ireland's most impressive monastic settlement. Founded by St. Kevin in the sixth century, the monastery flourished until the English destroyed it in 1398. A few hardy holy men continued to live here until it was finally abandoned during the Dissolution of the Monasteries in 1539. But pilgrims kept coming, especially on St. Kevin's Day, June 3. While much restoration was done in the 1870s, most of the buildings date from the 10th to 12th century.

In an Ireland without cities, these monastic communities were mainstays of civilization. They were remote outposts where ascetics gathered to commune with God. Today, Ireland is dotted with the reminders of this age: illuminated manuscripts, simple churches, and carved crosses.

The valley sights are split between the two lakes. The smaller, lower lake is just beyond the visitors center and nearer the best remaining ruins. The upper lake has scant ruins and feels like a state park. Walkers and hikers will enjoy a choice of nine different trails of varying lengths through the lush Wicklow countryside (longest loop takes four hours, hiking-trail maps available at visitors center).

The best ruins of Glendalough gather within 100 yards of its famous 110-foot-tall **round tower.** Highlights include the **cathedral,** well-preserved **St. Kevin's "kitchen"** (actually a church), and 10-foot tall **St. Kevin's Cross,** carved from a single block of granite. According to legend, if you hug this cross and can reach your hands around to touch your fingers on the other side, you'll have your wish granted.

The monastic ruins of Glendalough in the lush Wicklow Mountains

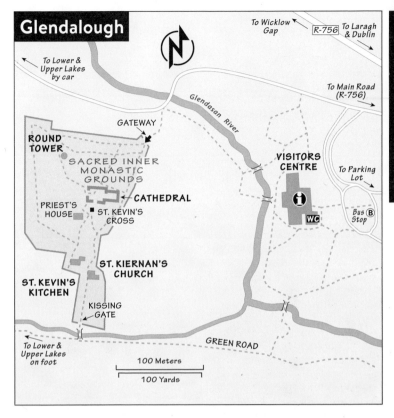

St. Kevin: the patron saint of dislocated shoulders.

Planning Your Visit: Summer tour-bus crowds are terrible all day on weekends and 11:00-14:00 on weekdays. If you're there at midday, your best bet is to take the once-daily, 45-minute tour of the site (only at 13:30, departs from visitors center). Otherwise, ask if you can tag along with a prebooked tour group's tour. If you're on your own, find the markers that give short descriptions of the ruined buildings.

Park for free at the visitors center. Visit the center; take the guided tour; wander the ruins surrounding the round tower on your own (free); or walk the traffic-free Green Road a half-mile to the upper lake, and then walk back to the visitors center and your car along the trail that parallels the public road (an easy, roughly one-mile loop). Or you can drive to the upper lake. If you're rushed, skip the upper lake.

Cost and Hours: Free to enter site, €4 for visitors center, €4 to park at upper lake; daily 9:30-18:00, mid-Oct-mid-March until 17:00, last entry 45 minutes before closing; tel. 0404/45352.

Kilkenny
and the
Rock of Cashel

If you're driving from Dublin (on Ireland's east coast) to Dingle (on Ireland's west coast), the best two stops to break the long journey across the Irish interior are Kilkenny, Ireland's finest medieval town; and the Rock of Cashel, a thought-provoking early Christian site crowning the Plain of Tipperary.

Counties Kilkenny and Tipperary ("Tipp" to locals) are blood rivals on the hurling field, with the lion's share of the GAA national championships split between them. Watch for sporting lads carrying their hurlies (ash-wood sticks with broad, flat ends) to or from school. These two counties also boast some of the finest agricultural land on this rocky and boggy island. Farm tractors rumble the back roads where it's not a long way to Tipperary.

KILKENNY AND THE ROCK OF CASHEL IN 1 DAY

Drivers connecting Dublin with Kinsale can stop in Kilkenny for lunch, and then tour the Rock of Cashel (allowing several hours) before ending up in Kinsale to spend the night.

For a longer visit, see the sights in Kilkenny (choose among the castle, Rothe House, cathedral, and ale tour) and enjoy an evening of traditional folk music in a pub.

I've listed accommodations for both Kilkenny and the Rock of Cashel. Kilkenny makes a good overnight for drivers from Dublin who want to visit Glendalough. Additional sights near Kilkenny include Jerpoint Abbey and Waterford's popular crystal factory. The Rock of Cashel is a fine overnight if you're driving between Dublin and Dingle (or Kenmare).

Kilkenny

KILKENNY AND THE ROCK OF CASHEL AT A GLANCE

In Kilkenny

▲**Kilkenny Castle** Historic castle and gardens, later converted into an opulent château, featuring a long gallery of portraits of dynastic Butler family aristocrats. **Hours:** Daily June-Aug 9:00-17:30, slightly shorter hours off-season. See page 108.

▲**Rothe House** Sprawling 17th-century merchant's townhouse complex consisting of three houses, three courtyards, and a garden displaying upper-crust Elizabethan life. **Hours:** April-Oct Mon-Sat 10:30-17:00, Sun 14:00-18:00; Nov-March closes at 16:30 and all day Sun. See page 109.

Between Kilkenny and Waterford

▲▲▲**Waterford Visitor Centre** Popular tour of glass factory with live demos and glittering sales shop. **Hours:** April-Oct Mon-Sat 9:00-16:15, Sun from 9:30. See page 115.

▲▲**Jerpoint Abbey** Informatively presented abbey ruins with carvings, bringing to life a monastic culture from 850 years ago. Hours: March-Oct daily 9:00-17:30; Nov daily 9:30-16:00; Dec-Feb shorter hours and closed Sat-Sun. See page 115.

▲▲*Dunbrody* **Famine Ship** Replica of a typical famine ship that brought emigrants to America, with many passengers succumbing to illness and death en route. **Hours:** Daily April-Sept 9:00-18:00, Oct-March 10:00-17:00. See page 115.

At Cashel

▲▲▲**Rock of Cashel** Ireland's best tangle of ecclesiastical ruins atop a rocky perch surveying the plains of Tipperary, visited by historic figures ranging from St. Patrick to Queen Elizabeth II. **Hours:** Daily 9:00-17:30 but stays open until 19:00 early June to mid-Sept, and closes at 16:30 in winter. See page 116.

KILKENNY

Lovely Kilkenny gives you a feel for salt-of-the-earth Ireland. Its castle and cathedral stand like historic bookends on a higgledy-piggledy High Street of colorful shops and medieval facades. A night in Kilkenny comes with plenty of traditional folk music in its pubs. It's nicknamed the "Marble City" for its nearby quarry (actually black limestone, not marble), and you can see white seashells fossilized within the black stone steps around town. While a small town today (fewer than 10,000 residents), Kilkenny has a big history: It was the capital of Ireland for a short spell in the turbulent 1640s. And of vital interest is the fact that actor George Clooney traces his roots to Kilkenny.

Orientation

Tourist Information: The TI is a block off the bridge in the 16th-century Shee Alms poorhouse (Mon-Sat 9:00-17:00, Sun 11:00-17:00 in summer, closed Sun Sept-May, Rose Inn Street, tel. 056/775-1500).

Walking Tour: Local guide **Pat Tynan** offers hour-long town walks that depart from the TI (€8; mid-March-Oct Mon-Sat at 10:30, 12:15, and 15:00, Sun at 11:15 and 12:30; Nov-mid-March Sat only; mobile 087-265-1745).

Bike Rentals and Tours: Kilkenny Cycling rents bikes for €15 a day (with a €50 refundable deposit). They provide safety gear, deliver bikes to your hotel on request (€1.50 charge), and have route maps. They also offer **biking and hiking tours** (€20, cash only, office in stone teahouse beside river—near parking lot on Bateman Quay, mobile 086-895-4961, www.kilkennycyclingtours.com).

Market: The square in front of Kilkenny Castle hosts a friendly produce, cheese, and crafts market on Thursdays (9:00-14:30).

Sights

▲KILKENNY CASTLE

Dominating the town, this castle is a stony reminder that the Anglo-Norman Butler family controlled Kilkenny for 500 years. The castle once had four sides, but Oliver Cromwell's army knocked down one wall when it took the castle, leaving it as the roughly "U" shape we see today.

Cost and Hours: €7, daily June-Aug 9:00-17:30, slightly shorter hours off-

Kilkenny Castle

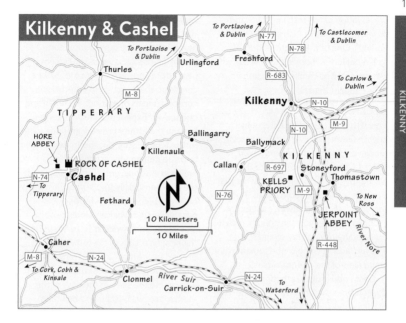

Kilkenny & Cashel

season, tel. 056/770-4100.

Visiting the Castle: Enter the castle gate, turn right in the courtyard, and head into the base of the turret. Here you'll find the continuously running 12-minute video explaining how the wooden fort built here by Strongbow in 1172 evolved into a 17th-century château. Then go into the main castle entrance (diagonally across the courtyard from the turret) to buy your entry ticket. You'll be free to walk through the castle. A pamphlet explains the exhibits, and you can also talk to stewards in the important rooms.

Now restored to its Victorian splendor, the castle's highlight is the beautiful family-portrait gallery, which puts you face-to-face with the wealthy Butler family ghosts.

Nearby: The **Kilkenny Design Centre,** across the street from the castle in some grand old stables, is full of local crafts and offers handy cafeteria-style lunches upstairs in the food hall (shops—Mon-Sat 10:00-19:00, Sun 10:00-17:00; food hall—daily 8:30-18:30, Thu-Sat until 21:30; tel. 056/772-2118, www.kilkennydesign.com).

▲ROTHE HOUSE

This is the crown jewel of Kilkenny's medieval architecture: a well-preserved merchant's house that expanded around interior courtyards as the prosperous Rothe family grew in the early 1600s.

Cost and Hours: €5.50; April-Oct Mon-Sat 10:30-17:00, Sun 14:00-18:00; Nov-March closes at 16:30 and all day Sun; Parliament Street, tel. 056/772-2893, www.rothehouse.com.

Visiting the Rothe House: Check out the graceful top-floor timberwork supporting the roof, which uses wooden dowels (pegs) instead of nails. The museum, which also serves as the County Kilkenny genealogy center, gives a glimpse of life here in late Elizabethan and early Stuart times. The walled gardens at the far back were a real luxury in their time.

The Rothe family eventually lost the house when Oliver Cromwell banished all Catholic landowners, sending them to live on less desirable land west of the Shannon River. In the late 1800s, the building housed the Gaelic League, devoted to the rejuvenation of Irish culture through preservation of the Irish language and promotion of native Irish sports (such as hurling). One of the future leaders of the 1916 rebellion—Thomas McDonagh, who was executed at Dublin's Kilmainham Gaol—taught here.

ST. CANICE'S CATHEDRAL

This 13th-century cathedral is early-English Gothic, rich with stained glass, medieval carvings, and floors paved in history. Check out the model of the old walled town in its 1641 heyday, as well as a couple of modest audiovisuals. The 100-foot-tall **round tower,** built as part of a long-gone pre-Norman church, recalls the need for a watchtower and refuge. The fun ladder-climb to the top affords a grand view of the countryside.

Cost and Hours: Cathedral-€4, tower-€3, combo-ticket for both-€6; June-Aug Mon-Sat 9:00-18:00, Sun 14:00-18:00; Sept-May slightly shorter hours and closed for lunch; tel. 056/776-4971, www.cashel.anglican.org.

SMITHWICK'S EXPERIENCE KILKENNY

Smithwick's (pronounced SMITH-icks) reddish ale was born in Kilkenny...and has been my favorite Irish beer since my first visit to Ireland. Older than Guinness (but now owned by the same parent company), Smithwick's marked its tercentennial (300th anniversary) in 2010. After a corporate shake-up in 2013, the brewery consolidated its operations in Dublin and opened an "Experience" visitors center here on the former brewery grounds.

Cost and Hours: €12, hourly 45-minute tours, 10 percent discount if booked online in advance, entry includes a pint at the tour's end, daily 10:00-18:00, last entry one hour before closing, tel. 056/778-6377, www.smithwicksexperience.com.

Visiting Smithwick's: Tours focus on the historic origins of the tasty ale, first brewed by the monks of St. Francis Abbey (the 14th-century ruins of the abbey lie adjacent to the site). In the days of the monks, beer was a safer and healthier alternative to local water sources that were often contaminated. I'll drink to that.

Like the Guinness Storehouse in Dublin, this is not a tour of a working brewery. It's a corporate-sponsored homage to the history of the brewery that once operated here.

St. Canice's Cathedral

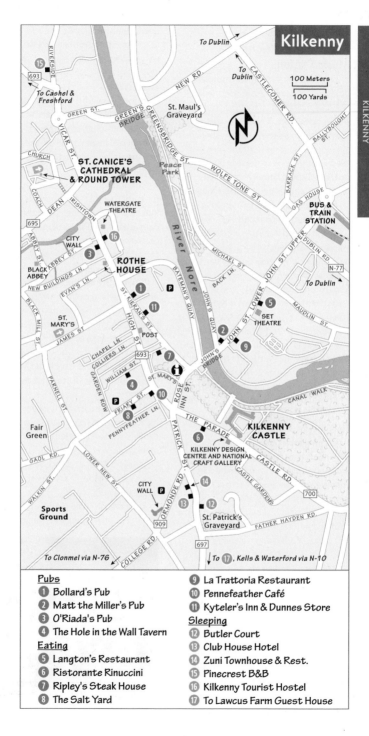

Kilkenny

Pubs

1. Bollard's Pub
2. Matt the Miller's Pub
3. O'Riada's Pub
4. The Hole in the Wall Tavern

Eating

5. Langton's Restaurant
6. Ristorante Rinuccini
7. Ripley's Steak House
8. The Salt Yard
9. La Trattoria Restaurant
10. Pennefeather Café
11. Kyteler's Inn & Dunnes Store

Sleeping

12. Butler Court
13. Club House Hotel
14. Zuni Townhouse & Rest.
15. Pinecrest B&B
16. Kilkenny Tourist Hostel
17. To Lawcus Farm Guest House

Experiences
Pubs and Traditional Music Sessions

Kilkenny has its fair share of atmospheric pubs. Visitors seeking fun trad music sessions may want to try the first three places listed here. Those seeking friendly conversation in utterly unvarnished Irish splendor should seek out the memorable duo at the end of these listings. A fun pub crawl could link all five of these places with less than 20 minutes of walking.

Bollard's Pub, an unpretentious landmark at the north end of St. Kieran's Street, is a good bet for lively traditional music sessions and good pub grub. Or sit out front under the awning and enjoy a pint as Kilkenny's humanity flows past you (music Tue and Thu-Fri at 21:00). Just down the same street is **Kyteler's Inn** ("KIT-lers"), with a stony facade and medieval cellar (music almost nightly in summer at 18:30, 27 St. Kieran's Street). You can saunter over John's Bridge to check out the tunes at **Matt the Miller's Pub,** with its multilevel, dark-wood interior (around 21:00 most nights, next to bridge on John Street across the river from the castle).

Lacking music but high on character, **O'Riada's** is an endangered species—a wonderful, old-fashioned place that your Irish grandfather would recognize and linger in (across from the Watergate Theatre at 25 Parliament Street). **The Hole in the Wall** is a tiny, restored Elizabethan tavern (1592) hidden down an alley. Owner Michael Conway, a cardiologist by day and a historian/playwright/actor/barman by night, presides over the speakeasy-like space as a labor of love. His music sessions can be an uninhibited go-for-broke thump-a-thon (he plays bass drum). He also writes and occasionally performs eclectic, history-based "singspiel" shows. Both take place in the larger, but equally ancient, timber-beamed upstairs hall (sporadic hours but always Fri-Sat from 20:00 and sometimes weeknights, call ahead, look for alley beside Bourkes shop at 17 High Street, mobile 087-807-5650, www.holeinthewall.ie).

Eating

Langton's is every local's first choice, serving high-quality Irish dishes under a labyrinthine, multi-chambered, Tiffany-skylight expanse (€12-18 lunches, €16-29 dinners, daily 12:00-22:30, 69 John Street, tel. 056/776-5133).

Ristorante Rinuccini serves classy, romantic, candlelit Italian meals (€11-18 lunches, €17-30 dinners, €28 three-course early-bird special before 19:00, reservations smart, daily 12:00-15:00 & 17:30-22:00, 1 The Parade, tel. 056/776-1575, www.rinuccini.com).

Ripley's Steak House delights carnivores (believe it or not) with choice cuts of locally raised beef. Try the flaky-crusted, veggie-stuffed steak hot pot (€20 two-course or €24 three-course meals, Wed-Fri 17:00-22:00, Sat 16:00-22:00, Sun 13:00-22:00, closed Mon-Tue, hidden down Butterslip Lane, tel. 056/777-0699).

The Salt Yard is an appealing Spanish-Irish fusion tapas bar featuring hearty paella dishes and Iberian wines (€15-27 meals, Tue-Wed 17:30-21:30, Thu-Sat 12:30-15:00 & 18:00-22:00, Sun 13:30-19:30, closed Mon, Friary Street, tel. 056/770-3644).

La Trattoria is the friendly, informal Italian option in town, presided over by

Kyteler's Inn

charming Giacomo (€14-25 dinners, €14 two-course early-bird special before 19:00, daily 12:00-22:00, 84 John Street, tel. 056/777-0907).

Zuni is a stylish splurge, offering international cuisine (€23 two-course and €28 three-course early-bird specials before 19:30 every night but Sat, daily 12:30-14:30 & 18:00-21:30, weekend reservations smart, 26 Lower Patrick Street, tel. 056/772-3999, www.zuni.ie).

Pennefeather Café, above the Kilkenny Book Centre, is good for a quick, cheap, light lunch (Mon-Fri 9:00-17:30, Sat until 17:00, closed Sun, 10 High Street, tel. 056/776-4063).

Kyteler's Inn serves decent pub grub in a timber-and-stone atmosphere with a heated and covered beer garden out back. Visit their fun 14th-century cellar and ask about their witch. Watch your head or risk leaving some of your DNA embedded in the low stone arches (Mon-Sat 12:00-21:00, Sun until 20:00, 27 St. Kieran's Street, tel. 056/772-1064).

Dunnes Stores has an ample selection of supplies for a grassy picnic (Mon-Sat 8:00-22:00, Sun 10:00-20:00, a few doors down from Kyteler's Inn on St. Kieran's Street).

Sleeping

The first three listings are more central, clustered within a block of each other along Lower Patrick Street. The next two are at the north end of town, but still just a short walk from the action. The last one is south of town.

$$$ Butler Court is Kilkenny's best lodging value. Ever-helpful Yvonne and John offer 10 modern, spacious rooms behind the beige, flag-draped archway. Bo the dog quietly patrols the courtyard (Sb-€60-80, Db-€75-120, Tb-€90-145, wheelchair-accessible, continental breakfast in room, will validate parking in nearby multistory garage on Ormonde Street for length of your stay, 14 Lower Patrick Street, tel. 056/776-1178, www.butlercourt.

Sleep Code

Abbreviations: S=Single, D=Double/Twin, T=Triple, Q=Quad, b=bathroom
   Price Rankings for Double Rooms: $$$ Most rooms €110 or more, $$ €70-110, $ €70 or less
   Notes: Room prices change; verify rates online or by email. For the best prices, book directly with the hotel.

com, info@butlercourt.com).

$$$ Club House Hotel, originally a gentlemen's sporting club, comes with 35 comfy bedrooms, fading Georgian elegance, a musty creakiness, and a palatial, well-antlered breakfast room (Sb-€50-75, Db-€100-130, best rates booked directly from hotel website, secure parking, Lower Patrick Street, tel. 056/772-1994, www.clubhousehotel.com, info@clubhouse hotel.com).

$$$ Zuni Townhouse, above a fashionable restaurant, has 13 boutique-chic rooms sporting colorfully angular furnishings. Ask about two-night weekend breaks and midweek specials that include a four-course dinner (Sb-€65-110, Db-€80-130, Tb-€100-165, parking in back, 26 Lower Patrick Street, tel. 056/772-3999, www.zuni.ie, info@zuni.ie).

$$ Pinecrest B&B has four nice rooms in a modern house on a quiet homey street, a 10-minute walk from the center of town (Sb-€50-70, Db-€70-90, Tb-€90-120, cash only, parking, Bishop Meadows, just off Freshford Road about 100 yards north of the roundabout to the Green's Bridge, tel. 056/776-3567, mobile 087-934-4579, pinecrestbnb@eircom.net, friendly Helen Heffernan).

$ Kilkenny Tourist Hostel, filling a fine Georgian townhouse with ramshackle fellowship in the town center, offers 60 cheap beds, a friendly-family room, a well-equipped members' kitchen, and a wealth of local information (dorm bed–€15-20, D–€36-46, T–€53-60, Q–€68-76, cash only, laundry service–€5, 2 blocks from cathedral at 35 Parliament Street, tel. 056/776-3541, www.kilkennyhostel.ie, info@kilkennyhostel.ie).

Near Kilkenny

$$$ Lawcus Farm Guest House is a quirky, seductive confection of rural comfort 10 miles south of Kilkenny between Kells Priory and the village of Stoneyford. Hosts Mark and Ann Marie have crafted a tasteful vibe from a passion for recycled materials and environmental sensitivity. A menagerie of friendly pets and farm animals shares the 20-acre property straddling the Kings River. Ask about the tiny secluded tree house (farmhouse—Sb-€50-70, Db-€100-120, Tb-€140-150, Qb-€190-210; tree house—Db-€350, 3-night minimum; cash only, parking, tel. 056/772-8949, mobile 086-603-1667, www.lawcus farmguesthouse.com, info@lawcusfarm guesthouse.com). To reach the farm, go south out of Kilkenny on N-10, which becomes R-713 after crossing over the M-9 motorway. Just as you enter the village of Stoneyford, turn right onto L-1023. Go 500 yards down that lane and watch for a brown sign directing you to turn right into a 100-yard gravel driveway.

Transportation
Arriving and Departing
BY TRAIN OR BUS

Kilkenny's train/bus station is four blocks from John's Bridge, which marks the center of town.

From Kilkenny by Train to: Dublin (6/day, 1.5 hours), **Waterford** (6/day, 45 minutes). For details, see www.irishrail.ie.

From Kilkenny by Bus to: Dublin (8/day, 2.5 hours), **Waterford** (2/day, 1 hour), **Cork** (4-5/day, 2 direct, 3.5 hours), **Tralee** (3/day, 5.5 hours, change in Cork), **Galway**

(3/day, 5 hours). For specifics, see www.buseireann.ie.

BY CAR

If you're arriving by car, the Market Yard Car Park behind Kyteler's Inn is handy for a few hours (€1.30/hour, daily 8:00-18:00, entry off Bateman's Quay). The multistory parking garage on Ormonde Street is the best long-term bet (€1.50/hour, or get the 3-day pass for €10 if staying overnight—it allows you to come and go; Sun-Thu 7:00-23:00, Fri-Sat 7:00-24:00). If parking overnight, wait until you depart to pay since some hotels will validate parking. Otherwise, you can use the pay-and-display meters on the street (€1.50/hour, enforced Mon-Sat 8:00-19:00).

BETWEEN KILKENNY AND WATERFORD

If you want to visit Waterford's popular crystal factory, here are a couple of sights to savor en route. The fast M-9 motorway links Kilkenny and Waterford in an hour. Alternatively, winding rural backroads with old stone bridges spanning placid rivers weave among tiny villages and abandoned mills to pastoral Jerpoint Abbey. Farther along, in the tiny port of New Ross is the Dunbrody Famine Ship. And in Waterford itself, you can see one of the most famous glassworks in the world.

The cloister at Jerpoint Abbey

▲▲JERPOINT ABBEY

Evocative abbey ruins dot the Irish landscape, but few are as well-presented as Jerpoint (founded in 1180). Its claim to fame is fine stone carvings on the sides of tombs and on the columns of the cloister arcade. If you visit only one abbey in Ireland, make sure it's this one. The well-versed guides bring the place alive again through their insight into the monastic culture that imprinted Ireland 850 years ago. Before leaving, ask for a map to navigate to the more secluded, nearby Kells Priory.

Cost and Hours: €4; March-Oct daily 9:00-17:30; Nov daily 9:30-16:00; Dec-Feb shorter hours and closed Sat-Sun; tel. 056/772-4623.

Getting There: It's located about 11 miles (17 km) south of Kilkenny or 2 miles (3 km) south of Thomastown, beside R-700.

Visiting the Abbey: The Cistercian monks, who came to Ireland from France in the 12th century, were devoted reformers bent on following the strict rules of St. Benedict. Their mission was to bring the wild Irish Christian church back in line with Rome. They steamrolled their belief system across the island and stamped the landscape with a network of identical monasteries. The Celtic Christianity that thrived in the Dark Ages was no match for the organization and determination of the Cistercians. For the next 350 years, these monasteries were the local religious authority.

What eventually did them in? King Henry VIII's marriage problems, his subsequent creation of the (Protestant) Church of England, and his eventual dissolution of the (Catholic) monasteries.

▲▲DUNBRODY FAMINE SHIP

Permanently moored on a river in the tiny port of New Ross, the *Dunbrody* is a full-scale reconstruction of a 19th-century three-masted bark built in Quebec in 1845. It's typical of the trading vessels that sailed empty to America to pick up goods. During the famine, ship owners found that they could make money on the westward voyage by offering transport to hungry Irish emigrants. Those who succumbed to "famine fever" (often typhus or cholera) were dumped overboard, earning the vessels the morbid moniker "coffin ships." Boats like this would arrive in America with only 50-80 percent of their original human cargo.

Cost and Hours: €8.50, daily April-Sept 9:00-18:00, Oct-March 10:00-17:00, 45-minute tours go 2/hour, last tour starts one hour before closing, upstairs café handy for lunch with nice views of the ship, tel. 051/425-239, www.dunbrody.com.

Getting There: The *Dunbrody* is in New Ross, a 30-minute drive southeast from Jerpoint Abbey via highway R700. During work hours, you'll need to feed the parking meters in the lot (€1/hour, free on Sun).

Visiting the Ship: Your visit starts with an audiovisual presentation on the life Irish emigrants were leaving behind, followed by coverage about the building of the vessel. Then you'll follow an excellent guide on board the ship, encountering a couple of grumpy passengers who tell vivid tales about life onboard. At the end, you'll get a glimpse of the new life Irish immigrants would encounter in New York. Most arrived filthy, illiterate, and often penniless.

Roots-seekers are welcome to peruse the computerized file of the names of the million immigrants who sailed on these ships from 1846 through 1865. For more about seeking your roots, see page 337.

▲▲▲WATERFORD VISITOR CENTRE

The oldest city in Ireland, Waterford is a plain, gray, workaday town of 45,000. Until recently, Waterford had the world's largest and most respected glassworks, with a tradition dating back to 1783. The economic downturn of 2008 shattered the market for luxury items like crystal, forcing the huge Waterford Crystal factory outside town to close. The company was bought by investors who opened a new, scaled-down factory in the town center. While 70 percent of Waterford Crystal is now manufactured by cheaper labor in Poland, Slovenia, and the Czech Republic, the finest glass craftsmen still reside here, where they create "prestige pieces." The one-hour tour of this hardworking factory is a joy. It's more intimate than the old, larger factory, and you're encouraged to interact with the craftsmen.

Cost and Hours: Tours–€13, depart every 30 minutes, April-Oct Mon-Sat 9:00-16:15, Sun from 9:30, shorter hours off-season, call to confirm; shop open longer hours; tel. 051/317-000, www.waterfordvisitorcentre.com.

Getting There: Waterford is located about a 30-minute drive southwest of New Ross via highway N25; or an hour south of Kilkenny via M-9 motorway. The Waterford Visitor Centre is conveniently located on a street called The Mall, an easy one-block walk south of Reginald's Tower.

Visiting the Factory: The tour begins with a bit of history and a look at an impressive six-foot-tall crystal grandfather clock. It then loses momentum with a pointless five-minute fireworks film montage set to a techno beat. Things pick up again when you meet the craftsmen in their element. Glassblowers magically spin glowing blobs of molten crystal into exquisite, recognizable shapes in minutes. The crystal is allowed to set and cool. Then glasscutters deftly cradle the fragile

creations against diamond-edged cutting wheels, creating intricate patterns. Afterward, visit the salesroom, surrounded by glittering temptations.

ROCK OF CASHEL

Rising high above the fertile Plain of Tipperary, the Rock of Cashel is one of Ireland's most historic and evocative sights. Seat of the ancient kings of Munster (c. A.D. 300-1100), this is where St. Patrick baptized King Aengus in about A.D. 450. Strategically located and perfect for fortification, the Rock was fought over by local clans for hundreds of years. Finally, in 1101, clever Murtagh O'Brien gave the Rock to the Church. His seemingly benevolent donation increased his influence with the Church, while preventing his rivals, the powerful McCarthy clan, from regaining possession of the Rock. As Cashel evolved into an ecclesiastical center, Iron Age ring forts and thatch dwellings gave way to the majestic stone church buildings enjoyed by visitors today. Queen Elizabeth II's history-making, four-day visit to Ireland in 2011 included a visit to the Rock.

Rick's Tip: Dress warmly. *Deceptively sheltered conditions in the parking lot may not reflect those on the high, windy, exposed Rock.*

Sights
▲▲▲ROCK OF CASHEL

If you have time, start by visiting the Sounds of History Museum under the Bru Boru Cultural Centre (at the base of the Rock; see page 122) to learn more about the Rock before you ascend. From there, it's a steep 100-yard walk up to the Rock itself. On this 200-foot-high outcrop of limestone, the first building you'll encounter is the 15th-century Hall of the Vicars Choral, housing the ticket desk, a tiny museum (with an original 12th-century high cross dedicated to St. Patrick and a

Crystal cutting at Waterford

few replica artifacts), and a 20-minute video (2/hour, shown in the hall's former dormitory). You'll also find a round tower, an early Christian cross, a delightful Romanesque chapel, and a ruined Gothic cathedral, all surrounded by my favorite Celtic-cross graveyard.

Cost and Hours: €7, families-€17, daily 9:00-17:30 but stays open until 19:00 early June to mid-Sept, and closes at 16:30 in winter, last entry 45 minutes before closing. Parking costs €4.50 (pay at the machine under the plexiglass shelter to the left of the exit before returning to your car).

Renovations: An extensive, essential restoration project is underway. It's likely that sections of the ruins—especially Cormac's Chapel—will be under scaffolding during your visit.

Tours: Call ahead for the tour schedule (included in admission, 45 minutes, tel. 062/61437). Otherwise, set your own pace with my self-guided tour.

WCs: Use the basic ones at the base of the Rock next to the parking lot or the nicer ones in the Bru Boru Centre below the parking lot (there are none up on the Rock).

Rick's Tip: **Crowds are worst** *June-Aug 11:00-15:00. Plan your visit for early or late in the day. If you're here* **at a peak time, tour the Rock first** *and save the movie, museum, and Hall of the Vicars Choral for the end of your visit.*

⊙ SELF-GUIDED TOUR

In a sense, architecture is the marriage of art (what can be imagined) and science (what's possible). When this union is blended to serve God, it's a potent mix. Nowhere else in Ireland can you better see the evolution of Irish devotion expressed in stone. This large lump of rock is a pedestal supporting a compact tangle of three dramatic architectural styles: early Christian (round tower and St. Patrick's high cross), Romanesque (Cormac's Chapel), and Gothic (the main cathedral).

• *Follow this tour counterclockwise around the Rock. To start the tour, climb the indoor stairs opposite the ticket desk.*

❶ **Hall of the Vicars Choral:** This is the youngest building on the Rock (early 1400s). It housed the minor clerics appointed to sing during cathedral services. These vicars—who were granted nearby lands by the archbishop—lived

The Rock of Cashel looms above the Tipperary countryside.

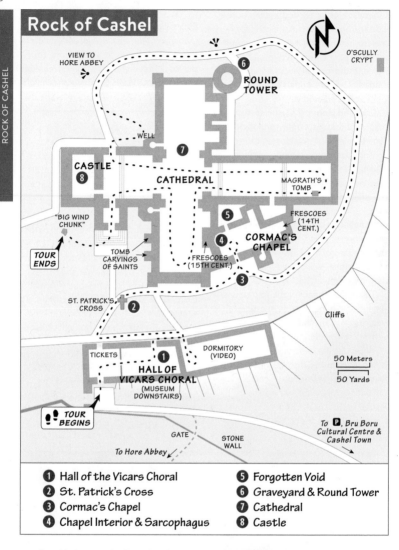

Rock of Cashel

VIEW TO
HORE ABBEY

O'SCULLY
CRYPT

6

ROUND
TOWER

WELL

7

CASTLE

8

CATHEDRAL

MAGRATH'S
TOMB

5

FRESCOES
(14TH
CENT.)

"BIG WIND
CHUNK"

4

CORMAC'S
CHAPEL

TOUR
ENDS

TOMB
CARVINGS
OF SAINTS

FRESCOES
(15TH CENT.)

3

ST. PATRICK'S
CROSS

2

Cliffs

TICKETS

1

DORMITORY
(VIDEO)

HALL OF
VICARS CHORAL
(MUSEUM
DOWNSTAIRS)

50 Meters

50 Yards

TOUR
BEGINS

GATE

STONE
WALL

To ⓟ, Bru Boru
Cultural Centre &
Cashel Town

To Hore Abbey

❶ Hall of the Vicars Choral
❷ St. Patrick's Cross
❸ Cormac's Chapel
❹ Chapel Interior & Sarcophagus
❺ Forgotten Void
❻ Graveyard & Round Tower
❼ Cathedral
❽ Castle

comfortably here, with a large fireplace and white, lime-washed walls (to reflect light and act as a natural disinfectant that discouraged bugs as well). Window seats gave the blessedly literate vicars the best light to read by. The furniture is original, but the oak timber roof is a reconstruction, built to medieval specifications using wooden dowels instead of nails. The large wall tapestry, showing King Solomon with the Queen of Sheba, contains intentional errors—to remind viewers that only God can create perfection.

The vicars, who formed a sort of corporate body to assist the bishop with local administration, used a special seal to authorize documents such as land leases. You can see an enlarged wooden copy of the seal (hanging above the fireplace), depicting eight vicars surrounding a seated organist. It was a good system—until some of the greedier vicars duplicated the seal for their own purposes, forcing the archbishop to curtail its use.

• Go outside the hall into the grassy space 50 feet away and find...

❷ St. Patrick's Cross: St. Patrick baptized King Aengus at the Rock of Cashel in about A.D. 450. Legend has it that St. Patrick, intensely preoccupied with the holy ceremony, accidentally speared the foot of the king with his crosier staff while administering the baptismal sacrament. But the pagan king stoically held his tongue until the end of the ceremony, thinking this was part of the painful process of becoming a Christian. Probably not that many other converts stepped forward that day.

This 12th-century cross, a stub of its former glory, was carved to celebrate the handing over of the Rock to the Church 650 years after St. Patrick's visit. Typical Irish high crosses use a ring around the cross' head to support its arms and to symbolize the sun (making Christianity more appealing to the sun-worshipping Celts). But instead, this cross uses the Latin design: The weight of the arms is supported by two vertical beams on each side of the main shaft, representing the two criminals who were crucified beside Christ (today only one of these supports remains).

On my first visit, more than 30 years ago, the original cross still stood here, outside. But centuries of wind and rain were slowly eroding away important detail, so the cross was moved into the adjacent museum (opposite the ticket desk) and replaced by this replica.

• Turn your back on St. Patrick's Cross, and walk about 100 feet slightly uphill along the gravel path beside the cathedral. Roughly opposite the far end of the Hall of the Vicars Choral is the entry to...

❸ Cormac's Chapel: As the wild Celtic Christian church was reined in and reorganized by Rome 850 years ago, new architectural influences from continental Europe began to emerge on the remote Irish landscape. This small chapel—Ireland's first and finest Romanesque church, constructed in 1134 by King Cormac MacCarthy—reflects this evolution. Travel in your imagination back to the 12th century, when this chapel and the tall round tower were the only stone structures on the Rock.

The "new" Romanesque style reflected the ancient Roman basilica floor plan. Its columns and rounded arches created an overall effect of massiveness and strength. Romanesque churches were like dark fortresses, with thick walls, squat towers, few windows, and minimal decoration. Irish stone churches of this period (like the one at Glendalough in the Wicklow Mountains) were simple rectangular buildings with few ornate stone carvings.

Legend says that the chapel's easy-to-cut sandstone was quarried 12 miles away, and the blocks were passed from hand to hand back to the Rock. (It's unlikely that they had the manpower to form a conga line that long—they probably used oxen-pulled carts.) The two square towers resemble those in Regensburg, Germany, further suggesting that well-traveled medieval Irish monks brought back new ideas from the Continent.

• The modern, dark-glass chapel door (always unlocked) is a recent addition to keep out nesting birds. Enter the chapel (remembering to close the door behind you) and let your eyes adjust to the low light.

❹ Chapel Interior: Just inside the chapel, on your left, is an empty stone **sarcophagus.** Nobody knows for sure whose body once lay here (possibly the brother of King Cormac MacCarthy). The damaged front relief is carved in the Scandinavian Urnes style. Vikings raided Ireland, intermarried with the Irish, and were melting into Irish society by the time this chapel was built. Some scholars interpret the relief design (a tangle of snakes and beasts) as a figure-eight lying on its side, looping back and forth forever, symbolizing the eternity of the afterlife.

With your back to the sarcophagus, let your eyes wander around the chapel interior. You're standing in the **nave,** lit by the three windows (partially blocked by the later cathedral, which is outside to the left) in the wall behind you. Overhead is a round vaulted ceiling with support ribs. The strong round arches support not only the heavy stone roof, but also the (unseen) second-story scriptorium chamber, where chilly monks, warmed only by candlelight, once carefully copied manuscripts.

The **chancel arch,** studded with fist-size heads, framed the altar (now gone). The lower heads are more grotesque, while those nearing the top become serene as they climb closer to God. The arch is off-center in relation to the nave, symbolic of Christ's head drooping to the side as he died on the cross.

Walk into the chancel and look up at the ceiling, examining the faint **frescoes,** a labor of love from 850 years ago. Frescoes are rare in Ireland because of the perpetually moist climate. (Mixing pigments into wet plaster worked better in dry climates like Italy's.) Once vividly colorful, then fading over time, these frescoes were further damaged during the Reformation. Such ornamentation was considered vain by Protestants, who piously whitewashed over them. These surviving frescoes were discovered under multiple layers of whitewash during painstaking modern restoration. The rich blue color came from lapis

lazuli, an expensive gemstone imported from Asia.

• *Walk through the other modern, dark-glass doorway (don't let the birds in), opposite the door you used to enter the chapel. You'll find yourself in a...*

❺ **Forgotten Void:** This enclosed space (roughly 30 feet square) was created when the newer cathedral was wedged between the older chapel and the round tower. Once the main entrance into the chapel, this forgotten doorway is crowned by a finely carved tympanum that decorates the arch above it. It's perfectly preserved because the huge cathedral shielded it from the wind and rain. The large lion (symbol of St. Mark's gospel) is being hunted by a centaur (half-man, half-horse) archer wearing a Norman helmet (essential conehead attire in the late Middle Ages).

As you exit the chapel (turning left), take a look at the more exposed and weathered tympanum outside, above the south entrance. The carved, bloated "hippo" is actually an ox, representing Gospel author St. Luke.

• *Tiptoe through the tombstones around the east end of the cathedral to the base of the round tower.*

❻ **Graveyard and Round Tower:** This graveyard still takes permanent guests— but only those put on a waiting list by their ancestors in 1930. A handful of these chosen few are still alive, and once they're gone, the graveyard will be considered full. The 20-foot-tall stone shaft at the edge of the graveyard, marking the O'Scully family

Ornate tomb at cathedral

Graveyard and round tower

crypt, was once crowned by an elaborately carved Irish high cross—destroyed during a lightning storm in 1976.

Look out over the **Plain of Tipperary.** Called the "Golden Vale," its rich soil makes it Ireland's most prosperous farmland. In St. Patrick's time, it was covered with oak forests (Ireland is now the most deforested nation in the EU). A path leads to the ruined 13th-century **Hore Abbey** in the fields below (free, always open and peaceful). The abbey is named for the Cistercian monks who wore simple gray robes, roughly the same color as hoarfrost (the ice crystals that form on morning grass).

Gaze up at the **round tower,** the first stone structure built on the Rock after the Church took over in 1101. The shape of these towers is unique to Ireland. Though you might think towers like this were chiefly intended as a place to hide in case of invasion, they were instead used primarily as bell towers and lookout posts. (Enemies could smoke out anyone inside the tower, and with enough warning, monks were better off concealing themselves in the countryside.) The tower stands 92 feet tall, with walls more than 3 feet thick. The doorway, which once had a rope ladder, was built high up not only for security, but also because having it at ground level would have weakened the foundation of the top-heavy structure. The interior once contained wooden floors connected by ladders, and served as safe storage for the monks' precious sacramental treasures. The tower's stability is impressive when you consider its age, the winds it has endured, and the shallowness of its foundation (only five feet below present ground level).

Continue walking around the cathedral's north transept, noticing the square "put-log" holes in the exterior walls. During construction, wooden scaffolding was anchored into these holes. After the structure was completed, the builders simply sawed off the scaffolding, leaving small blocks of wood embedded in the walls. With time, the blocks rotted away, and the holes became favorite spots for birds to build their nests.

On your way to the cathedral entrance, in the corner where the north transept joins the nave, you'll pass a small, easy-to-miss **well.** Without this essential water source, the Rock could never have withstood a siege and would not have been as valuable to clans and clergy. In 1848, a chalice was dredged from the well, likely thrown there by fleeing medieval monks intending to survive a raid. They didn't make it. (If they had, they would have retrieved the chalice.)

• Now enter the...

❼ Cathedral: Traditionally, the choir of a church (where the clergy celebrate Mass) faces east, while the nave stretches off to the west. Because this cathedral was squeezed between the preexisting chapel, round tower, and drinking well, the builders were forced to improvise—giving it an extra-long choir and a cramped nave.

Built between 1230 and 1290, the church's pointed arches and high, narrow windows proclaim the Gothic style of the period (and let in more light than earlier Romanesque churches). Walk under the central bell tower and look up at the rib-vaulted **ceiling.** The hole in the middle was for a rope used to ring the church bells. The wooden roof is long gone. When the Protestant Lord Inchiquin (who became one of Oliver Cromwell's generals) attacked the Catholic town of Cashel in 1647, hundreds of townsfolk fled to the sanctuary of this cathedral. Inchiquin packed turf around the exterior and burned the cathedral down, massacring those inside.

Ascend the terraces at the choir end of the cathedral, where the main altar once stood. Stand on the gravestones (of the 16th-century rich and famous) with your back to the east wall (where the narrow windows have crumbled away) and look back down toward the nave. The right wall of the choir is filled with graceful

Gothic windows, while the solid left wall hides Cormac's Chapel (which would have blocked any sunlight). The line of stone supports on the left wall once held the long, wooden balcony where the vicars sang. Closer to the altar, high on the same wall, is a small, rectangular window called the "leper's squint"—which allowed unsightly lepers to view the altar during Mass without offending the congregation.

The grand **wall tomb** on the left contains the remains of archbishop Miler Magrath, the "scoundrel of Cashel," who lived to be 100. From 1570 to 1622, Magrath was the Protestant archbishop of Cashel who simultaneously profited from his previous position as Catholic bishop of Down. He married twice, had lots of kids, confiscated the ornate tomb lid here from another bishop's grave, and converted back to Catholicism on his deathbed.

• *Walk back down the nave and turn left into the south transept.*

Take a peek into the modern-roofed wooden structure against the wall on your left. It's protecting 15th-century **frescoes** of the Crucifixion of Christ that were rediscovered during renovations in 2005. They're as patchy and hard to make out (and just as rare for Ireland) as the century-older frescoes in the ceiling of Cormac's Chapel. On the opposite side of this transept, in alcoves built into the wall, wonderful **carvings** of early Christian saints line the outside walls of tombs (look down at shin level).

• *Return to the nave and continue down to the far end. Exit the cathedral on the left, through the porch entrance.*

❽ Castle: Back outside, stand beside the huge chunk of wall debris and try to picture where it might have fit in the ruins above. This end of the cathedral was converted into an archbishop's castle in the 1400s (shortening the nave even more). Looking high into the castle's damaged top floors, you can see the bishop's residence chamber and the secret passageways that were once hidden in the thick

walls. Lord Inchiquin's cannons weakened the structure during the 1647 massacre, and in 1848, a massive storm (known as "Night of the Big Wind" in Irish lore) flung the huge chunk next to you from the ruins above.

In the mid-1700s, the Anglican Church transferred cathedral status to St. John's in town, and the archbishop abandoned the drafty Rock for a more comfortable residence, leaving the ruins that you see today.

BRU BORU CULTURAL CENTRE

Nestled below the Rock of Cashel parking lot, below the statue of the three blissed-out dancers, this center adds to your understanding of the Rock in its wider historical and cultural context. The highlight of the **Sounds of History Museum** downstairs is the exhibit showing the Rock's gradual evolution from ancient ring fort to grand church ruins—projected down onto a large disc that visitors gather around.

Those interested in Ireland's traditional music scene will enjoy the surprisingly good 15-minute film introduction to Irish trad music in the small museum theater.

Cost and Hours: Cultural Centre-free, Sounds of History Museum-€5; June-Aug Mon-Sat 9:00-18:00, closed Sun; Sept-May closes at 17:00 and on Sat-Sun; cafeteria, tel. 062/61122, www.bruboru.ie.

Performances: If you stay overnight in Cashel in summer, consider taking in a performance of the Bru Boru musical dance troupe in the center's large theater (€20, €50 with dinner, July-Aug Tue-Sat, dinner at 18:30, performance at 21:00).

TOWN OF CASHEL

The huggable town at the base of the Rock affords a good break on the long drive from Dublin to Dingle (**TI** open mid-March-Oct daily 9:30-17:30, Nov-mid-March closed Sat-Sun, tel. 062/61333). The Heritage Centre, next door to the TI, presents a modest six-minute audio explanation of Cashel's history around a walled town model. Parking requires a pay-and-display ticket from machines on the street (€1, enforced Mon-Sat 9:00-18:00, free Sun).

Eating

Near the Rock: Grab a basic soup-and-sandwich lunch at tiny, violet-colored **Granny's Kitchen** (daily 11:00-16:00, next to the parking lot at the base of the Rock). Popular **Chez Hans Café,** with the best lunch selection and biggest crowds, is 75 yards down the road from the parking lot (€16-20 meals, Tue-Sat 12:00-17:30, closed Sun-Mon). And 50 yards farther down that same road, you'll find **Rock House,** an enthusiastically hosted, cafeteria-style restaurant that's upstairs above O'Dwyer's pharmacy (daily 9:00-16:00, tel. 062/62299).

For a splurge dinner, look for the old stone church housing **Chez Hans,** the classy cousin of Chez Hans Café, listed above (€28-35 main courses, Tue-Sat 18:00-21:30, closed Sun-Mon, in an old church a block below the Rock, tel. 062/61177, www.chezhans.net).

In Town: Next door to the TI, **Feehan's Bar** is a convenient stop for a pub grub lunch (daily 12:00-16:00, tel. 062/61929). A couple of blocks farther into town, the **Cellar Pub** hides beneath Bailey's Hotel and serves satisfying dishes (€15-20 meals, daily 12:00-21:30, tel. 062/61937).

Super Valu is the town's supermarket (Mon-Sat 7:00-22:00, Sun 8:00-21:00, 30 Main Street).

Sleeping

If you spend the night in Cashel, you'll be treated to beautifully illuminated views of the ruins. The first listing is a classy hotel in the center of town (15-minute walk from the Rock). The rest are cozy, old-fashioned, and closer to the Rock.

$$$ Bailey's Hotel is Cashel's best boutique hotel, housed in a fine Georgian townhouse (1709). Its 19 refurbished rooms are large, inviting, and well-appointed, perched above a great cellar-pub restaurant (Sb-€75-80, Db-€110-120, Tb-€130-140, parking, 42 Main Street, tel. 062/61937, www.baileyshotelcashel.com, info@baileyshotelcashel.com).

$$ Joy's Rockside House B&B is closest to the Rock, resting on its lower slopes. With four large, fresh rooms (three with views of the Rock), it's the best value in Cashel (Sb-€60-70, Db-€80-90, Tb-€120-140, Qb-€160, cash only, parking, Rock Villas Street, tel. 062/63813, mobile 087-222-1676, www.joyrockside.com, joyrocksidehouse@eircom.net, Joan and Rem Joy).

$$ Cashel Lodge is a well-kept rural oasis housed in an old stone grain warehouse, 200 yards behind the Rock near the Hore Abbey ruins. Its seven comfortable rooms combine unpretentious practicality with Irish country charm (Sb-€47-55, Db-€75-90, Tb-€90-110, camping spots-€10/person, parking, Dundrum Road R-505, tel. 062/61003, www.cashel-lodge.com, info@cashel-lodge.com, Tom and Brid O'Brien).

$ Rockville House, 100 yards from the Rock, is a traditional place run by gentleman owner Patrick Hayes. The house itself has six fine rooms, and its old stablehouse, lovingly converted by Patrick, has five more (Sb-€35, Db-€58-60, Tb-€80, Qb-€90, cash only, 10 Dominic Street, tel. 062/61760, rockvillehse@eircom.net).

$ Wattie's B&B has three rooms that feel lived-in and comfy (Sb-€50-55, Db-€70-75, Tb-€90-98, cash only, parking, 14 Dominic Street, tel. 062/61923, www.wattiesbandb.ie, wattiesbandb@eircom.net, Maria Dunne).

Transportation

Cashel has no train station; the closest one is 13 miles away in the town of Thurles.

From Cashel by Bus to: Dublin (4/day, 3 hours), **Kilkenny** (3/day, 2.5 hours), **Waterford** (6/day, 2 hours). Bus info: www.buseireann.ie.

Kinsale

County Cork, on Ireland's south coast, is fringed with historic port towns and scenic peninsulas. The typical tour-bus route here includes Blarney Castle and Killarney—places where most tourists wear nametags. A major mistake many travelers make is allowing destinations into their itineraries simply because they're famous from a song or as part of a relative's big-bus-tour memory. If you have the misfortune to spend the night in Killarney town (next door in County Kerry), you'll understand what I mean. The town is a sprawling line of green Holiday Inns and outlet malls littered with pushy shoppers looking for plastic shamrocks.

Rather than kissing the spit-slathered Blarney Stone, spend your time enjoying the bustling, historic maritime town of Kinsale, which makes a great home base. The nearby port of Cobh was the last stop for the ill-fated *Titanic* and the beginning of a new life for many Irish emigrants bound for America. And if you can't go home without saying you kissed the Blarney Stone, it's a convenient stop when connecting to the Ring of Kerry or Dingle.

KINSALE IN 1 DAY

Kinsale is worth two nights and a day. Spend the morning checking out a few of the town's sights, and make sure to take Don and Barry's excellent Kinsale walking tour. After lunch at the Fishy Fishy Café, you could head out to Charles Fort for great bay views and insights into British military life in colonial Ireland. On the way back, stop for a pint at the Bulman Bar. Finish the day with a good dinner and live music in a pub.

With extra time, fit in a visit to Cobh. If you have Irish roots, your ancestors likely sailed from here. Coming from Kilkenny or the Rock of Cashel, you could visit Cobh on your way to Kinsale.

ORIENTATION

Historic Kinsale is delightful to visit. Thanks to the naturally sheltered bay barbed by a massive 17th-century star fort, you can submerge yourself in maritime history, from the Spanish Armada to the sailor who inspired Daniel Defoe's *Robinson Crusoe* to the *Lusitania*. Apart from all the history, Kinsale is laid-back, with a touch of wine-sipping class. Or, as a local told me with a wry smile, "Welcome to Happy Valley" (Eli Lilly manufactures its Prozac antidepressants just outside town).

Kinsale has a great natural harbor and is older than Cobh (the city of Cork's harbor town). While the town is prettier than the actual harbor, the harbor was its reason

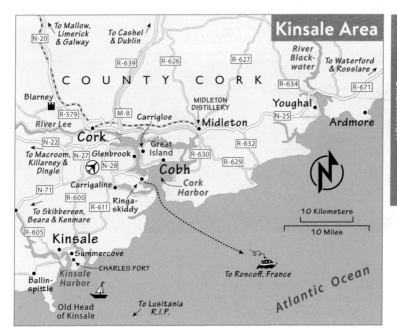

Kinsale Area

for being. Today, Kinsale is a vibrant bustle of 2,500 residents. The town's long and skinny old center is part modern marina (attracting wealthy yachters) and part pedestrian-friendly medieval town (attracting scalawags like us). It's an easy 20-minute stroll from end to end.

Tourist Information: The TI is at the head of the harbor across from the bus stop (July-Aug Mon-Sat 9:15-18:00, Sun 10:00-17:00; March-June and Sept-Nov Mon-Sat 9:30-17:00, closed Sun; shorter hours Dec-Feb; tel. 021/477-2234, www. kinsale.ie).

Market: Check out the lively open-air market on Wednesdays from June through September (9:00-14:00) in the town square on Market Quay, in front of Jim Edward's Steak & Seafood restaurant.

Bike Rental: Mylie Murphy's rents bikes from a handy spot near the Centra supermarket. They can recommend paths good for biking or walking that stretch around the harbor (€15/day, includes lock and helmet; Mon-Sat 9:30-18:00, closed Sun except June-Aug 12:00-17:00,

shorter hours in winter; arrangements can be made for pickup or drop-off, tel. 021/477-2703).

Taxi: Tom Conty can drive you where you need to go, including Cork Airport for €25 or Cork city for €30 (mobile 087-237-1022).

Rick's Tip: On the **first weekend in May, the Kinsale Rugby Sevens Tournament draws hundreds** *of loud and proud rowdy rugby fans. If you're not up for the scrum, then scram.*

Tours

▲▲**Don & Barry's Kinsale Historic Stroll:** To understand the important role Kinsale played in Irish, English, and Spanish history, join gentlemen Don Herlihy or Barry Moloney on a fascinating 1.5-hour walking tour (€7, daily April-mid-Oct at 11:15, additional early-bird tour May-Sept Mon-Sat at 9:15, no reservation necessary, meet outside the TI, private tours possi-

KINSALE AT A GLANCE

In Kinsale

▲▲**Don** & **Barry's Kinsale Historic Stroll** Duo of fascinating guides weave through town revealing the pivotal role Kinsale played in the history of the British Empire. **Hours:** Daily April-mid-Oct at 11:15, additional early tour May-Sept Mon-Sat at 9:15. See page 127.

▲▲**Charles Fort** Stout 17th-century fortress guarding harbor with great tour explaining British military life and featuring fine views; also the starting point of Scilly Walk—a fine harborside walk back into town. **Hours:** Daily mid-March-Oct 10:00-18:00, Nov-mid-March until 17:00. See page 133.

▲**Desmond Castle** Compact former customs house and prison housing the Museum of Wine, highlighting the thriving trade that existed for Irish wooden casks. **Hours:** Easter-Sept daily 10:00-18:00, closed Oct-Easter. See page 133.

▲**Kinsale Regional Museum** Grab-bag of knickknacks starring *Lusitania* debris beachcombed after the famous sinking, with coverage of the tribunal that took place here after the disaster. **Hours:** Wed-Sat 10:30-13:30, closed Sun-Tue. See page 134.

Nearby

▲**Cobh** Historic port with two worthwhile sights (both open daily): Titanic Experience (a simulation of the last day the ill-fated ship picked up passengers here) and Queenstown Story (an exhibit on Cobh's history as Ireland's busiest emigration port). **Hours:** Always open. See page 138.

Blarney Castle Overcrowded, commercial, touristy castle featuring the stone that visitors kiss to gain the gift of gab, surrounded by beautifully lush parkland. **Hours:** Mon-Sat 9:00-18:30, Sun 9:00-17:30, later in peak season, shorter hours in winter. See page 142.

ble, tel. 021/477-2873, www.historicstroll kinsale.com). Both guides are a joy to hear as they creatively bring Kinsale's past to life, place its story in the wider sweep of history, and make the stony sights more than just buildings. They collect payment at the end, giving anyone disappointed in the talk an easy escape midway through. Don't get hijacked by imitation tours that pretend to be recommended by me on my blog—ask for Don or Barry. This walk is Kinsale's single best attraction.

Ghost Walk Tour: This is not just any ghost tour; it's more Monty Python-style slapstick comedy than horror. Two actors (Brian and David) weave funny stunts and stories into a loose history of the town, offering an entertaining 1.25 hours of fun on Kinsale's after-dark streets (€10, April-Oct Sun-Fri at 21:00, no tours Sat, leaves from Tap Tavern, call ahead to confirm, mobile 087-948-0910). You'll spend the first 15 minutes in the back of the Tap Tavern—time to finish your drink and get to know some of the group. This tour doesn't overlap with the more serious historic town walk described earlier.

⊙ Kinsale Town Walk

Stroll the old part of town. The medieval walled town's economy was fueled by the harbor, where ships came to be stocked. The old walls defined the original town and created a small fortified zone that made taxation of goods coming in or going out easier. The wall followed what is now O'Connell Street and Main Street.

The subtle curves of Main Street trace the original coastline. Walking this street, you'll see tiny lanes leading to today's harbor. These originated as piers—just wide enough to roll a barrel down to an awaiting ship. The wall detoured inland to protect St. Multose Church, which dates from Norman times. In these days, worshippers sharpened their swords on the doorway of the church. Just like today, there were more right-handers than left-handers—check it out.

A block downhill from the church (across from today's Tap Tavern) was the town pound: a small enclosure where goods and livestock would be impounded until the owner could pay the associated tax. After the James and Charles forts

Wandering Kinsale

Kinsale

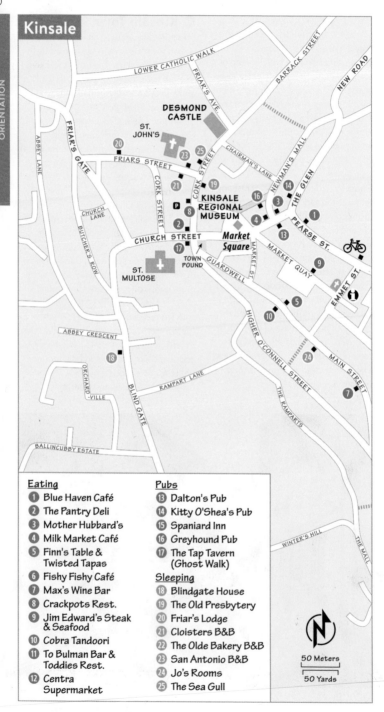

Eating
1. Blue Haven Café
2. The Pantry Deli
3. Mother Hubbard's
4. Milk Market Café
5. Finn's Table & Twisted Tapas
6. Fishy Fishy Café
7. Max's Wine Bar
8. Crackpots Rest.
9. Jim Edward's Steak & Seafood
10. Cobra Tandoori
11. To Bulman Bar & Toddies Rest.
12. Centra Supermarket

Pubs
13. Dalton's Pub
14. Kitty O'Shea's Pub
15. Spaniard Inn
16. Greyhound Pub
17. The Tap Tavern (Ghost Walk)

Sleeping
18. Blindgate House
19. The Old Presbytery
20. Friar's Lodge
21. Cloisters B&B
22. The Olde Bakery B&B
23. San Antonio B&B
24. Jo's Rooms
25. The Sea Gull

50 Meters

50 Yards

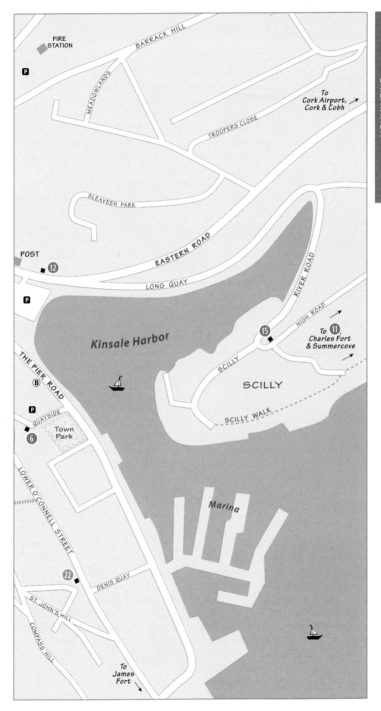

Kinsale is Key

Kinsale's perfect natural harbor has made this an important port since prehistoric times. Its importance peaked during the 16th, 17th, and 18th centuries, when it was the gateway to Spain and France—potentially providing a base for either of these two powers in cutting off English shipping.

In about 1500, the pope divided newly discovered lands outside Europe between Spain and Portugal. With the Reformation breaking Rome's lock on Europe, maritime powers such as England were ignoring the pope's grant. England threatened Spain's New World piñata, and Ireland was Catholic. Spain had an economic and a religious reason to defend the pope and Catholicism. The showdown between Spain and England was in Ireland. The excuse: to rescue the dear Catholics of Ireland from the terrible treachery of Protestant England.

So the Irish disaster unfolded. The Ulster chieftains Hugh O'Neill and Red Hugh O'Donnell and their clans had been waging guerilla battles against the English. With Spanish aid, they figured they could actually drive the English out of Ireland. In 1601, a Spanish fleet dropped off 3,000 soldiers, who established a beachhead in Kinsale. After the ships left, the Spaniards were pinned down in Kinsale by the English commander. In harsh winter conditions, virtually the entire Irish-clan fighting force left the north and marched to the south coast, thinking they could liberate their Spanish allies and win freedom from England.

The numbers seemed reasonable (8,000 Englishmen versus 3,000 Spaniards with 7,000 Irish clansmen). The Irish attacked on Christmas Eve in 1601. But, holding the high ground around fortified and Spanish-occupied Kinsale, a relatively small English force kept the Spaniards hemmed in, leaving the bulk of the English troops to rout the Irish, who were adept at ambushes but not at open-field warfare.

The Irish resistance was broken, and its leaders fled to Europe (the "flight of the Earls"). England made peace with Spain and began the "plantation" of mostly Scottish Protestants in Ireland (the seeds of today's Troubles in Ulster). England ruled the waves, and it ruled Ireland. The lesson: Kinsale is key. England eventually built two huge, star-shaped fortresses here to ensure control of the narrow waterway.

were built in the 1600s, the wall became obsolete—and also boxed in the town, preventing further expansion. The townspeople later disassembled the wall and used its ready-cut stones to build out the piers in the harbor.

What seems like part of the old center was actually built later on land reclaimed from the harbor. The town sits on the floor of a natural quarry, with easy-to-cut shale hills ideal for a ready supply of fill. Notice the mudflats in the harbor at low tide. Clear-cutting of the once-plentiful oak forest upriver (for shipbuilding and barrel-making) hastened erosion and silted up the harbor. By the early 1800s—when British ships needed lots of restocking for the Napoleonic Wars—Kinsale's port was slowly dying, and nearby Cobh's deepwater port took over the lion's share of shipping.

SIGHTS

▲▲CHARLES FORT

Kinsale is protected by what was Britain's biggest star-shaped fort—a state-of-the-art defense when artillery made the traditional castle obsolete (low, thick walls were tougher for cannons to breach than the tall, thin curtain walls of a castle). The British occupied it until Irish independence in 1922. Its interior buildings were torched in 1923 by anti-treaty IRA forces to keep it from being used by Free State troops during the Irish Civil War. Guided 45-minute tours (which depart on the hour—confirm at entry) engross you in the harsh daily life of 18th-century British soldiers and the few "lucky" wives allowed to live in the fort and earn their keep doing laundry for an army.

Before or after your tour, peruse the exhibits and audiovisuals in the barracks stores building. Spend a moment checking out the model of the fort. Great views await those who walk the walls.

Cost and Hours: €4, daily mid-March-Oct 10:00-18:00, Nov-mid-March until 17:00, last entry 45 minutes before closing, a half-mile south of town in Summercove, tel. 021/477-2263. A coffee-and-pastry café stands inside the walls, downhill across from the ticket office (daily May-Sept 10:00-18:00).

After Your Visit: For a beer or meal nearby, try Bulman Bar in Summercove, where the road runs low near the water on the way back to town (with small parking lot). And to see how easily the forts could bottle up this key harbor, pull over at the grand harbor viewpoint at the high point on the road back into town (between Summercove and The Spaniard pub).

Nearby: Without a car (and weather permitting), enjoy Kinsale's best 45-minute stroll back into town—with great harbor views—on the Scilly Walk pedestrian trail. The first couple hundred yards and last quarter-mile are on roads shared with traffic (and without sidewalks). But the middle 80 percent of the walk is along a lushly vegetated trail (trailhead on left after climbing 200 yards up the steep road from Bulman Bar; look for *Scilly Walk* sign and large cement slabs that block confused cars from entering the paved trail).

▲DESMOND CASTLE

This 15th-century fortified customs house has had a long and varied history.

Charles Fort guards Kinsale harbor.

It was the Spanish armory during Spain's 1601 occupation of Kinsale. Nicknamed "Frenchman's Prison," it served as a British prison and once housed 600 cramped prisoners of the Napoleonic Wars (not to mention earlier American Revolutionary War prisoners captured at sea—who were treated as rebels, not prisoners, and chained to the outside of the building as a warning to any rebellion-minded Irish). In the late 1840s, it was a famine-relief center.

Today, the evocative little tower comes with a scant display of its colorful history, as well as the modest two-room Museum of Wine, highlighting Ireland's little-known connection to the international wine trade. In the late Middle Ages, Kinsale was renowned for its top-quality wooden casks. Developing strong trade links with Bordeaux and Jerez, local merchants traded their dependable empty casks for casks full of wine. Later, Kinsale became a "designated wine port" for tax-collection purposes.

Cost and Hours: €4, Easter-Sept daily 10:00-18:00, closed Oct-Easter, last entry at 17:15; tours at 10:15, 12:00, 14:15, and 16:00; Cork Street, tel. 021/477-4855.

Desmond Castle

▲KINSALE REGIONAL MUSEUM

In the center of the old town, traffic circles the market, which later became a courthouse and is now the Regional Museum. Its Dutch architecture reflects the influence of Dutch-born King William of Orange at the end of the 1600s. Drop by at least to read the fun 1788 tax code for all Kinsale commercial transactions (outside at the front door).

Cost and Hours: Free, Wed-Sat 10:30-13:30, closed Sun-Tue, staffed by volunteers—hours can be erratic, Market Square, tel. 021/477-7930.

Visiting the Museum: The modest museum is worth a quick visit for its fun mishmash of domestic and maritime bygones. It also gives a good perspective on the controversial *Lusitania* tragedy. Kinsale had maritime jurisdiction over the waters 12 miles offshore, where the luxury liner was torpedoed in 1915. Hearings were held upstairs here in the courthouse shortly afterward to investigate the causes of the disaster—which helped propel America into World War I—and to paint the German Hun as a bloodthirsty villain. Claims by Germany that the *Lusitania* was illegally carrying munitions (and using innocent passengers as human shields) may have been inspired by the huge explosion and rapid sinking of the vessel. As the wreck slowly succumbs to a century of gravity and rust, it's collapsing on itself and the truth of its cargo may forever be lost in the ocean floor muck.

The museum displays are sparse, but include *Lusitania* flotsam such as a wicker deck chair and a US mail bag. A flickering black-and-white film shows the last happy glory days of the vessel in port. Apart from the *Lusitania* footage, you'll find a gritty model of medieval Kinsale surrounded by its once-proud walls. Perhaps even more memorable, in the side room is the boot of the 8-foot-3-inch Kinsale giant, who lived here in the late 1700s.

EATING

Back in the 1990s, when Ireland was just getting its cuisine act together, Kinsale was the island's self-proclaimed gourmet capital. While good restaurants are commonplace in Irish towns today, Kinsale still has an edge at mealtime. Local competition is fierce, and restaurants offer creative and tempting menus. Seafood is king. With so many options in the ever-changing scene, it's worth a short stroll to assess your options. Reservations are smart, especially if eating late or on a weekend. Restaurant connoisseurs can check the menu details of Kinsale's most famous restaurants online (www.kinsale restaurants.com).

Picnickers seek out the **Centra** supermarket (daily 8:00-22:00, Pearse Street).

Lunch

The following places are good for lunch, but only the Blue Haven also does dinner.

Inviting cafés are **Blue Haven Café,** with nice salads and mellow atmosphere (daily, at Blue Haven Hotel on Pearse Street), and **The Pantry,** your chance to try spiced lamb burger (Tue-Sat 9:00-18:00, closed Sun-Mon, across the street from St. Multose Church, tel. 021/477-4453).

Cheap and Cheery Lunches: Tiny **Mother Hubbard's,** packed with happy locals near Market Square, serves sandwiches or salads with coffee for under €10 (daily 8:30-14:30). The **Milk Market**

Café—right next door—offers burgers, pizza, and fish-and-chips.

Good Dinners in the Old Center

Colorfully fronted (but pricey) **Finn's Table** offers a refined vibe and a scrumptious menu ranging from lamb to lobster (€32.50 three-course dinners before 19:00; May-Oct Mon-Sat 18:00-22:00, closed Sun; Dec-April Thurs-Sat; closed Nov; 6 Main Street, tel. 021/470-9636).

Fishy Fishy Café has spacious seating (indoor, balcony, and terrace) and a wonderful fish menu. It's a good lunch or early dinner option. Look at the lobsters on death row in the tank and ponder this: Several years ago, a soft-hearted, deep-pocketed Buddhist tourist bought up the tank's entire supply of live lobsters and set them free in the bay (with stories to tell their crustacean cousins about how they'd been abducted by aliens). They've refilled the tank since. Owner Martin Shanahan's cooking prowess has led him to host a weekly cooking show on Irish TV (daily 12:00-21:00, reservations recommended, Pier Road, tel. 021/470-0415, www.fishyfishy.ie).

Wine-Bar Restaurants: Several atmospheric choices vie for your attention along the gently curving Main Street. **Max's Wine Bar** leads the pack, with subdued lighting and a menu that's big on quality seafood (€25 early-bird fixed-price meal before 19:30, daily 18:00-21:30, 48 Main Street, tel. 021/477-2443).

Crackpots sports distinctive ceramics created by owner Carole Norman in her romantically lit restaurant. Locally caught fish and organically grown veggies are menu staples, but don't overlook the duck, which gets rave reviews (great €25 three-course early-bird meal before 19:00, daily 18:00-22:00, 3 Cork Street, tel. 021/477-2847).

Jim Edward's Steak & Seafood keeps eaters happy in both the bar and the restaurant. Choose between the restaurant's maritime setting (€18-25 meals, dinner only) or simpler food in the no-nonsense bar (€12-18 meals). Arrive early or wait. While cheaper and less gourmet than other Kinsale eateries, it's a high-energy place that's clearly a local family favorite for its decent steaks, seafood, and vegetables (bar daily 12:30-22:00, restaurant daily 18:00-22:00, Market Quay, tel. 021/477-2541).

Ethnic Food: Walk around the old-town block for an array of inviting international eateries. **Twisted** is hip and youthful, serving Spanish tapas and lighter fare "with a twist" (5 Main Street, tel. 021/477-4218). **Cobra Tandoori** is good for tasty Punjabi/Indian cuisine (€11-16 plates, daily 16:00-23:30, 69 Main Street, tel. 021/477-7911).

Near Charles Fort

Bulman Bar and Toddies Restaurant serves seafood with seasonal produce. The mussels are especially tasty; on a balmy day or evening, diners take a bucket and a beer out to the seawall. This is the only way to eat on the water in Kinsale. The pub, strewn with fun decor and sporting a big fireplace, is also good for a coffee or beer after your visit to the fort (€15-20 lunches, €20-28 meals upstairs in fancy restaurant, daily 12:30-21:30, 200 yards toward Kinsale from Charles Fort in hamlet of Summercove, tel. 021/477-2131).

Pubs: Musical or Mellow

Kinsale's pubs are packed with atmosphere and live music (though not always traditional Irish). Rather than target a certain place, simply walk the area between Guardwell, Pearse Street, and the Market Square. Pop into each pub that has live music, and then settle in to your favorite. **Dalton's** and **Kitty O'Shea's** are good bets.

Irish music purists will be rewarded if they take the five-minute taxi ride (€8 one-way) out to the **Bulman Bar** near the base of Charles Fort. This is one of Kinsale's two most famous pubs for traditional Irish music sessions (Thu-Sat at 21:30, Sun at 17:00, get there early to ensure a seat, 200 yards toward Kinsale from Charles Fort in hamlet of Summercove, tel. 021/477-2131). Otherwise, get your trad fix at the charmingly claustrophobic **Spaniard Inn,** a 10-minute walk out to the Scilly peninsula across the harbor from town. It fills the center of a hairpin turn on the crest of the peninsula. The darkly atmospheric interior is about the size of a rail car, with the long bar taking up half the space, so only about 10 seats get an actual view of the musicians (most nights at 21:30, you'll stand all night unless you arrive before 20:30, tel. 021/477-2436).

I like the **Greyhound** for conversation or an introspective pint with a newspaper; there's no live music—it's just a scruffy, unpretentious throwback (off Newman's Mall, behind the Milk Market Café). **Tap Tavern** is another joint filled with characters who haven't changed in decades; it's presided over by Mary O'Neill, the unofficial godmother of Kinsale, and her slyly humorous son Brian, who runs the town's Ghost Tours. Check out the ancient holy well that came to light when they built their appealing back patio (corner of Church Street and Guardwell).

SLEEPING

Kinsale is a popular place in summer for yachters and golfers (who don't flinch at paying $250 for 18 holes out on the exotic Old Head of Kinsale Golf Course). It's wise to book your room in advance. I've listed peak-season prices. These places are all within a 10-minute walk of the town center.

$$$ **Blindgate House,** high up on the fringe of town behind St. Multose Church, offers 11 pristine rooms in fine modern comfort (Db-€100-140, tel. 021/477-7858, mobile 087-237-6676, www.blindgate house.com, info@blindgatehouse.com, Maeve Coakley).

$$$ **The Old Presbytery** is a fine, quiet house a block outside the commercial district, with a meandering floor plan, plush lounge, and 10 pleasant rooms. Listed in most guidebooks, it has lots of American guests. The breakfasts are a delight, the rooms are stocking-feet cozy, and Noreen McEvoy runs the place with a passion for excellence (standard Db-€95-130, bigger Db-€120-145, biggest Db-€135-165, Tb-€160, family Qb-€185, 2 Qb self-catering suites with no break-fast-€140-180, ask for Rick Steves discount with cash and this book, private parking, 43 Cork Street, tel. 021/477-2027, www.oldpres.com, oldpres@gmail.com).

$$ **Friar's Lodge** is a slate-shingled hotel, perched up the hill past St. John's Catholic Church. What its 18 spacious rooms lack in Old World character, they make up for in dependable quality. Three pleasant, self-catering cottages located up the slope behind their parking lot are great for families wanting their own space (Sb-€50-80, Db-€80-130, Tb-€100-160, Qb-€150-200, private parking, Friar Street, tel. 021/477-7384, www.friars-lodge.com, mtierney@indigo.ie).

$$ **Cloisters B&B** has four snug but bright and inviting rooms with a friendly atmosphere fostered by Orla Kenneally and Aileen Healy (Sb-€55-60, Db-€85-105, Tb-€115-130, 2 Friars Street, tel. 021/470-0680, www.cloisterskinsale.com, info@cloisterskinsale.com).

$ **The Olde Bakery B&B** makes you feel at home, with six quilt-bedded rooms, Lilly the loveable mute mutt, and a jovial breakfast at the kitchen table cooked up by charmingly chatty Chrissie and beekeeper Tom Quigley (D-€75-80, Db-€80-85, cash only, laundry service, 56 Lower O'Connell Street, tel. 021/477-3012, www.theoldebakerykinsale.com, olde bakery@gmail.com).

$ **San Antonio B&B** is a 200-year-old house with five rooms and a funky budget feel, lovingly looked after by gentleman Jimmie Conron (Sb-€50-55, Db-€80, Tb-€110-115, cash only, tel. 021/477-2341, mobile 086-878-9800, jimmiesan@yahoo.ie).

$ **Jo's Rooms** is a good value, offering five fresh, practical rooms in the center of town (Sb-€30-40, Db-€45-50, break-fast-€5-8 extra, cash only, small rooms with smaller double beds, 55 Main Street, mobile 087-948-1026, www.joskinsale.com, joskinsale@gmail.com).

$ **The Sea Gull,** perched up the hill right next to Desmond Castle, offers six retro-homey rooms. It's run by Mrs. Mary O'Neill, who also runs the Tap Tavern down the hill (S-€40, Sb-€45, Db-€70-80, Tb-€110, 10 percent discount with this

Sleep Code

Abbreviations: S=Single, D=Double/Twin, T=Triple, Q=Quad, b=bathroom
   Price Rankings for Double Rooms: $$$ Most rooms €120 or more, $$ €80-120, $ €80 or less
   Notes: Room prices change; verify rates online or by email. For the best prices, book directly with the hotel.

book in 2016, cash only, Cork Street, tel. 021/477-2240, mobile 087-241-6592, marytap@iol.ie).

TRANSPORTATION
Arriving and Departing
By Bus

Like many worthwhile corners of Ireland, Kinsale is not accessible by train; the nearest train station is in Cork, 15 miles north. But buses run frequently between Kinsale (on Pier Road, behind TI, at south end of town) and Cork's bus station (14/day Mon-Sat, fewer on Sun, 50 minutes).

In **Cork**, the bus station and train station are a 10-minute walk apart. The bus station (corner of Merchant's Quay and Parnell Place) is on the south bank of the River Lee, just over the nearest bridge from the train station (north of the river on Lower Glanmire Road).

From Cork by Train to: Dublin (hourly, 2.75 hours, www.irishrail.ie).

From Cork by Bus to: Dublin (every 2 hours, 3.5 hours), **Galway** (hourly, 4.5 hours), **Tralee** (hourly, 2.25 hours), **Kilkenny** (4-5/day, 2 direct, 3.5 hours). Bus info: tel. 021/450-8188 or www.bus eireann.ie.

By Car

Drivers should park the car and enjoy the town on foot. While Kinsale's windy medieval lanes are narrow and congested, parking is fairly easy. The most central lot is at the head of the harbor behind the TI (€1.50/hour, 2-hour maximum, use pay-and-display machine, exact coins required, enforced Mon-Sat 10:30-18:00, free on Sun). There's a big, safe, free parking lot across the street from St. Multose Church at the top of town, a five-minute walk from most recommended hotels and restaurants. Parking on the street is by pay-and-display machine (€1.50/hour, 2-hour maximum, enforced Mon-Sat 10:30-18:00, free on Sun).

NEAR KINSALE

COBH

If your ancestry is Irish, there's a good chance that Cobh, rated ▲, was the last Irish soil your ancestors had under their feet. Cobh (pronounced "cove") was the major port of Irish emigration in the 19th century. Of the six million Irish who have emigrated to America, Canada, and Australia since 1815, nearly half left from Cobh.

The first steam-powered ship to make a transatlantic crossing departed from Cobh in 1838—cutting the journey time from 50 days to 18. When Queen Victoria came to Ireland for the first time in 1849, Cobh was the first Irish ground she set foot on. Giddy, the town renamed itself "Queenstown" in her honor. It was still going by that name in 1912, when the *Titanic* made its final fateful stop here

before heading out on its maiden (and only) voyage...just over 100 years ago. To celebrate their new independence from British royalty in 1922, locals changed the town's name back to its original Irish moniker. Today the town's deep harbor attracts 60 cruise ships per year (with their large packs of eager visitors, though many pass through the town quickly).

Orientation

Cobh sits on a large island in Cork Harbor, connected to the mainland by a short bridge (on the north shore) or a handy drive-on ferry (on the west shore). The town's inviting waterfront is colorful yet salty, with a playful promenade. The butcher's advertisement reads, "Always

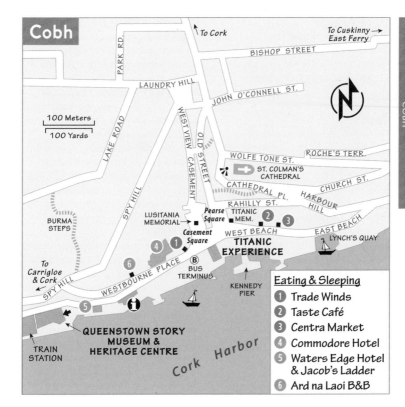

Cobh

To Cork

To Cuskinny →
East Ferry

BISHOP STREET

PARK RD.

LAUNDRY HILL

JOHN O'CONNELL ST.

LAKE ROAD

WEST VIEW

OLD STREET

CASEMENT

100 Meters
100 Yards

SPY HILL

WOLFE TONE ST.

ROCHE'S TERR.

ST. COLMAN'S
CATHEDRAL

CATHEDRAL PL.

CHURCH ST.

HARBOUR HILL

RAHILLY ST.

BURMA
STEPS

LUSITANIA
MEMORIAL →

Pearse
Square

TITANIC
MEM.

2

3

EAST BEACH

**Casement
Square**

WEST BEACH

LYNCH'S QUAY

4 **1**

**TITANIC
EXPERIENCE**

To
Carrigloe
& Cork

6

WESTBOURNE PLACE

B
BUS
TERMINUS

SPY HILL

KENNEDY
PIER

5

i

TRAIN
STATION

**QUEENSTOWN STORY
MUSEUM &
HERITAGE CENTRE**

Cork Harbor

Eating & Sleeping

1 Trade Winds
2 Taste Café
3 Centra Market
4 Commodore Hotel
5 Waters Edge Hotel
& Jacob's Ladder
6 Ard na Laoi B&B

pleased to meet you and always with meat to please you." There's a large *Lusitania* memorial on Casement Square and a modest *Titanic* memorial nearby on Pearse Square.

Rick's Tip: *If you're driving into Cobh, there's a* **two-hour parking maximum** *anywhere in town (first hour-free, second hour-€1, pay at machines on street).*

A hike up the hill to the towering Neo-Gothic St. Colman's Cathedral rewards you with a fine view of the port. To get to the cathedral, walk behind the *Lusitania* memorial, go under the stone arch, and strut up steep Westview Street, passing the photogenic row of colorful houses on your right (nicknamed the "deck of cards" by locals). After panting your way to the top, turn right—you can't miss the

St. Colman's Cathedral is a Cobh landmark.

cathedral steeple.

Tourist Information: The TI is in the Old Yacht Club on the harbor (Mon-Fri 9:00-17:30, Sat-Sun 10:30-17:00, tel. 021/481-3301, www.cobhharbour chamber.ie).

Tours

Michael Martin and his staff lead one-hour *Titanic* **Trail** walking tours of Cobh that give you unexpected insights into the tragic *Titanic* and *Lusitania* voyages, Spike Island, and Cobh's maritime history (€9.50, ask for Rick Steves discount—show this book when you pay, daily at 11:00, also 14:00 in summer with required pre-booking, call ahead to confirm tour times in winter, private tours available, meet in lobby of Commodore Hotel, tel. 021/481-5211, mobile 087-276-7218, www. titanic.ie, info@titanic.ie). Seriously interested travelers should look for his book, *RMS Lusitania: It Wasn't and It Didn't.*

Sights

▲THE *TITANIC* EXPERIENCE

It's stirring to think that this modest port town was the ship's final anchorage—and the last chance to get off. Occupying the former White Star Line building where the Titanic's final passengers boarded, this compact museum packs a decent punch as it recounts the story of the ship and its final moments.

Cost and Hours: €9.50, daily 9:00-18:00, last entry 45 minutes before closing, Casement Square, tel. 021/481-4412, www. titanicexperiencecobh.ie.

Visiting the Museum: As you look off the back balcony into the harbor, note the decayed pilings in front of you. These once supported the old pier and represent the passengers' last chance to turn back. One lucky surviving crewman with a pre-monition did.

Inside the museum, you travel room to room with your host, the ship's fourth mate, in audiovisual form. He meets you at the boarding dock, full of pride in the new vessel. He joins you in replicas of a posh first-class cabin and a no-frills third-class cabin before his commentary is interrupted by the sound of ice tearing at the hull. You then enter a small theater to view an animation that silently depicts the ship sinking in its steel-twisting, slow-motion ballet to the bottom (settling as two crunched hulls 600 yards apart and

12,000 feet deep).

The last stop is a room highlighting the luxurious ship's innovative firsts. It was one of the first equipped with a wireless "Marconi room" to send messages from sea to shore—or to other ships. *Titanic* was the first ever to issue an SOS message by Morse code. Another wall explains in grim detail the effects of hypothermia on the human body.

Before you leave, check out the list of 123 passengers who boarded the *Titanic* in Cobh. Your entry ticket has one of these passengers' names on it. See if you survived (you've got a 30 percent chance). A passenger with the same name as one of this book's co-authors is listed among the third-class passengers lost.

▲THE QUEENSTOWN STORY

Filling a harborside Victorian train station, this museum is an earnest attempt to make the city's history come to life. The topics—the famine, Irish emigration, Australia-bound prison ships, the sinking of the *Lusitania*, and the ill-fated voyage of the *Titanic*—are interesting enough to make it a worthwhile stop.

Cost and Hours: €9.50; May-Oct Mon-Sat 9:30-18:00, Sun 11:00-18:00; Nov-April until 17:00; last entry one hour before closing, handy café, Cobh Heritage Centre, tel. 021/481-3591, www.cobh heritage.com.

Visiting the Museum: Coverage of the *Titanic* and the *Lusitania* was beefed up for the centennials of these famous ships' sinking (2012 and 2015, respectively). You'll learn about one priest who got off the *Titanic* at Cobh. His photos of the early legs of the voyage are a priceless historical reference. But in general, the museum itself, while kid-friendly and engaging, is weak on actual historical artifacts. It reminds me of a big, interesting history picture book with the pages expanded and tacked on the wall.

Before departing, walk over to the Annie Moore statue next to the water, 25 yards from the front door. She emi-grated from Cobh to the US and was the first person to be processed through Ellis Island when it opened on January 1, 1892.

Nearby: Those with Irish roots to trace can use the Heritage Centre's **genealogy search service,** located right across from the Queenstown Story ticket booth. Since Cobh was the primary Irish emigration port, this can be a great place to start your search (€30 consultation and research assistance by appointment only, email ahead to book—genealogy@cobhheritage. com). See the sidebar on page 337 for more tips on researching your Irish heritage.

Eating

The **Trade Winds** pub (downstairs) and restaurant (upstairs) is the nicest place in town. It's near the Commodore Hotel, facing the waterfront at 16 Casement Square. I also like the **Jacob's Ladder** restaurant in Waters Edge Hotel. **Taste** is a hip sandwich joint, a couple of doors down from the *Titanic* memorial. For picnic fixings, there's the **Centra Market** (Mon-Sat 8:00-22:00, Sun from 9:00, facing the water on West Beach Street).

Sleeping

These hotels are all centrally located near the harbor, less than a five-minute walk from the Queenstown Story.

$$$ Commodore Hotel is a grand 165-year-old historic landmark with 40 rooms. This place was once owned by the Humbert family, wealthy Germans who opened it up to *Lusitania* refugees after the 1915 sinking. Its high-ceilinged rooms creak with Victorian character (Sb-€59-70, Db-€115-130, Tb-€170-190, Westbourne Place, tel. 021/481-1277, www.commodore hotel.ie, commodorehotel@eircom.net).

$$ Waters Edge Hotel, located 50 yards from the Queenstown Story, has 19 bright, modern rooms and a pleasant harbor-view restaurant (Sb-€70-100, Db-€80-150, Tb-€100-160, Yacht Club Quay, tel. 021/481-5566, www.watersedge hotel.ie, info@watersedgehotel.ie).

$ Ard na Laoi B&B is a friendly place with five fresh rooms (Sb-€40-50, Db-€60-70, Tb-€90-105, cash only, 15 Westbourne Place, tel. 021/481-2742, www.ardnalaoi.ie, info@ardnalaoi.ie, Michael O'Shea).

Transportation
Arriving and Departing
BY CAR

Driving between Cobh (on the Great Island) and Kinsale is 25 miles, takes an hour, and involves catching a small shuttle ferry between Carrigloe and Glenbrook (5 minutes, daily 7:00-22:00). But you don't want the ferry from Ringaskiddy (to France).

BY TRAIN

Cork's Kent Station has frequent service to Cobh (usually departs on the hour, returns on the half-hour, 25-minute trip, www.irishrail.ie).

BY PLANE

Some travelers (with limited time and no interest in urban Dublin) choose to start their trip to Ireland at **Cork Airport** in order to focus on the island's scenic south and west (airport code: ORK, tel. 021/431-3131, www.corkairport.com). Located four miles south of Cork city (on N-27/R-600 to Kinsale, a 30-minute drive away), it offers connecting flights from London Heathrow and Edinburgh on Aer Lingus, as well as from London's Stansted and Gatwick on Ryanair. More distant connections can be made from Munich, Amsterdam, Paris, Pisa, Prague, Warsaw, and Málaga (airport code: ORK, tel. 021/431-3131, www.corkairport.com). Citylink airport buses run hourly to Kinsale (only 4/day on Sunday) and less frequently to other destinations, including Galway (6/day, 4 hours).

To sleep near Cork Airport, consider **$$ Radisson Blu Cork Airport** (tel. 021/494-7500, www.radissonblu.com).

BLARNEY CASTLE

If you're driving between Kinsale and the Ring of Kerry, it's easy to stop here, though many find it a tourist trap. The town of Blarney is of no importance, and the 15th-century Blarney Castle is an empty hulk (with little effort put forth to make it meaningful or interesting). It's only famous as the place of tourist pilgrimage, where busloads line up to kiss a stone on its top rampart and get "the gift of gab." The stone's origin is shrouded in myth (perhaps brought back from the Holy Land by crusaders). The best thing about this overrated sight is the opportunity to watch a cranky man lower lemming tourists over the edge, belly up and head back, to kiss the stone while an automated camera snaps a photo—which will be available for purchase back by the parking lot. After a day of tour groups mindlessly climbing up here to perform this ritual, the stone can be literally slathered with spit and lipstick.

The tradition goes back to the late 16th century, when Queen Elizabeth I was trying to plant loyal English settlers in Ireland to tighten her grip on the rebellious island. She demanded that the Irish clan chiefs recognize the Crown, rather than the clan chiefs, as the legitimate titleholder of all lands. One of those chiefs was Cormac MacCarthy, Lord of Blarney Castle (who was supposedly loyal to the queen). He was smart enough never to disagree with

Kissing the Blarney Stone

Blarney Castle

the queen—instead, he would cleverly avoid acquiescing to her demands by sending a never-ending stream of lengthy and deceptive excuses, disguised with liberal doses of flattery (while subtly maintaining his native Gaelic loyalties). In her frustration, the queen declared his endless words nothing but "blarney."

While the castle is a shell, the surrounding grounds are beautiful and well-kept. There are even some hints of Ireland's pre-Christian past on the grounds;

you can see dolmens beside the trail in the forested Rock Close.

Cost and Hours: €13, Mon-Sat 9:00-18:30, Sun 9:00-17:30, later in peak season, shorter hours in winter, free parking lot, helpful TI, tel. 021/438-5252, www.blarney castle.ie.

Getting There: It's 5 miles northwest of Cork (the major city in south Ireland), 20 miles northwest of Cobh, and 24 miles north of Kinsale.

Kenmare
and the
Ring of Kerry

It's no wonder that visitors have been attracted to this dramatic chunk of Ireland since Victorian times. Mysterious ancient ring forts stand sentinel on mossy hillsides. A beloved Irish statesman maintained his ancestral estate here, far from 19th-century power politics. And early Christian hermit-monks left a lonely imprint of their devotion, in the form of simple stone dwellings atop an isolated rock crag far from shore...a holy retreat on the edge of the then-known world.

Today, it seems like every tour bus in Ireland makes the ritual loop around the scenic Ring of Kerry, using the bustling and famous tourist town of Killarney as a springboard, but I prefer to skip the town. Instead, make the tidy town of Kenmare your home base, and use my suggestions to cleverly circle the much-loved peninsula—entirely missing the convoy of tour buses.

If you only have time for one peninsula tour, I recommend Dingle (see comparison on page 160), but with more time, you could do both. Here's the most efficient way to do it:

KENMARE AND THE RING OF KERRY IN 1 DAY

All you need in compact Kenmare is one night and an early start the next day to drive the Ring of Kerry. The Ring is best driven clockwise, leaving Kenmare by 8:30; for specifics on the route, see page 160.

If you don't have a car for the Ring of Kerry, you can take a minibus tour from Kenmare, though it's not as enjoyable as driving the loop yourself.

Here's a good strategy for your entire visit, including your arrival and departure: Whether you're coming to Kenmare from Kinsale or another town, you'll likely drive through the town of Killarney. After Killar-

ney, you can visit any of these sights on your way to Kenmare: Muckross House, Killarney National Park, and the Kissane Sheep Farm.

Ideally you'd arrive in Kenmare in the late afternoon and see the town's sights, then get an early start on the Ring of Kerry in the morning. After driving the Ring, head to Dingle for the night.

Hardy hikers might consider adding another day to their itinerary to visit the rugged island of Skellig Michael. It requires overnighting in Portmagee or St. Finian's Bay nearby. Access is also unpredictable—boats are only able to reach it about five days out of seven due to rough seas, even in summer.

KENMARE

Cradled in a lush valley, this charming little town (known as Neidín, or "Little Nest," in Irish) hooks you with its rows of vividly colored shop fronts and go-for-a-stroll atmosphere. The nearby finger of the gentle sea feels more like a large lake, called the Kenmare River, just to confuse things. Far from the assembly-line tourism of Killarney town, Kenmare (rhymes with "been there") also makes a great launch-pad for enjoying the sights along the road around the Iveragh (eev-er-AH) Peninsula—known to shamrock lovers everywhere as the Ring of Kerry.

Orientation

Carefully planned Kenmare is shaped like an "X," forming two triangles. The upper (northern) triangle contains the town square (colorful market Wed in summer), the adjacent TI and Heritage Centre, and a cozy park. The lower (southern) triangle contains three one-way streets busy with shops, lodgings, and restaurants. Use the tall Holy Cross Church spire to get your bearings (across the street from northeast parking lot and gross public WCs).

Tourist Information: The helpful TI is on the town square (April-Oct Mon-Sat 9:30-17:00, closed Nov-March and Sun year-round, tel. 064/664-1233).

Internet Access: You'll find two public computers inside the front window of the post office.

Bike Rental: Finnegan's Corner rents bikes and has route maps (standard bike-€15/day, €20/24 hours, beefed-up road bike-€30/day; Mon-Sat 9:30-18:30, Sun 12:00-18:00; leave ID for deposit, office in gift shop at 37 Henry Street, across from post office, tel. 064/664-1083, www. finneganscornerkenmare.com).

Taxi: Try **Murnane Cabs** (mobile 087-236-4353) or **Kenmare Coach and Cab** (mobile 087-248-0800).

Parking: The town's two largest public parking lots (free overnight) cling to the two main roads departing town to the north (otherwise, free street parking is allowed for 2 hours).

Tours: Finnegan's Tours runs a variety of day tours by minibus, departing June through August from the TI at 10:00 and returning by 17:00 (€30 for any tour, route

Welcome to Kenmare.

KENMARE AND THE RING OF KERRY AT A GLANCE

In Kenmare

Ancient Stone Circle One of Ireland's most intact and easily accessible stone circles, over 3,000 years old. **Hours:** Always open. See page 149.

Kenmare Lace and Design Centre Modest cubbyhole with lovingly displayed examples of the lacemaking craftsmanship that impressed the Queen and put Kenmare on the map. **Hours:** May-mid-Oct Mon-Sat 10:00-13:00 & 14:15-17:00, closed mid-Oct-April and Sun year-round. See page 149.

The Ring of Kerry

▲▲▲**Driving the Ring of Kerry** Famous, scenic 120-mile loop road, featuring Iron Age ring forts, Daniel O'Connell's Derrynane estate, and grand views of the rugged coast and islands. See page 158.

▲▲**Kissane Sheep Farm** Working sheep farm on scenic hillside, with demonstrations of sheep shearing and dog herding. **Hours:** Most afternoons April-Sept by appointment only (minimum 15 people), closed Oct-March. See page 157.

▲▲**Muckross House and** ▲**Muckross Farms** Fine lakeside manor house surrounded by lush gardens, adjacent to folk park devoted to rural farm life over the past 200 years. **Hours:** House—daily 9:00-17:30, July-Aug until 18:30, shorter hours in winter. Farms—daily June-Aug 10:00-18:00, May and Sept daily 13:00-18:00, mid-March-April and Oct Sat-Sun only 13:00-18:00, closed Nov-mid-March. See page 155.

Killarney National Park Ireland's best National Park laced with hiking trails, waterfalls, and drives through old-growth forests dotted with postcard views of the lakes of Killarney. **Hours:** Always open. See page 156.

Side Trip

▲▲▲ **Skellig Michael** A craggy pinnacle of an island, topped with monks' huts, reachable by a boat (canceled in rough seas) from Portmagee, then a steep hike—an excursion for hardy hikers with extra time. See page 167.

depends on day: usually **Ring of Kerry** on Mon, Wed, and Fri; Ring of Beara on Tue; Glengarriff and Garnish Island on Thu; reserve a day in advance by phone or three days in advance by email, can book private tours for small groups with enough notice, tel. 064/664-1491, mobile 087-248-0800, www.kenmarecoachandcab. com, info@kenmarecoachandcab.com).

Sights

ANCIENT STONE CIRCLE

Of the 100 stone circles that dot southwest Ireland (Counties Cork and Kerry), this is one of the most accessible. More than 3,000 years old, it may have been used both as a primitive calendar and as a focal point for rituals. The circle has a diameter of 50 feet and consists of 15 stones ringing a large center boulder (possibly a burial monument). Experts think this stone circle (like most) functioned as a celestial calendar—it tracked the position of the setting sun to determine the two solstices (in June and December), which mark the longest and shortest days of the year.

Cost and Hours: €2, drop coins into honor box in hut by entry when attendant is away, always open.

Getting There: It's a five-minute walk from the TI. From the city center, face the TI, turn left, and walk 200 yards down Market Street, passing a row of cute 18th-century houses on your right. Beyond the row of houses, veer right through an unmarked modern gate mounted in stone columns, and continue 50 yards down the paved road. You'll pass the entry hut on your right. The stone circle is behind the adjacent hedge.

KENMARE LACE AND DESIGN CENTRE

A single large room (above the TI) displays the delicate lacework that put Kenmare on the modern map. From the 1860s until World War I, the Poor Clare convent at Kenmare was the center of excellence for Irish lacemaking. Inspired by antique Venetian lace, but creating their own unique designs, nuns taught needlepoint lacemaking as a trade to girls in a region struggling to get back on its feet in the wake of the catastrophic famine. Queen

Kenmare's ancient stone circle

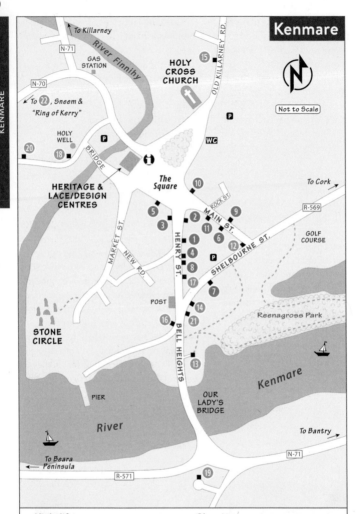

Kenmare

Not to Scale

HOLY CROSS CHURCH

To Killarney

River Finnihy

N-71

GAS STATION

N-70

To 22, Sneem & "Ring of Kerry"

HOLY WELL

BRIDGE

HERITAGE & LACE/DESIGN CENTRES

The Square

MARKET ST.

NEW RD.

HENRY ST.

STONE CIRCLE

POST

BELL HEIGHTS

PIER

OUR LADY'S BRIDGE

River

Kenmare

To Beara Peninsula

R-571

To Bantry

N-71

OLD KILLARNEY RD.

To Cork

R-569

ROCK ST.

MAIN ST.

SHELBOURNE ST.

GOLF COURSE

Reenagross Park

WC

Nightlife
1. Crowley's Pub
2. Foley's Pub

Eating
3. Jam Deli
4. The Purple Heather
5. Café Mocha
6. Murphy's Daybreak
7. The Lime Tree Rest.
8. Packies Restaurant
9. Mulcahy's Restaurant
10. Horse Shoe Pub & Rest.
11. P. F. McCarthy's Pub & Rest.

Sleeping
12. Lansdowne Arms Hotel/ Bold Thady Quill Bar
13. Sallyport House
14. Hawthorn House
15. Willow Lodge
16. Whispering Pines B&B
17. Virginia's Guesthouse
18. Limestone Lodge
19. Watersedge B&B
20. Rockcrest House
21. Kenmare Fáilte Hostel
22. To Parknasilla Hotel & Ring of Kerry Golf

Nuns' Lace

Sister Margaret Cusack, a.k.a. Sister Mary Francis Clare, lived in the town from 1862 to 1881, becoming the famous Nun of Kenmare. Her controversial religious life began when she decided to become an Anglican nun after her fiancé's sudden death. Failing to be accepted as one of Florence Nightingale's nurses during the Crimean War, she converted to Catholicism, joined the Poor Clare order as Sister Mary Francis Clare, and moved with the order to Kenmare. She became an outspoken writer who favored women's rights and lambasted the tyranny of the landlords during the Great Potato Famine (1845-1849). She eventually took church funds and attempted to set herself up as abbess of a convent in Knock. Her renegade behavior led to her leaving the Catholic faith, converting back to Protestantism, writing an autobiography, and lecturing about the "sinister influence of the Roman Church."

After the devastation of the famine, an industrial school was founded in Kenmare to teach trades to destitute youngsters. The school, run by the Poor Clare sisters, excelled in teaching young girls the art of lacemaking. Inspired by lace created in Italy, Kenmare lace caught the eye of Queen Victoria and became much coveted by Victorian society. Examples of it are now on display in the Victoria and Albert Museum (London), the Irish National Museum (Dublin), and the US National Gallery (Washington, DC).

Victoria commissioned five pieces of lace in 1885, and by the end of the century tourists began visiting Kenmare on their way to Killarney just for a peek at the lace. Nora Finnegan, who runs the center, usually has a work in progress to demonstrate the complexity of fine lacemaking to visitors.

Cost and Hours: Free, May-mid-Oct Mon-Sat 10:00-13:00 & 14:15-17:00, closed mid-Oct-April and Sun year-round, tel.

064/664-2978, mobile 087-234-6998, www.kenmarelace.ie.

Experiences
Horseback Riding
River Valley Riding Stables offers day treks for all levels of experience through beautiful hill scenery in the Roughty River Valley (adult-€20/hour, child-€15/hour, discounts for groups, long hours; located 7 miles east of Kenmare off R-569 near Kilgarvan, mobile 087-958-5895, rivervalleystables@hotmail.com).

Boating and Hiking
Star Sailing rents boats, gives sailing lessons, and organizes hill walks. Hop on a small two-person sailboat (€45/1 hour), a six-person boat (€60/1 hour), or a kayak (single-€20/hour, double-€36/hour). Phone ahead to reserve boats (daily 10:00-17:00, located 5 miles southwest of Kenmare on R-571 on Beara Peninsula,

courtesy shuttle can pick you up in Kenmare, tel. 064/664-1222, www.staroutdoors.ie; adjacent Con's Restaurant is open daily 12:00-20:00).

Golfing

Another way to experience Ireland's 40 shades of green is to splurge on a scenic day on the links. The **Kenmare Golf Club** is right on the edge of town (€35 greens fee June-Aug, €25 Sept-May, on R-569 toward Cork, tel. 064/664-1291, www.kenmaregolfclub.com). Or try the **Ring of Kerry Golf and Country Club** (weekdays-€50 greens fee, weekends-€60, prebook on weekends, 4 miles west of town on N-70, tel. 064/664-2000, www.ringofkerrygolf.com).

Nightlife

Wander the compact Kenmare town triangle and stick your head in wherever you hear something you like. Music usually starts at 21:30 (although some pubs have early 18:30 sessions—ask at the TI) and ranges from Irish traditional sessions to sing-along strummers. **Crowley's** is an atmospheric shoebox of a pub with an unpretentious clientele. **Foley's** jug-stacked window invites you in for a folksy songfest. The Lansdowne Arms Hotel sponsors live traditional sessions in their **Bold Thady Quill Bar.**

Eating

Make a reservation or get a table early, as many finer places book up later in the evening during the summer. Pub dinners are a good value and easier on the budget, but pub kitchens close earlier than restaurants.

Lunch

Soup-and-sandwich lunch options abound. **Jam** is a handy deli that can make sandwiches or wraps to go for picnics (Mon-Sat 8:00-17:00, Sun 10:00-17:00 except closed Sun Oct-May, Henry Street). **The Purple Heather** has great

salads and omelets (€10-17 meals, Mon-Sat 11:00-17:00, closed Sun, Henry Street, tel. 064/664-1016). **Café Mocha** is a basic €6 sandwich shop (Mon-Fri 9:00-17:30, Sat-Sun 10:00-17:00, on the town square, tel. 064/664-2133). **Murphy's Daybreak** supermarket is a good place to stock up for a Ring of Kerry picnic (Mon-Sat 8:00-22:00, Sun 9:00-21:00, Main Street).

Dinner

The Lime Tree Restaurant occupies the former Lansdowne Estate office, which gave more than 4,000 people free passage to America in the 1840s. These days, it serves delicious, locally caught seafood dishes in a modern yet cozy dining hall. It's wise to reserve ahead (€18-27 meals, April-Oct daily 18:30-21:30, closed Nov-March, Shelbourne Street, tel. 064/664-1225).

Packies is a popular bistro that has a leafy, low-light interior and cottage ambience, and serves traditional cuisine with French influence. Their seafood gets rave reviews (€23-34 meals, Mon-Sat 18:00-22:00, closed Sun, reservations wise, Henry Street, tel. 064/664-1508).

Mulcahy's Restaurant has a jazz-mellowed, elegant atmosphere and creatively presented gourmet dishes. Given the Indian, Japanese, and American influences, there's always a good vegetarian entrée (€20-29 meals, Thu-Tue 17:00-22:00, closed Wed, reservations smart, Main Street, tel. 064/664-2383).

Horse Shoe Pub and Restaurant, specializing in steak and spareribs, somehow turns rustic farm-tool decor into a romantic candlelit sanctuary (€17-25 meals, Mon-Fri 12:00-15:00 & 17:00-22:00, Sat-Sun 17:00-22:00, Main Street, tel. 064/664-1553).

P. F. McCarthy's Pub and Restaurant feels like a sloppy saloon, serving reasonable salad or sandwich lunches and filling dinner fare (€15-22 meals, Mon-Sat 10:30-21:00, closed Sun, 14 Main Street, tel. 064/664-1516).

Sleeping

$$$ Lansdowne Arms Hotel is the town's venerable grand hotel, with generous public spaces. This centrally located, 200-year-old historic landmark rents 26 large, crisp rooms (Sb-€60-85, Db-€80-150, music in pub until late on Fri-Sat, parking, corner of Main and Shelbourne Streets, tel. 064/664-1368, www.lansdownearms.com, info@lansdownearms.com).

$$$ Sallyport House, a classy, tranquil house with five rooms filled with antique furniture, has been in Helen Arthur's family for generations. Ask her to point out the foot-worn doorstep that was salvaged from the local workhouse and built into her stone chimney (Sb-€70-110, Db-€100-140, Tb-€130-160, closed Nov-mid-March, cash only, no kids, parking, 5-minute walk south of town before crossing Our Lady's Bridge, tel. 064/664-2066, www.sallyporthouse.com, port@iol.ie).

$$ Hawthorn House is a fine, modern, freestanding house with a lounge, a warm and friendly hostess, and 10 comfy rooms sporting fine woodwork courtesy of Mr. O'Brien, who's also a carpenter. Its quiet residential location is just a block from all the pub and restaurant action (Db-€90-100, Tb-€120-140, Qb-€140, parking, Shelbourne Street, tel. 064/664-1035, www.hawthornhousekenmare.com, hawthorn@eircom.net, Mary and Noel O'Brien). Their two modern, self-catering apartments next door work well for those wanting to linger (weekly rentals).

$$ Willow Lodge, on the main road at the edge of town, feels American-suburban, with friendly hosts and seven comfortable rooms (Sb-€65-90, Db-€85-100, Tb-€135-150, Qb-€145-160, cash only, Wi-Fi, parking, 100 yards beyond Holy Cross Church, tel. 064/664-2301, www.willowlodgekenmare.com, willowlodgekenmare@yahoo.com, jovial Paul and talkative Gretta Gleeson-O'Byrne).

$$ Whispering Pines B&B offers five rooms with sincere, traditional Irish hospitality in a spacious house warmed by the presence of hostesses Mary Fitzgerald and daughter Kathleen (June-Sept only, Sb-€45-60, Db-€76-80, Tb-€110, cash only, at the edge of town on Bell Height, tel. 064/664-1194, www.whisperingpineskenmare.com, wpines@eircom.net).

$ Virginia's Guesthouse, ideally located near the best restaurants, is well kept by Neil and Noreen. Its nine rooms are fresh, roomy, and appealing (Sb-€35-50, Db-€50-80, Tb-€70-110, optional breakfast extra, 36 Henry Street, tel. 086/372-0625, www.virginias-kenmare.com, virginias.guesthouse@gmail.com).

$ Limestone Lodge stands rock-solid beside a holy well, with five cozy rooms in a quiet location. Friendly hosts Sinead and Siobhan Thomas are experts on Kenmare's famous lace, and Casey, their wiggly Jack Russell terrier, is an expert at being cute (Sb-€35-50, Db-€70-80, Tb-€80-99, Qb-€100-132, cash only, parking, tel. 064/664-2231, mobile 087-757-4411, www.limestonelodgekenmare.com, info@limestonelodgekenmare.com).

$ Watersedge B&B is a mile south of town, serenely isolated on a forested hillside overlooking the estuary. The modern house has four clean, colorful rooms and a kid-pleasing backyard (Sb-€40-50, Db-€64-70, Tb-€75-80, cash only, parking, tel. 064/664-1707, mobile 087-

413-4235, www.watersedgekenmare.com, watersedgekenmare@gmail.com, Noreen and Vincent O'Shea). To get here, drive south over Our Lady's Bridge, bear left, immediately look for the B&B sign, and take the first right onto the road heading uphill. Go a hundred yards up the paved road, then—at the end of the white cinder-block wall (on left)—turn right onto the gravel lane and drive 50 yards to the dead-end. It's worth it.

$ Rockcrest House is secluded down a leafy lane, with six large rooms and a fine front-porch view (Sb-€35-50, Db-€65-80, Tb-€90-110, cash only; as you pass the TI heading north out of town, take the first left after crossing the bridge; tel. 064/664-1248, mobile 087-904-3788, www.visit-kenmare.com, info@visit-kenmare.com, Marian and David O'Dwyer). Ask about their two self-catering cottage rentals.

$ Kenmare Fáilte Hostel (fawl-chuh) maintains 34 budget beds in a well-kept, centrally located building with more charm than most hostels. It is run by Finnegan's Corner bike rental folks directly across street (€18 dorm beds in rooms without bath, D-€44, Db-€52, T-€60, Tb-€69, Q-€76, Qb-€88, closed mid-Oct-April, Shelbourne Street, tel. 064/664-2333, mobile 087-711-6092, www.kenmarehostel.com, info@kenmarehostel.com).

$$$ Parknasilla Hotel is a 19th-century luxury hotel, located 35 minutes' drive west of Kenmare, with 82 rooms and 500 plush acres of a subtropical park overlooking the wild Atlantic Ocean. The tranquility, combined with old-fashioned service and Victorian elegance, makes this a good stop for anyone interested in luxuriating on the Ring of Kerry. Originally an old railroad hotel for Romantic Age tourists, in recent decades it has been a ritual splurge for Irish families and wedding groups (Db-€129-199, higher July-Aug, 19th-century diversions like croquet, park walks, see website for details and complex pricing

scheme, tel. 064/667-5600, www.park nasillahotel.ie, info@parknasillahotel.ie).

Transportation

Kenmare has no train station (the nearest is in Killarney, 20 miles away) and only a few bus connections (www.buseireann.ie). Most buses transfer in Killarney.

From Kenmare by Bus to: Killarney (4/day, 45 minutes), **Tralee** (3/day, 2 hours), **Dingle** (3/day, 3 hours, change in Killarney), **Kinsale** (3/day, 3.5-4.25 hours, 2 changes), **Dublin** (4/day, 6.75-7.75 hours, change in Killarney and Limerick).

KILLARNEY

Killarney's value is its location. For most tour organizers, the town is the logical jumping-off point for excursions around the famous Ring of Kerry peninsula. If you're approaching the region from Kinsale, drive through Killarney and hop on the Ring to visit Muckross House, Killarney National Park, and the Kissane Sheep Farm (in the mountains) en route to Kenmare. By taking a bite out of the Ring the day before you sleep in Kenmare, you'll be better situated to drive most of the remainder of the Ring of Kerry loop the next day. Get an early start from Kenmare and you should be able to avoid the worst of the bus traffic on the Ring.

Killarney is a household word among American tourists. Springing from the bus and train station are a few colorful streets lined with touristy shops and restaurants. If you're traveling in the region without a car, you'll have to stop here. The Killarney bus and train stations flank the big, modern Killarney Outlet Centre mall. If you have a layover between connections, walk five minutes straight out from the front of the mall, and check out Killarney's shop-lined High Street and New Street. The **TI** is a 15-minute walk from the train station, on Beech Street.

Sights near Killarney

▲▲MUCKROSS HOUSE AND ▲MUCKROSS FARMS

Perhaps the best stately Victorian home you'll see in the Republic of Ireland, Muckross House (built in 1843) is magnificently set at the edge of Killarney National Park. It's adjacent to Muckross Farms, a fascinating open-air farm museum that shows rural life in the 1930s. Besides the mansion and farms, this regular stop on the tour-bus circuit also includes a fine garden idyllically set on a lake and an information center for the national park. The poignant juxtaposition of the magnificent mansion and the humble farmhouses illustrates in a thought-provoking way the vast gap that once separated rich and poor in Ireland.

Cost and Hours: House–€9, farms–€9, €15 combo-ticket includes both (Heritage Cards not accepted for farms). House open daily 9:00-17:30, July-Aug until 18:30, shorter hours in winter, last entry one hour before closing. Farms open daily June-Aug 10:00-18:00, May and Sept daily 13:00-18:00, mid-March-April and Oct Sat-Sun only 13:00-18:00, closed Nov-mid-March, tel. 064/667-0144, www.muckross-house.ie.

Getting There: Muckross House is conveniently located for a break on the long ride from Kinsale or Cashel to Dingle or Kenmare. From Killarney, follow signs to Kenmare, where you'll find Muckross House three miles (5 km) south of town. As you approach from Killarney, you'll see a small parking lot two miles before the actual parking lot. This is used by horse-and-buggy bandits to hoodwink tourists into thinking they have to pay to clip-clop to the house. Giddy-up on by to find a big, safe, and free parking lot right at the mansion.

Tours: The only way to see the interior of the house is with the 45-minute guided tour, which gives meaning to your visit (included with admission, offered frequently throughout the day). Book your tour as soon as you arrive (they can fill up). Then enjoy a walk in the gardens or lunch in their better-than-average cafeteria until your tour begins.

Visiting the House and Farms: A visit to **Muckross House** takes you back to the Victorian period—the 19th-century boom time, when the sun never set on the British Empire and the Industrial Revolution (born in England) was chugging the world into the modern age. Of course, Ireland was a colony back then, with big-shot English landlords. During the Great Potato Famine of 1845-1849, most English gentry lived very well—profiting off the export of their handsome crops to lands with greater buying power—while a third of Ireland's population starved.

Muckross House feels lived-in (and it was, until 1933). Its fine Victorian furniture is arranged around the fireplace under Waterford crystal chandeliers and lots of antlers. You'll see Queen Victoria's bedroom (ground floor, since she was afraid of house fires). The owners of the house spent a couple of years preparing for the royal visit in 1861, eager to gain coveted titles and nearly bankrupting themselves in the process. The queen stayed only

Muckross House

three nights and her beloved Prince Albert died soon after the visit. The depressed queen never granted the titles that the grand house's owners had so hoped for.

The house exit takes you through an **information center** for Killarney National Park, with a relaxing 15-minute video on "Ireland's premier national park," featuring lots of geology, flora, and fauna (free, shown on request).

The **garden** is a hit for those with a green thumb, and a €1.50 booklet makes the nature trails interesting. A bright, modern cafeteria (with indoor/outdoor seating) faces the garden. The adjacent crafts shop shows weaving and pottery-making in action.

The **Muckross Traditional Farms** consists of six different vintage farmhouses. The farms are strung along a mile-long road, with an old bus shuttling those who don't want to hike (free, 4/hour).

For those interested in Irish farm life from the 1920s until electricity arrived in 1955, this is a great experience—but only if you engage the attendants in conversation. Each farm is staffed by a Kerry local who enjoys telling tales of life on the farm in the old days. When they first got electricity in 1955, they'd pull on their rubber Wellington boots for safety and nervously "switch it on." Poor farmers could afford electricity only with the help of money from relatives in America. No one dreamed of actually heating the house with electricity. Children slept six to a bed, "three up and three down...feet in your face." You'll learn what happened when you had the only radio in the area, and how one flagstone on the mud floor was enough for the fiddler and dancer to set the beat. Probe with your questions... get personal.

KILLARNEY NATIONAL PARK

As you drive from Killarney to Kenmare, heading south on N-71, you'll sweep through scenic Killarney National Park (just south of Killarney town) on the most mountainous stretch of the Ring of Kerry.

This 25,000-acre park is Ireland's oldest, established in 1932. Glacially sculpted rock ridges cradle three large lakes teeming with trout and salmon, making them popular for sport fishing.

Hikers enjoy an easy 10-minute stroll along a mossy trail from the roadside up to **Torc Waterfall** (look for small parking lot beside N-71, 2 miles—3 km—south of Muckross House), then lace up their boots to take on more strenuous trails beyond. If you go early or late in the day, keep an eye out for Ireland's only native herd of red deer. The park's old-growth oak, yew, and alder groves are the best preserved in Ireland, and rhododendrons explode beside the road in late May and June.

Take a quiet moment to contemplate your lush surroundings. This is what the majority of Ireland looked like 8,000 years ago, before Neolithic man settled and began rudimentary slash-and-burn farming. Later English colonial harvesting of timber exacerbated the deforestation

Torc Waterfall in Killarney National Park

process. Today, Ireland has the smallest proportion of forested land—10.5 percent—of any EU nation.

Enjoy expansive lake views from **Ladies View,** right beside the N-71 road, half a mile (1 km) from the park's southern exit. Just south of the park exit, you'll pass long, thin Looscaunagh Lough (beside the road on the left). A few hundred yards farther, the Black Valley opens up beneath you on the right. This remote valley was the last chunk of Ireland to get electricity—in 1978. The highest bump on the distant ridge across the Black Valley to the west is Carrauntoohil, Ireland's tallest mountain at 3,400 feet.

▲▲KISSANE SHEEP FARM

Animal lovers will enjoy an hour's visit to this hardworking 2,500-acre Irish farm, perched on a scenic slope above the Black Valley. John Kissane, whose family has raised sheep here for five generations, gives hands-on demonstrations of sheep shearing. John (or his brother Noel) explains the process and invites you to touch the pile of fresh wool afterward. You can feel the lanolin, which acts as natural waterproofing for the sheep and is extracted from the wool to sell to pharmaceutical firms (synthetic manufacturing has driven the price of wool so low, it's not worth selling otherwise). But the highlight of any visit is the demonstration of sheepherding by the highly alert family dogs (border collies trained here since puppyhood). John commands the dogs from afar using an array of verbal calls and hand signals.

This is a working farm—demonstration times fluctuate depending on necessary farm work. Call ahead for times (usually in the afternoon), or check the current schedule on their website, under "Sheep Dog Demonstration Calendar."

Cost and Hours: €7, most afternoons April-Sept by appointment only (minimum 15 people), closed Oct-March, tel. 064/663-4791, mobile 087-260-0410, www.kissanesheepfarm.com.

Getting There: It's on N-71 between Ladies View and Moll's Gap. To continue on to Kenmare, continue driving south on N-71. Going over Moll's Gap (WCs and Avoca Café beside parking lot), you'll descend into Kenmare. The rugged, bare rock on either side of the road was rounded and smoothed by the grinding action of glaciers over thousands of years. In the distance to the north (on your right) you can see the Gap of Dunloe, a perfect example of a U-shaped glacial valley notch.

RING OF KERRY

The Ring of Kerry (the Iveragh Peninsula) has been the perennial breadwinner of Irish tourism for decades now. Lassoed by a winding coastal road (the Ring), this mountainous, lake-splattered region comes with breathtaking scenery and the highest peak in Ireland. While a veritable fleet of tourist buses circles it each day, they generally stay together and stop at the same handful of attractions. Therefore, if you avoid those places at rush hour, the Ring feels dramatic, isolated, unspoiled.

Armed with a good map and a reliable alarm clock, you can avoid the crowds and enjoy one of the most rewarding days in Ireland. To include a boat trip out to the remote, evocative island of Skellig Michael, add another day and plan an

Kissane Sheep Farm

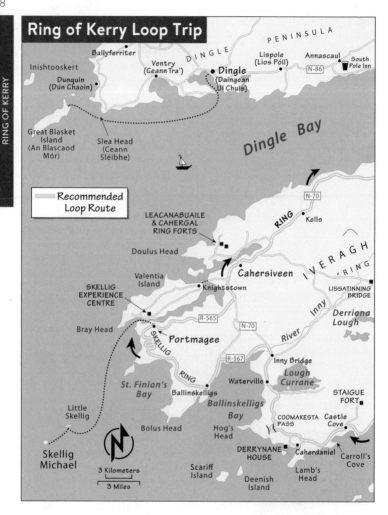

Ring of Kerry Loop Trip

DINGLE PENINSULA

Ballyferriter

Inishtooskert

Dunquin
(Dún Chaoin)

Ventry
(Ceann Trá')

Dingle
(Daingean
Uí Chuis)

Lispole
(Lios Póil)

Annascaul

South
Pole Inn

N-86

Great Blasket
Island
(An Blascaod
Mór)

Slea Head
(Ceann
Sléibhe)

Dingle Bay

Recommended
Loop Route

N-70

RING

Kells

LEACANABUAILE
& CAHERGAL
RING FORTS

Doulus Head

IVERAGH

RING

Cahersiveen

Valentia
Island

Knightstown

LISSATINNING
BRIDGE

SKELLIG
EXPERIENCE
CENTRE

R-565

N-70

River

Inny

Derriana
Lough

Bray Head

SKELLIG

Portmagee

RING

R-567

Inny Bridge

Lough
Currane

St. Finian's
Bay

Ballinskelligs

Waterville

Little
Skellig

Ballinskelligs
Bay

STAIGUE
FORT

Bolus Head

Hog's
Head

COOMAKESTA
PASS

Castle
Cove

Skellig
Michael

N

DERRYNANE
HOUSE

Caherdaniel

Carroll's
Cove

3 Kilometers

3 Miles

Scariff
Island

Deenish
Island

Lamb's
Head

overnight in the Portmagee area. (Note that there aren't lots of ATMs throughout the Ring; bring sufficient cash with you from Kenmare.)

Without a car, take a one-day minibus tour of the Ring of Kerry from Kenmare; see page 147.

▲▲▲Driving the Ring of Kerry

You can explore the Ring (primarily on N-70) in one satisfying day.

Leave Kenmare by 8:30 and head clockwise (against the prevailing tour-bus traffic). Allow time for stops at Staigue Fort (45 minutes) and Derrynane House (1 hour), and get to Waterville before noon. To entirely miss the chain of tour buses, get to Waterville by 11:00; shortly after that, leave the main drag for the Skellig Ring (with a road that's too narrow for big buses). Plan to have lunch out on the Skellig Ring, either as a picnic on the lovely beach at St. Finian's Bay, or in Portmagee. By the time you rejoin the main route, the tour buses are gone. On the last

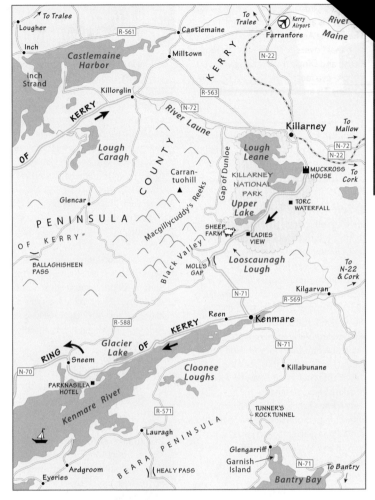

half of the route, there are two more hour-long stops: the Skellig Experience Centre (near Portmagee) and two additional big ring forts (near Cahersiveen).

The two most photogenic coastal stretches are out near the tip of the peninsula: between Caherdaniel and Waterville (on the Ring of Kerry) and from Ballinskelligs to Portmagee (on the Skellig Ring).

The only downside of going against all the bus traffic is that, on the narrow parts of the Ring road, buses always have the right-of-way. It's up to you to back up to the nearest wide spot in the road to let a less-nimble bus get through a tight curve. But every year I notice that the road has been improved and bottlenecks widened. There are also lots of scenic-view pull-outs. With an early start, you can avoid these hassles: On my last circuit, I got to Waterville by 11:30, then slipped happily into the bus-free Skellig Ring...and didn't have to pass a single bus all day.

Smart drivers equip themselves with a good map before driving the Ring of Kerry loop. Consider the *Complete Road Atlas of*

Survey (€10-13, sold
ookstores in Ireland).
l series provides a useful
both the Iveragh (Ring of
gle peninsulas, giving you
l for the terrain (€9, sold
in many ... d bookstores in County
Kerry).

Rick's Tip: *The flat, inland, northeastern section of the Ring, from Killorglin to Killarney on N-72, is* **skippable.**

➲ Self-Guided Tour

Here's a self-guided sightseeing tip sheet for my preferred clockwise route, kilometer by kilometer. If you do any exploring, you'll likely get hopelessly off pace, but the kilometer references still help—just do the arithmetic to figure out how far various stops are from each other. Several of these stops are explained in far greater detail later in this chapter, in the same order in which they're listed here. To understand your options, read the rest of this chapter before you start on your tour.

0 km: Leave Kenmare.

17.6 km: On the right is Glacier Lake, with a long, smooth limestone "banister" carved by a glacier 10,000 years ago.

22.8 km: The posh 19th-century Parknasilla Hotel is a great stop for tea and scones.

26 km: Visit the town of Sneem.

40.4 km: Turn off for the Staigue Fort.

41.5 km: On the left, enjoy great views of the Beara Peninsula beyond a ruined hospital with IRA ties (it was funded about 1910 by a local Englishwoman sympathetic to the Irish Republican cause). No one wants to touch these ruins today out of fear of "kicking up a beehive."

43.5 km: Carroll's Cove has a fine beach with some of the warmest water in Ireland, grand views of Kenmare Bay, a trailer park, and "Ireland's only beachside bar."

46.4 km: Take the turnoff for

The Ring of Kerry vs. the Dingle Peninsula

If I had to choose one spot to enjoy the small-town charm of traditional Ireland, it would be Dingle and its history-laden scenic peninsula. But the Ring of Kerry—a much bigger, more famous, and more touristed peninsula just to its south—is also great to visit. If you go to Ireland and don't see the famous Ring of Kerry, your uncle Pat will never forgive you. Here's a comparison to help with your itinerary planning.

Both peninsulas come with a scenic loop drive. Dingle's is 30 miles. The Ring of Kerry is 120 miles. Both loops come with lots of megalithic wonder. Dingle's prehistory is more intimate, with numerous evocative stony structures. The Ring of Kerry's prehistory shows itself in three massive ring forts—far bigger than anything on Dingle.

Dingle town is the perfect little Irish burg—alive with traditional music pubs, an active fishing harbor, and the sturdy cultural atmosphere of an Irish-speaking Gaeltacht region. You can easily spend three fun nights here. In comparison, Kenmare (the best base for the Ring of Kerry loop) is pleasant but forgettable. Those spending a night on the west end of the Ring of Kerry find a rustic atmosphere in Portmagee (the base for a cruise to magical Skellig Michael).

Both regions are beyond the reach of the Irish train system and require a car or spotty bus service to access. Both offer memorable scenery, great restaurants, warm B&B hospitality, and similar prices. The bottom line: With limited time, choose Dingle. If you have a day or two to spare, the Ring of Kerry is also a delight.

Derrynane House (home of Daniel O'Connell).

50.4 km: Enjoy brilliant views for the next two kilometers to Coomakesta Pass.

52.4 km: The Coomakesta Pass lookout point (700-foot altitude) offers grand vistas in both directions.

54.5 km: Watch for fine views of the Skellig Islands.

56.4 km: Notice the ruins of famine villages on both sides of the road.

59.6 km: In the town of Waterville, you'll see a sculpture of Charlie Chaplin on the left. Waterville is also home to the Butler Arms Hotel—a fine stop for tea and scones in its Charlie Chaplin room (with lots of photos of the silent-film icon and his young wife frolicking as they lived well in Ireland).

65 km: After rejoining the main road, cross the small bridge that's locally famous for salmon fly-fishing. Take the first left (R-567) for the Skellig Ring loop (follow brown *Skellig Ring* signs through Ballinskelligs, and then scenically to Portmagee). At this point, you've left the big-bus route.

75 km: St. Finian's Bay lies about halfway around, with a pleasant picnic-friendly beach that's been discovered by surfers (no WCs). Just before the bay is the small, modern Skelligs Chocolate Factory, with free, tasty samples as well as a café for coffee and muffins. This stop is especially fun for kids (Mon-Fri 10:00-17:00, Sat-Sun 12:00-17:00, tel.

066/947-9119, www.skellig com).

80 km: Photographers and w. want to turn left into the driveway ι. advertises "Best View in County Kerry. Park and pay the €4 fee at the B&B reception. Then walk 10 minutes straight up the gravel road, where you'll be confronted by a dramatic coastal cliff that opens up onto what may indeed be the best view in County Kerry. The beehive huts nearby are replicas, but true to the originals.

83 km: You reach Portmagee, a small port town and jumping-off point for boats to the Skellig Islands.

83.2 km: Cross the bridge to the Skellig Experience Centre. You're now on Valentia Island, its name hinting at medieval trading connections with nearby Spain—which lies due south. Dinosaur hunters may want to detour and follow the signs to the modest but ancient tetrapod tracks, frozen in stone, on the north side of the island.

91.2 km: At the church in Knightstown, turn left for the Knightstown Heritage Museum.

93 km: Return to the main road and go through Knightstown to the tiny ferry (€6/car, runs constantly 8:00-21:00, 1-km trip).

95 km: Leaving the ferry, rejoin N-70 (the main Ring of Kerry route), turning left for the town of Cahersiveen. From here, you can detour a few kilometers to two impressive stone ring forts, Cahergal and Leacanabuaile.

Lakes of Killarney

St. Finian's Bay

The Ring Forts of Kerry

The Ring of Kerry comes with three awe-inspiring prehistoric ring forts—among the largest and best preserved in all of Ireland. **Staigue Fort** (near the beginning of my clockwise Ring route) is the most impressive and is in a desolate setting. The two others—**Cahergal** and **Leacanabuaile,** side by side just north of Cahersiveen (closer to the end of the Ring, after Valentia Island)—are easier to visit and plenty evocative. Each ring fort is about a 4-kilometer (2.5-mile) side-trip off the main drag. If you're trying to beat the tour-bus convoy, Staigue Fort is problematic because it eats up morning time before the buses have passed you. The Cahersiveen ring forts are your last stop in the Ring of Kerry, when bus traffic is of no concern.

All of these ring forts have the same basic features. The circular drystone walls were built sometime between 500 B.C. and A.D. 300 without the aid of mortar or cement. About 80 feet across, with walls 12 feet thick at the base and up to 25 feet high, these brutish structures would have taken 100 men six months to complete. Expert opinion is divided on the reason they were built, but most believe that the people who built them would have retreated here at times of tribal war. Civilization was morphing from nomadic hunter-gatherers to settled farmers, so herders could have used these forts to gather their valuable cattle inside and protect them from rustlers. Other experts see the round design as a kind of amphitheater, where clan chieftains would have gathered for important meetings or rituals. However, the ditch surrounding the outer walls of Staigue Fort suggests a defensive, rather than ceremonial, function. Without written records, we can only imagine the part these magnificent piles of finely stacked stones played in ancient dramas.

100 km: Return to N-70 at Cahersiveen and follow signs for *Glenbeigh* and *Killorglin.* Enjoy views of the Dingle Peninsula across Dingle Bay to your left (you can see the harbor and Ersk Tower) and Inch Beach.

The rest of the loop is less scenic. At Killorglin, you've seen all there is to see. From here, go either to Dingle (left) or to Kenmare/Killarney/Kinsale (right).

Sneem

Although it's inundated by tour buses daily from 14:00 to 16:00, Sneem is peaceful and laid-back the rest of the day. This humble town has two entertaining squares. The Irish joke, "As we're in Kerry, the square on the east side is called South Square and the one on the west is called North Square." On the first (South) square, you'll see a statue of Steve "Crusher" Casey, the local boy who reigned as world champion heavyweight wrestler (1938-1947). A sweet peat-toned stream gurgles under the one-lane bridge connecting the two Sneem squares. The North Square features a memorial to former French president Charles de Gaulle's visit (Irish on his mother's side, de Gaulle came here for two weeks of R&R after his final retirement from office in 1969). Locals call the memorial "da gallstone."

Between Sneem and Portmagee
▲STAIGUE FORT

This impressive ring fort is worth a stop on your way around the Ring (drop €1 in the gray donation box beside the gate, always open). While viewing the imposing pile of stone, read "The Ring Forts of Kerry" sidebar.

Getting There: The fort is 2.5 miles (4 km) off the main N-70 road up a narrow rural access lane (look for signs just after the hamlet of Castle Cove). Honk on blind corners to warn oncoming traffic as you drive up the hedge-lined lane.

▲DERRYNANE HOUSE

This is the home of Daniel O'Connell, Ireland's most influential pre-independence politician, whose tireless nonviolent agitation gained equality for Catholics 185 years ago. The coastal lands of the O'Connell estate that surround Derrynane (rhymes with MaryAnn) House are now a national historic park. A visit here is a window into the life of a man who not only liberated Ireland from the last oppressive anti-Catholic penal laws, but also first developed the idea of a grassroots movement—organizing on a massive scale to achieve political ends without bloodshed (see sidebar).

Cost and Hours: €4; May-Sept daily 10:30-18:00; April and Oct Wed-Sun

Statue of Steve "Crusher" Casey

10:30-17:00, closed Mon-Tue; closed Nov-March; last entry 45 minutes before closing, tel. 066/947-5113.

Getting There: Just outside the town of Derrynane, pick up a handy free regional map from the private TI inside the brown Wave Crest market, which is a great place to buy picnic food (TI open daily May-Sept 9:00-18:00, closed Oct-April, tel. 066/947-5188). One mile after the market, take a left and follow the signs into Derrynane National Historic Park.

Visiting the House: The house has a quirky floor plan. Ask about the next scheduled 20-minute audiovisual show, which fleshes out the highlights of O'Connell's turbulent life and makes the contents of the house more interesting.

Downstairs in the study, look for the glass case containing the pistols used in O'Connell's famous duel. Beside them are his black gloves, one of which he always wore on his right hand when he went to Mass (out of remorse for the part it played in taking a man's life). The dining room is lined with family portraits. Upstairs in the drawing room, you'll find his ornately carved chair with tiny harp strings and wolfhound collars made of gold. In a drawer in an upstairs bedroom is a copy of O'Connell's celebrated speech imploring the Irish not to riot when he was arrested. And in another upstairs room is his deathbed, brought back from Genoa.

The coach house (out back) shows off the enormous grand chariot that carried O'Connell through throngs of joyous Dubliners after his release from prison in 1844. He added the small chapel wing to the house in gratitude to God for his release.

Portmagee

Just a short row of snoozy buildings lining the bay, Portmagee is the best harbor for boat excursions out to the Skellig Islands (see "Getting There" on page 168). It's a quiet village with a handful of B&Bs, two pubs, a bakery, a market, and no ATMs—

the closest ATM is 6 miles (10 km) east in Cahersiveen. On the rough harborfront, a slate memorial to sailors lost at sea from here reads, "In the nets of God may we be gathered."

A 100-yard-long bridge connects Portmagee to gentle Valentia Island, where you'll find the Skellig Experience Centre (on the left at the Valentia end of the bridge). A public parking lot is at the Portmagee end of the bridge, with award-winning WCs (no kidding: look for the proudly displayed "Irish Toilet of the Year 2002 runner-up" plaque).

EATING

These options all line the waterfront (between the pier and the bridge to Valentia Island). **The Moorings** is a nice restaurant with great seafood caught just outside its front door (€16-24 dinners, Tue-Sun 18:00-22:00, closed Mon, reservations wise, tel. 066/947-7108, www. moorings.ie). The **Bridge Bar,** next door, does traditional pub grub. Call ahead to check on their traditional music and dance schedule (€12-18 meals, daily 10:00-20:30, live music Fri and Sun nights, tel. 066/947-7108). The **Fisherman's Bar** is less flashy, with more locals and cheaper prices (€12-20 meals, daily 10:00-21:00,

tel. 066/947-7103).

For picnic supplies, **O'Connell's Market** is the only grocery (Mon-Sat 9:00-19:00, Sun 9:30-12:30). **Skellig Mist Bakery** can make basic lunch sandwiches to take on Skellig boat excursions (daily 9:00-17:30, tel. 066/947-7250).

SLEEPING

The first two listings are in town. The last listing is south of Portmagee, on St. Finian's Bay.

$$$ Moorings Guesthouse feels like a small hotel, with 17 rooms, a pub and a fine restaurant downstairs, and the most convenient location in town, 50 yards from the end of the pier (Sb-€50-80, Db-€90-120, Tb-€110-145, Qb-€160-190, tel. 066/947-7108, www.moorings. ie, moorings@iol.ie, Gerard and Patricia Kennedy).

$$ Portmagee Heights B&B is a modern, solid slate home up above town, renting eight fine rooms. Hostess Monica Hussey can arrange Skellig boat trips (Db-€70-90, Tb-€105-135, Qb-€130-180, cash only, on the road into town, tel. 066/947-7251, www.portmageeheights.com, portmageeheights@gmail.com).

$$ Beach Cove B&B offers three comfortable, fresh, and lovingly decorated

Portmagee's harbor

Daniel O'Connell (1775-1847)

Born in Cahersiveen and elected from Ennis as the first Catholic member of the British Parliament, O'Connell was the hero of Catholic emancipation in Ireland. Educated in France at a time when punitive anti-Catholic laws limited schooling for Irish Catholics at home, he witnessed the carnage of the French Revolution. Upon his return to Ireland, he saw more bloodshed during the futile Rebellion of 1798.

Abhorring all this violence, O'Connell dedicated himself to peacefully gaining equal rights for Catholics in an Ireland dominated by a wealthy Protestant minority. He formed the Catholic Association with a one-penny-per-month membership fee and quickly gained a huge following. Although Catholics weren't allowed to hold office, he ran for election to Parliament anyway and won a seat in 1828. His unwillingness to take the anti-Catholic Oath of Supremacy initially kept him out of Westminster, but the moral force of his victory caused the government to concede Catholic emancipation the following year.

Known as "the Liberator," O'Connell began working toward his next goal—repealing the Act of Union with Britain. When his massive "monster meeting" rallies attracted thousands, his popularity spooked the British authorities, who threw him in jail on trumped-up charges of seditious conspiracy in 1844. He was soon released because his trial was deemed unfair, and perhaps partly because the authorities feared that his incarceration could provoke further unrest. When the Great Potato Famine hit in 1845, some Irish protesters advocated for violent action against the British, which O'Connell had long opposed. He died two years later in Genoa on his way to Rome, but his ideals lived on: His Catholic Association was the model of grassroots organization for the Irish, both in their homeland and in America.

rooms in splendid isolation four miles south of Portmagee, beside the pretty beach at St. Finian's Bay (100 yards from the Skelligs Chocolate Factory). Charming Bridie O'Connor will arrange a boat trip out to the Skelligs for you. Her cottage out back has two double rooms, ideal for families (Db-€80-85, Tb-€115, cottage without breakfast-€140, tel. 066/947-9301, mobile 087-139-0224, www.stayatbeach cove.com, beachcove@eircom.net).

Valentia Island

These two sights are on Valentia Island, across the bridge from Portmagee.

SKELLIG EXPERIENCE CENTRE

Whether or not you're actually sailing to Skellig Michael (described later), this little center (with basic exhibits and a fine 15-minute film) explains it well—both the story of the monks and the natural environment.

Cost and Hours: €5, daily July-Aug 10:00-19:00, until 18:00 in spring and fall, closed late-Nov-mid-March, last entry one hour before closing, call ahead outside of peak season as hours may vary, on Valentia Island beside bridge linking it to Portmagee, tel. 066/947-6306, www. skelligexperience.com.

Boat Trips: The Skellig Experience Centre arranges two-hour boat trips, circling both Skellig Michael and Little

Evolution in Ireland: Tetrapods to Telegraphs

Evolution, literacy, communication—Ireland has played a starring role in all three.

Many Irish paleontologists believe that the fossilized tetrapod tracks preserved on Valentia Island are the oldest in Europe. It was here that some of the first fish slithered out of the water on four stubby legs 385 million years ago, onto what would become the Isle of Saints and Scholars. Over time, those tetrapods evolved into the ancestors of today's amphibians, reptiles, birds, mammals...and humans, with the desire to record their thoughts and history, and communicate with others across the miles.

Irish scribes—living in remote outposts like the Skellig Islands just off this coast—kept literate life alive in Europe through the darkest depths of the so-called Dark Ages. In fact, in about the year 800, Charlemagne imported monks from this part of Ireland to be his scribes.

Just more than a thousand years later, in the mid-19th century, Paul Julius Reuter—who provided a financial news service in Europe—knew his pigeons couldn't fly across the Atlantic. So he relied on ships coming from America to drop a news capsule overboard as they rounded this southwest corner of Ireland. His boys would wait in boats with nets to "get the scoop." They say Europe learned of Lincoln's assassination (1865) from a capsule tossed out of a boat here.

The first permanent telegraph cables were laid across the Atlantic from here to Newfoundland, giving the two hemispheres instantaneous electronic communication. Queen Victoria was the first to send a message—greeting American president James Buchanan in 1858. The cable broke more than once, but it was finally permanently secured in 1866. Radio inventor Guglielmo Marconi achieved the first wireless transatlantic communication from this corner of Ireland to America in 1901.

Today, driving under the 21st-century mobile-phone and satellite tower that crowns a hilltop above Valentia Island, while gazing out at the Skellig Islands, a traveler has to marvel at humanity's progress—and the part this remote corner of Ireland played in it.

Skellig (without actually bringing people ashore)—perfect for those who want a close look without the stair climb and vertigo that go with a visit to the island (€30, sailing daily about 14:45 and returning by 17:00, weather permitting, depart from Valentia Island pier, 50 yards below the Skellig Experience Centre).

VALENTIA HERITAGE MUSEUM

The humble Knightstown schoolhouse, built in 1861, houses an equally humble museum. You'll learn about tetrapods (those first fish to climb onto land—which locals claim happened here). You'll also follow the long story of the expensive, frustrating, and heroic battle to lay telegraph cable across the Atlantic, which finally succeeded in 1866, when the largest ship in the world connected this tiny island of Valentia with Newfoundland.

Cost and Hours: €3.50, daily April-Sept 10:30-17:00, closed Oct-March, tel. 066/947-6411, www.valentiaisland.ie.

Rick's Tip: *If you're interested in* **tetra-pods**, *the actual* **"first footprints"** *are a 15-minute drive from the museum, on a rugged bit of rocky shoreline, a 10-minute hike below a parking lot. Get details locally.*

Cahergal and Leacanabuaile Ring Forts

Crowning bluffs in farm country, 2.5 miles (4 km) off the main road at Cahersiveen, these two windy and desolate forts are each different and worth a look. Just beyond the Cahersiveen town church at the tourist office, turn left, cross the narrow bridge, turn left again, and follow signs to the ancient forts—you'll see the huge stone structures in the distance. You'll hike 10 minutes from the tiny parking lot (free, always open, no museum). Both forts are roughly 100 yards off the road (uphill on the right) and are 200 yards from each other. For details, see "The Ring Forts of Kerry" sidebar, earlier.

SKELLIG MICHAEL

A trip to this jagged, isolated pyramid—the Holy Grail of Irish monastic island settlements—rates as a truly memorable ▲▲▲ experience. After visiting Skellig Michael a hundred years ago, Nobel Prize-winning Irish playwright George Bernard Shaw called it "the most fantastic and impossible rock in the world."

Rising seven miles offshore, the Skelligs (Irish for "splinter") are two gigantic slate-and-sandstone rocks crouched aggressively on the ocean horizon. The larger of the two, Skellig Michael, is more than 700 feet tall and a mile around, with a tiny cluster of abandoned beehive huts clinging near its summit like stubborn barnacles. The smaller island, Little Skellig, is home to a huge colony of gannet birds (like large, graceful seagulls with six-foot wingspans), protected by law from visitors setting foot onshore.

Skellig Michael (dedicated to the archangel) was first inhabited by sixth-century Christian monks. Inspired by earlier hermit-monks in the Egyptian desert,

Leacanabuaile ring fort

they sought the purity of isolation to get closer to God. Neither Viking raids nor winter storms could dislodge them, as they patiently built a half-dozen small, stone, igloo-like dwellings and a couple of tiny oratories. Their remote cliff-terrace perch is still connected to the sea 600 feet below by an amazing series of rock stairs. Viking Olav Trygvasson, who later became king of Norway and introduced Christianity to his country, was baptized here in 956.

Chiseling the most rudimentary life from solid rock, the monks lived a harsh, lonely, disciplined existence here, their colony surviving for more than 500 years. They collected rainwater in cisterns and lived off fish and birds. To supplement their meager existence, they traded bird eggs and feathers with passing boats for cereals, candles, and animal hides (used for clothing and for copying scripture). They finally moved their holy community ashore to Ballinskelligs in the early 1100s. But Christian pilgrims continued to visit Skellig Michael for centuries as penance...edging out onto a ledge to kiss a stone cross that has since toppled into the ocean.

Getting There

To book a boat trip from Portmagee (€60, May-Sept), contact **Patrick Murphy** (mobile 087-234-2168, www.esatclear.ie/~skelligsrock), **Joe Roddy** (mobile 087-284-4460, www.skelligstrips.com), or **Brendan Casey** (mobile 087-228-7519).

Boat trips normally depart Portmagee at 10:00 (depending on tides), sail for an hour, leave you on the island from roughly 11:00 until 13:30, and get you back into Portmagee by 14:30 (with plenty of time to drive on to Dingle). Fifteen small boats (from Portmagee, Ballinskelligs, Waterville, and Valentia Island) have permits to land on Skellig Michael. Each boat can carry a dozen passengers. This limits the number of daily visitors and minimizes the impact on the sensitive island ecosystem.

Bring your camera, a sandwich lunch (easy to buy at the Skellig Mist Bakery in Portmagee), water, sunscreen, rain gear, hiking shoes, and a sense of wonder.

Weather Warning: Landing on Skellig Michael is highly weather-dependent. If the seas are too choppy, the boats cannot safely drop people at the concrete island pier (it's a bit like jumping off a trampoline onto an ice rink). Excursions are sched-

Skellig Michael

uled to run daily from Easter to late September, but experienced boat captains say they are able to bring visitors ashore roughly five days out of seven in an average summer week.

Your best bet is to reserve a room near Portmagee or St. Finian's Bay—whichever best fits your itinerary. (It's possible to sleep in Kenmare and get up early to drive two hours straight to Portmagee—but you'll be frustrated by not having time to enjoy the Ring's attractions along the way.) Then call a few days in advance to make a boat reservation. Keep your fingers crossed for good weather. Contact the boat operator on the morning of departure to get the final word. If the seas are too rough, he can tell from Portmagee and will make a decision that morning whether to go (rather than taking passengers halfway out, then turning back).

Visiting Skellig Michael

Since you'll have only 2.5 hours to explore the island, begin by climbing the seemingly unending series of stone stairs to the monastic ruins (600 vertical feet of uneven steps with no handrails). Save most of your photographing for the way down. Photo-bugs who linger too long below risk missing the enlightening 20-minute free talk among the beehive huts, given by guides who camp on the island from April through October. Afterward, poke your head into some of the huts and try to imagine the dark, damp, and devoted life of a monk here more than 1,000 years ago. After rambling through the ruins, you can give in to the puffin-spotting photo frenzy as you wander back down the stairs.

The two lighthouses on the far side of the island are now automated, and access to them has been blocked off. There are no WCs or modern shelters of any kind on Skellig Michael.

If you visit between late April and early August, you'll be surrounded by fearless rainbow-beaked puffins, which nest here in underground burrows. Their bizarre swallowed cooing sounds like a distant chainsaw. These portly little birds live off fish, and divers have reported seeing them 20 feet underwater in pursuit of their prey.

In summer of 2014, the ruggedly exotic Skellig Michael was used as a filming location for the final scene of the sci-fi epic *Star Wars VII: The Force Awakens*. To keep the filming top-secret, the Irish Navy was called in to enforce a two-mile exclusionary zone around the island. But controversy soon arose: UNESCO voiced concerns about the impact on the island's fragile ecosystem, especially the native seabirds who are sensitive to disturbances and might be spooked into seeking other nesting grounds.

Your return boat journey usually includes a pass near Little Skellig, which looms like an iceberg with a white coat of guano—courtesy of the 20,000 gannets that circle overhead like feathered confetti. These large birds suddenly morph into sleek darts when pursuing a fish, piercing the water from more than 100 feet above. You're also likely to get a glimpse of gray seals lazing on rocks near the water's edge.

Dingle Town
and Peninsula

For over 35 years, my Irish dreams have been set here on the sparse but lush Dingle Peninsula. This westernmost tip of Ireland offers just the right mix of far-and-away beauty, isolated wanders, and ancient wonders—all within convenient reach of its main town.

Although Dingle is crowded in summer, it still feels like the fish and the farm really matter. A half-dozen fishing boats sail from here, tractors leave tracks down the main drag, and a faint whiff of peat fills the nighttime streets.

Locals are fond of saying, "The next parish over is Boston." When I asked a local if he was born here, he thought for a second and said, "No, it was about six miles down the road." I asked his friend if he'd lived here all his life. He said, "Not yet."

Dingle feels so traditionally Irish because it's part of the Gaeltacht, a region where the government subsidizes the survival of the Irish language and culture. While English is always there, the signs, chitchat, and songs come in Irish Gaelic. Children carry Gaelic footballs to class and the local preschool brags it's "ALL Gaelic."

DINGLE TOWN AND PENINSULA IN 2 DAYS

Take one day to sightsee and relax in Dingle town. Take my self-guided walks (through town and to the harbor), look for the dolphin, marvel at the chapel's stained-glass windows, have an excellent dinner, and enjoy trad music in the pubs.

On your second day, explore the 30-mile loop around the peninsula by bike or car (see route specifics on page 193). By spending at least two nights, you'll feel more like a local on your second evening in the pubs. It's not uncommon to find Americans slowing way down in Dingle.

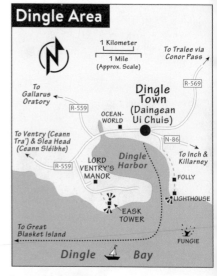

Dingle Area

1 Kilometer
1 Mile (Approx. Scale)

To Tralee via Conor Pass

R-569

To Gallarus Oratory

R-559

OCEAN-WORLD

Dingle Town (Daingean Uí Chuis)

N-86

To Ventry (Ceann Trá) & Slea Head (Ceann Sléibhe)

R-559

LORD VENTRY'S MANOR

Dingle Harbor

To Inch & Killarney

FOLLY

LIGHTHOUSE

EASK TOWER

To Great Blasket Island

FUNGIE

Dingle Bay

DINGLE TOWN

Of the peninsula's 10,000 residents, 1,500 live in Dingle town (Daingean Ui Chuis). It's just large enough to have all the necessary tourist services and a steady nocturnal beat of Irish traditional music. Its streets, lined with ramshackle but playfully painted shops and pubs, run up from a rain-stung harbor always busy with fishing boats and sailboats.

In 1970, the movie *Ryan's Daughter* introduced the world to Dingle. The trickle of Dingle fans has grown to a flood as word of its musical, historical, gastronomical, and scenic charms—not to mention its friendly dolphin—has spread. But it's still a peaceful town. The courthouse (1832) is open one hour a month. The judge does his best to wrap up business within a half hour. During the day, you'll see teenagers—already working on ruddy beer-glow cheeks—roll kegs up the streets and into the pubs in preparation for another night of music and craic (fun conversation and atmosphere).

Rick's Tip: *Expect* **crowds throughout July and August,** *especially during events like the* **Dingle Races** *(early Aug),* **Dingle Regatta** *(early to mid-Aug), and the* **Blessing of the Boats** *(end of Aug). The* **first Mondays in May, June, and August** *are Bank Holidays, giving Ireland's workers three-day weekends that they often spend in Dingle.*

Orientation

Dingle hangs on a medieval grid of streets between the harborfront (where the bus to Tralee, with the nearest train station, stops) and Main Street (three blocks inland). Nothing in town is more than a 15-minute walk away. Street numbers are used only when more than one place is run by a family of the same name. Most locals know most locals, and people on the street are fine sources of information.

Tourist Information: The TI has a great town map (free) and a staff who know the town, but less about the rest of the peninsula (July-Aug Mon-Sat 9:00-18:00, Sun 10:00-17:00, shorter hours off-season, on Strand Street by the water, tel. 066/915-1188).

The Mountain Man, a hiking shop run by local guide Adrian Curran, is a clearinghouse for information on outdoor activities, recreation, and peninsula tours (daily June-mid-Sept 9:00-21:00, mid-Sept-May 9:00-18:00, just off harbor at Strand Street, tel. 066/915-2400, www.themountainmanshop.com).

Farmers Market: On Fridays, vendors sell their fresh produce, homemade marmalade, and homespun crafts (mid-April-mid-Oct 9:00-15:00, across the street from SuperValu grocery store in a small parking lot).

Money: Two banks in town face each other across Main Street (Mon-Fri 10:00-16:00, Mon until 17:00, closed Sat-Sun) and have ATMs. Expect to use cash (rather than credit cards) to pay for most peninsula activities.

Internet Access: The Old Forge Internet Café is friendly and central, and has Wi-Fi (Mon-Fri 10:00-17:00, Sat 11:00-16:00, closed Sun, Holyground). The old **library** has Wi-Fi and a printer. Its three terminals are often busy (Mon-Sat 10:00-17:00, Thu until 20:00, closed Sun, Green Street).

Bike Rental: Try **Paddy's Bike Hire.** Plan on leaving €20, plus a driver's license or passport, as a security deposit (€15/day, includes helmet and lock, daily 9:00-19:00, directly across Dykegate from An Café Liteartha, tel. 066/915-2311).

Taxi: Try **Diarmuid Begley** (mobile 087-250-4767), Sean with **S.O.L. Cabs** in Dingle (mobile 087-660-2323), or **Tom Kearney** out in Dunquin (mobile 087-933-2264).

Travel Agency: Maurice O'Connor at **Galvin's Travel Agency** can book plane tickets, as well as ferry rides to

DINGLE TOWN AND PENINSULA AT A GLANCE

In Dingle Town

▲▲**Harry Clark Windows of Díseart** Glorious display of Art Nouveau-style stained glass craftsmanship, adorning the walls of a former convent chapel. **Hours:** Mon-Fri 9:00-13:00 & 14:00-17:00, Sat 10:00-16:00, closed Sun, shorter hours off-season. See page 179.

▲**Fungie** Friendly dolphin in the harbor and the star of the one-hour sightseeing cruises. **Hours:** Cruises run daily 11:00-17:00, depending on demand. See page 180.

▲**Oceanworld** Earnest presentation of mostly local sealife, spiced with species from arctic and tropical environments, making a good, kid-friendly, rainy-day retreat. **Hours:** Daily 10:00-18:00, shorter hours off-season. See page 181.

▲**Bike and Hike to Eask Tower** Moderate bike ride followed by steep schlep on foot up to the remote Eask Tower and its stunning 360-degree hilltop views of the region. See page 181.

The Dingle Peninsula

▲▲▲**Slea Head Loop Drive** This compact 30-mile road takes the better part of a day (by car, bike, or minivan tour) to link the most intimate historic sights and memorable coastal views in Ireland. See page 193.

▲▲**Great Blasket Centre** Insightful tribute to the storytelling skill and hardscrabble fishing life of a lost culture that inhabited the Blasket Islands up until the early 1950s. **Hours:** Easter-Oct Mon-Sat 10:00-18:00, Sun 11:00-18:00, closed Nov-Easter. See page 203.

What's in a Name: Dingle or Daingean Ui Chuis?

Linguistic politics have stirred up a controversy over the name of this town and peninsula. As a Gaeltacht, the entire region gets subsidies from the government, which supports the survival of the traditional Irish culture and language. A precondition of this financial support is that towns use their Irish Gaelic name. In 2005, well-meaning government officials in Dublin dictated that Dingle convert its name to the Irish Gaelic "An Daingean" ("on DANG-un"). But as it turns out, four separate Irish towns are named Daingean ("fortress"), so in 2012 Dingle's name was changed again—to Daingean Ui Chuis ("Fortress of the Husseys," a Norman founding family back in the late Middle Ages).

The town has resisted these dictates from Dublin. Dingle has become so wealthy from the tourist trade that it sees its famous name as a trademark, and doesn't want to become "the cute tourist town with the unpronounceable name, formerly known as Dingle." While official road signs identify the town only as *Daingean Ui Chuis*, you'll notice that many have been modified by a crude *DINGLE*, stenciled by stubborn locals. In town, most businesses, all tourist information, and nearly all people—locals and tourists alike—refer to it as Dingle.

For the sake of clarity, in this book I follow the predominant convention: Dingle instead of Daingean Ui Chuis. But for ease of navigation, I've also included the place's Irish name in parentheses. For a list of these bilingual place names, see the sidebar on page 192.

Britain (Mon-Fri 9:30-18:00, Sat 9:30-14:00, closed Sun, John Street, tel. 066/915-1409).

Tours: Sciuird (SKEW-erd, Irish for "excursion") **Archaeology Tours** are offered by Tim Collins, the retired Dingle police chief, and his son Michael, who give serious 2.5-hour minibus tours. Dress for the weather. In a gale storm with horizontal winds, Tim kept telling me, "You'll survive it" (€25, departing at 10:30 and 14:00, depending upon demand; to put your name on the list, drop by the Eileen Collins Kirrary B&B at Dykegate and Grey's Lane or call 066/915-1606 or mobile 086-854-9560).

Dingle Bay Charters offers harbor boat cruises (€10, 1 hour, runs several times daily), a ferry to Great Blasket Island (see page 203), ecotours, sea-fishing excursions, and boat rentals (office around corner from TI, tel. 066/915-1344, mobile 087-672-6100, www.dinglebaycharters.com).

Dingle Walks
⊙ *Town Walk*

This quick, self-guided circle through town gives you a once-over-lightly historical overview and good orientation.

Start at the **"old roundabout"** (next to O'Flaherty's pub, not the "new roundabout" by the hospital), which replaced the big bridge over the town river in the 1980s. Step out to the tiny pedestrian bridge (toward the bay) with the black wrought-iron railing. This was the original train line coming into Dingle (the westernmost train station in all of Europe from 1891 to 1953). The train once picked up fish here; its operators boasted that the cargo would be in London markets within 24 hours. The narrow-gauge tracks ran right along the harborfront. All the land beyond the old buildings you see today has been reclaimed from the sea. Look inland and find the building on the left with the slate siding (the back wall of O'Flaherty's pub) facing the worst storms coming in from the sea. This was the typical design for 19th-century weather-proofing. The radio tower marks the salm-on-pink police station.

Cross the roundabout and walk 20 yards along the river up "The Mall" to the two stubby red-brick **pillars** that mark the entry to the police station. These pillars are all that remain of the 19th-century British Constabulary, which afforded a kind of Green Zone for British troops when they tried to subdue the local insurgents here. It was burned down in 1922, during the Civil War; the present building dates from 1938.

The big white **crucifix** across the street and 50 yards up The Mall is a memorial to heroes who died in the 1916 Uprising. In the people's language, it says "For honor and glory of Ireland, 1916 to 19___." The date is unfinished until Ireland is united and free. The names listed are of patriots executed by the English, and one who died while on a hunger strike.

At the *Russels B&B* sign, take 15 paces up the driveway to see an old stone etched with a cross sitting atop the fence (on the right). This marks the site of a former **Celtic holy well,** a sacred spot for people here 2,000 years ago. Back across the street, check out the gurgling stream straddled by a couple of houses.

A few yards up is another much-honored spot: the distribution center for **Guinness.** From this warehouse, pubs throughout the peninsula are stocked with beer. The wooden kegs have been replaced by what locals fondly call "iron lungs."

Farther up and across the street is the 19th-century **courthouse.** Once a symbol of British oppression, today it's a laid-back place where, on the last Friday of each month, the roving County Kerry judge drops by to adjudicate cases (mostly domestic disputes and drunken disorderliness). Next door, with the blue walls, is

Medieval Dingle

The wet sod of Dingle is soaked with medieval history. In the dimmest depths of the Dark Ages, peace-loving, bookish monks fled the chaos of the Continent and its barbarian raids. They sailed to the drizzly fringe of the known world—to places like Dingle. These monks kept literacy alive in Europe, and later provided scribes to Charlemagne, who ruled much of central Europe in the year 800.

It was from this peninsula that the semi-mythical explorer-monk St. Brendan is said to have set sail in the sixth century in search of a legendary western paradise. Some think he beat Columbus to North America by almost a thousand years.

Dingle was a busy seaport in the late Middle Ages. Dingle and Tralee were the only walled towns in Kerry. Castles stood at the low and high ends of Dingle's Main Street, protecting the Normans from the angry and dispossessed Irish outside. Dingle was a gateway to northern Spain—a three-day sail due south. Many 14th- and 15th-century pilgrims left from Dingle for the revered Spanish church in Santiago de Compostela, thought to house the bones of St. James.

the popular **Courthouse Pub.**

The next intersection is the "Small Bridge" (a stream runs under the road). Continuing straight would take you up the road a few miles to the ruggedly scenic Conor Pass. Instead, turn left into the commercial heart of the town, up **Main Street.** The old stagecoach from Tralee ended at Dingle's first hotel, Benners (halfway up on the left), with its Georgian facade and door surviving.

Across the street, up a short gravel

alley, is St. James' Church. Since the 13th century, a church has stood here (just inside the medieval wall). Today, it's Anglican on Sundays and filled with great traditional music several nights a week (schedule on gate). In 2003, a mid-winter concert series sprang up at the church, featuring internationally known artists seeking an intimate venue. It became known as the "Other Voices" series and grew to become an annual event. Perhaps the best-known performance was by the late Amy Winehouse, whose "One Shining Moment" TV concert was filmed here in 2006.

Continue uphill and poke your head into two of Dingle's most unapologetically traditional drinking holes, which face each other across Main Street: **Ó Curráin's** (on the right) and **Foxy John's** (on the left). Like many Irish pubs, these two throwbacks were originally shops by day and pubs by night. Decades ago, small-town pubs often also served as the town morgue (because they had the only large refrigerated space in town)—where you could literally drink until you dropped.

At the first intersection, take a left onto Green Street. The brownish-red building on your right (as you turn the corner) was once intended to be the residence-in-exile for Marie-Antoinette. Her escape from execution in Paris had been arranged by an Irish officer who owned this house and was employed by the Habsburgs. But Marie-Antoinette refused to leave her husband and children (see the plaque near the front door).

Down the street on the right, pop into the beautiful, modern St. Mary's Church. The convent behind it shows off its delightful **Díseart windows** (described later, under "Sights" in Dingle). Wander in the backyard to check out the tranquil nuns' cemetery, with its white-painted iron crosses huddling peacefully together under a big copper beech tree. Across from St. Mary's is the **Dick Mack's Pub,** another traditional pub well worth a peek, even for non-drinkers.

Green Street leads past lots of inviting boutiques, estate agents (showing the current price of houses here), and the library. The **library,** a gift from the Carnegie Foundation, has a shelf of tourist-information books and a small exhibit (in the foyer and upstairs) about local patriot Thomas Ashe and the Blasket Island

Courthouse Pub

Díseart windows

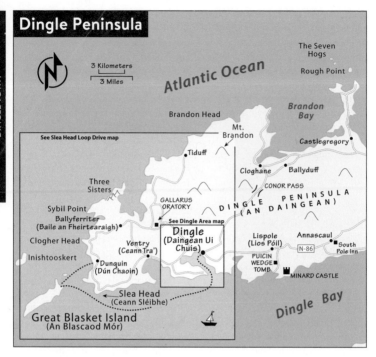

Dingle Peninsula

3 Kilometers
3 Miles

Atlantic Ocean

The Seven Hogs

Rough Point

Brandon Head

Brandon Bay

Mt. Brandon

Castlegregory

See Slea Head Loop Drive map

Tiduff

Cloghane   Ballyduff

CONOR PASS

Three Sisters

GALLARUS ORATORY

DINGLE   PENINSULA (AN DAINGEAN)

Sybil Point
Ballyferriter
(Baile an Fheirtearaigh)

See Dingle Area map

Dingle
(Daingean Uí Chúis)

Lispole
(Lios Póil)

Annascaul

N-86   South Pole Inn

Clogher Head

Ventry
(Ceann Trá')

PUICIN WEDGE TOMB

Inishtooskert

Dunquin
(Dún Chaoin)

MINARD CASTLE

Slea Head
(Ceann Sléibhe)

Great Blasket Island
(An Blascaod Mór)

Dingle Bay

writers. The best historic photos you'll find in town decorate the library's walls with images of 19th-century Dingle. Green Street continues to the Strand, where a right turn takes you to the harbor.

The **harbor** was built on land reclaimed (with imported Dutch expertise) in 1992. The string of old stone shops facing the harbor was the loading station for the railway that hauled the fish from Dingle until 1953. Walk out to the end of the break-water—recently paved and illuminated at night. The Eask Tower, on the distant hill, helped ships locate Dingle's hidden harbor in pre-radar days (though it was built primarily as a famine-era make-work project). The fancy manor house (now a school) across the harbor was built in the 18th century by Lord Ventry, a big-shot landlord. Near the dolphin statue, you'll find an office where you can get information about the various boat excursions.

● Harbor Walk

This easy stroll along the harbor out of town gives you a chance to see Fungie the dolphin. It takes about 1.5 hours round-trip. Head east from the old roundabout (just past O'Flaherty's pub) and walk uphill past the Esso station. Just after Bambury's B&B, take a right, then immediately bear left (toward the cell-phone tower). You'll head downhill and soon spot a tiny Irish Coast Guard station beside the bay. Turn left at the station,

Dingle's harbor

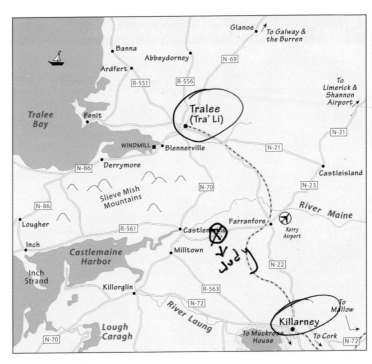

climbing the steps over the low wall and following the seashore path to the mouth of Dingle Harbor (passing Hussey's folly, an empty two-story shell of a tower built by a 19th-century fat cat). Ten minutes beyond that is a two-story (white with red trim) lighthouse. This is Fungie's neighborhood. If you see tourist boats out, you're likely to see the dolphin. The trail continues another half-mile to dramatic cliff views and an intimate beach.

Sights

▲▲HARRY CLARK WINDOWS OF DÍSEART

Just behind Dingle's St. Mary's Church stands St. Joseph's Convent and Díseart (dee-SHIRT, rhymes with "T-shirt"), containing a beautiful Neo-Gothic chapel built in 1884. The sisters of this order, who came to Dingle in 1829 to educate local girls, worked heroically during the famine. During Mass in the chapel, the Mother Superior would sit in the covered stall in the rear, while the sisters—filling the carved stalls—chanted in response.

The chapel was graced in 1922 with 12 windows—the work of Ireland's top stained-glass man, Harry Clark. Long appreciated only by the sisters, these special windows—showing six scenes from the life of Christ—are now open to the public. The convent has become a center for sharing Christian Celtic culture and spirituality.

Cost and Hours: €3, Mon-Fri 9:00-13:00 & 14:00-17:00, Sat 10:00-16:00, closed Sun, shorter hours off-season, tel. 066/915-2476, www.diseart.ie.

Visiting the Chapel: Enjoy a quick orientation by the attendant, followed by a 15-minute recorded narration explaining the chapel and its windows. The scenes (clockwise from the back entrance) are the visit of the Magi, the Baptism of Jesus, "Let the little children come to me," the Sermon on the Mount, the Agony in the Garden, and Jesus appearing to Mary

Tom Crean, Unsung Antarctic Explorer

Kerrymen are a hardy lot, and probably none more so than Antarctic explorer Thomas Crean. In 1901, Crean volunteered to join the crew of the RSS *Discovery*. Onboard were Captain Robert Falcon Scott and other soon-to-be famous explorers, including Ernest Shackleton. Their mission: to be the first men to reach the South Pole.

The effort required pulling sleds laden with supplies across miles of ice in extreme conditions. Crean quickly gained his mates' respect for his hard work, calm presence, and cheerful (if tuneless) singing. The *Discovery* Expedition pushed the boundaries of Antarctic exploration, but didn't reach the pole (Britain's second attempt, in 1909 under Shackleton, got much closer before also turning back).

Determined to try again, Scott handpicked Crean for the crew for the *Terra Nova* Expedition (1910-1913). Early on, Crean saved some expedition members stranded on a drifting ice floe—encircled by orcas—by leaping between floating chunks of ice, then scaling an ice wall to get help. Later, Crean and two others were the last support team ordered to turn back as Scott made the final push to the pole. Having come so close, the otherwise unshakable Crean wept at the news. Near the end of the 730-mile return trip, Crean's two mates, sick and freezing, could go no farther. Exhausted and provisioned with only three cookies and two sticks of chocolate, Crean made a nonstop, solo, 35-mile march through a blizzard to reach help, saving his mates' lives. (Though Scott's party did reach the pole, a Norwegian team led by Roald Amundsen beat them to it—by a month; Scott and his men didn't survive the trip back.)

Crean's most famous act of heroism took place on his third and final polar expedition (1914-1917), led by Shackleton. Their ship, the *Endurance*, was crushed by ice, marooning the crew on Elephant Island. Hoping to find help at a whaling station, Shackleton, Crean, and four others sailed a modified open lifeboat 800 miles in 17 days to South Georgia Island. There they were forced to hike across the rugged, unexplored interior to reach the station on the other side. A ship was sent to rescue the exhausted and malnourished crew, all of whom had miraculously survived the 18-month ordeal.

Crean never did reach the South Pole himself, turning down Shackleton's request to join him on his next (and final) trek. But Crean distinguished himself as a hero among explorers—who named both a mountain and a glacier after him in Antarctica—and was honored by King George V. In 1920, he retired from the navy, returned to County Kerry. He married, bought a pub, and stashed his medals away, never again speaking of his experiences.

Magdalene. Each face is lively and animated in the imaginative, devout, medieval, and fun-loving style of Harry Clark, whom locals talk about as if he's the kid next door.

▲ FUNGIE

In 1983, a dolphin moved into Dingle Harbor and became a local celebrity. Fungie (FOON-ghee, with a hard *g*) is the darling of the town's tourist trade and one reason you'll find so many tour buses parked along the harbor. A recent study theorizes that he may be one of a half-dozen dolphins that were released from "Dolphinariums" (under pressure from animal rights activists) on the southern coast of Britain. This would account for Fungie's comfort around humans...and British accent. As Fungie is getting on in years, locals admit that he doesn't come up as often as he used to. But regardless, Fungie is still a fun guy.

Tour boats thrive by baiting passengers with the chance of an up-close Fungie encounter, then motoring out to the mouth of the harbor; don't pay unless you see the dolphin (€16, kids-€8, one-hour trips depart daily 11:00-17:00 depending on demand, behind TI at Dolphin Trips office, tel. 066/915-2626, www.dingle dolphin.com).

To actually swim with Fungie, rent wetsuits at Brosnan's B&B (Cooleen Street, tel. 066/915-1146 or mobile 087-273-4970) and catch the early morning 8:00-10:00 trip (€25 for the boat trip, €20 for the wetsuit, minimum 6 people or they won't go).

▲OCEANWORLD

This aquarium offers 300 different species of fish, including local species and a colorful Amazon collection. It's also the easiest way to see Fungie the dolphin: on video. Other highlights are the penguin exhibit, with tuxedo torpedoes darting underwater and the petting pool featuring rays, which are fortunately unplugged.

Cost and Hours: €13, families with children (4-6 people)-€34-40, daily 10:00-18:00, shorter hours off-season, cafeteria, just past harbor on west edge of town, tel. 066/915-2111, www.dingle-oceanworld.ie.

Experiences
▲Bike and Hike to Eask Tower

Here's a good compromise for those wanting more exercise than a mellow harbor walk. Lazybones can skip the bike portion of the following excursion and just drive to the trailhead.

Rent a bike in town and pedal west past the aquarium, going left at the roundabout that takes you over the bridge onto R-559 toward Slea Head. After about three kilometers (two miles), turn left at the brown sign to *Holden's Leather Work-*

Fungie, Dingle's resident dolphin

shop. A narrow leafy lane leads another three kilometers to a hut on the right marked *Eask Tower* (the tower looms on the bare hill above). Pay the €2 trail fee at the hut (if unattended, feed the honor box) and hike straight up the hill. Pace yourself on this steep trail. You'll zigzag around sheep and tiptoe over their droppings. You'll also need to navigate through (and possibly climb) a couple of waist-high, metal-rung gates. After 45 minutes, you'll have huffed and puffed up to the stone signal tower on the crown of the hill. Enjoy fantastic views of Dingle town (to the north) and Dingle Bay with the Iveragh Peninsula (home of the Ring of Kerry to the south). Try to spot the two jagged Skellig Islands off the distant tip of the Iveragh Peninsula. The right-hand island (farthest from the mainland) was home to the monastic Skellig hermitage for more than five centuries. Those islands were once the edge of the known world.

Horseback Riding

Dingle Horse Riding takes out beginners and experienced riders on excursions (€35/hour for a beginner trail ride, €75/2-hour ride, €125/half-day, €175/full day, call ahead to book, follow Main Street out of Dingle, turn right at sign, tel. 066/915-2199, www.dinglehorseriding. com). **Long's Horseriding Centre** is farther out on the peninsula, just past Ventry (look for sign on right)—an easy stop for bikers or drivers doing the Slea Head Loop (€30/one-hour beach ride, €60/two-hour beach and mountain trail ride, short rides often depart at 10:00, call to book, tel. 066/915-9034, mobile 087-225-0286, www.longsriding.com). In either case, mountain rides are only for advanced riders, and all horses come with English-style saddles (no horns for hanging on).

Golf

Dingle Pitch & Putt's humble 18 holes (ranging from 30 to 70 yards in length) offer a relaxing diversion for average duffers on a green headland overlooking the harbor (€8, includes gear, April-Oct daily 10:00-19:00, closed Nov-March, 20-minute walk out of town—over bridge take first left and then your first right, curling behind Milltown House, tel. 066/915-2020).

Biking outside Dingle Town

Eask Tower

Located out west, near the wildly scenic tip of the Dingle Peninsula and the town of Ballyferriter, **Ceann Sibéal/Dingle Links** offers a round of golf in a hard-to-beat setting (€55 green fees 9:00-16:00, €35 outside those hours, open daily till dusk, Baile an Fheirtearaigh, 9 miles west of Dingle town, tel. 066/915-6255, www.dinglelinks.com).

Nightlife
▲▲▲PUBS

Traditional pub music is Dingle town's best experience. Even if you're not into pubs, give these a whirl. Dingle is renowned among traditional musicians as a good place to get work ("€40 a day, tax-free, plus drink"). The town has piles of pubs that feature music most nights, and with nary a cover charge. The scene is a decent mix of locals, Americans, and Germans. Music normally starts at 21:30-ish, and the last call for drinks is at "half eleven" (23:30), sometimes later on weekends. For a seat near the music, arrive early. If the place is chockablock with people, power in and find breathing room in the back. By midnight, the door is usually closed and the chairs are stacked.

While two pubs, the **Small Bridge Bar** (An Droichead Beag) and **O'Flaherty's,** are the most famous for their atmosphere and devotion to traditional Irish music, make a point to wander the town and follow your ear. Smaller pubs may feel a bit foreboding to a tourist, but rest assured that people—locals as well as travelers—are out for the *craic*. Irish culture is very accessible in the pubs; they're like highly interactive museums waiting to be explored. If you sit at a table, you'll be left alone. But stand or sit at the bar and you'll be engulfed in conversation with new friends. Have a glass in an empty, no-name pub and chat up the publican. Pubs are no longer smoky, but can be stuffy and hot, so leave your coat at home. I know it's going to be a great trad music session when my eyeglasses steam up as I enter.

Pub Crawl: The best place to start a pub crawl is at **O'Flaherty's,** the first music pub in Dingle, located on Holyground Street. Quietly intense owner

Enjoying the pub experience

Fergus O'Flaherty, a fixture since my first visit to Dingle, can belt out a song as he joins a varying lineup of loyal local musicians. Talented Fergus sings and plays a half-dozen different instruments during almost nightly traditional-music sessions. His domain has a high ceiling and is dripping in old-time photos and town memorabilia—it's unpretentious, cluttered fun.

Moving up Strand Street, find **John Benny Moriarty's.** Its dependably good traditional-music sessions come with John himself joining in on accordion when he's not pouring pints.

Then head up Green Street. **Dick Mack's Pub,** across from the church, is nicknamed "the last pew." This was once a tiny leather shop that expanded into a pub at night. Today, Dick Mack's keeps the old leather-shop ambience but sells only drinks, with several rooms, a fine snug (private booth, originally designed to allow women to drink discreetly), ample beer choices, and a fascinating ambience. Notice the Hollywood-type stars on the sidewalk outside, recalling famous visitors. The pub was established in 1899 by Dick Mack (master of the westernmost train station in Europe), whose mission was to provide "liquid replenishment" to travelers. The grandson of the original Dick Mack runs the place today. A painting in the window shows Dick Mack II with the local gang.

Green Street climbs to Main Street, where two more Dick Mack-type places are filled with locals deep in conversation (but no music): **Foxy John's** (a hardware shop by day) and **Ó Curráin's** (across the street, a small clothing shop by day).

A bit higher up Main Street is **McCarthy's Bar,** a smoke-stained relic. It's less touristy and has occasional traditional-music sessions on its little stage. Wander down Main Street. The **Dingle Pub** is well established as *the* place for folk-ballad singing rather than the churning traditional beat of an Irish folk session. At the bottom of Main Street, **Small Bridge Bar** offers live music nightly. These days, its dimly lit confines are popular with a younger, late-night crowd.

And the **Court House Pub** is a steamy hideaway with low ceilings and high-caliber musicians. Owner Tommy O'Sullivan is a guitar-strumming fixture on the

Dick Mack's Pub

trad music scene (on The Mall, next to the old gray courthouse).

Off-Season: From October through April, the music semi-hibernates. But on weekends, your best bets are the Small Bridge Bar, O'Flaherty's, the Court House Pub, and John Benny Moriarty's.

▲▲Folk Concerts

If you're not a night owl, these are your best opportunities to hear Irish traditional music in a more controlled, early evening environment. Keep in mind that in these settings, many of the musicians find flash photography to be an irritating distraction.

Top local musicians offer a quality evening of live, acoustic, traditional Irish music in **St. James' Church** (100 seats), just off Main Street. These concerts are organized by local piper Eoin Duignan, whose command of the melodic *uileann* bagpipes is a highlight most nights. Surprisingly, this humble church is the home venue of the acclaimed "Other Voices" winter concert TV series that has drawn the likes of Amy Winehouse, Sinéad O'Connor, and Donovan (€13 in advance,

€15 at the door; May-Oct Mon, Wed, and Fri at 19:30; see sign on church gate or, for more details or to book a ticket, drop by the Whole Food Vegetarian Café, Paul Geaneys Pub, Leac a Ré craft shop, or Siopa Ceoil music shop; mobile 087-284-9656).

The **Siopa Ceoil** music shop hosts intimate "unplugged" traditional Irish music sessions in its cramped but cozy 35-seat venue (€15, includes a tasty Irish coffee during break between sets; May-Sept Tue, Thu, and Sat at 19:30; 2 The Colony, tel. 066/915-2618, mobile 087-914-5826, www.siopaceoil.ie).

Cinema

Dingle's film club (50-60 locals) meets at **The Phoenix** on Tuesdays year-round at 20:30 for coffee and cookies, followed by a film at 21:00. The leader runs it almost like a religion, with a sermon on the film before he rolls it. The regular film schedule for the week is posted on the door (€8 for film, anyone is welcome; theater on Dykegate).

Eating

While the top-end restaurants charge on average €20-30, some serve good-value, early-bird specials from 17:30 to 19:00. You can eat well for €15-19 in Dingle's pubs and ethnic eateries. Many cheap and cheery lunch places close at 18:00. Most pubs stop serving food at about 21:00 (to make room for their beer drinkers and musicians). Anyone will serve tap water for free.

Fine Dining

All of these restaurants are good; I've listed them in the order of my personal preference.

Chart House Restaurant serves contemporary cuisine in a sleek, well-varnished dining room. Settle back into the shipshape, lantern-lit, harborside ambience. The menu is shaped by what's fresh and seasonal. The chef, who has

Music performance at St. James' Church

Dingle Restaurants & Pubs

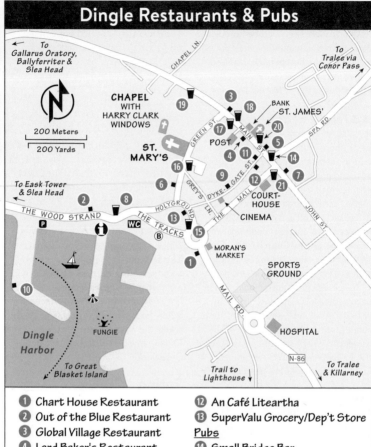

To Gallarus Oratory, Ballyferriter & Slea Head

To Tralee via Conor Pass

CHAPEL LN.

CHAPEL
WITH
HARRY CLARK
WINDOWS

BANK
ST. JAMES'

200 Meters
200 Yards

ST.
MARY'S

POST

GREEN ST.

MAIN ST.

SPA RD.

To Eask Tower
& Slea Head

GREY'S LN.

DYKE ST.

GATE ST.

THE MALL

COURT-
HOUSE

CINEMA

THE WOOD STRAND

HOLYGROUND

THE TRACKS

P

WC

B

JOHN ST.

MORAN'S
MARKET

SPORTS
GROUND

Dingle
Harbor

FUNGIE

MAIL RD.

HOSPITAL

To Great
Blasket Island

Trail to
Lighthouse

N-86

To Tralee
& Killarney

1 Chart House Restaurant
2 Out of the Blue Restaurant
3 Global Village Restaurant
4 Lord Baker's Restaurant
5 James G. Ashe Pub/Rest. & Whole Food Vegetarian Café
6 Fenton's Restaurant
7 The Half Door
8 John Benny Moriarty's
9 An Canteen Restaurant
10 Fishbarr
11 The Wren's Nest

12 An Café Liteartha
13 SuperValu Grocery/Dep't Store

Pubs

14 Small Bridge Bar
15 O'Flaherty's Pub
16 Dick Mack's Pub
17 Foxy John's Pub
18 Ó Curráin's Pub
19 McCarthy's Bar
20 Dingle Pub
21 Court House Pub

a Tuscan connection and a passion for South African wines, is committed to always offering a good vegetarian entrée (€20-30 dinners, daily 18:00-22:00 except closed Mon Oct-May, reservations wise, at roundabout at base of town, tel. 066/915-2255, www.thecharthousedingle.

com, Jim McCarthy).

Out of the Blue Seafood-Only Restaurant is the locals' choice for just plain great fresh fish. The interior is bright and elegantly simple. The menu—not printed, but on a chalkboard—is dictated by what the fishermen caught that morning. If they're closed, you know there's been a storm and the fishermen couldn't go out. The €15-19 lunches and heartier €21-30 dinners are artfully presented, with a touch of nouvelle cuisine and certainly no chips (Thu-Tue 12:30-15:00 & 17:00-21:30, closed Wed and after a storm, some outdoor picnic-table seating, reservations smart, just past the TI, facing the harbor on The Waterside, tel. 066/915-0811, www.outoftheblue.ie).

At **Global Village Restaurant,** Nuala Cassidy and Martin Bealin—with inspiration gleaned from his world travels—concoct their favorite dishes. Martin has a passion for making things from scratch and giving dishes a creative twist. No chips, no deep-fat-fried anything. It's an eclectic, healthy, fresh seafood-eaters' place (€25-30 dinners, good salads, early-bird special served 17:30-18:45; March-Oct daily 17:30-22:00, Nov-Feb open Fri-Sun only; top of Main Street, tel. 066/915-2325, mobile 087-917-5920).

Lord Baker's is the venerable elder among fine Dingle dining options. John Moriarty and his family concoct quality dishes served in a friendly yet refined atmosphere. The seafood soup is a memorable specialty (daily 12:30-14:00 & 18:00-22:00, €24 two-course meals, €28 three-course meals, reservations smart, Main Street, tel. 066/915-1277 or 066/915-2174, www.lordbakers.ie).

James G. Ashe Pub and Restaurant, an old-fashioned joint, is popular with locals for its nicely presented, top-quality, traditional Irish food and seafood at good prices. Check out the photos of Gregory Peck, who was related to the Ashe family and visited the pub often. I like their beef-and-Guinness stew (€15-25 dinners, early-bird special 17:30-19:00, daily 12:00-15:00 & 17:30-21:30, Main Street, tel. 066/915-0989).

Fenton's is good for seafood meals with a memorable apple-and-berry-crumble dessert (€23-30 main courses, early-bird specials before 19:00, open

Sleep Code

Abbreviations: S=Single, D=Double/Twin, T=Triple, Q=Quad, b=bathroom
   Price Rankings for Double Rooms: $$$** Most rooms €100 or more, **$$** €70-100, **$ €70 or less
   Notes: Room prices change; verify rates online or by email. For the best prices, book directly with the hotel.

Tue-Sun 18:00-21:30, closed Mon, reservations smart, on Green Street down the hill below the church, tel. 066/915-2172, mobile 087-248-2487, www.fentonsrestaurantdingle.com).

The Half Door, at the top of the town, is one of Dingle's long-established top-notch restaurants, satisfying diners with hearty portions. While elegant, the dining room feels a bit congested (€30-40 meals, early-bird special 17:30-18:30; Mon-Sat 12:30-14:00 & 18:00-21:30, closed Sun, reservations smart, on John Street, tel. 066/915-1600, www.halfdoor.ie).

Inexpensive Dinners

John Benny Moriarty's is a waterfront pub dishing up traditional Irish fare with a relatively cozy interior. John, the proprietor, hopes people will come here for dinner and stay for a drink and enjoy his nightly live music (€12-16 hearty dinner plates, food daily 12:30-21:30, music after 21:30, The Pier).

An Canteen hides out up the street across from the cinema, offering home-cooking made with fresh seasonal produce, served up in an unpretentious atmosphere for great prices (€15-22 meals, Thu-Tue 17:00-21:00, closed Wed, Dykegate Street, mobile 086-660-3778).

Whole Food Vegetarian Café is a peaceful place serving healthy soups,

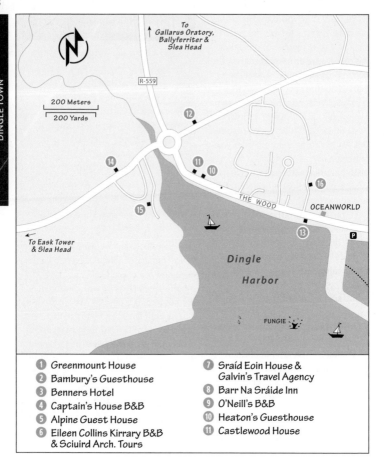

To
Gallarus Oratory,
Ballyferriter &
Slea Head

R-559

200 Meters
200 Yards

THE WOOD

OCEANWORLD

To Eask Tower
& Slea Head

Dingle

Harbor

FUNGIE

1. Greenmount House
2. Bambury's Guesthouse
3. Benners Hotel
4. Captain's House B&B
5. Alpine Guest House
6. Eileen Collins Kirrary B&B
   & Sciuird Arch. Tours
7. Sraíd Eoin House &
   Galvin's Travel Agency
8. Barr Na Sráide Inn
9. O'Neill's B&B
10. Heaton's Guesthouse
11. Castlewood House

salads, pancakes, fruit smoothies, and home-baked cakes. Its serene back garden is perfect for enjoying a light lunch (Wed-Sat 12:00-17:00, closed Sun-Tue except July-Aug, Lower Main Street, mobile 087-741-6947).

Fishbarr has all the cinder-block charm you'd expect in a great fish-and-chips lunch joint. It's off the beaten path at the end of the modern yacht pier, with outdoor tables to track the boating action in the bay (May-Sept daily 11:00-15:00, closed Oct-April, cash only, mobile 086-378-8584).

The Wren's Nest is a mellow coffeehouse, reflecting musician-owner John Ryan's philosophical demeanor. This lunch-only refuge, with an ultra-appealing back garden, serves wholesome omelets, sandwiches, cakes, and tea. A small corner stage hosts occasional open-mic acoustic music gigs; you can also check out the schedule of bodhran and music lessons (daily 11:00-17:00, Dykegate Street, mobile 086-177-3119).

An Café Liteartha, a simple refuge hidden behind a wonderfully cluttered bookstore, serves soup and sandwiches to a good-natured crowd of Irish speakers (daily 10:00-18:00, Sept-May until 17:00 and closed Sun, Dykegate Street, tel. 066/915-2204).

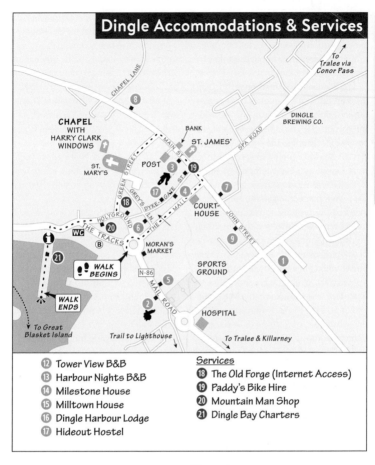

Dingle Accommodations & Services

⑫ Tower View B&B
⑬ Harbour Nights B&B
⑭ Milestone House
⑮ Milltown House
⑯ Dingle Harbour Lodge
⑰ Hideout Hostel

Services
⑱ The Old Forge (Internet Access)
⑲ Paddy's Bike Hire
⑳ Mountain Man Shop
㉑ Dingle Bay Charters

Picnics

The **SuperValu** supermarket/department store, at the base of town, has everything and stays open late (Mon-Sat 8:00-21:00, Sun until 19:00, daily until 22:00 July-Aug). Smaller groceries, such as **Centra,** are scattered throughout the town (Mon-Sat 8:00-21:00, Sun until 18:00, on Main Street). Consider a grand-view picnic out on the end of the newer pier (as you face the harbor, it's the pleasure-boat pier on your right). You'll find picnic tables on the harbor side of the roundabout and benches along the busy harborfront.

Sleeping

Prices vary with the season, with winter cheap and August tops.

In or near the Town Center

$$$ **Greenmount House** sits among chilly palm trees in the countryside at the top of town. A five-minute hike up from the town center, this guesthouse commands a fine view of the bay and mountains. Gary Curran runs one of Ireland's best B&Bs, with two fine rooms (Db-€70-110), three superb rooms (Db-€100-140), and seven sprawling suites (Db-€120-160) in a modern building with lavish public areas and breakfast in a solarium. Seek out the hot

tub in their back-garden cabin (reserve in advance, most rooms at ground level, parking, top of John Street, tel. 066/915-1414, www.greenmounthouse.ie, info@greenmounthouse.ie).

$$$ Bambury's Guesthouse, hosted by cheerful Bernie Bambury, is big and modern with views of grazing sheep and the harbor. The 12 rooms are airy and comfy (Sb-€80, Db-€100-120, Tb-€150, less off-season, family deals; coming in from Tralee it's on your left on Mail Road, 2 blocks before Esso station; tel. 066/915-1244, www.bamburysguesthouse.com, info@bamburysguesthouse.com).

$$$ Benners Hotel was the only hotel in town a hundred years ago. It stands bewildered by the modern world on Main Street, with sprawling public spaces and 52 abundant, overpriced rooms (Db-€120-200 July-Aug, €140-165 May-June and Sept, €110-135 Oct-April, discounts on website, tel. 066/915-1638, www.dinglebenners.com, info@dinglebenners.com).

$$$ Captain's House B&B rents three suites in the town center. Mary, whose mother ran a guesthouse before Dingle was discovered, provides a continental breakfast for her guests (suites-€120-200, entry on Dykegate Street, tel. 066/915-1531, www.captainshousedingle.com, captigh@eircom.net, Jim and Mary Milhench).

$$ Alpine Guesthouse looks like a Monopoly hotel, and is fittingly comfortable and efficient. Its 14 bright and fresh rooms come with pastoral views, a cozy lounge, and friendly owner Paul O'Shea (Sb-€45-60, Db-€70-96, Tb-€90-120, Qb-€100-130, less off-season, ask for Rick Steves discount with this book, easy parking, Mail Road, tel. 066/915-1250, www.alpineguesthouse.com, alpinedingle@eircom.net). Driving into town from Tralee, this will be the first lodging on your right, next to the sports field and a block uphill from the Dingle Esso station.

$$ Eileen Collins Kirrary B&B, which takes up a quiet corner in the town center, is run by the same Collins family that does archaeological tours of the peninsula. They offer five fine rooms, great prices, a large garden, and a homey friendliness (Db-€70-80, cash only, tel. 066/915-1606 or mobile 087-150-0017, Kirrary House, just off The Mall on Avondale at Dykegate and Grey's Lane, www.collinskirrary.com, collinskirrary@eircom.net, Eileen Collins). They also rent a cozy, family-friendly, self-catering cottage that sleeps five people (minimum 3-night stay); a couple of hundred yards high up behind town, it has Dingle's best views.

$$ Sraíd Eoin House offers five pleasant, top-floor rooms above Galvin's Travel Agency (Db-€70-80, Tb-€90-100, Qb-€100-120, ask for Rick Steves discount with cash and this book, John Street, tel. 066/915-1409, www.sraideoinbnb.com, sraideoinhouse@hotmail.com, friendly Kathleen and Maurice O'Connor).

$$ Barr Na Sráide Inn, central and hotel-like, has 29 basic rooms (Sb-€35-55, Db-€70-110, Tb-€100-150, family deals, self-service laundry, bar, parking, past McCarthy's pub on Upper Main Street, tel. 066/915-1331, www.barrnasraide.com, barrnasraide@eircom.net).

$ O'Neill's B&B is homey and friendly, with six decent rooms on a quiet street at the top of town (Db-€65-70, cash only, parking, John Street, tel. 066/915-1639, www.oneillsbedandbreakfast.com, info@oneillsbedandbreakfast.com, Mary and Stephen O'Neill).

Beyond the Pier

These accommodations are a 10-15-minute walk from Dingle's town center. They tend to be quieter, since they are farther from the late-night pub scene.

$$$ Heaton's Guesthouse, big, peaceful, and comfortable, is on the water just west of town at the end of Dingle Bay—a five-minute walk past Oceanworld on The Wood. The 16 thoughtfully appointed rooms come with all the amenities (Db-

€78-130, suite Db-€118-170, less off-season, creative breakfasts, parking, The Wood, tel. 066/915-2288, www.heatons dingle.com, info@heatonsdingle.com, David Heaton).

$$$ **Castlewood House** is a palatial refuge with 12 tasteful rooms, classy furnishings, and delicious breakfasts. The breakfast room and patio have a wonderful view of Dingle Harbor (Sb-€65-110, Db-€85-170, Tb-€120-195, parking, The Wood, tel. 066/915-2788, www.castle wooddingle.com, info@castlewooddingle. com, Brian and Helen Heaton).

$$ **Tower View B&B** is a big, bright-yellow modern home just outside of town on a lovely wooded lot. This kid-friendly mini-farm, with pettable animals, rents eight fine rooms (Sb-€55-65, Db-€70-90, Tb-€100-120, Qb-€120-140, cash only, just past the roundabout on the west side of town on High Road, tel. 066/915-2990, www.towerviewdingle.com, info@tower viewdingle.com, Mary and Robbie Griffin).

$$ **Harbour Nights B&B** weaves together a line of old row houses to create a 14-room guesthouse facing the harbor (Sb-€50-70, Db-€60-80, Tb-€90-110, parking, just past the aquarium on The Wood, tel. 066/915-2499, mobile 087-686-8190, www.harbournightsguest house.com, info@dinglebandb.com, Seán and Kathleen Lynch).

Beyond the Bridge

A couple of worthwhile lodging options lie beyond the roundabout and bridge at the western end of town, a 20-minute walk from the center. These work best for drivers, as the heavily-trafficked, unlit bridge has no sidewalks (making it a dicey crossing for pedestrians, especially at night).

$$ **Milestone House** has six warmly decorated rooms, great views of Dingle Harbor, an ancient boundary stone in the front yard, and wonderful breakfasts. Friendly Barbara and Michael Carroll are brimming with sightseeing tips (Sb-€50-55, Db-€80-100, Tb-€120-150, Qb-€140-160, cash only, parking, tel. 066/915-1831, www.milestonedingle.com, milestone dingle@eircom.net).

$$ **Milltown House** has a secluded setting across Dingle Bay. With friendly giant Seamus the Irish wolfhound at large, it sports a pleasant glass breakfast conservatory and 10 comfortable rooms, 5 with fine bay views. Robert Mitchum slept here during the filming of *Ryan's Daughter*. Staffed primarily by friendly, nomadic, college-age youngsters, this grand guesthouse is worth considering (Sb-€80-100, Db-€90-135, seaview Db-€110-165, Tb-€150-175, less off-season, ask for Rick Steves discount with this book, cozy bar, tel. 066/915-1372, mobile 083-147-7363, www.milltownhouse.com, info@milltown house.com).

Hostels and Dorms

$ **Dingle Harbour Lodge** is a hostel-hotel hybrid with 29 rooms on the edge of town. You have the feeling of being a guest in a comfy hotel without the fancy prices (bunk in dorm room-€25-30, Db-€70-130, Tb-€80-140, family rooms, up a long driveway off The Wood past the aquarium, tel. 066/915-1577, www.dingleharbour lodge.com, info@dingleharbourlodge. com).

$ **Hideout Hostel** has 36 beds and is friendly and central, just across the lane from the movie theater. Michael (MEE-hall) grew up on this street and manages a relaxed, fun atmosphere while screening out loud stag/hen-party gangs (bunk in dorm room-€18, additional nights-€15, Db-€50, family room available, Dykegate Street, tel. 066/915-0559, www.thehide outhostel.com, info@thehideouthostel. com).

Transportation
Arriving and Departing

Tralee (Tra' Li), 30 miles from Dingle, is the region's transportation hub, with the nearest train station to Dingle. Most bus

All Roads Lead to Daingean Ui Chuis

The western half of the Dingle Peninsula is part of the Gaeltacht, where locals speak the Irish Gaelic language. In an effort to ward off English-language encroachment, all place names on road signs were controversially changed to Irish-only in the past decade. As you travel along Slea Head Drive (known as Ceann Sléibhe in Irish), refer to this cheat sheet of the most useful destination names. A complete translation of all Irish place names is included in the Gazetteer section at the back of the *Complete Road Atlas of Ireland* by Ordnance Survey.

English Name	Irish Gaelic Name	Pronounced
Dingle	*Daingean Ui Chuis*	DANG-un e koosh
Ventry	*Ceann Tra'*	k'yown (rhymes with crown) thraw
Slea Head	*Ceann Sléibhe*	k'yown SHLAY-veh
Dunquin	*Dún Chaoin*	doon qween
Blasket Islands	*Na Blascaodai*	nuh BLAS-kud-ee
Great Blasket Island	*An Blascaod Mór*	on BLAS-kade moor
Ballyferriter	*Baile an Fheirtearaigh*	BALL-yuh on ERR-ter-ig
Reasc Monastery	*Mainistir Riaisc*	MON-ish-ter REE-isk
Gallarus	*Gallaras*	GAHL-russ
Kilmalkedar	*Cill Mhaoil-cheadair*	kill moyle-KAY-dir
Annascaul	*Abhainn an Scáil*	ow'en on skahl
Lispole	*Lios Póil*	leesh pohl
Tralee	*Tra' Li*	traw lee

trips also make connections in Tralee. For more info, see Tralee's "Transportation" section at the end of this chapter.

BY BUS

Dingle has no bus station and only one bus stop; it's on the waterfront behind the SuperValu supermarket (look for the bus shelter with the roof made from an over-turned black *currach* boat). Most bus trips out of Dingle require at least one or two easy transfers (bus info tel. 01/836-6111).

From Dingle by Bus to: Galway (5/day, 6.5 hours), **Dublin** (4/day, 8-9 hours, transfer in Tralee and Limerick), **Rosslare** (1/day, 9 hours), **Tralee** (5/day, fewer off-season and Sun, 1.5 hours).

BY CAR

Drivers choose two roads into Dingle town: the narrow but exciting Conor Pass road; or the faster, easier, N-86 through Lougher and Annascaul (Abhainn an Scáil). Either route is 30 miles (48 km) from Tralee.

On a clear day, Conor Pass comes with incredible views over Tralee Bay and Brandon Bay. On the north slope approaching the pass, pull out at the waterfall. From here, there's a fun five-minute scramble to a dramatic glacier-created lake. Pause also at the summit viewpoint to look down on Dingle town and harbor.

If you're not staying overnight (i.e., parking at your B&B), use the waterfront parking lot extending west from the TI

(€1/hour, pay at meter in lot and display on dashboard, daily 8:00-18:00).

Ferry Shortcut: If you're connecting Dingle with the Burren or Doolin, use the Killimer-Tarbert ferry connection to avoid the 80-mile detour around the Shannon River. If you're going straight to or from Galway, the inland Limerick route is faster. But the ferry route is more scenic and direct to the Cliffs of Moher and the Burren (hourly, 20 minutes, no need to reserve, tel. 065/905-3124, www.shannon ferries.com).

BY PLANE
Kerry Airport, halfway between Tralee and Killarney, is a one-hour drive from Dingle. Short puddle-jumper flights connect the region to Dublin and make a visit to Dingle possible even for travelers with limited time. For more on Kerry Airport, see the end of this chapter.

DINGLE PENINSULA LOOP

Worth ▲▲▲, the Dingle Peninsula loop around Slea Head is about 30 miles (47 km) long and must be driven in a clockwise direction. It's easy by car, or it's a demanding four hours by bike—if you don't stop to catch your breath. Cyclists should plan on an early start (preferably by 9:00) to allow for enough time for rest, sightseeing, and lunch.

The Dingle Peninsula is 10 miles wide and runs 40 miles from Tralee to Slea Head. The top of its mountainous spine is Mount Brandon—at 3,130 feet, it's the second-tallest mountain in Ireland (after a nearby peak above Killarney that's almost 500 feet higher). While only a few tiny villages lie west of Dingle town, the peninsula is home to 50,000 sheep.

Slea Head Loop Drive
There are many great guided tours of the peninsula (see page 175), but this self-guided tour allows you to do it on

your own. I've provided distances to help locate points of interest—in kilometers so you can follow along with your rental-car odometer.

If you're driving, check your odometer at Oceanworld, as you leave Dingle (ideally, reset your odometer to zero). Even if you get off track or are biking, you can subtract the kilometers listed below to figure out distances between points. To get the most out of your trip, read through this entire section before departing. Then go step-by-step (staying on R-559 the entire way and following the brown *Ceann Sléibhe/Slea Head Drive* signs most of the way—through kilometer 37.7). Roads are very congested from mid-July to late August.

⊙ *Self-Guided Tour*
0.0 km: Leave Dingle town west along the waterfront, at Oceanworld. Driving out of town, on the left you'll see a row of humble "two up and two down" flats from a 1908 affordable-housing government initiative. Today, even these little places cost more than €200,000.

0.5 km: There's an eight-foot tide here. The seaweed was used to make formerly worthless land arable. (Seaweed is a natural source of potash—it's organic farming, before it was trendy.) Across the Milltown River estuary, the white **Milltown House** was Robert Mitchum's home for a year during the filming of *Ryan's Daughter*. (Behind that is a scruffy pitch-and-putt range—described on page 182.) Look for the narrow mouth of this blind harbor (in the distance at the opposite end of the bay, where Fungie the dolphin frolics) and the Ring of Kerry beyond that. Dingle Bay is so hidden that ships needed the Eask Tower to find its mouth.

0.7 km: At the roundabout, turn left over the bridge. On the far side, the blue building on the right was the site of a corn-grinding mill in the 18th century (you'll get a glimpse of the huge black waterwheel snug behind it). Today it's a

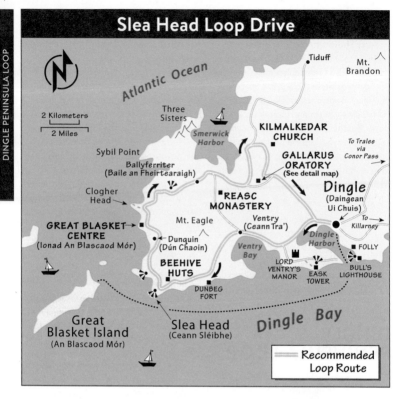

Slea Head Loop Drive

Atlantic Ocean

Tiduff

Mt. Brandon

Three Sisters

Smerwick Harbor

KILMALKEDAR CHURCH

To Tralee via Conor Pass

Sybil Point

GALLARUS ORATORY
(See detail map)

Ballyferriter
(Baile an Fheirtearaigh)

Clogher Head

REASC MONASTERY

Dingle
(Daingean Ui Chuis)

GREAT BLASKET CENTRE
(Ionad An Blascaod Mór)

Mt. Eagle

Ventry
(Ceann Tra')

To Killarney

Dunquin
(Dún Chaoin)

Dingle Harbor

FOLLY

BEEHIVE HUTS

Ventry Bay

LORD VENTRY'S MANOR

EASK TOWER

BULL'S LIGHTHOUSE

DUNBEG FORT

Great Blasket Island
(An Blascaod Mór)

Slea Head
(Ceann Sléibhe)

Dingle Bay

2 Kilometers
2 Miles

Recommended Loop Route

modern warehouse that shelters the **Dingle Distillery**. Not far beyond that, you'll go by the junction (on the right) where you'll complete this loop trip later. The gas station on your left is a handy spot to top up your tank (there aren't many gas options beyond this point).

1.3 km: The Milestone B&B is named for the stone **pillar** (*gallaun* in Irish) in its front yard. This pillar may have been a prehistoric grave or a boundary marker between two tribes. Half of the stone's length is buried underground. This peninsula, literally an open-air museum, is dotted with more than 2,000 such monuments dating from the Neolithic Age (4000 B.C.) through early Christian times. Another stone pillar stands in the field across the street (100 yards away, on the left), in the direction of the distant yellow manor house of Lord Ventry. The pillar's

Reasc standing stone

function today: cow scratcher.

Lord Ventry, whose family came to Dingle as post-Cromwellian War land-lords in 1666, built this mansion in about 1750. Today it houses an all-Irish-language boarding school for 140 high school girls.

As you drive past the **Ventry estate,** you'll pass palms, magnolias, and exotic flora, which were introduced to Dingle by Lord Ventry. The Gulf Stream is the source of the mild climate (it rarely snows here), which supports subtropical plants. Consequently, fuchsias—imported from Chile and spreading like weeds—line the roads all over the peninsula and redden the countryside from June through September. More than 100 inches of rain a year gives this area its "40 shades of green."

The old red-sandstone and slate-roof cottages along the roadside housed Ventry estate workers in the 1840s.

3 km: A brown sign reading *Holden's Leather Workshop* leads up a road to the left. This is the narrow lane that eventually leads to the trailhead up to **Eask Tower** (see page 181 for details on this active hiking/biking option).

4.6 km: Stay off the "soft margin" as you enjoy views of Ventry Bay, its four-mile-long beach (to your right as you face the water), and distant Skellig Michael, which you'll see all along this part of the route. **Skellig Michael**—an island jutting up like France's Mont St. Michel—contains the rocky remains of a sixth-century monastic settlement. Next to it is a smaller island, Little Skellig—a breeding ground for gannets (seagull-like birds with six-foot wingspans). In 1866, the first transatlantic cable was laid from nearby Valentia Island to Canada's Newfoundland. It was in use until 1965. Mount Eagle (1,660 feet), rising across the bay, marks the end of Ireland.

In the town of **Ventry**—a.k.a. Ceann Tra'—Irish is the first language. Ventry is little more than a bungalow holiday village today. Urban Irish families love to come here in the summer to immerse their kids in the traditional culture and wild nature. A large hall at the edge of the village is used as a classroom where big-city students come on field trips to learn the Irish language.

Just past the town, a lane leads left to a fine beach and mobile-home vacation community. An information board explains the history, geology, and bird life of this bay. The humble trailer park has

Slea Head loop drive

no running water or electricity. Locals like it for its economy and proximity to the beach. From here, a lane also leads inland to **Long's Horseriding Centre.**

During World War II, a German U-boat churned into this bay and put 28 Greek sailors ashore on this beach (and therefore onto neutral Irish soil). They were survivors from a merchant ship that the sub had sunk...not the kind of humanitarian gesture that German U-boat captains were known for making.

5.2 km: The bamboo-like **rushes** on either side of the road are the kind used to make the local thatched roofs. Thatching, which nearly died out because of the fire danger, is more popular now that anti-flame treatments are available. It's not the cheapest roofing alternative, however, as it's expensive to pay the few qualified thatchers who remain in Ireland. Black-and-white magpies fly overhead.

8.6 km: The Irish football (GAA) star Páidí Ó Sé (Paddy O'Shea) was a household name in Ireland. He won eight all-Ireland football titles for Kerry as a player. He then trained the Kerry team for many years, and then ran the pub on the left. A heroic **statue** stands outside today (also notice

the tiny grocery on the right; easy beach access from here).

9.2 km: The plain blue **cottage** hiding in the trees 100 yards off the road on the left (view through the white gate, harder to see in summer when foliage is thickest) was kept cozy by Tom Cruise and Nicole Kidman during the filming of *Far and Away*. Just beyond are fine views of the harbor and Dingle's stone tower.

10.7 km: *Taisteal go Mall* means "go slowly"; there's a red-colored, two-room **schoolhouse** on the right (20 students, two teachers). In summer it's used for Irish Gaelic courses for kids from the big cities. On the left is the small Celtic and Prehistoric Museum, a quirky private collection of prehistoric artifacts collected by a retired busker (musician) named Harris (€5, daily 10:00-17:30).

11.1 km: The circular mound (which looks like an elevated hedge) on the right is a late-Stone Age **ring fort.** In 500 B.C., it was a petty Celtic chieftain's headquarters—a stone-and-earth stockade filled with little thatched dwellings. These "Raths" survived untouched through the centuries because of superstitious beliefs that they were "fairy forts." While this site

Horseback riding on the beach

is unexcavated, archaeologists have found evidence that people have lived on this peninsula since well before 4000 B.C.

11.7 km: Look ahead up Mount Eagle at the patchwork of stone-fenced fields.

12.5 km: Dunbeg Fort (50 yards downhill on the left) is made up of a series of defensive ramparts and ditches around a central *clochan* (€3, includes video at nearby Stone House, May-Sept 9:00-18:00). A chunk of the fort was lost in February 2014, when waves from fierce winter storms caused a quarter of it to fall into the sea. Forts like this are the most important relics left from Ireland's Iron Age (500 B.C.-A.D. 500).

The modern stone-roofed dwelling across the street was built to blend in with the landscape and the region's ancient rock-slab architecture (A.D. 2000). It's the **Stone House,** a friendly restaurant with an adjacent visitors center, where you can check out a 10-minute video that gives a bigger picture of the prehistory of the peninsula (included with Dunberg Fort ticket). A traditional *currach* boat is permanently dry-docked in the parking lot.

12.6 km: Roughly 50 yards up the hill is a thatched **cottage** abandoned by a family named Kavanaugh 165 years ago, during the famine. With a few rusty and chipped old artifacts and good descriptions, it offers an evocative peek into the simple lifestyles of the area in the 19th century (€3, family-€10, May-Oct daily 10:00-17:00, closed Nov-April, tel. 066/915-6241, mobile 087-762-2617).

13.4 km: A group of **beehive huts** (*clochans*) is a short walk uphill (€3, daily 9:30-19:00, WC). These mysterious stone igloos, which cluster together within a circular wall, are a better sight than the similar group of beehive huts a mile down the road. Look over the water for more Skellig views.

Farther on, you'll ford a stream. There's never been a bridge here; this bit of road—nicknamed the "upside-down bridge"—was designed as a ford.

Building a Rock Fence

The Emerald Isle is as rocky as it is green. When the English took the best land, they told the Irish to "go to hell or go to Connaught" (the rugged western part of Ireland where the soil was particularly poor and rocky). Every spring, farmers "harvest" rocks driven up by the winter frost in order to plant more edible fare. Over generations, Irish farmers stacked these rocks into fences, which still divide so much of the land.

The fences generally have no visible gates. But upon closer look, you'll see a "V" built into the wall by larger rocks, which are then filled in with smaller rocks. When a farmer needs to move some cattle, he slowly unstacks the smaller rocks, moves the cattle through, and then restacks them. Flying low over western Ireland, the fields—alligatored by these rock fences—seem to stretch forever. And nearly all have these labor-intensive V-shaped gates built in.

14.9 km: Pull off to the left at this second group of beehive huts. Look downhill at the rocky field—in the movie *Far and Away*, that's where Lord Ventry evicted

Beehive hut

(read: torched) peasants from their cottages. Even without Hollywood, this is a bleak and godforsaken land. Look above, at the patches of land slowly made into **farmland** by the inhabitants of this westernmost piece of Europe. Rocks were cleared and piled into fences. Sand and seaweed were laid on the clay, and in time it was good for grass. The created land, if at all tillable, was generally used for growing potatoes; otherwise, it was only good for grazing. Much of it has fallen out of use now. Look across the bay at the Ring of Kerry in the distance and ahead at the Blasket Islands (**Na Blascaodai**).

16.1 km: At **Slea Head** (Ceann Sléibhe)—marked by a crucifix, a pullout, and great views of the Blasket Islands (described later)—you turn the corner on this tour. On stormy days, the waves are "racing in like white horses."

16.9 km: Pull into the parking lot (at *Dún Chaoin* sign) for **views** of the Blasket Islands and Dunmore Head (the westernmost point in Europe) and to review the roadside map (which traces your route) posted in the parking lot. The scattered village of Dunquin (Dún Chaoin) has many ruined rock homes abandoned

during the famine. Some are fixed up, as this is a popular place these days for summer homes. You can see more good examples of land reclamation, patch by patch, climbing up the hillside. Mount Eagle was the first bit of land that Charles Lindbergh saw after crossing the Atlantic on his way to Paris in 1927. Villagers here were as excited as he was—they had never seen anything so big in the air. About a kilometer down a road on the left, a plaque celebrates the 30th anniversary of the filming of *Ryan's Daughter*. From here, a trail leads down to a wild beach.

19.3 km: The Blasket Islands' residents had no church or cemetery on the island. This was their **cemetery.** The famous Blascaod storyteller Peig Sayers (1873-1958) is buried in the center. At the next intersection, drive down the lane that leads left (100 yards) to a small stone marker (hiding in the grass on the left) commemorating the 1588 shipwreck of the *Santa María de la Rosa* of the Spanish Armada. Below that is the often-tempestuous Dunquin Harbor. Island farmers—who on a calm day could row across in 30 minutes—would dock here and hike 12 miles into Dingle to sell their produce.

View from Slea Head

19.4 km: Back on the main road, follow signs to the *Ionad An Blascaod Mór* **(Great Blasket Centre).** You'll pass a village school from 1914 (its two teachers still teach 18 students, grades 1-6).

22.3 km: Leave the Slea Head Drive, turning left for the Great Blasket Centre (provides a worthwhile introduction to Blasket Islands—see page 203; also has a good cafeteria).

23.1 km: Back at the turnoff, head left (sign to *Louis Mulcahy Pottery*).

23.2 km: *Ryan's Daughter* film buffs will take a left turn here (a gravel lane) to visit the **schoolhouse** built for crucial scenes in that movie. Drive down the lane a hundred yards and park at the dead end. Walk the trail another hundred yards (through a couple of kissing gates), and you'll see the schoolhouse below, ringed by a low stone wall. Never intended to be a permanent structure, it's the only building still standing from that outdoor movie set of more than 40 years ago—and it's falling apart, too. But the lonely setting is memorable.

24.5 km: Passing land that was never reclaimed, think of the work it took to pick out the stones, pile them into fences, and bring up sand and seaweed to nourish the clay and make soil for growing potatoes. Look over the water to the island aptly named **"Sleeping Giant"**—see his hand resting happily on his beer belly.

24.9 km: Grab the **scenic pullout.** The view is spectacular. Ahead, on the right, study the top fields, untouched since the planting of 1845, when the potatoes didn't grow, but rotted in the ground. The faint vertical ridges of the potato beds can still be seen—a reminder of the Famine (easier to see a bit later). Before the Famine, 40,000 people lived on this peninsula. After the Famine, the population was so small that there was never again a need to farm so high up. Today, only 10,000 live on the peninsula.

The lousy farmland on both sides of the straight stretch of road was stripped of seven feet of peat (turf) in the 19th

century. The land may have provided a lot of warmth back then...but it provides no food today.

A breezy 15-minute walk leads out to **Clogher Head.** The dirt road stretches off to the left and peters out after 200 yards. But it's all open ground and easy to navigate. Just step carefully over bog puddles and head uphill through the rocky heather to the lumpy summit. There you'll be rewarded with postcard-worthy panoramic views.

30 km: The town of **Ballyferriter** (Baile an Fheirtearaigh), established by a Norman family in the 12th century, is the largest on this side of Dingle. The pubs serve grub, and the old schoolhouse is a museum. Its modest exhibits provide the best coverage of this very historic peninsula (€2.50, hours vary but usually June-Sept daily 10:00-17:30, closed Oct-April, tel. 066/915-6100, www.westkerry museum.com). The early Christian slab cross in front of the schoolhouse looks real. Tap it...it's fiberglass—a prop from the *Ryan's Daughter* bus-stop scenes.

31.9 km: At the T-junction, signs direct you left to *Daingean Ui Chuis* (Dingle, 11 km). Go left, via *Gallaras* (and still following *Ceann Sléibhe/Slea Head Drive* signs). Take a right over the barely noticeable yellow bridge, following signs to *Gallaras*.

32 km: A few yards beyond the bridge, you'll pass the Tigh Bhric pub on the right. Fifty yards up on the right is the easy-to-miss sign to *Mainistir Riaise* (Reasc Monastery); detour right up the lane. After 0.3 kilometers (up the unsigned turnout on your right), you'll find the scant remains of the walled **Reasc Monastery,** dating from the 6th to 12th centuries (free, always open). The inner wall divided the community into sections for prayer and business (cottage industries helped support the monastery). In 1975, only the stone pillar was visible, as the entire site was buried. The layer of black tar paper (near the base of the walls) marks where the original rocks stop and the excavators' reconstruction begins. The stone pillar is Celtic (c. 500 B.C.; pictured on page 194).

When the Christians arrived in the fifth century, they didn't throw out the Celtic society. Instead, they carved a Maltese-type cross over the Celtic scrollwork. The square building was an oratory (church—you'll see an intact oratory at the next stop). The round buildings would have been clochans—those stone igloo-type dwellings. One of the cottage industries operated by the monastery was a dou-ble-duty kiln. Just outside the wall (oppo-site the oratory, past the duplex *clochan*, at the bottom end), find a stone hole with a passage facing the southwest wind. This was the kiln—fanned by the wind, it was used for cooking and drying grain. Locals would bring their grain to be dried and ground, and the monks would keep a 10 percent tithe. With the arrival of the Normans in the 12th century, these small religious communities were replaced by relatively big-time state and church governments.

32.8 km: Return to the main road, and continue to the right.

34.6 km: At the big hotel (Smerwick

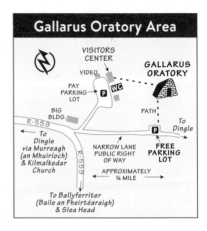

Harbor), turn left following the sign to *Gallaras* (Gallarus Oratory; rhymes with walrus).

35.6 km: At the big building (with the *camping* sign), make a hard right up the long lane bordered by hedges. To park for free near the **Gallarus Oratory**, continue along this lane (between the dashed lines) for a quarter-mile, to a five-car park-ing lot—which occasionally fills up (be prepared to cooperate with other drivers exiting this small lot). From the free park-

Gallarus Oratory

ing lot, a sign points you up the fuchsia-hedge-lined path leading you to the oratory (about 100 yards away).

If, however, you don't mind paying €3 to park, veer left just at the start of the hedge-lined lane into a large paved parking area. Nearby is a small visitors center with a coffee shop, WC, and video theater. I prefer to park for free in the small lot (especially since it's closer to the oratory). But many will appreciate the large lot, handy WC, and informative 17-minute video overview of the Dingle Peninsula's historic sights (daily 9:00-20:00, Oct-April until 19:00, tel. 066/915-5333). This visitors center is the business initiative of a man who simply owns the adjacent land—not the oratory. If you park in his lot, you'll have to pay the fee, even if you skip the facilities and walk up the public right-of-way lane.

The Gallarus Oratory, built about 1,300 years ago, is one of Ireland's best-preserved early Christian churches. Shaped like an upturned boat, its finely fitted dry-stone walls are still waterproof. Lower your head (notice how thick the walls are), walk inside, and give your eyes a moment to adjust to the low light. A simple, small

arched window offers scant daylight to the opposite wall, where the altar would have stood. Picture the interior lit by candles during medieval monastic services. It would have been tough to fit more than about a dozen monks inside (especially if they decided to do jumping jacks). Notice the holes once used to secure covering at the door, and the fine alternating stonework on the corners.

From the oratory, return to the main road and continue, following the brown *Ceann Sléibhe/Slea Head Drive* signs. If instead you continue up the narrow lane from the free parking lot, you'll end up on R-559 (a shortcut to Dingle that misses the Kilmalkedar Church ruins).

37.7 km: Bear right at the fork and immediately take a right at the next fork. Here you leave the Slea Head Drive and head for Dingle (10 km away) by staying on R-559 (do not follow Slea Head Drive from this point onward).

39.5 km: The ruined church of Kilmalkedar (Cill Mhaoil-cheadair, on the left) was the Norman center of worship for this end of the peninsula. It was built when England replaced the old monastic settlements in an attempt to centralize

Ruined church of Kilmalkedar

their rule. The 12th-century Irish Romanesque church is surrounded by a densely populated graveyard (which has risen noticeably above the surrounding fields over the centuries). In front of the church, you'll find the oldest medieval tombs, a stately early Christian cross (substantially buried by the rising graveyard and therefore oddly proportioned), and a much older ogham stone. This stone, which had already stood here 900 years when the church was built, is notched with the mysterious Morse code-type ogham script used from the third to seventh centuries. It marked a grave, indicating this was a pre-Christian holy spot. The hole was drilled through the top of the stone centuries ago as a place where people would come to seal a deal—standing on the graves of their ancestors and in front of the house of God, they'd "swear to God" by touching thumbs through this stone. You can still use this to renew your marriage vows (free, B.Y.O. spouse). The church fell into ruin during the Reformation.

40.2 km: Continue uphill, overlooking the water. You'll pass another **"fairy fort"** (Ciher Dorgan) on the right, dating back to 1000 B.C. (free, go through the rusty kissing gate). The bay stretched out below you is Smerwick Harbor. In 1580 a force of 600 Italian and Spanish troops (sent by the pope to aid a rebellion against the Protestant English) surrendered at this bay to the English. All 600 were massacred by the English forces, which included Sir Walter Raleigh.

41.7 km: At the crest of the hill, enjoy a three-mile-long coast back into Dingle town (sighting, as old-time mariners did, on the Eask Tower).

46.3 km: *Tog Bog E* means "take it easy." At the T-junction, turn left. Then turn right at the roundabout.

47.5 km: You're back in Dingle town. Well done.

BLASKET ISLANDS

This rugged group of six islands (Na Blascaodai) off the tip of Dingle Peninsula is close to the soul of Ireland. Today, Great Blasket—the largest and easiest island to visit—is little more than a ghost town overrun with rabbits on a peaceful, grassy, three-mile-long poem.

Blasket Islands

Life here was hard, but the sea provided for all, and no one went hungry. Each family had a cow, a few sheep, and a plot of potatoes. They cut their peat from the high ridge and harvested fish from the sea. To these folk, World War I provided a bonus, as occasional valuable cargo washed ashore from merchant ships sunk by U-boats. There was no priest, pub, or doctor. Because they were not entirely dependent upon the potato, island inhabitants survived the Famine relatively unscathed. These people formed the most traditional Irish community of the 20th century—the symbol of ancient Gaelic culture.

From this simple but proud fishing/farming community came three writers of international repute whose Gaelic works—basically tales of life on Great Blasket Island—have been translated into many languages. You'll find *Peig* (by Peig Sayers) and *The Islandman* (Thomas O'Crohan) in shops everywhere. But the most readable and upbeat is *Twenty Years A-Growing* (Maurice O'Sullivan), a somewhat true, Huck Finn-esque account of the author's childhood and adolescence and of island life as it was a hundred years ago.

The population of Great Blasket Island (An Blascaod Mór), once home to as many as 160 people, dwindled until the government moved the last handful of residents to the mainland in 1953. The island's café closed down some time ago, but the simple hostel reopened on a seasonal basis in 2014.

If you visit, you can explore the ghost town, and take the easy hike along the ridge running down the center of the island over spongy moss terrain. Bring everything you need (picnic lunch, water, rain gear), and plan on having no shelter if a squall blows in.

Getting to the Blasket Islands

In summer, various boats run between Dingle town and the Blasket Islands. The ride (which may include a quick look at Fungie the dolphin) traces the spectacular coastline all the way to Slea Head. The boats offer similar services from Dingle town and operate when there's enough demand. These boats also do three-hour ecotours for those interested in puffins, dolphins, and seals. The tricky landing at Great Blasket Island's primitive and slippery boat ramp makes getting off a challenge and landing virtually impossible in wet weather (€35 same-day round-trip; departs from the marina pier in Dingle at 11:00 and 14:00; returns from Great Blasket at 15:00 and 18:30, includes 45-minute ride each way with 2-3 hours to explore the island, call to confirm sailing times—or for more details on the €50 ecotours—tel. 066/915-1344 or mobile 087-672-6100).

Sights

▲▲GREAT BLASKET CENTRE (IONAD AN BLASCAOD MÓR)

This sight isn't on the Blasket Islands, but on the mainland facing the islands. It's an essential stop before visiting the islands—or a good place to learn about them without making the crossing. It fits neatly into the Dingle Peninsula Loop Trip.

This state-of-the-art Blascaod and Gaelic heritage center gives visitors the

Great Blasket Centre

best look possible at the language, literature, and way of life of Blasket Islanders. The building's award-winning design mixes interpretation and the surrounding countryside. Its spine, a sloping village lane, leads to an almost sacred view of the actual island. Watch the exceptional 20-minute video (shows on the half-hour), then hear the sounds, read the poems, browse through old photos, and gaze out the big windows at those rugged islands. Even if you never got past limericks, the poetry of these people—so pure and close to each other and nature—will have you dipping your pen into the cry of the birds.

Cost and Hours: €4, Easter-Oct Mon-Sat 10:00-18:00, Sun 11:00-18:00, closed Nov-Easter, fine cafeteria, well-signposted on the Slea Head Drive near Dunquin/Dún Chaoin, tel. 066/915-6444.

TRALEE

Tralee (traw-LEE) is County Kerry's transit hub. Many travelers will pass through, whether by car, train, or bus. Some stay an hour to see the sights.

This amiable town, near the base of the Dingle Peninsula, comes alive for the famous Rose of Tralee International Festival, usually held in mid-August. It's a celebration of arts and music, culminating in the election of the Rose of Tralee—the most beautiful woman at the festival (no matter which country she was born in, as long as she has Irish heritage).

Sights

▲KERRY COUNTY MUSEUM

Easily the best place to learn about life in Kerry, this museum (located in Ashe Memorial Hall in the center of town) has three parts: Kerry slide show, museum, and medieval-town walk.

Cost and Hours: €5; daily 9:30-17:30, Oct-May until 17:00 and closed Sun-Mon; tel. 066/712-7777, www.kerrymuseum.ie.

Visiting the Museum: Get in the mood by relaxing for 10 minutes through the Enya-style continuous slide show of Kerry's spectacular scenery. Then wander through 7,000 years of Kerry history in the museum (well-described, no need for free headphones). The Irish joke that when a particularly stupid guy moved from Cork to Kerry, he raised the average IQ in both counties—but this museum is pretty well done. It starts with good background info on the archaeological sites of Dingle, progresses through Viking artifacts found in the area, and goes right up to a video showing highlights of the Kerry football team (a fun look at Irish football, which is more like rugby than soccer). Good coverage is given to adventurous Kerryman Tom Crean, who survived three Antarctic expeditions with Scott and Shackleton (see page 180). The lame finale is a stroll back in time on a re-creation of Tralee's circa-1450 Main Street. Before leaving, horticulture enthusiasts will want to ramble through the rose garden in the adjacent park.

BLENNERVILLE WINDMILL

On the western edge of Tralee, just off the N-86 Dingle road, spins a restored mill originally built in 1780. Its eight-minute video tells the story of the windmill, which ground grain to feed Britain as that country steamed into the Industrial Age. In the 19th century, Blennerville was a major port

Tralee

for America-bound emigrants. It was also the home port where the *Jeanie Johnston* was built. This modern-day replica of a 19th-century ship tours Atlantic ports, explaining the Irish emigrant experience. Most of the time, it's docked and available to tour in Dublin, on the north shore of the River Liffey (see page 73).

Cost and Hours: €5 gets you a one-room emigration exhibit, the video, and a peek at the spartan interior of the working windmill; April-Oct daily 9:00-18:00, closed Nov-March, last entry 45 minutes before closing, tel. 066/712-1064.

Transportation
Arriving and Departing
BY TRAIN AND BUS

Travelers headed to or from Dingle will likely go through Tralee. The town's bus station (bus info tel. 066/716-4700) is across the parking lot from the train station (train info tel. 066/712-3522).

From Tralee by Train to: Dublin (every 2 hours, 6/day on Sun, 1 direct in morning, otherwise change in mellow Mallow, 4 hours), **Killarney** (8/day, 35 minutes).

By Bus to: Dingle (5/day, fewer off-season and on Sun, 1.5 hours), **Galway** (8/day, 4.5 hours), **Doolin/Cliffs of Moher** (2/day, 5 hours), **Ennis** (6/day, 3.5 hours, change in Limerick), **Rosslare** (2/day, 7.5 hours), **Shannon** (7/day, 3 hours), **Dublin** (7/day, 6 hours).

BY PLANE

Kerry Airport is a 20-minute drive from Tralee and a one-hour drive from Dingle. It's just off the main N-22 road, halfway between Killarney and Tralee. It has a half-dozen handy rental-car outlets and an ATM (airport code: KIR, tel. 066/976-4644, www.kerryairport.ie). Dingle Shuttle Bus is your best connection to Dingle town, but you must reserve in advance (€20/person one-way, minimum 3 passengers, mobile 087-250-4767, www.dingleshuttlebus.com). You can also connect to the airport via taxi (€25 from Tralee, €75 from Dingle) or bus (3/day to Dingle via Tralee). The Kerry Airport offers connecting flights from **Dublin** on Aer Lingus (2/day, www.aerlingus.com). International destinations served from this tiny airport include London's Stansted and Luton airports as well as Frankfurt Hahn airport.

Blennerville windmill stands proudly outside Tralee.

County Clare

Those connecting Dingle in the south with Galway up the coast to the north can take a joyride through the tidy villages and fascinating landscape of County Clare.

Overlooking the Atlantic, the dramatic Cliffs of Moher offer tenderfeet a thrilling hike. The Burren is a unique, windblown limestone moonscape that hides an abundance of flora, fauna, caves, and history. Ennis is a workaday city with a medieval history and a market bustle—ideal for anyone tired of the tourist crowds. If you stick around long enough to enjoy evening entertainment, join a tour-bus group in a castle for a medieval banquet in Kinvarra or meet up with traditional Irish music enthusiasts from around Europe for tin-whistling in Doolin.

COUNTY CLARE IN 1 DAY

A car is the best way to experience County Clare and the Burren. The region can be an enjoyable daylong drive-through. None of the sights takes long to see—but do get out and walk a bit.

If you have more time, you could take a walking tour (of the Cliffs of Moher or the Burren) or a cruise from Doolin (to see the Cliffs of Moher and Aran Island of Inisheer). For an overnight stay, good choices are Doolin and Ennis.

If you're driving from Dingle to Galway in one day, here's the best way to do it: Take the ferry shortcut (instead of the main N-21 road via Limerick that would add an 80-mile drive around the Shannon estuary to your journey). To reach the Tarbert-Killimer car ferry from Dingle, drive north from Tralee on N-69 via Listowel to Tarbert (hourly ferry, 20 minutes, no need to reserve, tel. 065/905-3124, www.shannonferries.com).

From Killimer, drive north on N-67 via Kilkee and Milltown Malbay. The village of Lahinch makes a good lunch stop. Then drive the coastal route to the Cliffs of Moher for an hour-long break. (You could wait to eat at the cafeteria at the cliffs, but big-bus tour groups can clog it at midday in summer.) The scenic drive from the cliffs through the Burren, with a few stops (covered in my self-guided tour), takes about two hours to Kinvarra and another hour from there to Galway. Consider partaking in the 17:30 medieval banquet at Dunguaire Castle, near Kinvarra.

By Train or Bus: If you're using trains or buses, your gateways to this region are Ennis from the south and Galway from the north. Linking the smaller sights within County Clare and the Burren by bus is still difficult: Book a one-day tour instead, out of Ennis or Galway.

Rick's Tip: *Visit an* **ATM in Ennis, Galway, or Lahinch** *before you enter this region. There are no ATMs in Doolin, Kilfenora, or Ballyvaughan.*

COUNTY CLARE AT A GLANCE

▲**Ennis** County's main market town (a great overnight base for nearby Shannon Airport) sporting fun trad music pubs, historic abbey ruins, and nearby Craggaunowen open-air folk park. See page 210.

▲▲▲**Cliffs of Moher** Steep cliffs bordered by a cliff-top trail—offering majestic, breathtaking coastal views—perched precariously 600 feet above the churning Atlantic. **Hours:** Trail always open. Visitors center—Daily May-Sept 9:00-19:30, gradually closing later toward midsummer—as late as 21:00 July-Aug, Oct-April 9:00-17:00. See page 217.

▲▲**The Burren** Desolate but botanically diverse, a limestone wonderland for hikers, sheltering evocative 4,000-year-old burial structures that witnessed man's transition from hunter-gatherer to farmer-herder. See page 220.

▲**Doolin** A friendly crossroads town drawing great musicians to its pubs and serving as an easy base for cruising along the Cliffs of Moher and day-tripping to the Aran Island of Inisheer. See page 218.

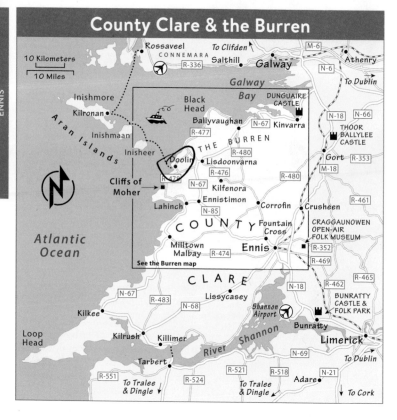

County Clare & the Burren

ENNIS

This bustling market town (pop. 24,000), rated ▲, is a handy transportation hub, with good rail connections to Limerick, Dublin, and Galway. Just 15 miles from Shannon Airport, it makes a good first- or last-night base for travelers not locked into Dublin flights. It also offers a chance to wander around an Irish town that is not reliant upon the tourist dollar (though not shunning it either). The great boxer Muhammad Ali visited the town in 2008 after discovering that one of his great-grandfathers had been born in Ennis. Locals credit his success to his fightin' Irish side.

Orientation

The center of Ennis is a tangle of contorted streets (often one-way). Use the steeple of Saints Peter and Paul Cathedral and the Daniel O'Connell monument column (at either end of the main shopping drag, O'Connell Street) as landmarks.

Tourist Information: The TI is just off O'Connell Street Square (July-Aug daily 9:30-17:30; March-June and Sept-Dec Mon-Fri 9:30-17:00, Sat 9:30-13:00, closed Sun; Jan-Feb Mon-Fri 9:30-17:00, closed Sat-Sun; tel. 065/682-8366).

Taxi: A good local bet is **Burren Taxis** (tel. 065/682-3456).

Walking Tours: Jane O'Brien leads 1.5-hour walking tours of Ennis departing from the TI (€8, mid-May-mid-Sept

Mon-Tue and Thu-Sat at 11:00; no tours Wed, Sun, and off-season; mobile 087-648-3714, www.enniswalkingtours.com).

Bus Tours: Barratt Tours runs bus tours of the Cliffs of Moher and the Burren (€27, May-Sept daily, Oct-April Sat only, departing from the TI at 10:30 and returning by 17:30, call to confirm schedule, tel. 061/333-100, mobile 087-237-5986, www.4tours.biz).

Sights

CLARE MUSEUM

This small but worthwhile museum, housed in the large TI building, has eclectic displays about ancient ax heads, submarine development, and local boys who made good—from 10th-century High King Brian Boru to 20th-century statesman Eamon de Valera. Coverage includes the Battle of Dysert O'Dea in 1318. One of the few Irish victories over the invading Normans, it delayed English domination of most of County Clare for another 200 years.

Cost and Hours: Free, Mon-Sat 9:30-13:00 & 14:00-17:30, closed Sun year-round and Mon Oct-May, tel. 065/682-3382, www.clarelibrary.ie.

ENNIS FRIARY

The Franciscan monks arrived here in the 13th century, and the town grew up around their friary (which is like a monastery). Today, it's still worth a look for its 15th-century limestone carvings (protected by a modern roof to keep their details from further deterioration).

Cost and Hours: €4, sometimes includes tour—depends on staffing, April-Sept daily 10:00-17:30, closed Oct-March, tel. 065/682-9100.

Visiting the Friary: If more than one guide is on duty, ask for a brief intro to the five carvings taken from the McMahon family tomb. The last one, of Christ rising on the third day, has a banner with a tiny swastika. But look closely: it's rotating as the rising sun would (the opposite of the infamous symbol of Nazism). Despite the swastika's detestable WWII association, it's actually a centuries-old symbol of good luck (the word "swastika" comes from Sanskrit and means "good"). Postwar visitors, unaware of the symbol's older meaning, misunderstood it and tried to rub it out of the carving, thus its very faint presence today.

The guides can also fully explain the crucifixion symbolism in the 15th-century *Ecce Homo* carving on a nearby pillar. Every item surrounding Christ on the cross has its own purposeful meaning (nothing on this carving is done just for the sake of decoration). It's an intriguing glimpse into how illiterate worshippers 600 years ago could understand icons even though they couldn't read.

Near Ennis

▲CRAGGAUNOWEN

This open-air folk museum nestles in a pretty forest, an easy 20-minute drive east of Ennis. All the structures are replicas, except for the small 16th-century tower house, which the park was built

Craggaunowen tower house

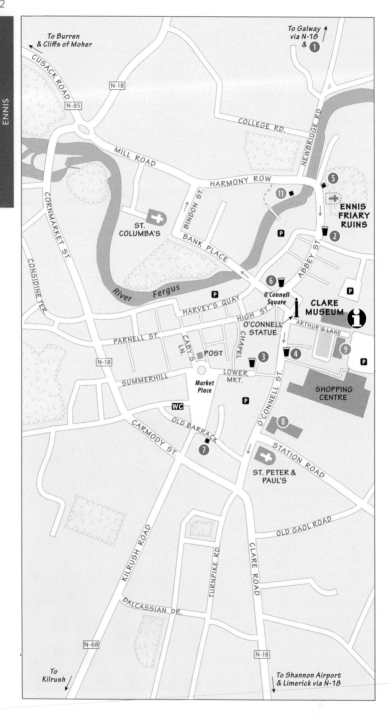

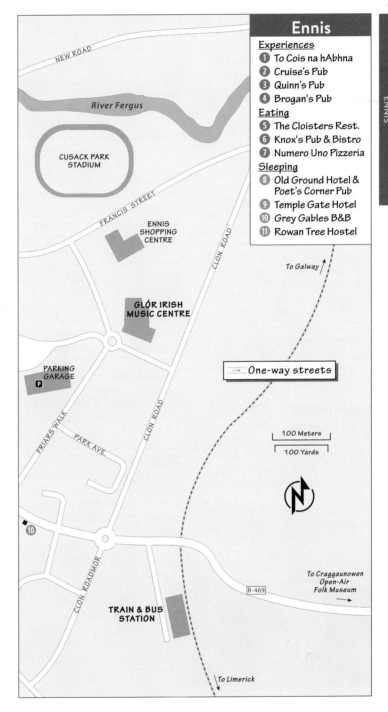

Ennis

Experiences
1. To Cois na hAbhna
2. Cruise's Pub
3. Quinn's Pub
4. Brogan's Pub

Eating
5. The Cloisters Rest.
6. Knox's Pub & Bistro
7. Numero Uno Pizzeria

Sleeping
8. Old Ground Hotel & Poet's Corner Pub
9. Temple Gate Hotel
10. Grey Gables B&B
11. Rowan Tree Hostel

NEW ROAD

River Fergus

CUSACK PARK STADIUM

FRANCIS STREET

ENNIS SHOPPING CENTRE

CLON ROAD

To Galway

GLÓR IRISH MUSIC CENTRE

PARKING GARAGE

→ One-way streets

FRIARS WALK

PARK AVE.

CLON ROAD

100 Meters

100 Yards

N

10

CLON ROADMOR

To Craggaunowen Open-Air Folk Museum

R-469

TRAIN & BUS STATION

To Limerick

around. A friendly weaver, spinning her wool on the castle's ground floor, is glad to tell you the tricks of her fuzzy trade. A highlight is the Crannog, a fortified Iron Age thatch-roofed dwelling built on a small man-made island, which gives you a grubby idea of how clans lived 2,000 years ago. A modern surprise hides in a corner of the park under a large glass teepee: the *Brendan*, the original humble boat that scholar Tim Severin sailed from Ireland to North America in 1976 (via frosty stepping stones like Iceland and Greenland). He built this boat out of tanned hides, sewn together using primitive methods, to prove that Ireland's St. Brendan may indeed have been the first to discover America, 900 years before Columbus and 500 years before the Vikings.

Cost and Hours: €9, Easter-Sept daily 10:00-17:00, shorter hours off-season, last entry one hour before closing, tel. 061/367-178, www.shannonheritage.com.

Getting There: The park is well-signposted nine miles (15 km) east of Ennis off R-469, which leads out of town past the train station.

Experiences
Glór Irish Music Centre

The town's modern theater center (*glór* is Irish for "sound") connects you with Irish culture. It's worth considering for traditional music, dance, or storytelling performances.

Cost and Hours: €12-25, year-round usually at 20:00, 5-minute walk behind TI,

Friar's Walk, ticket office open Mon-Sat 10:00-17:00, closed Sun, tel. 065/684-3103, www.glor.ie.

Rick's Tip: **Skip the commercialized Bunratty Castle and Folk Park,** *near the Shannon Airport, past Limerick on the road to Ennis. Leave it to the jet-lagged, big-bus American tour groups.*

Cois na hAbhna

This original stage show, housed in the local Cois na hAbhna Hall, is a fine way to spend an evening. Like other ongoing Comhaltas-sponsored cultural productions, it's a celebration of Irish performing arts. The show is presented in two parts. The first features great Irish music, song, and dance. After the break, you're invited to kick up your heels and take the floor as the dancers teach some famous Irish set dances. Phone ahead to see if a *ceilidh* (Irish dance gathering) is scheduled on off nights.

Cost and Hours: €10-15, sporadically May-Sept Wed and Fri at 20:30, call ahead to confirm, at edge of town on N-18 Galway road, tel. 065/682-4276, www.cois nahabhna.ie.

Traditional Music

Live music begins in the pubs at about 21:30. The best is **Cruise's** on Abbey Street, with music nightly year-round and good food (bar is cheaper than restaurant, tel. 065/682-8963). Other pubs offering weekly traditional music nights (generally on weekends, but schedules vary) are **Quinn's** on Lower Market Street (tel. 065/682-8148) and **Brogan's** on O'Connell Street (tel. 065/682-9480). The **Old Ground Hotel** hosts live music year-round in its pub (Thu-Sun, open to anyone); although tour groups stay at the hotel, the pub is low-key and feels real, not staged.

Craggaunowen

The Voyage of St. Brendan

It has long been part of Irish lore that St. Brendan the Navigator (A.D. 484-577) and 12 followers sailed from the southwest of Ireland to the "Land of Promise" (what is now North America) in a *currach*—a wood-frame boat covered with ox hide and tar. According to a 10th-century monk who poetically wrote of the journey, St. Brendan and his crew encountered a paradise of birds, were attacked by a whale, and suffered the smoke of a smelly island in the north before finally reaching their Land of Promise.

The legend and its precisely described locations still captivate modern readers. Parts of the tale hold up: The smelly island could well be the sulfuric volcanoes of Iceland. Other parts seem like devoted delirium: The holy monks claimed to have come upon Judas, chained to a rock in the middle of the ocean for all eternity.

A British scholar of navigation, Tim Severin, re-created the entire journey in 1976-1977. He and his crew set out from Brendan Creek in County Kerry in a *currach*. The prevailing winds blew them to the Hebrides, the Faeroe Islands, Iceland, and finally to Newfoundland. While this didn't successfully prove that St. Brendan sailed to North America, it did prove that he could have. (You can visit Tim Severin's boat at the Craggaunowen open-air folk museum.)

According to his 10th-century biographer, "St. Brendan sailed from the Land of Promise home to Ireland. And from that time on, Brendan acted as if he did not belong to this world at all. His mind and his joy were in the delight of heaven."

Eating

The Cloisters is next door to Ennis Friary, inhabiting equally historic 800-year-old walls. Its steak, lamb, and fish dishes are the best in town and are served in a tasteful atmosphere (€20-29 dinners served upstairs Tue-Sun 17:30-21:00, €13-19 bar menu served downstairs Tue-Sun 12:30-17:30, both sections closed Mon, Abbey Street, tel. 065/686-8198).

The **Old Ground Hotel** serves up hearty meals in its Poet's Corner pub (€10-15 lunches, €15-22 dinners, daily 12:00-21:00).

I like **Knox's Pub & Bistro** for better than average pub grub (daily 12:00-21:00, on Abbey Street, tel. 065/682-287). Or try one of the places mentioned under "Traditional Music," earlier.

The simple **Numero Uno Pizzeria** is good for an easy pub-free dinner (Mon-Sat 12:00-23:00, Sun from 15:00, on Old Barrack Street off Market Place, tel. 065/684-1740).

Sleeping

With central locations in mind, I've listed two fancy hotels that you'll share with tour groups, a B&B, and a hostel. Book direct.

$$$ Old Ground Hotel is a stately, ivy-covered 18th-century manse with 105 rooms and a family feel. Pan Am clipper pilots stayed here during the early days of transatlantic seaplane flights (Sb-€85-105, Db-€100-170, Db suite-€160-210, best rates online, 2-night weekend stays include a dinner, a few blocks from station at intersection of Station Road and O'Connell Street, tel. 065/682-8127, www.flynnhotels.com/Old_Ground_Hotel_Ennis, reservations@oldgroundhotel.ie).

$$$ Temple Gate Hotel's 70 rooms are more modern and less personal (Db-€80-140, Db suite-€150-190, rates lower off-season, just off O'Connell Street, in courtyard with TI, tel. 065/682-3300, www.templegatehotel.com, info@templegatehotel.com).

$$ Grey Gables B&B has 12 tastefully decorated rooms (Sb-€35-40, Db-€70-75, Tb-€99, Qb-€125, cash only, wheelchair access, parking, on Station Road 5 minutes from train station toward town center, tel. 065/682-4487, mailto:marykeane.ennis@eircom.net, Mary Keane).

$ Rowan Tree Hostel is a well-run budget option, centrally located beside the gurgling River Fergus. It incorporates a grand old gentleman's club into its modern additions with better-than-expected private rooms and tidy dorm rooms sleeping from 4 to 14. A pleasant café/bar rounds out the complex (dorm bed-€15-25, Sb-€30-40, Db-€49-69, Tb-€66-78, Qb-€79-99, on Harmony Row next to the bridge, coin laundry, kitchen, lockers, tel. 065/686-8687, www.rowantreehostel.ie, info@rowantreehostel.ie).

Transportation
Arriving and Departing
BY CAR

If you're not spending the night in Ennis (i.e., stowing your car at your B&B), parking is best in one of several pay-and-display lots (€1.30/hour, enforced Mon-Sat 9:30-17:30, free on Sun, pay at meter in lot and display ticket on dashboard, usually 3-hour maximum). The centrally located multistory lot on Market Place Square charges €5 per day (Mon-Sat 7:30-19:30, closed Sun).

BY TRAIN OR BUS

Ennis' train and bus station is located southeast of town, a 15-minute walk from the town center. To reach town, exit the station parking lot and turn left on Station Road, passing through a roundabout and past the Grey Gables B&B. Turn right after the Old Ground Hotel onto O'Connell Street.

From Ennis by Train to: Galway (5/day,

1.5 hours), **Limerick** (9/day, 40 minutes), **Dublin** (7/day, 3.5-4 hours, change in Limerick, Limerick Junction, or Athenry). Train info: Tel. 065/684-0444, www.irishrail.ie.

From Ennis by Bus to: Galway (hourly, 1.5 hours), **Dublin** (almost hourly, 4-5.5 hours), **Limerick** (hourly, 1 hour), **Ballyvaughan** (1/day, 2-3 hours), **Tralee** (6/day, 3.5 hours, change in Limerick), **Doolin** (5/day, 1.5-2.5 hours). Bus info: Tel. 065/682-4177, www.buseireann.ie.

BY PLANE

Shannon Airport is about 15 miles south of Ennis. The major airport in western Ireland comes with far less stress than its overcrowded counterpart in Dublin (airport code: SNN, airport tel. 061/712-000, www.shannonairport.ie). It has a TI (daily 6:30-19:30, Oct-May until 17:30, tel. 061/471-664), ATMs, Wi-Fi, a change bureau, and a baggage storage desk. Direct flights link to New York, Boston, London, Edinburgh, and various destinations on the European continent.

From Shannon Airport by Bus to: Ennis (bus #51 runs between the airport and the Ennis train station hourly, 20 minutes after the hour starting at 8:20, 30 minutes), **Galway** (hourly, 1.75 hours), **Limerick** (hourly, 30-50 minutes, can continue to Tralee—2 hours more, and Dingle—4/day, another 2 hours; bus tel. 061/313-333, www.buseireann.ie).

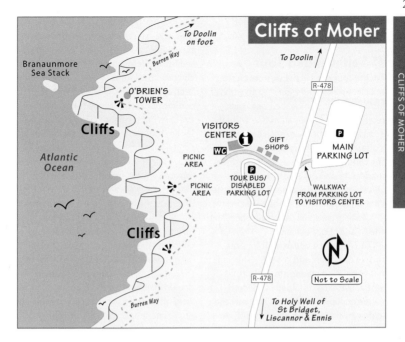

Sleeping near the Airport: Consider **$$$ Park Inn by Radisson Shannon Airport** (tel. 061/471-122, www.parkinn.com).

CLIFFS OF MOHER

The Cliffs of Moher live up to their name: They're called the Cliffs of "More"... because who would visit the Cliffs of Less? For five miles, the dramatic cliffs soar as high as 650 feet above the Atlantic. It's a sight worth ▲▲▲, and one of Ireland's great natural thrills.

Getting There

The Cliffs of Moher are located on R-478, south of Doolin. The parking lot across the road from the visitors center is for the general public; pay the attendant as you drive in. The lot next to the visitors center is for tour buses and disabled visitors.

If you're without wheels, it's easiest to get here on a bus tour out of Galway or Ennis; check the companies listed on page 222 (tours generally include the Burren).

Or—to see (but not visit) the cliffs—you can take a boat from Doolin, with either **Doolin2Aran Ferries** (tel. 065/707-5949, mobile 087-245-3239, www.doolin2 aranferries.com) or **O'Brien Line** (tel. 065/707-5555, www.obrienline.com). Boats depart from the pier in Doolin (same dock as Aran Islands boat, €20, runs daily April-Oct, 3/day, weather and tides permitting, call or go online for sailing schedule and to reserve).

Orientation

Cost: €6/person, includes parking and admission to the visitors center and its Atlantic Edge exhibit (buy tickets online for a 10 percent discount). It costs €2 to climb O'Brien's Tower.

Hours: Daily May-Sept 9:00-19:30, gradually later closing times toward midsummer—as late as 21:00 July-Aug, Oct-April 9:00-17:00.

Information: You'll find a TI and ATM in the visitors center—the Tolkienesque building tucked under the grassy hillside—flanked by six hobbit garages housing gift shops (across the street from the parking lot). Tel. 065/708-6141, www.cliffsof moher.ie.

⊙ Self-Guided Tour

For this tour, start in the **visitors center,** built in a concentric-circle layout with local stone. Upstairs is the Long Dock restaurant (which serves coffee and sub-stantial cafeteria-style meals until 19:00); a photo diorama showing aerial views of the cliffs and underwater photos of local marine life; and the toilets, where you can enjoy a huge panoramic photo of the cliffs on the stall doors as you wait in line. Downstairs is a small café, a gift shop, and the Atlantic Edge exhibit.

The **Atlantic Edge exhibit** focuses mainly on natural and geological history, native bird and marine life, and virtual interactive exhibits aimed at children (often occupied by adults). You may even learn why the cliffs are always windy. A small theater with an IMAX-style screen shows *The Ledge,* a film following a gannet who's a Jonathan Livingston Seagull wan-nabe, as he flies along the cliffs and then dives underwater, encountering puffins, seals, and even a humpback whale along the way.

After leaving the visitors center, walk 200 yards to the **cliff** edge and along the wall of the local Liscannor slate. Notice the squiggles made by worms, eels, and snails long ago when the slate was still mud on the seafloor.

For years, the Irish didn't believe in safety fences: just natural selection. Any-one could walk right up to the cliffs, until numerous fatal accidents prompted the hiring of "rangers"—ostensibly there to answer your questions and lead guided tours, but mainly to keep you from getting too close to the edge (wind gusts can be sudden, strong, and deadly).

O'Brien's Tower, built in 1835, marks the highest point of the cliffs (but isn't worth the fee to climb...30 feet up doesn't improve the views much). Hike five min-utes up to the tower and look to the north

(your right). In the distance, on windy days, you can see the Aran Islands wearing their white necklace of surf.

Nearby: Before leaving the area, drivers can take 10 minutes to check out the **Holy Well of St. Bridget,** located beside the tall column about a half-mile (1 km) south of the cliffs on the main road to Liscannor. In the short hall leading into the hillside spring, you'll find a treasure of personal and religious memorabilia left behind by devoted visitors seeking cures and bless-ings. A trickle of water springs from the hillside at the far end. To the right of the simple hall entrance is a stairway heading up into a peaceful graveyard. Be sure to check out the wishing tree (sometimes called a fairy bush or rag tree) halfway up the left side of the stairway. It's usually draped in ribbons tied to branches. These were offerings to saints as part of a healing ritual. The simple gray column outside was a folly erected over 150 years ago by a local landlord with money and ego to burn.

DOOLIN

Rated ▲, Doolin has long been a mecca for Irish musicians, who came together here to play before a few lucky aficio-nados: music lovers would come here directly from Paris or Munich. Now that the town is on the tourist map, the crowds and the foreigners have overwhelmed the musicians, and the quality of music is not as reliable. I prefer Dingle's richer music scene. Still, as long as fans crowd the pubs, the *bodhrán* beat goes on.

Orientation

The "town" is just a few homes and shops strung out along a valley road from the tiny harbor. Residents generally divide Doolin into an Upper and Lower Village. The Lower Village is the closest thing to a commercial center (with a couple of pubs and a couple of music shops).

Tourist Information: The TI at Hotel

Doolin in the Upper Village books lodging and Aran Islands boat trips (mid-March–Oct daily 9:00-19:00, tel. 065/707-5642).

Taxi: Try **Dial-A-Cab** (mobile 086-812-7049 or 087-290-2060).

Services: The Lodge Doolin, which rents rooms, offers an Internet café (€3/30 minutes, free to lodgers, daily 8:00-21:00) and a launderette (drop-off only, pick up clothes in 6 hours, no self-service, same hours as café). The staff can also recommend horseback riding, hiking, and fishing options.

Experiences
Traditional Music
Doolin is famous for three pubs, all featuring Irish folk music: Nearest the harbor, in the Lower Village, is **Gus O'Connor's Pub** (tel. 065/707-4168). A mile farther up the road, the Upper Village—straddling a bridge—is home to two other destination pubs: **McGann's** (tel. 065/707-4133) and **McDermott's** (tel. 065/707-4328). Music starts in the pubs between 21:30 and 22:00, finishing at about midnight. Get there before 21:00 if you want a place to sit, or pop in later and plan on standing. The *craic* is fine regardless. Pubs serve decent dinners before the music starts.

Cliffs of Moher Walks and Cruises
From Doolin, you can hike up the Burren Way along the coast for three miles to the Cliffs of Moher. Local guide and farmer Pat Sweeny operates **Doolin Cliff Walk,** leads walking tours that depart daily at 10:00 from O'Connor's Pub. The five-mile walk to the cliffs takes three hours and is not safe for kids under age 10; you catch the 13:30 bus back to Doolin (€5, May-Sept, mobile 086-822-9913, www.doolincliffwalk.com, phone ahead to reserve and check weather/trail conditions).

Two companies offer boat cruises along the Cliffs of Moher: **Doolin2Aran Ferries** (tel. 065/707-5949, mobile 087-245-3239, www.doolin2aranferries.com) and **O'Brien Line** (tel. 065/707-5555, www.obrienline.com). Boats depart from the pier in Doolin (same dock as Aran Islands boat, €20, runs daily April-Oct, 3/day, weather and tides permitting, call or go online for sailing schedule and to reserve).

Eating
Cullinans is the only gourmet option, it faces the T-intersection as you come down the hill into the Upper Village (Easter-Sept Mon-Tue and Thu-Sat 18:00-21:00, closed Sept-Easter and Wed and Sun year-round, reservations smart in summer, tel. 065/707-4183).

The **Ivy Cottage** in the Lower Village, just past the bridge, has a pleasant, leafy tea garden out front. They do a dish of the day as well as simple sandwiches, quiche, or chowder (daily 10:00-18:00). Next door, the **Sea Salt** chipper uses the same kitchen and does reasonable fish-and-chips to take away and enjoy with the coastal view of your choice (daily 12:00-21:00).

Strolling the Cliffs of Moher

Doolin pub

Doolin's reputation for pub grub is consistently good. In the Lower Village, try **Gus O'Connor's Pub,** and in the Upper Village, give **McGann's** a spin. **Mac's Daybreak** is the town market (Mon-Sat 8:30-20:00, Sun 9:00-20:00, on R-478 above town next to the Harbour View B&B).

Sleeping

$$ Harbour View B&B is a fine modern house with six rooms, overlooking the coast a mile from the Doolin fiddles. Amy Lindner keeps the place immaculate, and serves bread from a bakery out back (Sb-€50-65, Db-€70-100, Tb-€99-135, on main road halfway between Lisdoonvarna and Cliffs of Moher, next to Aran View Market and gas station, tel. 065/707-4154, www.harbourviewdoolin.com, clarebb@eircom.net).

$$ The Lodge Doolin is a modern compound of four stone buildings with 21 bright, airy, good-value rooms (Sb-€35-45, Db-€60-80, Tb-€90-110, Qb-€100-140, located halfway between Upper and Lower Villages, tel. 065/707-4888, mobile 087-223-9638, www.doolinlodge.com, info@doolinlodge.com). The lodge offers a grab bag of handy amenities.

$$ Half Door B&B is the coziest place around, with six woody rooms and a pleasant sun porch. It's just a short walk from the best pubs in the Upper Village (Sb-€45-60, Db-€70-85, Tb-€115-120, Qb-€140, family room, cash only, a keg's roll from McDermott's pub, tel. 065/707-5959, www.halfdoordoolin.com, ann@halfdoordoolin.com).

$ Doolin Hostel, right in the Lower Village with 90 beds, caters creatively to the needs of backpackers in town for the music. Friendly Anthony and Dierdre are on top of the local scene (dorm bed-€16-25, Db-€53-69, Tb-€64-82, Qb-€70-100, kitchen, Lower Village, mobile 087-282-0587, www.doolinhostel.ie, anthony@doolinhostel.ie).

Transportation
From Doolin by Bus to: Galway (5/day, 1.5-2 hours), **Ennis** (5/day, 1.5-2.5 hours). Buses depart from the Doolin Hostel.

From Doolin by Ferry to the Aran Islands: For the full rundown on ferries from Doolin, see page 264. In short, if you want to day-trip from Doolin, go with either **Doolin2Aran Ferries** (tel. 065/707-5949, mobile 087-245-3239, www.doolin2aranferries.com) or **O'Brien Line** (tel. 065/707-5555, www.obrienline.com), both of which take you to the closest island, Inisheer (with time to explore), then back along the Cliffs of Moher. If you want to visit either or both of the farther islands—Inishmaan and Inishmore—plan on an overnight, due to the transit time involved.

THE BURREN

Burren literally means the "rocky place." This 10-square-mile limestone plateau, worth ▲▲, is so barren that a disappointed surveyor in the 1650s described it as "a savage land, yielding neither water enough to drown a man, nor a tree to hang him, nor soil enough to bury him." Evidently, he wasn't much of a botanist: The Burren is a unique ecosystem, with flora that has managed to adapt since the last Ice Age, 10,000 years ago. It's also rich in prehistoric and early Christian sites, including dozens of Iron Age stone forts. When the first human inhabitants of the Burren arrived about 6,000 years ago, they cut down its trees with short-sighted slash-and-burn methods, which accelerated erosion of the topsoil (already scoured to a thin layer by glaciers). Those ancient people are partially responsible for the stark landscape we see today.

Tours
Walking Tours
Most travelers zip through the seemingly barren Burren without stopping, grateful for the soft soil they garden back home. But healthy hikers and armchair natural-

Hotel Doolin

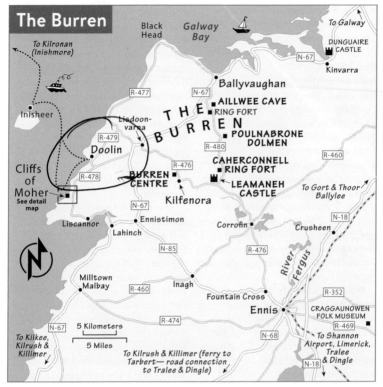

The Burren

To Galway

Black Head
Galway Bay

DUNGUAIRE CASTLE
N-67
Kinvarra

To Kilronan (Inishmore)

Inisheer

R-477
N-67
Ballyvaughan
AILLWEE CAVE
RING FORT

THE BURREN

POULNABRONE DOLMEN

Lisdoon-varna
R-479
Doolin
R-480
R-460

R-476
CAHERCONNELL RING FORT

Cliffs of Moher
See detail map
R-478
BURREN CENTRE
LEAMANEH CASTLE

To Gort & Thoor Ballylee

Kilfenora
N-67

Liscannor
Ennistimon
Lahinch
Corrofin
Crusheen
N-18

N-85
R-476

River Fergus

Milltown Malbay
R-460
Inagh
Fountain Cross
R-352

Ennis
CRAGGAUNOWEN FOLK MUSEUM
R-469

To Kilkee, Kilrush & Killimer
N-67
5 Kilometers
5 Miles
N-68
To Shannon Airport, Limerick, Tralee & Dingle

To Kilrush & Killimer (ferry to Tarbert— road connection to Tralee & Dingle)
N-18

COUNTY CLARE
THE BURREN

ists should slow down and take a closer look. Be sure to wear comfortable shoes for the wet, uneven, rocky bedrock. These local guides can bring the harsh landscape to life.

From Ballyvaughan (at the northern entrance to the Burren): **Shane Connolly** leads in-depth, three-hour guided walking tours, explaining the region's history, geology, and diverse flora, and the role humans have played in shaping this landscape. This proud farmer really knows his stuff (€15, daily at 10:00 and 15:00, call to book and confirm meeting place in Ballyvaughan, tel. 065/707-7168, http://homepage.eircom.net/~burrenhillwalks).

From Kilfenora (at the southern entrance to the Burren): **Tony Kirby** leads regularly scheduled two-hour "Heart of Burren Walks" during the summer, and the rest of the year by appointment. His

expertise peels back the rocky surface to reveal the surprisingly fascinating natural and human history that has created this unique region (€20, June-Aug Tue-Thu at 14:30, Fri-Sun at 10:30, meet at the Burren Centre in Kilfenora, tel. 065/682-7707, mobile 087-292-5487, www.heartofburrenwalks.com, info@heartofburrenwalks.com).

From Oughtmama (roughly halfway between Ballyvaughan and Kinvarra): The **Burren Wild Tour** offers interactive walking tours of the Burren. Their motto, "Don't be nuts, get off the bus," distinguishes their active hiking focus from sedate bus tours. They offer two tours: The first is a gentle one-hour walk (€10, daily at 10:30); the second is a more rugged 2.5-hour hike (€25, by appointment only, at 12:15, mobile 087-877-9565, www.burrenwalks.com). Both walks start from the Connolly family farm near the village of Oughtmama, inland from Bell-harbour; call ahead for directions.

Bus Tours

From Galway: Three companies—**Lally Tours, Healy Tours,** and **Galway Tour Company**—run standard all-day bus tours (€25-45, up to 25 percent discount if you book online). Their similar tours of the Burren do a loop south of Galway, covering Kinvarra, Aillwee Cave, Poulnabrone Dolmen, and the Cliffs of Moher (on a 2-hour lunch stop). Galway Tour Company also offers an all-day tour connecting the Cliffs of Moher, Doolin (lunch stop), and the island of Inisheer—a handy way to get a quick taste of an Aran Island and the cliffs in one day. For specifics, see page 232.

From Ennis: **Barratt Tours** runs bus tours of the Cliffs of Moher and the Burren (€27, May-Sept daily, Oct-April Sat only, departing from TI at 10:30 and returning by 17:30, call to confirm schedule, tel. 061/333-100, mobile 087-237-5986, www.4tours.biz).

⊙ Burren Driving Tour

This self-guided drive from Kilfenora to Ballyvaughan offers the best quick swing through the historic Burren.

• *Begin in the town of Kilfenora, eight kilometers (5 miles) southeast of Lisdoonvarna, at the T-intersection where R-476 meets R-481.*

Kilfenora

This town's hardworking, community-run **Burren Centre** shows an informative 10-minute video explaining the geology and botany of the region, and then ushers you into its enlightening museum exhibits (€6, daily June-Aug 9:30-17:30, mid-March-May and Sept-Oct 10:00-17:00, closed Nov-mid-March, tel. 065/708-8030, www.theburrencentre. ie). You'll also see copies of a fine eighth-century golden collar and ninth-century silver brooch (now in Dublin's National Museum).

The ruined **church** next door has a couple of 12th-century crosses, but isn't much to see. Mass is still held in the church, which claims the pope as its bishop. As the smallest and poorest diocese in Ireland, Kilfenora was almost unable to function after the Great Potato Famine, so in 1866 Pope Pius IX supported the town as best he could—by personally declaring himself its bishop.

For lunch in Kilfenora, consider the cheap and cheery **Burren Centre Tea Room** (daily 9:30-17:30, located at far back of building) or the more atmospheric **Vaughan's Pub.** If you're spending the night in County Clare, make a real effort to join the locals at the fun set-dancing get-togethers run by the Vaughans in the **Barn Pub,** adjacent to their regular pub. This dance scene is a memorable treat (€5, Sun at 21:30, mid-May-mid-Sept also Thu at 21:30, call ahead to confirm schedule, tel. 065/708-8004).

Leamaneh Castle

Cloudgazing in the Burren

• *To continue from Kilfenora into the heart of the Burren, head east out of town on R-476. After about five kilometers (3 miles), you'll come to the junction with northbound R-480. Take the sharp left turn onto R-480, and slow down to gaze up (on the left) at the ruins of...*

Leamaneh Castle

This ruined shell of a fortified house is closed to everyone except the female ghost that supposedly haunts it. From the outside, you can see how the 15th-century fortified tower house (the right quarter of the remaining ruin) was expanded 150 years later (the left three-quarters of the ruin). The castle evolved from a refuge into a manor, and windows were widened to allow for better views as defense became less of a priority.

• *From the castle, continue north on R-480 (direction: Ballyvaughan). After about eight kilometers (5 miles), you'll hit the start of the real barren Burren. Keep an eye out for the next stop.*

Caherconnell (Cahercommaun) Ring Fort

One of many ring forts in the area, you can see the low stone profile of Caherconnell to the left on the crest of a hill just off the road. You can park in the gravel lot and walk up to the small visitors center and handy café for an informative 20-minute film followed by a quick wander through the small fort. The fort sometimes features a sheepherding demo with dogs (generally at 12:00 and 15:00—call to confirm).

Cost and Hours: €7, €9.50 includes sheepherding demo, daily July-Aug 10:00-18:00, Easter-June and Sept-Oct 10:30-17:30, closed Nov-Easter, tel. 065/708-9999, www.caherconnell.com.

• *The stretch from the ring fort north to Ballyvaughan offers the starkest scenery. Soon you'll see a 10-foot-high stone structure a hundred yards off the road to the right (east, toward an ugly gray metal barn). Pull over for a closer look.*

Poulnabrone Dolmen

While it looks like a stone table, this is a portal tomb. Two hundred years ago, locals called this a "druids' altar." Five thousand years ago, it was a grave chamber in a cairn of stacked stones. Amble over for a look. (It's crowded with tour buses at midday, but it's all yours early or late.)

Poulnabrone Dolmen

Botany of the Burren

The Burren is a story of water, rock, geological force, and time, supporting the greatest diversity of plants in Ireland. It's an orgy of cross-pollination that attracts more insects than Doolin does music lovers—even beetles help out. Limestone, created from layers of coral, seashells, and mud, is the bedrock of the Burren. (The same formation resurfaces 10 miles or so out to sea to form the Aran Islands.)

Geologic forces in the earth's crust heaved up the land, and the glaciers swept it bare and shattered it like glass under their weight—dropping boulders as they receded. Rain, reacting naturally with the limestone to create a mild but determined acid, slowly drilled potholes into the surface. Rainwater cut through weak zones in the limestone, leaving crevices on the surface and one of Europe's most extensive systems of caves below. Algae grew in the puddles, dried into a powder, and combined with bug parts and rabbit turds (bunnies abound in the Burren) to create a very special soil. Plants and flowers fill the cracks in the limestone. Grasses and shrubs don't do well here, and wild goats eat any trees that try to grow, giving tender flowers a chance to enjoy the sun. Different flowers appear throughout the months (they're best in June and July), sharing space rather than competing. Mediterranean and Arctic wildflowers bloom side by side here—as they do nowhere else.

Wander about for some quiet time with the wildflowers and try to think like a geologist. You're walking across a former seabed, dating from 250 million years ago when Ireland was at the equator (before continental drift nudged it north). Look for white smudges of fossils. Stones embedded in the belly of an advancing glacier ground the scratches you see in the rocks. The rounded boulders came south from Connemara, carried on a giant conveyor belt of ice, then left behind when the melting glaciers retreated north.
• As you drive away from the dolmen (continuing north), look for the 30-foot-deep sinkhole beside the road on the right (a collapsed cave). From here, R-480 winds slowly downhill for about six kilometers (4 miles), eventually leaving the rocky landscape behind and entering a comparatively lush green valley. Watch for a broad left bend in the road with a grove of trees beside the road on the left and park in the gravel pull-out on the right, just opposite the grove. (It's not marked, but if you reach the Aillwee Cave right turn, you've gone 50 yards too far.) Get out of the car and carefully cross the busy road to find a...

Hidden Ring Fort
This grove of trees hides a gorgeous secluded ring fort (free and unattended). Walk the rim of the circular earthen ring, stepping over roots, and notice the swampy moat beneath the outer edge. As Iron Age ring forts go, this one has a mystical vibe appreciated by others. Find the old stump in the center of the fort where old coins have been left undisturbed in the hopes of wishes coming true. A quiet 10 minutes here can be magic.
• Just beyond, on the right, you'll find the turn up to...

Aillwee Cave
As this is touted as "Ireland's premier show cave," I couldn't resist a look. While

fairly touristy and not worth the time or money if you've seen a lot of caves, it's the easiest way to sample the massive system of caves that underlie the Burren. Your guide walks you 300 yards into the plain but impressive cave, giving a serious 40-minute geology lesson. During the Ice Age, underground rivers carved countless caves such as this one. Brown bears, which became extinct in Ireland a thousand years ago, found them great for hibernating.

Rick's Tip: *If you take the tour, also* **take a sweater**: *The cave is a constant 50°F.*

Just below the cave (and on the same property) is the **Burren Birds of Prey Centre,** with caged owls, eagles, hawks, and falcons (bird demonstrations likely at 12:00, 14:00, and 16:00—but call for daily schedule).

Adjacent to the cave, the **Hawk Walk** gets visitors face-to-beak with a Harris hawk, "the world's only social raptor." After a brief training session, an instructor leads a small group on a 45-minute hike up a nearby mountain trail. Those paying the stiff €70 fee get to launch and call back the bird to perch on their arm (limited slots, must reserve).

Cost and Hours: Cave-€12, bird center-€10, €18 combo-ticket includes both sights but not Hawk Walk; open daily at 10:00, last tour at 18:30 July-Aug, otherwise 17:30, Dec-Feb call ahead for limited tours; clearly signposted just south of

The lush mystery of a hidden ring fort

Ballyvaughan, tel. 065/707-7036, www.aillweecave.ie.

• *Continuing on, our final destination is...*

Kinvarra

This tiny town, between Ballyvaughan and Galway (30 minutes from Ballyvaughan and an hour from Galway), is waiting for something to happen in its minuscule harbor. It faces Dunguaire Castle, a four-story tower house from 1520 that stands a few yards out in the bay.

The touristy but fun **Dunguaire Castle medieval banquet** is Kinvarra's most worthy attraction (€50, cheaper if you book online, mid-April-mid-Oct Fri-Tue at 17:30 and sometimes at 20:45, closed Wed-Thu and mid-Oct-mid-April, reservations tel. 061/360-788, castle tel. 091/637-108, www.shannonheritage.com). **Warning:** This company also operates banquets at two other castles in the region, so be sure that you make your reservation for the correct castle.

The evening is as intimate as a gathering of 55 tourists under one time-stained, barrel-vaulted ceiling can be. You get a decent four-course meal with wine (or mead if you ask sweetly), served amid an entertaining evening of Irish tales and folk songs. Remember that in medieval times, it was considered polite to flirt with wenches. It's a small and multitalented cast: one harpist and three singer/actors who serve the "lords and ladies" between tunes. The highlight is the 40-minute stage show, which features songs and poems by local writers, and comes with dessert.

You can visit the castle itself by day without taking in an evening banquet (€6, daily 10:00-16:30).

Sleeping in Kinvarra: **$$ Cois Cuain B&B** is a small but stately house with a garden, overlooking the square and harbor of the most charming village setting you'll find. Mary Walsh rents three super-homey rooms (Db-€60-75, cash only, The Quay, tel. 091/637-119).

Galway

With 76,000 people, Galway feels like a boomtown—rare in Western Ireland. Until the recession hit in 2008, it was the fastest growing city in Ireland. It's still its most international city: One out of every four residents was born outside of Ireland.

While Galway has a long and interesting history, precious little from old Galway survives. What does remain has the interesting disadvantage of being built in the local limestone, which, even if medieval, looks like modern stone construction.

What the lively university town lacks in sights it makes up for in ambience. Wander its medieval streets, with their delightful mix of colorful facades, labyrinthine pubs, weather-resistant street musicians, and steamy eateries. After dark, blustery Galway heats up, with a fine theater and a pub scene that even attracts Dubliners. Visitors mix with old-timers and students as the traditional music goes round and round.

Galway is well-connected by train to Dublin. And it's a convenient jumping-off point for visiting the Aran Islands (a Gaelic cultural preserve), the Burren (an area of geologic and prehistoric interest, to the south), and the Connemara (a region steeped in Irish history, to the north).

GALWAY IN 1 DAY

Galway's sights are little more than pins on which to hang the old town. The joy of Galway is its street scene. Although you could see the town's sights in a couple of hours, the best part of Galway is its nightlife—starring traditional music.

Here are efficient plans:

By Car: Spend two nights in Galway and the day visiting the Aran Islands. For example: If you're driving north from Dingle, visit the Cliffs of Moher and the Burren en route, and spend the night in Galway. In Galway, stroll from Eyre Square to Galway Bay, seeking out a pub with music. On the next day, visit the Aran Islands (Inishmore), then return to Galway to enjoy another music-filled evening. Take off early the following day to drive through the region of Connemara on your way to Northern Ireland.

By Public Transportation and Tour: Arrive in Galway by train or bus. Spend two nights there, and use your full day for a day trip to the Aran Islands (my top choice), the Burren and Cliffs of Moher, or the Connemara region. Tour companies make day trips to all three regions cheap and easy.

GALWAY AT A GLANCE

▲ **Medieval Galway's "Latin Quarter"** Half-mile-long pub and shopping zone linking Eyre Square to Galway Bay, dotted with old Norman architecture and weather-proof street musicians. See page 233.

▲ **Eyre Square** Grassy fair-weather community gathering spot, location of beloved JFK speech and haven for Frisbee tossers and dog walkers. See page 235.

▲ **Cathedral of St. Nicholas** Town's 50-year-old center of worship with richly appointed interior and quirky mosaic honoring JFK at the foot of Christ's Ascension. See page 235.

▲ **Salthill** Unpretentious suburb with a popular swimming beach and waterfront promenade, fun for strollers, joggers, and cyclists. See page 236.

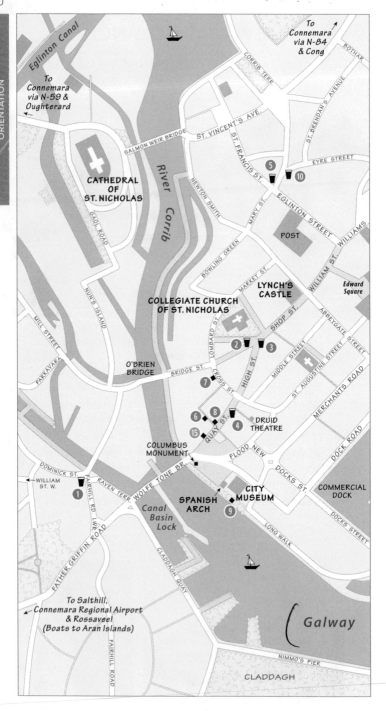

Eglinton Canal

To
Connemara
via N-59 &
Oughterard

To
Connemara
via N-84
& Cong

CORRIB TERR.

BOTHAR

ST. BRENDAN'S AVENUE

SALMON WEIR BRIDGE

ST. VINCENT'S AVE.

ST. FRANCIS ST.

EYRE STREET

River Corrib

CATHEDRAL
OF
ST. NICHOLAS

GAOL ROAD

NEWTON SMITH

MARY ST.

5

10

EGLINTON STREET

WILLIAM ST.

WILLIAMS

POST

BOWLING GREEN

MARKET ST.

LYNCH'S
CASTLE

Edward
Square

MILL STREET

NUN'S ISLAND

COLLEGIATE CHURCH
OF ST. NICHOLAS

SHOP ST.

APPLEGATE STREET

PARKAVARA

LOMBARD ST.

O'BRIEN
BRIDGE

BRIDGE ST.

CROSS ST.

HIGH ST.

2

3

MIDDLE STREET

ST. AUGUSTINE STREET

MERCHANTS ROAD

7

6

8

15

QUAY ST.

4

DRUID
THEATRE

DOCK ROAD

COLUMBUS
MONUMENT

FLOOD

NEW

DOCKS ST.

COMMERCIAL
DOCK

DOMINICK ST.

WILLIAM
ST. W.

FAIRHILL RD. LWR.

RAVEN TERR.

WOLFE TONE BR.

1

SPANISH
ARCH

9

CITY
MUSEUM

DOCKS STREET

FATHER GRIFFIN ROAD

Canal
Basin
Lock

CLADDAGH QUAY

LONG WALK

To Salthill,
Connemara Regional Airport
& Rossaveel
(Boats to Aran Islands)

Galway

FAIRHILL ROAD

NIMMO'S PIER

CLADDAGH

Galway Bay Hotel

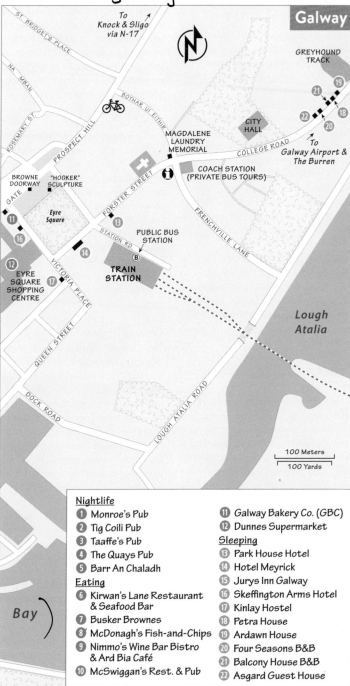

To
Knock & Sligo
via N-17

GREYHOUND
TRACK

St BRIDGET'S PLACE

NA MBAN

ROSEMARY ST.

PROSPECT HILL

BÓTHAR UÍ EITHIR

MAGDALENE
LAUNDRY
MEMORIAL

CITY
HALL

COLLEGE ROAD

To
Galway Airport &
The Burren

BROWNE
DOORWAY

"HOOKER"
SCULPTURE

GATE

Eyre
Square

FORSTER STREET

COACH STATION
(PRIVATE BUS TOURS)

STATION RD

PUBLIC BUS
STATION

FRENCHVILLE LANE

EYRE
SQUARE
SHOPPING
CENTRE

VICTORIA PLACE

TRAIN
STATION

Lough
Atalia

QUEEN STREET

DOCK ROAD

LOUGH ATALIA ROAD

100 Meters
100 Yards

Bay

Nightlife
1 Monroe's Pub
2 Tig Coili Pub
3 Taaffe's Pub
4 The Quays Pub
5 Barr An Chaladh
Eating
6 Kirwan's Lane Restaurant
& Seafood Bar
7 Busker Brownes
8 McDonagh's Fish-and-Chips
9 Nimmo's Wine Bar Bistro
& Ard Bia Café
10 McSwiggan's Rest. & Pub

11 Galway Bakery Co. (GBC)
12 Dunnes Supermarket
Sleeping
13 Park House Hotel
14 Hotel Meyrick
15 Jurys Inn Galway
16 Skeffington Arms Hotel
17 Kinlay Hostel
18 Petra House
19 Ardawn House
20 Four Seasons B&B
21 Balcony House B&B
22 Asgard Guest House

ORIENTATION

The center of Galway is Eyre Square. Within two blocks of the square, you'll find the TI, Aran boat offices, a tour pickup point, accommodations, and the train station. The train and public bus station butt up against Hotel Meyrick, a huge gray railroad hotel that overlooks and dominates Eyre Square. The inviting old town lies between Eyre Square and the river. From Eyre Square, Williams Gate leads a pedestrian parade right through the old town (changing street names several times) to Wolfe Tone Bridge. Nearly everything you'll see and do is within a few minutes' walk of this spine.

Tourist Information

The well-organized **TI,** located a block from the bus/train station, has brochures and booking services (daily 9:00-17:30, Sun off-season until 11:45, Forster Street, tel. 091/537-700, www.discover ireland.ie).

Tours
In Galway
▲**Hop-On, Hop-Off City Bus Tours** offer a good introduction to the city. Two companies compete for your euros, with similar schedules and prices, departing from the TI on Forster Street and stopping at the cathedral, Salthill (beachfront promenade), and the Spanish Arch. These double-decker buses can't penetrate the winding medieval back streets, but you can get off, explore, and hop back on later. **Galway City** buses are blue (€10, April-Sept daily at 11:00, 12:30, 14:00, and 15:30, tel. 091/524-728, mobile 087-679-8525, www.galwaybustours.ie). **Lally's** buses are yellow (€12, April-Sept daily at 10:30, 12:00, 13:30, and 15:00, tel. 091/562-905, www.lallytours.com).

Walking Tours in this town are full of stories waiting to be told. **Galway Walking Tours** are led by Fiona Brennan, who takes her guests on leisurely 1.5-hour explorations of the city (€10, mobile 087-290-3499, www.galwaywalkingtours. com, fiona@galwaywalkingtours.com). **Liam Silke** comes from one of Galway's oldest families and still serves as Galway's town crier as he leads 1.5-hour tours (€10, departs at 11:30 from TI, tel. 091/588-897, mobile 086-348-0958, www.walkingtours galway.com, info@walkingtoursgalway. com).

Galway Region

Three Galway-based companies offer tours of nearby regions, including the Burren, Cliffs of Moher, Aran Islands, and Connemara (€25-45). They include **Galway Tour Company** (tel. 091/566-566, www.galwaytourcompany.com); **Lally Tours** (tel. 091/562-905, www.lallytours. com); and **Healy Tours** (tel. 091/770-066, www.healytours.ie). Galway Tour Company also has a land-and-sea tour that covers the Cliffs of Moher, Doolin, and the Aran Island of Inisheer.

Tours leave from Galway's coach station on Fairgreen Road, across from the TI. They depart at 9:45 (except for Galway Tour Company's Moher/Doolin/Inisheer tour, which leaves at 9:00) and get you back by about 17:30. Check online or call to confirm the exact time and itineraries. Generally, you'll get discounts for booking online or signing up for more than one tour. Drivers take cash only; to pay with a credit card, book online or at Galway's TI.

Galway bus tour

Helpful Hints

Markets: On Saturdays year-round and Sundays in summer, a fun market clusters around St. Nicholas' Church (all day, best 9:00-14:00).

Bike Rental: On Yer Bike offers rentals for a pleasant ride out to the end of Salthill's beachfront promenade and back (€10/day, Mon-Fri 10:00-19:00, Sat 10:00-18:00, Sun 15:00-18:00, 42 Prospect Hill, tel. 091/563-393, mobile 087-942-5479, www.onyourbikecycles.com).

Taxi: Try **Big-O-Taxis** (tel. 091/585-858).

Rick's Tip: Expect **huge crowds and higher prices** *during the* **Galway Arts Festival** *(mid-to-late-July, www.galwayartsfestival.com) and* **Galway Oyster Festival** *(late Sept, www.galwayoysterfest.com).*

SIGHTS

▲Medieval Galway's "Latin Quarter"

From the top of Eyre Square, Williams Gate—named for the old main gate of the Norman town wall that once stood here—is the spine of medieval Galway. While the road changes names several times (Williams Gate, then Shop, High, and Quay streets), it leads generally downhill to the River Corrib, straight past the following sights.

LYNCH'S CASTLE

Now the Allied Irish Bank, Galway's best late-15th-century fortified townhouse was the home of the Lynch family—the most powerful of the town's 14 tribes—and the only one of their mansions to survive. More than 80 Lynch mayors ruled Galway in the 16th and 17th centuries.

COLLEGIATE CHURCH OF ST. NICHOLAS

This church, located a half-block off the main street on the right, is the finest medieval building in town (1320), and is dedicated to St. Nicholas of Myra, the patron saint of sailors. Columbus is said to have worshipped here in 1477, undoubtedly contemplating a scary voyage. Its interior is littered with obscure town history (free entry but €3 suggested donation). Consider attending an **evening concert** of traditional Irish music in this atmospheric venue (see "Nightlife," later). A wonderful **open-air market** surrounds the church on Saturdays year-round and also on Sundays in summer.

THE QUAYS

This pub was once owned by "Humanity Dick," an 18th-century Member of Parliament who was the original animal-rights activist. His efforts led to the world's first conviction for cruelty to animals in 1822. It's worth a peek inside for its lively interior. The lane just before it leads to the...

DRUID THEATRE

This 100-seat venue offers top-notch contemporary Irish theater. Although the theater company is often away on tour, it's worth checking their schedule online

Lynch's Castle

Galway Legends and Factoids

Because of the dearth of physical old stuff, the town milks its legends. Here are a few that you'll encounter repeatedly:

- In the 15th century, the mayor, one of the Lynch tribe, condemned his son to death for the murder of a Spaniard. When no one in town could be found to hang the popular boy, the dad—who loved justice more than he loved his son—did it himself.
- Columbus is said to have stopped in Galway in 1477. He may have been inspired by tales of the voyage of St. Brendan, the Irish monk who is thought by some (mostly Irish) to have beaten Columbus to the New World by almost a thousand years.
- On the main drag, you'll find a pub called The King's Head. It was originally given to the man who chopped off the head of King Charles I in 1649. For his safety, he settled in Galway—about as far from London as an Englishman could get back then.
- William Joyce, born in America, spent most of his childhood in Galway and later was seduced by fascist ideology in the 1930s. He moved to Germany and became "Lord Haw-Haw," infamous as the radio voice of Nazi propaganda during World War II. After the war, he was hanged in London for treason. His daughter had him buried in Galway.

or dropping by to see if anything's playing tonight (€20-30 tickets, Chapel Lane, tel. 091/568-660, www.druid.ie).

Directly across the alley from the theater door you'll find the **Hall of the Red Earl.** Wall diagrams and storyboards explain that these are the dusty foundations of Galway's oldest building, once the 13th-century hall of the Norman lord Richard DeBurgo (free, closed Sun).

SPANISH ARCH
Overlooking the River Corrib, this makes up the best remaining chunk of the old city wall. A reminder of Galway's former importance in trade, the Arch (c. 1584) is the place where Spanish ships would unload their cargo—primarily wine.

CITY MUSEUM
Fragments of old Galway are kept in this modern museum, located just behind the Spanish Arch. Temporary exhibitions by local artists are on the upper two floors. Check out the intact Galway "hooker"

fishing boat hanging from the ceiling. The ground floor houses the permanent exhibits: prehistoric and ancient Galway-related treasures, such as medieval pottery, Iron Age ax heads, and Bronze Age thingamajigs.

Cost and Hours: Free, Tue-Sat 10:00-17:00, Sun 12:00-17:00, closed Mon, handy café with cheap lunches, tel. 091/532-460, www.galwaycitymuseum.ie.

Galway's waterfront at Spanish Arch

More Sights

▲EYRE SQUARE

On a sunny day, grassy Eyre Square is a popular hangout. In the Middle Ages, it was a field just outside the town wall. The square is named for the mayor who gave the land to the city in 1710. While still called Eyre Square, it now contains John F. Kennedy Park—established in memory of the Irish-American president's visit in 1963 when he filled this space with adoring Irish for one of his speeches, a few months before he was assassinated. Though Kennedy is celebrated as America's first Irish-Catholic president, several US presidents were descended from Protestant Ulster stock (Barack Obama is part Irish, with roots in County Offaly). Take a look at the JFK bust near the kids' play area, which commemorates his visit.

Walk to the rust-colored "Hooker Sculpture," built in 1984 to celebrate the 500th anniversary of the incorporation of the city. The sails represent Galway's square-rigged fishing ships ("hookers") and the vessels that made Galway a trading center so long ago. The Browne Doorway, from a 1627 fortified townhouse, is a reminder of the 14 family tribes that once ruled the town (see Lynch's Castle, listed earlier, to get a feel for an intact townhouse). Each had a town castle— much like the towers that characterize the towns of Tuscany, with their feuding noble families. So little survives of medieval Galway that the town makes a huge deal of any remaining window or crest. Check out the 14 colorful flags lining the western edge of the square, each one with a different original Norman founding-tribe name.

The Eyre Square Shopping Centre—a busy, modern shopping mall (see the arcaded entry from the square)—contains a short stretch of the old town wall that includes two reconstructed towers (and an antique market).

▲CATHEDRAL OF ST. NICHOLAS

Opened by American Cardinal Cushing in 1965, this is one of the last great stone churches built in Europe.

Cost and Hours: Free, church bulletins at doorway list upcoming Masses and concerts, located across Salmon Weir Bridge on outskirts of town, tel. 091/563-577.

Visiting the Cathedral: The interior is a treat—mahogany pews set on green Connemara marble floors under a Canadian cedar ceiling. The acoustically correct cedar enhances the church's fine pipe organ. Two thousand worshippers sit on three sides facing the central altar. A Dublin woman carved the 14 larger-than-life Stations of the Cross. The carving above the chapel (left of entry) is from the old St. Nicholas church. Explore the modern stained glass. Find the Irish Holy Family—with Mary knitting and Jesus offering Joseph a cup of tea. The window depicting the Last Supper is particularly creative—find the 12 apostles.

Next, poke your head into the side chapel with a mosaic of Christ's resurrection (if you're standing in the nave facing the main altar, it's on the left and closest

The River Corrib glides through Galway.

to the front). Take a closer look at the profiled face in a circular frame, below and to the right of Christ—the one looking up while praying with clasped hands. It's JFK, nearly a saint in Irish eyes at the time this cathedral was built.

Outer Galway
▲SALTHILL
This small resort town packs pubs, a splashy water park, and amusement centers up against a fine, mile-long beach promenade (Ireland's longest). For beach time, a relaxing sunset stroll, or late-night traditional music, Salthill hops.

Good for a rainy day, the **Atlantaquaria Aquarium** features touch tanks, native Irish aquatic life, and some Amazonian species (€11.50, Mon-Fri 10:00-17:00, Sat-Sun 10:00-18:00, The Promenade, tel. 091/585-100, www.nationalaquarium.ie).

Getting There: To get to Salthill, catch bus #401 from Eyre Square in front of the AIB bank, next to Meyrick Hotel (runs 7:00-23:00).

EXPERIENCES

Nightlife
▲ Traditional Irish Music
Galway, like Dingle and Doolin, is a mecca for good Irish music (nightly 21:30-23:30). But unlike Dingle and Doolin, this is a university town (enrollment: 12,000), and many pubs are often overrun with noisy students. Still, your chances of landing a seat close to a churning band surrounded by new Irish friends are good any evening of the year.

In Pubs: Touristy and student pubs are found and filled along the main drag down from Eyre Square to the Spanish Arch, and across Wolfe Tone Bridge, along William Street West and Dominick Street. If it happens to be Tuesday, cross the bridge and start at **Monroe's,** with its vast, music-filled interior (trad music Tue and Sun at 21:30, set-dancing Tue at 21:00, a

Magdalene Laundries Memorial

Recent documentaries and films, such as *The Magdalene Sisters* and *Philomena*, have highlighted the plight of unmarried, pregnant Irish women who were incarcerated and put to work doing laundry as virtual slaves. Viewing pre-marital pregnancy as one step short of prostitution, various Catholic orders operated these infamous "Magdalene laundries." (No such stigma applied to the men involved.) Across from the TI (at 47 Forster Street), a modest and easy-to-miss statue stands on the site of one such facility, operated by the Sisters of Mercy, which opened in 1824, with a capacity of 110 young women, and closed in 1984, with 18 inmates remaining. It's estimated that upwards of 10,000 women passed through the Magdalene laundry system. Magdalene survivors claim that they were held against their will, forced to work without pay, and physically abused...and their children were sold for adoption. The Irish government apologized in 2013 for turning a blind eye to the mistreatment of these women, who were imprisoned out of sight, often with the consent of their shamed families.

mixed bag of folk/rock music other nights, Dominick Street, tel. 091/583-397, www.monroes.ie). Several other pubs within earshot frequently feature trad music.

Pubs known for Irish music along the main drag include **Tig Coili,** featuring Galway's best trad sessions (Mon-Sat at 18:00 and 21:00, Sun at 14:00 and 21:00, intersection of Main Guard Street and High Street, tel. 091/561-294, www.pubsdirect.ie/tigcoili); **Taaffe's** (nightly music sessions at 17:30, Shop Street, across from St. Nicholas Church, tel. 091/564-066);

and **The Quays,** with a young scene (trad music most nights at 21:30, sporadic schedule, Quay Street, tel. 091/568-347). A bit off the main drag, scruffy **Barr An Chaladh** offers nightly trad or ballad sessions and more locals (3 Daly's Place, tel. 091/895-762).

At a Church: The **Collegiate Church of St. Nicholas** is the mellow medieval venue for "Tunes in the Church," with a rotating lineup of accomplished trad musicians. The 1.5-hour concerts are fun for early birds who don't want to stay up to catch the same great players in a local pub later that night (€15; July-Aug Mon, Wed, and Fri at 20:00; where High Street and Shop Street intersect, mobile 087-962-5425, www.tunesinthechurch.com).

Trad on the Prom

This fine traditional-music and dance troupe was started by Galway-born performers who returned home after years of touring with *Riverdance* and *The Chieftains.* So popular that it's lasted for more than a decade, their performance is a great way to enjoy live step dancing and accomplished musicians in a fairly intimate venue.

Cost and Hours: €30, mid-May-Sept only, shows at 21:00 Tue, Thu, and Sun—call or check online to confirm, and best to reserve ahead online; in Galway Bay Hotel, 30-minute walk west of town along the Salthill promenade or short ride on bus #401 from Eyre Square; tel. 091/582-860, mobile 087-2388-489, www.tradon theprom.com.

EATING

This college town is filled with colorful, inexpensive eateries. People everywhere seem to be enjoying their food.

At the Bottom of the Old Town

Each of these places is within a block or two of Jurys Inn.

Kirwan's Lane Restaurant & Seafood Bar is considered Galway's best dining experience. The seafood bar downstairs and the restaurant up top have the same hours. Both are dressy places where reservations are required (€17-25 lunches, €24-30 dinners, daily 12:30-14:30 & 18:00-22:00, no lunch on Sun, on Kirwan's Lane a block from Jurys Inn, tel. 091/568-266,

Trad music in Galway

www.kirwanslane.com).

Busker Brownes, with three eateries in one sprawling block, is popular for its good, cheap food. Enter on Cross Street for the restaurant and walk to the back for better seating, or enter on Kirwan's Lane for the ground-floor pub; the third section is upstairs from the pub (€11-22 meals, daily 10:30-21:30, cleanse your palate with jazz sessions Sun at 13:00 and Mon at 21:30, Cross Street and Kirwan's Lane, tel. 091/563-377).

McDonagh's Fish-and-Chips is a favorite among residents. It has a fast, cheap, all-day chipper on one side and a sit-and-stay-awhile dinner-only restaurant on the other side. If you're determined to try Galway oysters, remember that they're in season only from September through April. At other times, you'll eat Pacific oysters—go figure (€12 lunch, €15-25 in restaurant, €20 two-course early-bird special served 17:00-18:45; chipper open Mon-Sat 12:00-22:00, Sun 16:00-22:00; restaurant open Mon-Sat 17:00-22:00, closed Sun; 22 Quay Street, tel. 091/565-001).

Nimmo's Wine Bar Bistro and **Ard Bia Café** peacefully coexist in an old stone warehouse behind the Spanish Arch. The upstairs is a mellow hangout with great cheese platters and wine. The candlelit ambience is fine any night, even for a cup of coffee (€15-24 meals, café lunches Tue-Sat 12:00-15:30, wine-bar dinners Tue-Sun 18:00-21:30, closed Mon, Long Walk Street, tel. 091/561-114 or 091/539-897).

Near Eyre Square

McSwiggan's, with a downstairs pub and upstairs restaurant, is a maze of wooden stairways, brick walls, and hidden alcoves, serving hearty traditional Irish meals (€12-18 lunches, €17-25 dinners, daily 12:00-22:30, Eyre Street, tel. 091/568-917).

The **Galway Bakery Company (GBC)** is a popular, basic place for a quick Irish meal (€12-18 meals in ground-floor cafeteria, pricier restaurant upstairs, daily 12:00-21:00, 7 Williams Gate, near Eyre Square, tel. 091/563-087).

Supermarket: You can get to **Dunnes** through the Eyre Square Shopping Centre or around the corner at tiny Castle Street, off the pedestrian Williams Gate (Mon-Sat 9:00-19:00, Thu-Fri until 21:00, Sun 11:00-19:00, supermarket in basement).

Galway's "Latin Quarter"

Lots of smaller grocery shops are scattered throughout town.

SLEEPING

There are three price tiers for most beds in Galway: off-season, high season (Easter-Oct), and charge-what-you-like festivals and race weekends. I've listed high-season rates. B&Bs simply play the market. If you're on a tight budget, call around and see where the best prices are. All B&Bs include a full "Irish fry" breakfast.

Rick's Tip: *The* **Galway Races** *are heaven for lovers of horse racing and hell for everyone else (late July-early Aug, mid-Sept, and late Oct, www.galwayraces.com);* **prices double for food and lodging.**

Hotels

For a fancy place, Park House Hotel offers the best value. For a budget hotel, go to Jurys Inn. For cheap beds, hit the hostel.

$$$ Park House Hotel, a plush, business-class hotel, is ideally located a block from the train station and Eyre Square. Its 84 spacious rooms come with all the comforts you'd expect (Db-€109-199, online discounts, expensive full Irish breakfast-€12.50, pay parking, elevator, great restaurant, helpful staff, Forster Street, tel. 091/564-924, www.parkhousehotel.ie, reservations@parkhousehotel.ie).

$$$ Hotel Meyrick, filled with palatial Old World elegance and 97 rooms, marks the end of the Dublin-Galway train line and the beginning of Galway. Since 1845, it has been Galway's landmark hotel...JFK stayed here in 1963 when it was the Great Southern (Db-€169-219, some discounts during slow times, best rates when you book online, at the head of Eyre Square, tel. 091/564-041, www.hotelmeyrick.ie, reshm@hotelmeyrick.ie).

$$$ Jurys Inn Galway has 130 American-style rooms in a modern hotel, centrally located where the old town hits the

river. It attracts lots of tour groups. The big, bright rooms have double beds and huge modern bathrooms (Db-€89-139 Sun-Thu, €119-169 Fri-Sat; prices depend on season, breakfast-€10, elevator, pay parking, Quay Street, tel. 091/566-444, US tel. 800-423-6953, www.jurysinns.com, jurysinngalway@jurysinns.com).

$$$ Skeffington Arms Hotel feels more Irish than other hotels in town, but is furnished in a modern style. Centrally located on Eyre Square, it sits above a nightclub with noise from fun-loving stag/hen partygoers on weekends (Sb-€79-129, Db-€99-189, Tb-€139-229, Qb-€179-249, online discounts, Eyre Square, tel. 091/563-173, www.skeffington.ie, reception@skeffington.ie).

$ Kinlay Hostel is a no-nonsense place just 100 yards from the train station, with 224 beds in bare, clean, and simple rooms, including 15 doubles/twins. Easygoing people of any age feel welcome here, but if you want a double, book well ahead—several months in advance for weekends (dorm bed-€18-33, Sb-€48-60, Db-€60-70, elevator, self-service kitchen, baggage storage, laundry service-€8.50/load, on Merchants Road just off Eyre Square, tel. 091/565-244, www.kinlaygalway.ie, info@kinlaygalway.ie).

Sleep Code

Abbreviations: S=Single, D=Double/Twin, T=Triple, Q=Quad, b=bathroom
   Price Rankings for Double Rooms: $$$** Most rooms €120 or more, **$$** €60-120, **$ €60 or less
   Notes: Room prices change; verify rates online or by email. For the best prices, book directly with the hotel.

B&Bs

Clustered on College Road (near the greyhound-racing stadium) are an array of homey and reasonably priced lodging options. On foot, these B&Bs are about a 10-minute walk from Eyre Square (from the train or bus stations, walk up Forster Street, which turns into College Road). The following places are lined up like battleships and all have free parking. They're quieter than the rowdy weekend scene at bigger hotels in the city center. Although there are other B&Bs on this road, my favorites are the ones where the owner lives on-site and shows pride of ownership.

$$ Petra House rents nine fresh rooms, including a family room, in a peaceful-feeling brick building with an elegant sitting room. The owners, Joan and Frank Maher, keep everything lovingly maintained. Breakfasts are a highlight (Sb-€50-75, Db-€70-120, Tb-€110-150, Qb-€120-160, 29 College Road, tel. 091/566-580, 087/451-1711, www.petrahousegalway.net, petrahouse@eircom.net).

$$ Ardawn House is a welcoming B&B with nine fine, comfortable rooms. The Guilfoyles—friendly Breda and Antarctic explorer Mike—are great sources for local tips (Sb-€55-75, Db-€70-120, Tb-€110-150, Qb-€120-160, 31 College Road, near stadium on right, tel. 091/568-833, www.ardawnhouse.com, info@ardawnhouse.com).

$$ Four Seasons B&B is well kept, with seven inviting rooms hosted by Eddie and Helen Fitzgerald (Sb-€45-60, Db-€70-100, Tb-€90-120, Qb-€120-150, 23 College Road, tel. 091/564-078, www.fourseasonsgalway.com, info@fourseasonsgalway.com).

$$ Balcony House B&B rents eight pleasant rooms. Teresa Coyne provides treats in your room on arrival (Sb-€45-60, Db-€80-120, Tb-€105-140, Qb-€140-160, 27 College Road, tel. 091/563-438, www.aaabalconyhouse.com, info@aaabalconyhouse.com).

$$ Asgard Guesthouse offers eight restful rooms and an appealing glass-atrium breakfast room (Sb-€45-80, Db-€70-120, Tb-€90-150, Qb-€140-200, 21 College Road, tel. 091/566-855, www.galwaycityguesthouse.com, info@galwaycityguesthouse.com, Mary O'Flynn).

TRANSPORTATION

Arriving and Departing
By Train and Bus

Trains and most buses share the same station, virtually on Eyre Square (which has the nearest ATMs). The train station can store your bag (€2.50/day, Mon-Fri 8:00-18:00, closed Sat-Sun). To get from the station to the TI, go left on Station Road as you exit the station (toward Eyre Square), and then turn right on Forster Street.

Don't confuse the public bus station (in same building as the train station) with the coach station (a block away, across the street from the TI), which handles only privately owned coaches: These include Citylink buses from Dublin and Dublin's airport, as well as regional day-tour buses.

TRAIN AND BUS CONNECTIONS

From Galway by Train to: Dublin (8/day, 2.5-3 hours), **Limerick** (4/day, 2 hours), **Ennis** (5/day, 1.5 hours). For **Belfast** and **Tralee,** you'll change in or near Dublin. Train info: tel. 091/561-444, www.irishrail.ie.

From Galway by Bus to: Dublin (hourly, 3.5 hours; also see Citylink, below), **Kilkenny** (3/day, 5 hours), **Cork** (hourly, 4.5 hours), **Ennis** (hourly, 1.5 hours), **Shannon Airport** (hourly, 2 hours), **Cliffs of Moher** (8/day in summer, some with change in Ennis, 2 hours), **Doolin** (5/day, 1.5 hours), **Limerick** (hourly, 1.5-2.5 hours), **Dingle** (5/day, 6.5 hours), **Tralee** (8/day, 4.5 hours), **Westport** (5-7/day, 2-4 hours), **Rosslare** (2/day, 7.5-8 hours), **Belfast** (every 2 hours, 6 hours, change in Dublin), **Derry** (6/day, 5.5

hours). Bus info: tel. 091/562-000, www.buseireann.ie.

Citylink Buses runs cheap and fast bus service from the coach station (across from the TI) to: **Dublin** (arriving at Bachelor's Walk, a block from Tara Street DART station; hourly, 2.5 hours), **Dublin Airport** (hourly, 3 hours), and **Cork Airport** (6/day, 4 hours). Bus info: tel. 091/564-164, www.citylink.ie.

By Car

Drivers staying overnight at a College Road B&B can park there for free (each has a small lot in front). Hotels charge about €10 per day for parking. For day-trip parking, the most central and handiest parking garage is under the Jurys Inn Galway in the town center (Mon-Sat 8:00-1:00 in the morning, Sun 9:00-18:00). Otherwise, you'll have to buy a pay-and-display ticket and put it on your dashboard (2-hour maximum, buy from machines on street).

Travelers continuing on to Northern Ireland should get an early start. Allow a day for the drive from Galway to Portrush.

BEST OF THE REST

CONNEMARA AND MAYO

If you have a car, you could easily spend a day exploring the wild western Irish fringe known as Connemara and straying into historic County Mayo. Gaze up at the peak of Croagh Patrick, the mountain from which St. Patrick supposedly banished the snakes from Ireland. Pass through the desolate Doo Lough Valley on a road stained with tragic famine history. Bounce on a springy peat bog, and drop in at a Westport pub owned by a member of the Chieftains, the well-known traditional Irish music group. This beautiful area also claims a couple of towns—Cong and Leenane—where classic Irish movies were filmed, as well as the photogenic Kylemore Abbey.

Connemara in 1 Day

By Car: I describe a counterclockwise loop trip from Galway, but if you're following my 14-day itinerary, your visit through Connemara could be as short as stopping in Cong and Westport before heading north to Portrush. For a longer one-way trip, you could take the western part of the loop from Galway to Westport. Consider which sights most appeal to you, and base your decision on that.

By Tour: From Galway, three companies (Lally, Healy, and Galway) run day-long bus tours of this region; see page 232.

Connemara Driving Tour

This self-guided loop trip takes a full day and involves five hours of driving, not including stops (almost 200 miles/320 km, using Galway as your base). Start early (by 9:00), so your day will be less rushed. Those wanting to slow down and linger can sleep in Westport. These country roads, punctuated by blind curves and surprise bumps, are shared by trucks, tractors, cyclists, more tractors, and sheep. Drive sanely, and bring rain gear and your sense of humor. This is rural Ireland with all the trimmings.

Take along a good map (Ordnance Survey atlases are widely sold in Ireland). Before you start, study the loop connecting these points: Galway, Cong, Westport, Louisburgh, Leenane, Kylemore Abbey, Clifden, Roundstone, and back to Galway.

Route Summary: Take N-84 north out of Galway; the road becomes R-334 in Headford. At Cross, take R-346 into Cong and R-345 back out again. At Neale, go north, putting you back on R-334. Pick up

N-84 again as it winds through Ballinrobe to Partry. Take R-330 from Partry to Westport for lunch.

At Westport, if you're heading on to Portrush, take N-5 east. But if you're continuing the loop back to Galway, go west on R-335 through Louisburgh and south through Doo Lough Valley all the way to Leenane. Meet N-59 in Leenane and take it to Kylemore Abbey, continuing to Letterfrack and Connemara National Park. Continue south to Clifden, where you'll turn off onto R-341. Hug the coast through Roundstone before finding the junction with N-59 near Recess. Follow N-59 back to Galway via Maam Cross and Oughterard.

Galway to Cong

From Galway's Eyre Square, drive north out of town on Prospect Hill Road. Follow the signs at each roundabout in the direction of Castlebar onto N-84. You'll soon be out of Galway's suburbs and crossing miles of flat bogland laced with simple rock walls.

• At Headford, keep straight through town as the road changes names to R-334. At Cross, take R-346 to Cong. You'll pass the grand, gray gateway of Ashford Castle (on the left) as you approach the town.

Cong

Plan to spend an hour in Cong (1.5 hours if you include the Ashford Castle grounds). Cross the small bridge and park in front of the abbey. Drop into the TI across from the abbey entrance for a map (generally Mon-Sat 10:00-17:00, closed Sun and Oct-April, tel. 094/954-6542). There are no banks or ATMs in Cong (the closest ATM is 10 miles away in Ballinrobe). Public WCs are 50 yards down the street across from the **Quiet Man cottage.** That's right, pilgrim, this is where John Wayne and Maureen O'Hara filmed *The Quiet Man* in 1951 (€5, mid-March-Oct daily 10:30-16:00, closed Nov-mid-March, tel. 094/954-6089). Fuel up with coffee at

the **Hungry Monk Café** (Tue-Sun 10:00-17:00, closed Mon, on Abbey Street) or lunch at the **Crows Nest Pub** (daily 12:00-18:00, Main Street).

We're here for the ruins of **Cong Abbey,** built in the early 1100s, when Romanesque was going out and Gothic was coming in. Its famous Cross of Cong, which supposedly held a splinter of the True Cross, is now on display in Dublin's National Museum.

Take a walk through the cloister and down the gravel path behind the abbey. The forested grounds are lush, and the stream water is incredibly clear. The monks fished for more than sinners. They built the modest **Monks' Fishing Hut,** just over the footbridge, right on the bank so that the river flowed underneath. They lowered a net through the floor and attached a bell to the rope; whenever a fish was netted, the bell would ring.

To reach **Ashford Castle** from the abbey, face the Romanesque/Gothic main entrance and go left around the corner of the abbey, walking 15 minutes down the pleasant forested lane onto the grounds of the castle, which is hidden behind the trees. The castle evolved from the original, modest Norman keep into this sprawling Victorian complex that rents some of the finest rooms in all of Ireland. Casual gawkers are discouraged inside.

• Take R-345 out of Cong (left turn opposite the main stone gateway to the grounds of

Monks' Fishing Hut

Ashford Castle). Heading north, you'll pass through the tiny hamlet of Neale.

At Neale, go north on R-334, then take N-84 from Ballinrobe to Partry. At Partry, turn left off N-84 onto R-330 in the direction of Westport (the easy-to-miss turnoff is just after you pass the thatch-roofed Village Inn).

Westport

On arrival in Westport, park along the Mall under the trees that line the shallow canal-like river. This is a planned town with a genteel vibe, built in the Georgian style in the late 1700s to support the adjacent estate of Westport House (skip it for a better manor at Muckross House). It's a good place for a relaxed lunch and some exploration on foot.

As you stroll the South Mall in front of St. Mary's Church, you'll pass the bust of Westport-born **Major John MacBride,** one of the more colorful rebels of the 1916 Easter Uprising. He had previously fought with the Boers against the British, then wed beautiful stage actress Maude Gonne (much to the consternation of Maude's jealous suitor W. B. Yeats, who immortalized MacBride as a "vain-glorious lout").

MacBride unexpectedly wandered into a band of rebels marching into position in Dublin and joined them; he was among the 14 executed at Kilmainham Gaol after the failed rising.

The **TI** is on Bridge Street (March-Oct Mon-Fri 9:00-17:30, Sat until 16:30 except July-Aug until 17:30, closed Sun except July-Aug 10:00-17:00; shorter hours and closed Sun Nov-Feb; tel. 098/25711).

For a short visit, free **parking** is allowed on the street for two hours; for longer stays, park at your B&B or use the pay-and-display lots (€0.70/first hour, €0.30/hour after that, pay at meter and display ticket on dashboard, enforced Mon-Fri 8:30-19:00, Sat 10:00-18:00, free on Sun).

NIGHTLIFE

Irish music fans seek out **Matt Molloy's** pub (sessions at 21:30, arrive by 20:30 or stand all night, Bridge Street, tel. 098/26655). Molloy isn't just the owner of the pub—he's also a flutist for the Chieftains, the group credited with the worldwide resurgence of Irish music over the past 50 years.

Ashford Castle

EATING

Most of your best bets are clustered on Bridge Street. For dinner, head to **J. J. O'Malleys'** restaurant (daily 17:00-22:00, Bridge Street, tel. 098/27307). **Mangos Seafood Restaurant** serves the town's best fish (daily 17:45-22:30, July-Aug also serves lunch 12:30-15:00, Bridge Street, tel. 098/24999). Casual **Madden's Bistro** is on the ground floor of the Clew Bay Hotel (daily 12:30-21:00, James Street, tel. 098/28088).

SLEEPING

Westport is the best place along this route to spend a night. Try good-value **$$ Boulevard Guesthouse** (cash only, www.boulevard-guesthouse.com), modern **$$$ Clew Bay Hotel** (www.clewbay hotel.com) or budget **$ Old Mill Hostel** (www.oldmillhostel.com).

• *Leave Westport heading west on R-335 (or east on N-5 if heading to Portrush). After about eight kilometers (five miles) on R-335, as you're driving along scenic Clew Bay, you'll reach a wide spot in the road called Murrisk. Stop here. In the field on your right (opposite Campbell's Pub) is the...*

Coffin Ship

This bronze ship sculpture is one of the most powerful famine memorials that you'll see in Ireland. It's a "coffin ship," like those of the late 1840s that carried sick and starving famine survivors across the ocean in hope of a new life. Unfortunately, many of the ships contracted to take the desperate emigrants were barely seaworthy. The poor were weak from starvation and vulnerable to "famine fever," which they then spread to others in the cramped holds of these awful ships. Many who lived through the six- to eight-week journey died shortly after reaching their new country. Look at the skeletons swirling around the ship's masts and contemplate the fact that famine still exists in the modern world.

• *Across the road from the coffin ship is...*

Croagh Patrick

This mountain rises 2,500 feet above the bay. In the fifth century, St. Patrick is said to have fasted on its summit for the 40 days of Lent. It's from here that he supposedly rang his bell, driving all the snakes out of Ireland. The snakes never existed, of course, but they represent the pagan beliefs that Patrick's newly arrived Christianity replaced. Every year on the last Sunday of July, some 30,000 pilgrims hike three hours up the rocky trail to the summit in honor of St. Patrick and celebrate Mass in a modest chapel on the top.

Hikers should allow three hours to reach the top and two hours to get back down (bring plenty of water, sunscreen, and rain gear). There is a primitive WC on the summit, 30 yards below the chapel. The trail is easy to follow, but the upper half of the mountain is a steep slope of loose, shifting scree that can bang or turn exposed ankles. Both times I've climbed this, I've been glad I wore boots.

• *Continue west on R-335. Passing through Louisburgh, you'll turn south to enter some of the most rugged and desolate country in Ireland.*

Doo Lough Valley

Signs of human habitation vanish from the bogland, and ghosts begin to appear beside the road. About 13 kilometers (8 miles) south of Louisburgh, stop at the simple gray-stone cross on the left. The lake ahead is Doo Lough (Irish for "Black Lake"). This is the site of one of the saddest famine tales.

County Mayo's rural folk were the hardest hit when the Great Potato Famine came in 1845. In the winter of 1849, about 600 starving Irish walked 12 miles from Louisburgh to Delphi Lodge, hoping to get food from their landlord, but they were turned away. Almost 200 of them died on the walk back. Today, an annual walk commemorates the tragedy.

• *Continue south on R-335. You'll get a fine view of* **Aasleagh Falls** *on the left. In late*

May, the banks below the falls explode with lush, wild, purple rhododendron blossoms. Cross the bridge after the falls, and turn right onto N-59 toward Leenane. You'll drive along Killary Harbor, an Irish example of a fjord. This long, narrow body of water was carved by an advancing glacier.

Leenane

This crossroads is a good place for a break. The 1990 movie *The Field*, starring Limerick-born Richard Harris, was filmed here. Take a glance at the photos of the making of the movie on the wall of **Hamilton's Pub.** Drop into the **Leenane Sheep and Wool Centre** (on the left as you enter town) to see interesting wool-spinning and weaving demonstrations (€5, April-Oct daily 9:30-18:00, closed Nov-March; tel. 095/42323, www.sheepandwool centre.com).

• *As you continue west on N-59, notice the rows of blue floats in Killary Harbor. They're there to mark mussel farms growing on hanging nets in the cold seawater. As you climb out of the fjord valley about eight kilometers (five miles) past Leenane, you'll pass (on the left) some areas that offer good, close looks at a turf cut in a peat bog.*

A Slog on the Bog

Walk a few yards onto the spongy green carpet. (Watch your step on wet days to avoid squishing into a couple of inches of water.) Find a dry spot and jump up and down to get a feel for it. Have your companion jump; you'll feel the vibrations 30 feet away.

These bogs once covered almost 20 percent of Ireland. As the climate got warmer at the end of the last Ice Age, plants began growing along the sides of the many shallow lakes and ponds. When the plants died in these waterlogged areas, there wasn't enough oxygen for them to fully decompose. Over the centuries, the moss built up, layer after dead layer, helping to slowly fill in the lakes.

It's this wet, oxygen-starved ecosystem that has preserved ancient artifacts so well, many of which can be seen in Dublin's National Museum. Most bizarre are the wrinkled bog mummies (some of them close to 2,000 years old), found so intact that their eyelashes, hairstyles, and last meals can be identified. They were likely sacrifices to the pagan gods of Celtic times.

People have been cutting, drying, and

Doo Lough Valley

burning peat as a fuel source for more than a thousand years. The cutting usually begins in April or May, when drier weather approaches. You may see stacks of "turf" piled up to dry along recent cuts. In the past few decades, bogs have been recognized as a rare habitat, and conservation efforts have been encouraged. The sweet, nostalgic smell of burning peat is increasingly rare.

• *Continue west on N-59. The road soon crosses a shallow lake, with a great view of Kylemore Abbey to the right. But don't stop here—you'll get a better photo from the parking lot, a few hundred yards ahead. Pull into the lot and take a few minutes to enjoy the view (gate closes at 18:00).*

Kylemore Abbey

This Neo-Gothic country house was built by the wealthy English businessman Mitchell Henry in the 1860s. After World War I, refugee Benedictine nuns from Belgium took it over and ran it as an exclusive girls' boarding school—which peaked at 200 students—until it closed in 2010. The Indiana-based University of Notre Dame recently signed a 30-year lease to use part of the facility for sum-mer classes and student housing. The nuns still live upstairs, but you can visit the half-dozen open rooms downstairs that display the Henry family's cushy lifestyle. Hourly tours of the abbey and its gardens are so-so; better to just enjoy the setting (€13 combo-ticket for abbey and gardens, daily March-Oct 9:00-18:00, shorter hours off-season, tel. 095/52001, www.kylemoreabbeytourism.ie).

• *Heading west from the abbey, you'll drive less than eight kilometers (five miles) to the town of Letterfrack. Pass through the town and go left off N-59 to reach...*

Connemara National Park

This park encompasses almost 5,000 acres of wild bog and mountain scenery. The visitors center displays worthwhile exhibits of local flora and fauna, (free, park open daily year-round, visitors center open daily June-Aug 9:30-18:30, March-May and Sept-Oct 10:00-17:30, closed Nov-Feb, last entry 45 minutes before closing, tel. 095/41054, www.heritage ireland.ie). Nature lovers may want to reverse the direction of my driving loop to enjoy a two-hour walking tour with a park naturalist. Call ahead to confirm walking

Kylemore Abbey, a Connemara landmark

Coastal Connemara

tour schedules, and bring rain gear and hiking shoes (July-Aug Wed and Fri at 11:00, departs from visitors center).

• If you're running short on time, you could stay on N-59 the whole way back to Galway. But I prefer to turn south off N-59 in Clifden to enjoy a scenic coastal loop on R-341.

Coastal Connemara

The essence of scenic Connemara—rocky yet seductive—is captured in this 38-kilometer (24 miles) lumpy loop on R-341. The 12 peaks of Connemara loom deeper inland. In the foreground, broad shelves of bare bedrock are netted with stone walls, which interlock through the landscape. The ocean slaps the hardscrabble shore. Fishermen cast into lakes, and ponies trot in windswept fields. Abandoned, roofless stone cottages stand mute, keeping their stories to themselves. The only settlement on this loop to speak of is Roundstone, a perfect place to stop for a cup of coffee before turning home.

• R-341 links back up with N-59 near Recess. At the junction with N-59, turn right, and follow Galway signs back through Recess, Maam Cross, and Oughterard. Our tour is over.

Aran Islands

Strewn like limestone chips hammered on the jagged west coast, the three Aran Islands—Inishmore, Inishmaan, and Inisheer—confront the wild Atlantic with stubborn grit. Steep, rugged cliffs fortify the southern flanks of each island. Windswept rocky fields, stitched together by stone walls, blanket the interiors. And the island's precious few sandy beaches hide in coves that dimple the northern shores. During the winter, severe gales sweep through; because of this, most of the settlements on the islands are found on the more sheltered northeastern side.

There's a stark beauty about the Aran Islands, the villages, and the simple lives their inhabitants eke out of a mean sea and less than six inches of topsoil. In the past, people made a precarious living here from fishing and farming. The scoured bedrock offered little in the way of soil, so it was created by the islanders—the result of centuries of layering seaweed with limestone sand and animal dung. Fields are small, divided by several thousand miles of "drystone" wall (made without mortar). Nowadays, tourism boosts the islands' economy. The islands are a Gaeltacht—a Gaelic cultural preserve. If you hear a strange language on the streets and wonder where those people are from, it's Irish, and so are they. But they happily speak English for their visitors.

I cover two of the three islands. The largest island, Inishmore (9 miles by 2 miles), is the most populated, popular, and interesting—starring Dún Aenghus, the must-see Iron Age fort. Inishmore is easy to visit when you're in Galway, near the mainland port of Rossaveel, from where you sail to Inishmore. And flights from Galway take you to any of the islands.

For most, the big island is quiet enough. But less touristy Inisheer is a good alternative if you're staying in Doolin, a

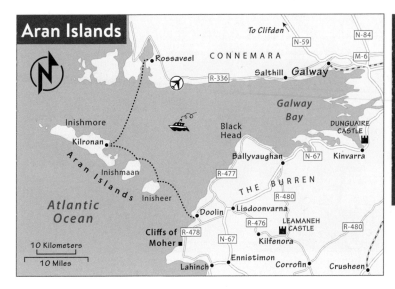

Aran Islands

INISHMORE IN 1 DAY

Most travelers visit Inishmore (Inis Mór) as a day trip by boat from Galway. Here's a good framework for the day: Leave Galway at 9:00 on the shuttle bus to Rossaveel, where you'll catch the 10:30 boat. You'll step off the boat in Kilronan

at about 11:15. Arrange minivan transport or rent a bike, visit the Dún Aenghus fort, and grab a bite at one of the two simple cafés near the base of the Dún Aenghus fort trail (or bring a picnic). Explore the island during low tide, and depart on the boat when high tides return between 16:00 and 18:00. You can squeeze an extra two or three hours out of your day trip

ARAN ISLANDS AT A GLANCE

On Inishmore (best reached from Galway)

▲▲▲**Dún Aenghus** Remote 2,000-year-old Iron Age ring fort, perched on a cliff with breathtaking coastal views and surrounded by a defensive ring of sharp stones. **Hours:** March-Oct daily 9:00-18:00, Nov-Dec daily 9:30-16:00, Jan-Feb Wed-Sun 9:30-16:00 and closed Mon-Tue. See page 255.

▲**Island Minivan Tours** Dependable, weather-proof transport between the island's sights, driven by gift-of-gab locals who contribute random, humorous, and occasionally factual commentary en route. See page 255.

Seven Churches and St. Enda's Church Ruins of two separate early Christian communities at opposite ends of the island, both reachable by minivan, bike, or pony trap. See page 256.

Black Fort, St. Benen's Church, and the Worm Hole Three separate, isolated ancient sites scattered across the island, offering dramatically windswept vistas reachable only by rocky and rewarding hikes. See page 257.

On Inisheer (best reached from Doolin)

Small, quiet-island alternative to Inishmore's hectic day-tripper scene, featuring modest sights that include the ruins of O'Brien's Castle, the sand-sunken St. Cavan's Church, and the beached *An Plassy* shipwreck. See page 261.

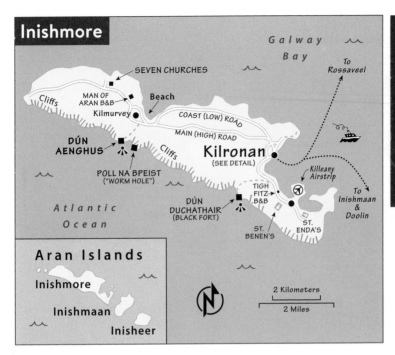

Inishmore

G a l w a y
B a y

To
Rossaveel

SEVEN CHURCHES

MAN OF
ARAN B&B   Beach

Cliffs

Kilmurvey

COAST (LOW) ROAD

MAIN (HIGH) ROAD

DÚN
AENGHUS

Cliffs

Kilronan
(SEE DETAIL)

Killeany
Airstrip

POLL NA BPEIST
("WORM HOLE")

TIGH
FITZ
B&B

To
Inishmaan
&
Doolin

A t l a n t i c

DÚN
DUCHATHAIR
(BLACK FORT)

ST.
BENEN'S

ST.
ENDA'S

O c e a n

Aran Islands

Inishmore

Inishmaan

Inisheer

2 Kilometers

2 Miles

by booking an early flight over and a late flight back from Connemara Regional Airport near Rossaveel.

Staying Overnight: Travelers spending the night can savor the quiet time before and after the day-trip crowds. Here's how I'd suggest you spend your arrival day: Since most day-trippers make a beeline straight off the boat to Dún Aenghus, head in the opposite direction to check out the subtle charms of the less-visited eastern end of the island. Buy a picnic at the Spar supermarket in Kilronan. Then walk to either the ruins of tiny St. Benen's Church (an easy 45-minute hike one way from Kilronan, on a ridge just past the Tigh Fitz B&B) or the rugged Black Fort ruins (a rocky 1-hour scramble one way from Kilronan). Save Dún Aenghus for later in the afternoon, after the midday crowds have subsided (allow an hour at Dún Aenghus, closes at 18:00 March-Oct, off-season at 16:00, last entry one hour before closing).

Enjoy an evening in the pubs and take a no-rush midmorning boat trip or flight back to the mainland the next day.

INISHMORE

Today, the 800 people of Inishmore (literally "the big island") greet as many as 2,000 visitors a day. The vast majority of these are day-trippers, washing ashore with the docking of each ferry. Everyone arrives at Kilronan, the Aran Islands' biggest town, though it's just a village. Their goal is the blockbuster sight: the striking Dún Aenghus fort, set on a sheer cliff.

Minivans, bike shops, and a few men in pony carts sop up the tourists. Most opt for taking a minivan from the dock for a 2.5-hour visit to Dún Aenghus, grabbing a simple lunch, and then spending an hour or two browsing through the few shops or sitting at a picnic table outside a pub with a pint of Guinness.

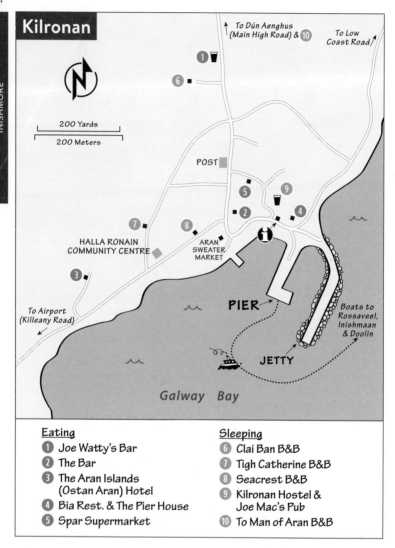

Kilronan

To Dún Aenghus
(Main High Road) & ⑩

To Low
Coast Road

① 🍺

⑥

N

200 Yards
200 Meters

POST

⑤   ⑨
② ④

⑦   ⑧   ℹ️

HALLA RONAIN
COMMUNITY CENTRE

ARAN
SWEATER
MARKET

③

To Airport
(Killeany Road)

PIER

Boats to
Rossaveel,
Inishmaan
& Doolin

JETTY

Galway Bay

Eating
① Joe Watty's Bar
② The Bar
③ The Aran Islands
   (Ostan Aran) Hotel
④ Bia Rest. & The Pier House
⑤ Spar Supermarket

Sleeping
⑥ Clai Ban B&B
⑦ Tigh Catherine B&B
⑧ Seacrest B&B
⑨ Kilronan Hostel &
   Joe Mac's Pub
⑩ To Man of Aran B&B

Orientation

Your first stop on Inishmore is the town of Kilronan, huddling around the pier. There are about a dozen shops and B&Bs, about half as many restaurants, and a couple of **bike-rental huts** (regular bikes-about €10/day plus €10 deposit; snazzy electric bikes-€25/day plus €20 deposit; for biking tips, see page 260).

A few blocks inland up the high road,

you'll find the best folk-music **pub** (Joe Watty's), a **post office** (Mon-Fri 9:00-13:00 & 14:00-17:30, Sat 9:00-13:00, closed Sun), and a tiny **bank** across from the roofless Anglican church ruins (open only on Wed 10:30-12:30 & 13:30-15:00, plus Thu June-Aug). A friendly **Internet café** lurks behind the stony Aran Sweater Market building, across from the high cross, and shows the *Man of Aran* film (€1/10 minutes, €5/hour, May-Sept daily 10:00-20:00, shorter hours in winter).

The Spar **supermarket,** two blocks inland from the harbor, has the island's only **ATM.**

Rick's Tip: *Bring cash or get it when you arrive.* **Most B&Bs and many other businesses don't accept credit cards.**

Tourist Information: Kilronan's TI is helpful, but don't rely on it for accommodations; the B&B owners who work with the TI are out of town and desperate (daily 10:00-17:00, July-Aug until 18:00, shorter hours in winter, faces the harbor, tel. 099/61263).

The TI offers free maps of the island (though your ferry operator may have already given you one). This map is all the average day-tripper or leisure biker will need to navigate. But serious hikers who plan on scampering out to the island's craggy fringes will want to invest in the detailed black-and-white *Oileáin Árann* map and companion book by Tim Robinson (€16, sold at the Internet café behind the Aran Sweater Market, and at some bookstores in Galway).

Public **WC**s are 100 yards beyond the TI on the harbor road.

Tours

Fewer than 100 vehicles roam the island, and most of them seem to be minivans offering ▲ island tours. A line of vans (seating 8-18 passengers) awaits the arrival of each ferry, offering €10 island tours. They're basically a shared taxi service that will take you to the various sights, drop you off, and return at an agreed time to take you to the next attraction.

Chat with a few drivers to find one who likes to talk. On my tour, I learned that 800 islanders live in 14 villages (actually just crossroads), with three elementary schools and three churches. Most islanders own a small detached field where they keep a couple of cows (sheep are too

much trouble). When pressed for more information, my guide explained that there are 400 types of flowers and 19 types of bees on the island. Then he pointed to the 2,000-year-old ring fort on the hilltop and grinned, saying, "It's so popular with visitors that we plan to build another 2,000-year-old ring fort next year."

The tour, a convenient time-saver, zips you to the end of the island for a quick stroll in the desolate fields, gives you 15 minutes to wander through the historic but visually unimpressive Seven Churches, and then drops you off for two hours at Dún Aenghus (30 minutes to hike up, 30 minutes at the fort, 20-minute hike back down, 40 minutes in café for lunch or shopping at drop-off point) before running you back to Kilronan. These sights can be linked together in various sequences, but the trailhead crossroads below Dún Aenghus—with two cafés—makes the best lunch stop. Ask your driver to take you back along the smaller coastal road (scenic beaches and sunbathing seals at low tide).

Sights

▲▲▲DÚN AENGHUS (DUN AONGHASA)

The stone fortress hangs spectacularly and precariously on the edge of a cliff

Dún Aenghus

200 feet above the Atlantic. The crashing waves seem to say, "You've come to the end of the world." Gaze out to sea and consider this: Off this coast, Hy Brasil—a phantom island cloaked in mist—was said to pop into view once every seven years. This mythical place appeared on maps as late as the mid-1600s.

Little is known about this 2,000-year-old Iron Age fort. Its concentric walls are 13 feet thick and 10 feet high. As an added defense, the fort is ringed with a commotion of spiky stones, sticking up like lances, called *chevaux-de-frise* (literally, "Frisian horses," named for the Frisian soldiers who used pikes to stop charging cavalry). Slowly, as the cliff erodes, hunks of the fort fall into the sea.

Dún Aenghus doesn't get crowded until after 11:00; if you can, get there early or late. A small museum (housing the ticket office and controlling access to the trail) displays aerial views of the fort and tells the story of its inhabitants.

Warnings: Rangers advise visitors to wear sturdy walking shoes and watch kids closely; there's no fence between you and a crumbling 200-foot cliff overlooking the sea. Also, be very careful about unexpected gusts of wind and uncertain footing near the edge (uneven rocky ground that begs to be tripped on). The Irish don't believe in litigation, just natural selection.

Cost and Hours: €4; March-Oct daily 9:00-18:00, Nov-Dec daily 9:30-16:00, Jan-Feb Wed-Sun 9:30-16:00 and closed Mon-Tue; last entry one hour before closing, 5.5 miles from Kilronan, tel. 099/61008. From June through August, guides at the trailhead answer questions and can sometimes give free tours up at the fort if you call ahead.

SEVEN CHURCHES
(NA SEACHT TEAMPAILL)

Close to the western tip of the island, this gathering of ruined chapels, monastic houses, and fragments of a high cross dates from the 8th to 11th century. The island is dotted with reminders that Chris-

tianity was brought to the islands in the fifth century by St. Enda, who established a monastery here. Many great monks studied under Enda. Among these "Irish apostles" who started Ireland's "Age of Saints and Scholars" (A.D. 450-800) was Columba (Colmcille in Irish), the founder of a monastery on the island of Iona in Scotland—home of the Irish monks who produced the Book of Kells. Check out the ornate gravestones (best detail on sunny days) of the "seven Romans," located in the slightly elevated back corner of the graveyard, farthest from the road. These pilgrims came here from Rome in the ninth century, long after the fall of the Roman Empire.

KILMURVEY

The island's second village sits below Dún Aenghus. With a gaggle of homes, a B&B, a great sheltered swimming beach, and a pub, this is the place for peaceful solitude. This narrowest section of the island also has the best grazing land, a fact not lost on the local landlord who claimed it for himself.

Seven Churches

Currach and Navogue Boats

These are the traditional fishing boats of the west coast of Ireland—lightweight and easy to haul. In your coastal travels, you'll see a few actual *currach* or *navogue* boats—generally retired and stacked where visitors can touch them and ponder the simpler age when they were a key part of the economy. The *currach* (manned by three oarsmen) is native to the Aran Islands, while the *navogue* (four oarsmen) is native to the Dingle Peninsula. The boats were easy to make: Cover a wooden frame with canvas (originally cowhide) and paint with tar. A currach's advantage was maneuverability on the sea and ease in getting into and out of the water. Its disadvantage was its fragility when hauling anything other than men or fish. When transporting sheep, farmers would lash each sheep's pointy hooves together and place it carefully upside-down in the *currach*—so it wouldn't puncture the frail craft's canvas skin.

THE WORM HOLE (POLL NA BPEIST)

Off the beaten path and accessible only by hiking, this site takes the "logic" out of geo-*logic*. It's a large, perfectly rectangular, 40-by-100-foot seawater-filled pool, cut by nature into the flat coastal bedrock. You'd swear that God used a cake knife to cut out this massive slab—just to mess with us. The Worm Hole was formed when the limestone fractured at right angles and a cave underneath (cut by wave and tidal action) collapsed just so. To add to the surreal scene, Red Bull Energy Drink has twice featured this site in its annual cliff-diving competition (search YouTube for thrilling video clips).

Boulder-hopping your way across the narrowest section of the island, you'll find the Worm Hole beneath the island's southern cliffs, one mile straight south of Kilmurvey's fine beach. It's signposted from the Main Road, but Tim Robinson's detailed map (see "Tourist Information," earlier) is handy for navigating here.

ANCIENT SITES NEAR KILLEANY

The quiet eastern end of Inishmore offers ancient sites in evocative settings for overnight visitors with more time, or for those seeking rocky hikes devoid of crowds. First, get a good hiking map from the Internet café behind the Aran Sweater Market. Then consider assembling a picnic to fuel up either before or after you spend a couple of hours exploring these sights on foot. Ask the folks in town for directions (almost always a memorable experience in Ireland).

Closest to the road, amid the dunes one mile past the Tigh Fitz B&B and just south of the airport, is the eighth-century **St. Enda's Church** (Teaghlach Einne). Protected from wave erosion by a stubborn breakwater, it sits half-submerged in a sandy graveyard, surrounded by a sea of sawgrass and peppered with tombstones. St. Enda is said to be buried here, along with 125 other saints who flocked to Inishmore in the fifth century to learn from him.

St. Benen's Church (Teampall Bheanáin) perches high on a desolate ridge opposite the Tigh Fitz B&B. Walk up the stone-walled lane, passing a holy well and

St. Benen's Church

the stubby remains of a round tower. Then take another visual fix on the church's silhouette on the horizon, and zigzag up the stone terraces to the top. The 30-minute hike up from the B&B pays off with a great view. Dedicated to St. Benen, a young disciple of St. Patrick himself, this tiny (12 foot by 6 foot) 10th-century oratory is aligned north-south (instead of the usual east-west) to protect the doorway from prevailing winds.

About a five-minute walk past the Tigh Fitz B&B (on your left as you head toward the airport), you'll notice an abandoned stone pier and an adjacent, modest medieval ruin. This was **Arkin Fort,** built by Cromwell's soldiers in 1652 using cut stones taken from the round tower and the monastic ruins that once stood below St. Benen's Church. The fort was used as a prison for outlawed priests before they were sent by English authorities to the West Indies to be sold into slavery.

Hidden on a remote, ragged headland an hour's walk from Kilronan to the south side of the island, you'll find the **Black Fort** (Dún Duchathair). After Dún Aenghus, this is Inishmore's most dramatic fortification. A good map is essential to navigate here. Built on a promontory with cliffs on three sides, its defenders would have held out behind drystone ramparts, facing the island's interior attackers. Watch your step on the uneven ground, be ready to course-correct as you go, and chances are you'll have this windswept ruin all to yourself. Imagine the planning and cooperative effort that went into building these life-saving structures 2,000 years ago, before Gore-Tex and granola bars.

Experiences
Pub Music

Kilronan's pubs offer music sporadically on summer nights. Nothing is dependably scheduled, so ask at your B&B or look for posted notices on the front of the Spar supermarket or post office. **Joe Watty's Bar,** on the high road 100 yards past the post office, is worth the 10-minute walk from the dock. Its appealing front porch goes great with a pint, and Irish folk music warms the interior most nights. The more central **Joe Mac's Pub** (next to the hostel) and **The Bar** (next to the high cross at the base of the high road) are also possibilities.

The Black Fort

Dancing

The **Halla Ronain community center** becomes a dance hall on a few Saturday nights, when from midnight to 2:00 in the morning, locals have a *ceilidh* (KAY-lee), the Irish equivalent of a hoedown. Ask at the TI to see if one is scheduled during your stay.

Events

The last weekend in June, Inishmore shakes off its slumber and kicks up its heels at the annual three-day **Patrún** celebration, with boat races and a fun run. June 23 is **St. John's Eve Bonfire Night,** a Christian/pagan tradition held the night before St. John's Day, close to (but not on) the summer solstice. Each community stokes a raging fire around dusk, and dozens are visible not only on the island, but also on distant shores.

Eating

There are few restaurants in Kilronan and none are fancy. Plan on comfort food at reasonable prices.

I like the friendly vibe and tasty grub up the hill at **Joe Watty's Bar.** It also has pleasant front-porch seating. Try the chicken goulash with a pint and stick around for the music (€15-22 meals, daily April-Oct 12:30-15:30 & 17:00-21:00, tel. 099/20892).

The **Aran Islands Hotel** has a modern pub serving simple soup-and-sandwich lunches and hot dinners (€12-24, daily 12:30-14:30 & 18:00-21:00, tel. 099/61104).

The Pier House operates the dependable **Bia Restaurant** on the ground floor of its guesthouse (€12-18 lunches, €18-25 dinners, daily May-Sept 11:00-22:00, tel. 099/61811).

In addition, Kilronan's modest cafés dish up hearty soup, soda bread, sandwiches, and tea.

The **Spar** supermarket has all the groceries you'll need (June-Aug Mon-Sat 9:00-20:00, Sun 10:00-17:00; Sept-May Mon-Sat 9:00-18:00, closed Sun).

Sleeping

This is a rustic island. Many rooms are plain, with sparse plumbing. Luxury didn't make the leap from the mainland. Only the Aran Islands (Ostan Aran) Hotel and The Pier House take credit cards—others are cash only.

In Kilronan

$$$ The **Aran Islands (Ostan Aran) Hotel** is the only modern option on the island. Its 20 rooms have the comforts you'd expect (four sport large harbor-facing porches). Beware of loud weekend stag/hen parties drawn to their downstairs pub (Db-€78-118, Tb-€117-147, 10-minute walk east of the dock on the coast road heading toward Killeany, tel. 099/61104, www.aranislandshotel.com, info@aranislandshotel.com).

$$$ **The Pier House** stands solidly, 50 yards from the pier, offering 12 decent rooms, a good restaurant downstairs, and sea views from many of its rooms (Sb-€55-60, Db-€70-100, Tb-€105-120, tel. 099/61417, www.pierhousearan.com, pierhousearan@gmail.com).

$$ **Clai Ban,** the only really cheery place in town, is run by friendly Marion and Bartley Hernon. Their six rooms and warm hospitality are worth the 10-minute uphill walk from the pier. The place is

patrolled by their affectionate and pudgy Corgi, Guinness (Sb-€50-70, Db-€60-70, Tb-€90-105, Qb-€110-120, cash only, walk past bank out of town and down lane on left, tel. 099/61111, claibanhouse@gmail.com).

$$ Tigh Catherine is a well-kept B&B with four homey rooms overlooking the harbor (Sb-€45-50, Db-€70, Tb-€90, cash only, on Church Road up behind the Halla Ronain community center, tel. 099/61464, mobile 087-980-9748, catherineandstiofain@gmail.com, Catherine Mulkerrin).

$$ Seacrest B&B offers six uncluttered rooms in a central location behind the Aran Sweater Market (Sb-€45-50, Db-€70, Tb-€90, cash only, tel. 099/61292, mobile 087-161-6507, seacrestaran@gmail.com, Geraldine and Tom Faherty).

$ Kilronan Hostel, overlooking the harbor near the TI, is cheap but noisy above Joe Mac's Pub (dorm bed-€18-25, self-service kitchen, tel. 099/61255, www.kilronanhostel.com, kilronanhostel@gmail.com).

Elsewhere on Inishmore

$$$ Man of Aran B&B, as classy as a thatched cottage can be, is in the peaceful countryside four miles outside of Kilronan, toward the western end of the island. Weigh the isolation against the fact that the five rooms are quiet and rustic, with fireplaces. The restaurant serves €18-25 meals (with homegrown vegetables and herbs) only to overnight guests. The setting is pristine—this is where much of the movie of the same name was filmed more than 80 years ago (S-€55, Sb-€60, D-€80, Db-€90, reserve well in advance, closed Nov-Feb; 4 miles/6.5 km from Kilronan, bear right 100 yards after passing Kilmurvey Beach before Dún Aenghus turnoff; tel. 099/61301, www.manofaran cottage.com, manofaran@eircom.net, Maura and Joe Wolf).

Getting Around Inishmore

Just about anything on wheels functions as a **taxi** here. A trip from Kilronan to Dún Aenghus to the Seven Churches and back to Kilronan costs €10 per person in a shared minivan. These range in capacity from 8 to 18 passengers. **Pony carts** cost about €50 for two people (€80 for 4) for a trip to Dún Aenghus and back.

Biking is great. Before heading out, check that your bike seat is correctly extended and stable enough so that you can comfortably extend both legs as you pedal. (The most frequent bike-rental complaint is a seat that won't stay in place and slowly slips down...cramping your legs when you're far down the island.) Take it for a short test spin while you're still near the rental shop.

Novice bikers should be aware that the terrain is hilly and there are occasional headwinds and unpredictable showers (figure 30 minutes to ride from Kilronan to start of trailhead up to Dún Aenghus). Cyclists should take the high road over and the low road back—fewer hills, scenic shoreline, and at low tide, a dozen seals basking in the sun. Keep a sharp lookout along the roads for handy, modern limestone signposts (with distances in kilometers) that point the way to important sights. They're in Irish, but you'll be clued in by the small metal depictions of the sights embedded within them.

Biking outside Kilronan

INISHEER

Inisheer (Inis Oír) offers a vivid glimpse of Aran Island culture and has an engaging smorgasbord of salty but modest sights. The roughly circular little island has only a quarter of the land area and population of Inishmore—my island of choice. But Inisheer's close proximity to the mainland makes it an easy 25-minute boat journey from Doolin and a good option for those with limited time who aren't going north to Galway (which is closer to the port of Rossaveel, where you sail to Inishmore).

To maximize your time on Inisheer, take an early boat from Doolin.

Orientation

You'll dock on the north side of the island in its only settlement. Facing inland with your back to the pier, you'll be able to see nearly all of the island's landmarks (except for the *An Plassy* shipwreck and the light-house on the southern shore). Although a handful of pony carts and minivan drivers meet you at the pier, I'd rely on them only on a rainy day (€10, but prices are soft... negotiate).

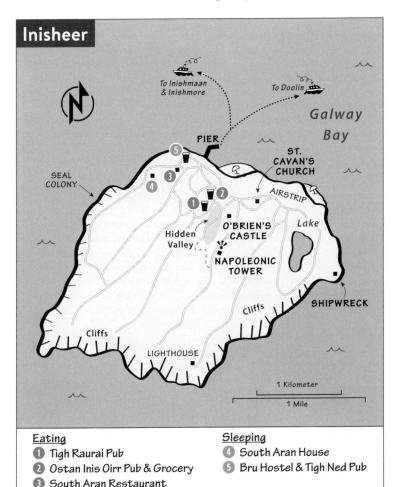

Eating
1. Tigh Raurai Pub
2. Ostan Inis Oirr Pub & Grocery
3. South Aran Restaurant

Sleeping
4. South Aran House
5. Bru Hostel & Tigh Ned Pub

For me, the joy of compact Inisheer is seeing it on a bike ride or a long breezy walk. The bike-rental shop is right at the base of the pier (€10/day, no deposit necessary "unless you look suspicious"). Any of the boat operators in Doolin can give you a free map of the island showing Inisheer's primitive road network. That's all you'll need to navigate.

The island has several pubs and one small grocery store, but no ATMs. All of the sights, with the exception of the lonely lighthouse on the southern coast, are concentrated on the northern half of an already small island.

Inisheer lacks the dramatic (and much higher) coastal cliffs of Inishmore, but has its own craggy, photogenic charms.

⊙ Inisheer Tour

The sights on this self-guided tour are free, open all the time, and marked on your free boat company map. See them in the order listed, from west to east, across the northern half of the island. If you bike rather than hike, be prepared to walk the bike up (or down) short, steep hills.

O'BRIEN'S CASTLE
(CAISLEAN UI BHRIAIN)

The ruins of this castle dominate the hill-top and are visible from almost anywhere on the northern half of the island. It's a steep 20-minute walk from the pier up to the castle ruins. The small castle was built as a tower house refuge around 1400 by the O'Brien clan from nearby County Clare. It sits inside a low wall of a much older Iron Age ring fort. Cromwell's troops destroyed the castle in 1652, leaving the evocative ruins you see today.

If you've huffed your way up to O'Brien's Castle, then go another easy five minutes to the **Napoleonic Tower** (An Tur Faire), which was built in the early 1800s to watch for a feared French invasion that never took place. The views from this highest point on the island are worth it.

• *Consult your map and continue walking (south) on the paved road into the heart of the island. Take your first right turn, roughly 100 yards after the Napoleonic Tower, onto a rocky, grassy cow lane that zigzags downhill into a lush* **hidden valley,** *displaying the prettiest mosaic of ivy-tangled rock walls and small green fields I've seen anywhere on the Aran Islands. Unholster your camera and fire away.*

Once you've wound your way back down to the main north-shore road again, turn right and continue east with the airstrip on your left. On your right, you'll soon see a time-passed graveyard up atop a sandy hill. Hike the 50 yards up into the graveyard to find...

ST. CAVAN'S CHURCH
(TEAMPALL CHAOMHAIN)

St. Cavan was the brother of St. Kevin, who founded the monastery at Glendalough in the Wicklow Mountains (see page 102). In the middle of the graveyard is a sunken sandpit holding the rugged roof-

Sleepy Inisheer

O'Brien's Castle

less remains of an 11th-century church. The shifting sand dunes almost buried it before sawgrass stabilized the hill. St. Cavan's reputed gravesite is protected by a tiny modern structure worth poking your head into for its candlelit atmosphere. Local folklore held that if you spent a night sleeping on the tomb lid, your particular illness would be cured.

• *Walk back down to the north-shore road and head out on the coast road (to the southeast) 30 minutes to the remote...*

SHIPWRECK OF THE *AN PLASSY*

This freighter was wrecked offshore on Finn's Rock in 1960. But islanders worked with the coastal patrol to help rescue the crew with no loss of life. A couple of weeks later the unmanned ship was washed high up onto the rocky shore, where it still sits today, a rusty but fairly intact ghost ship with a broken back. The fierce winter winds and record-breaking waves of 2013 shifted the wreck, further weakening it, and discussions are under way to remove it as it deteriorates. A local told me, "We may have to go out some night with lanterns to bring in a new shipwreck." Beware of turning an ankle on the unstable footing of the rounded cobbles thrown up by the surf near the wreck.

• *With more time, consult your map and seek out the remaining intimate church ruins and holy wells that the island has to offer. Or head back to town for a beverage while you await the return ferry.*

Eating

Inisheer's three main pubs offer decent pub grub (usually 12:30-20:30). **Tigh Raurai Pub** (House of Rory) is the epicenter of island social life (from the pier, head east to the edge of the beach and turn right—inland—up a narrow lane for 100 yards). Just below it, closer to the beach, is **Ostan Inis Oirr Pub** (Hotel Inisheer) with a colorful collage of international flags draping the pub's ceiling. **Tigh Ned Pub** (House of Ned) is right next door to Bru Hostel, near the pier on the north-shore road. Life could be worse than to sit outside at their appealing front tables on a summer evening, enjoying a pint in the salt air.

For a mellow evening meal, try the **South Aran Restaurant,** a five-minute walk west of the pier on the north-shore

The wreck of the An Plassy

road (daily 18:00-21:00, tel. 099/75073, mobile 087-340-5687).

Picnic lovers flock to the island's small **grocery**, Siopa XL, behind Ostan Inis Oirr Pub and below Tigh Raurai Pub (Mon-Sat 9:00-17:00, Sun 10:00-15:00).

Sleeping

A scattering of B&Bs dots the northern half of the island. Here are two good options:

$$ South Aran House is a quiet, well-run place with five spic-and-span, black-and-white rooms. Friendly Enda and Maria Conneely are generous with local tips and also run the nearby South Aran Restaurant, where you'll have breakfast (Sb-€45-55, Db-€70-90, an easy 10-minute walk west of the pier on north-shore road, call ahead with your ferry arrival time so they can meet you with keys, tel. 099/75073, mobile 087-340-5687, www.southaran.com, info@southaran.com). Their small rental cottage sleeps two (€100).

$ Bru Hostel is a simple, economical, 40-bed option just 100 yards west of the pier, next to Tigh Ned Pub (€20 dorm beds, includes continental breakfast, open May-Sept, tel. 099/75024, radharcnamara@hotmail.com).

TRANSPORTATION

Arriving and Departing
By Ferry
FROM ROSSAVEEL (NEAR GALWAY) TO INISHMORE

Island Ferries sails to Inishmore from Rossaveel, a port 20 miles west of Galway. The company sells tickets at the Galway TI and runs a 45-minute shuttle bus from Galway to the Rossaveel dock (3/day April-Oct, 2/day Nov-March, 45-minute crossing).

Coming from Galway, allow two hours in transit one-way, including the 45-minute shuttle bus ride (€25 round-trip boat crossing plus €7 round-trip for Galway-Rossaveel shuttle bus, 10 percent discount if you book online, WCs on board). Catch shuttle buses from Galway on Queen Street, a block behind the Kinlay Hostel (check-in 1.5 hours before sailing); shuttles return to Galway immediately after each boat arrives.

Here is the typical ferry schedule: April-Oct from Rossaveel at 10:30, 13:00, and 18:30; from Inishmore at 8:15, 12:00, 16:00, and 17:00 (plus 18:30 July-Aug). Confirm the latest schedule online at www.aranislandferries.com.

Island Ferries has two offices in Galway: on Forster Street across from the TI and across from Kinlay Hostel on Merchants Road (tel. 091/568-903, after-hours tel. 091/572-273).

Beware: The boat you take out to the islands may not be the same as the one you come back on. And sometimes you'll board by walking up the gangplank of one boat and walking across its deck to another boat docked beside or behind it. Make sure to ask.

Drivers: Go straight to the ferry landing in Rossaveel, passing several ticket agencies and pay parking lots. At the boat dock, you'll find a convenient parking lot and a small office that sells tickets for Island Ferries. Check to see what's going when and for how much.

FROM DOOLIN TO THE ARAN ISLANDS

Boats from Doolin can be handy, though the scene at the ferry dock is a confusing mosh pit of competition. Two ferry companies operate from three ticket huts with one thing in mind: snaring your business. They have similar schedules and might honor the other's return tickets if you decide you want to return at a different time. Prices can vary with the intensity of the competition.

Note that Doolin's ferries can be canceled in bad weather. The town's new deep-water pier will make departures more dependable, though the larger boats sailing from Rossaveel (near Galway) will always be less weather-dependent.

From Doolin, your best day trip is sailing to Inisheer, the closest Aran Island. Although ferry companies can take you all the way to Inishmore (promising to get you there in an hour's time), the journey—with brief stops at the other islands—actually takes more than 1.5 hours, leaving you with very little time to explore Inishmore before you have to turn around and sail back to Doolin. If you want to go as far as Inishmore, consider staying overnight there.

With a car, Doolin is easy to reach, and parking is free beside the pier, even overnight. Without a car, it's easier to get to Galway and Rossaveel, then cruise to Inishmore.

No matter which company you choose in Doolin, it's smart to check online for discounts, and call a day or two ahead to confirm schedules and prices.

Doolin2Aran Ferries is run by friendly Donie Garrihy and his family. Confirm their schedules online (to Inisheer: €15 same-day round-trip, 4/day, 30 minutes, departs at 10:00, 11:00, 13:00, and 17:30, returns at 8:15, 11:15, 14:00, and 16:45). They also offer a fun €25 triangular day trip that takes you from Doolin to Inisheer, drops you off on Inisheer for about four hours, then sails along the base of the Cliffs of Moher before docking back in Doolin (departs at 9:00, has you back in Doolin by 16:00, runs April-Oct, tel. 065/707-5949, mobile 087-245-3239, www.doolin2aranferries.com).

O'Brien Line, run by Bill O'Brien, has been at it the longest, with similar sched-ules and occasionally cheaper prices. They also offer a cruise along the base of the Cliffs of Moher that includes a stop at Inisheer (tel. 065/707-5555, www.obrienline.com).

By Plane

Aer Arann Islands, a friendly and flexible little airline, flies daily from Connemara Regional Airport, stopping at all three islands (3/day, up to 11/day in peak season, €25 one-way if boating back, €49 round-trip, groups of 4 or more pay €44 each, 10-minute flight, tel. 091/593-034, www.aerarannislands.ie, info@aerarannislands.ie). These eight-seat planes get booked up—reserve two or three days in advance with a credit card. Connemara Regional Airport is 20 slow miles west of Galway; allow 45 minutes for the drive, plus 30 minutes to check in before the scheduled departure. A cheap minibus shuttle runs from Victoria Hotel off Eyre Square in Galway an hour before each flight. Be sure to reserve a space on the shuttle bus at the same time you book your flight. The Kilronan airport on Inishmore is minuscule. A cheap minibus shuttle travels the two miles between the airport and Kilronan (where the bus stops behind the Aran Sweater Market).

From May through September, a sightseeing-only Aer Arann flight leaves from the same airport at 12:00 each day. You'll fly above all three Aran Islands with an extra swoop past the Cliffs of Moher (€60, 40 minutes, may not go if not enough people sign up).

Northern

The island of Ireland was once the longest-held colony of Great Britain. Unlike its Celtic cousins, Scotland and Wales, Ireland has always been distant from London—a distance due more to its Catholicism than the Irish Sea.

Four hundred years ago, Protestant settlers from England and Scotland were strategically "planted" in Catholic Ireland to help assimilate the island into the British economy. In 1620, the dominant English powerbase in London first felt entitled to call both islands—Ireland as well as Britain—the "British Isles" on maps (a geographic label that irritates Irish Nationalists to this day). These Protestant settlers established their own cultural toehold on the island, laying claim to the most fertile land. Might made right, and God was on their side. Meanwhile, the underdog Catholic Irish held strong to their Gaelic culture on their ever-diminishing, boggy, rocky farms.

Over the centuries, British rule hasn't been easy. By the beginning of the 20th century, the sparse Protestant population could no longer control the entire island. When Ireland won its independence in 1921 (after a bloody guerrilla war against British rule), 26 of the island's 32 counties became the Irish Free State, ruled from Dublin with dominion status in the British Commonwealth—similar to Canada's level of sovereignty. In 1949, these

Ireland

26 counties left the Commonwealth and became the Republic of Ireland, severing all political ties with Britain. Meanwhile, the six remaining northeastern counties—the only ones with a Protestant majority—chose not to join the Irish Free State and remained part of the UK.

But embedded within these six counties—now joined as the political entity called Northern Ireland—was a large, disaffected Catholic minority who felt they'd been sold down the river by the drawing of the new international border. Their political opponents were the "Unionists"—Protestants eager to defend the union with Britain, who were primarily led by two groups: the long-established Orange Order, and the military muscle of the newly mobilized Ulster Volunteer Force (UVF). This was countered on the Catholic side by the Irish Republican Army (IRA), who wanted all 32 of Ireland's counties to be united in one Irish nation—their political goals were "Nationalist."

In World War II, the Republic stayed neutral while the North enthusiastically supported the Allied cause—winning a spot close to London's heart. Derry (a.k.a. Londonderry) became an essential Allied convoy port, while Belfast lost more than 800 civilians during four Luftwaffe bombing raids in 1941. After the war, the split between North and South seemed permanent,

Northern Ireland Almanac

Official Name: Since Northern Ireland is not an independent state, there is no official country name. Some call it Ulster, while others label it the Six Counties. Population-wise, it's the smallest country of the United Kingdom (the other three are England, Wales, and Scotland).

Population: Northern Ireland's 1.8 million people are about 45 percent Protestant (mostly Presbyterian and Anglican) and 40 percent Catholic. Another 5 percent profess different religions, and 10 percent claim no religious ties. English is far and away the chief language, though Irish Gaelic is also spoken in staunchly Nationalist Catholic communities.

Despite the country's genetic homogeneity, the population is highly segregated along political, religious, and cultural lines. Roughly speaking, the eastern seaboard is more Unionist, Protestant, and of English-Scottish heritage, while the south and west (bordering the Republic of Ireland) are Nationalist, Catholic, and of Irish descent. Cities are often clearly divided between neighborhoods of one group or the other. Early in life, locals learn to identify the highly symbolic (and highly charged) colors, jewelry, music, names, and vocabulary that distinguish the cultural groups.

Latitude and Longitude: 54°N and 5°W. It's as far north as parts of the Alaskan panhandle.

Area: 5,400 square miles (about the size of Connecticut), constituting a sixth of the island. Northern Ireland includes 6 of the island's traditional 32 counties.

Geography: Northern Ireland is shaped roughly like a doughnut, with the UK's largest lake in the middle (Lough Neagh, 150 square miles and a prime eel fishery). The terrain comprises gently rolling hills of green grass, rising to the 2,800-foot Slieve Donard. The weather is temperate, cloudy, moist, windy, and hard to predict.

Biggest Cities: Belfast, the capital, has 300,000 residents. Half a million people—nearly one in three Northern Irish—inhabit the greater Belfast area. Derry (called Londonderry by Unionists) has 85,000 people.

Economy: Northern Ireland's economy is more closely tied to the UK than to the Republic of Ireland. Sectarian violence has held back growth, and the economy gets subsidies from the UK and the EU. Traditional agriculture (potatoes and grain) is fading fast, though modern techniques and abundant grassland make Northern Ireland a major producer of sheep, cows, and grass seed. Modern software and communications companies are replacing traditional manufacturing. Shipyards are rusty relics, and the linen industry is now threadbare; both are victims of cheaper labor available in Asia.

Currency: Northern Ireland uses the pound (£), not the euro.

Exchange rate: £1 = about $1.60.

Government: Northern Ireland is not a self-governing nation, but is part of the UK, ruled from London by Queen Elizabeth II and Prime Minister David Cameron, and represented in Parliament by 18 elected Members of Parliament. For 50 years (1922-1972), Northern Ireland was granted a great deal of autonomy and self-governance, known as "Home Rule." The current National Assem-

bly (108-seat Parliament)—after an ineffective decade of political logjams—has recently begun to show signs of rejuvenation.

Politics are dominated, of course, by the ongoing debate between Unionists (who want to preserve the union with the UK) and Nationalists (who want to join the Republic of Ireland). Two high-profile and controversial figures have been at opposite ends of this debate: the elderly firebrand Reverend Ian Paisley for the Unionists (who now serves in the British House of Lords); and assassination-attack survivor Gerry Adams of Sinn Fein, the political arm of the IRA (who now serves in the Republic of Ireland's parliament). In a hopeful development in the spring of 2007, the two allowed themselves to be photographed together across a negotiation table (a moment both had once sworn would never happen) as London returned control of the government to Belfast.

Flag: The official flag of Northern Ireland is the Union flag of the UK. But you'll also see the green, white, and orange Irish tricolor (waved by Nationalists) and the Northern Irish flag (white with a red cross and a red hand at its center), which is used by Unionists.

Northern Ireland Terminology

Ulster (one of Ireland's four ancient provinces) consists of nine counties in the northern part of the island of Ireland. Six of these make up Northern Ireland (pronounced "Norn Iron" by locals), while three counties remain part of the Republic.

Unionists—and the more hardline, working-class **Loyalists**—want the North to remain in the UK. The **Ulster Unionist Party** (**UUP**), the political party representing moderate Unionist views, is currently led by Mike Nesbitt (Nobel Peace Prize co-winner David Trimble led the UUP from 1995 to 2005). The **Democratic Unionist Party** (**DUP**), led by Peter Robinson (protégé of the late founder Reverend Ian Paisley) and supported by parliamentarian Jeffery Donaldson, takes a harder stance in defense of Unionism. The **Ulster Volunteer Force** (**UVF**), the **Ulster Freedom Fighters** (**UFF**), and the **Ulster Defense Association** (**UDA**) are the Loyalist paramilitary organizations mentioned most frequently in newspapers and on spray-painted walls.

Nationalists—and the more hardline, working-class **Republicans**—want a united and independent Ireland ruled by Dublin. The **Social Democratic Labor Party** (**SDLP**), founded by Nobel Peace Prize co-winner John Hume and currently led by Margaret Ritchie, is the moderate political party representing Nationalist views. **Sinn Fein** (shin fayn), led by Gerry Adams (working closely with Martin McGuinness), takes a harder stance in defense of Nationalism. The **Irish Republican Army** (**IRA**) is the Nationalist paramilitary organization (linked with Sinn Fein) mentioned most often in the press and in graffiti.

To gain more insight into the complexity of the **Troubles**, the 90-minute documentary *Voices from the Grave* provides an excellent overview (easy to find on YouTube). Also check out the University of Ulster's informative and evenhanded Conflict Archive at http://cain.ulst.ac.uk/index.html.

and Britain invested heavily in Northern Ireland to bring it solidly into the UK fold.

In the Republic of Ireland (the South), where 94 percent of the population was Catholic and only 6 percent Protestant, there was a clearly dominant majority. But in the North, at the time it was formed, Catholics were still a sizable 35 percent of the population—enough to demand attention. To maintain the status quo, Protestants considered certain forms of anti-Catholic discrimination necessary. It was this discrimination that led to the Troubles, the conflict that filled headlines from the late 1960s to the late 1990s.

Four hundred years ago (during the Reformation), this was a fight over Prot-

estant and Catholic religious differences. But over the last century, the conflict has been not about faith, but about politics: Will Northern Ireland stay part of the UK, or become part of the Republic of Ireland? The indigenous Irish of Northern Ireland, who generally want to unite with Ireland, happen to be Catholic (like their cousins to the south). The descendants of the Scottish and English settlers, who generally want to remain part of Britain, happen to be Protestant (like their beloved monarch).

Partly inspired by Martin Luther King Jr. and the civil rights movement in America—beamed into Irish living rooms by the new magic of television news—in the

Northern Ireland Politics

NATIONALISTS
(MOSTLY CATHOLICS)
"Feel Irish""

UNIONISTS
(MOSTLY PROTESTANTS)
"Feel British"

ALLIANCE
David Ford

SINN FEIN
Gerry Adams
Martin McGuinness

SDLP
Margaret Ritchie
John Hume
(retired)

UUP
Mike Nesbitt
David Trimble
(retired)

DUP
Peter Robinson
Jeffrey Donaldson
Ian Paisley
(deceased)

MODERATES

REPUBLICANS

LOYALISTS

GREEN

ORANGE

Not to scale &
not all opinions shown

1960s the Catholic minority in Northern Ireland began a nonviolent struggle to end discrimination, advocating for better jobs and housing. Extremists polarized issues, and demonstrations—also broadcast on TV news—became violent. Unionists were afraid that if the island became one nation, the relatively poor Republic of Ireland would drag down the comparatively affluent North, and that the high percentage of Catholics would spell repression for the Protestants. As Unionist Protestants and Nationalist Catholics clashed in 1969, the British Army entered the fray. Their role, initially a peacekeeping one, gradually evolved into acting as muscle for the Unionist government. In 1972, a tragic watershed year, more than 500 people died as combatants moved from petrol bombs to guns, and a new, more violent IRA emerged. In that 30-year (1968-1998) chapter of the struggle for an independent and united Ireland, more than 3,000 people were killed.

A 1985 agreement granted Dublin a consulting role in the Northern Ireland government. Unionists bucked this idea, and violence escalated. That same year, Belfast City Hall draped a huge, defiant banner under its dome, proclaiming, *Belfast Says No.*

In 1994, the banner came down. In the 1990s—with Ireland's membership in the EU, the growth of its economy, and the weakening of the Catholic Church's influence—the consequences of a united Ireland became slightly less threatening to the Unionists. Also in 1994, the IRA declared a cease-fire, and the Protestant Ulster Volunteer Force (UVF) followed suit.

Nationalist mural on Falls Road

The Nationalists wanted British troops out of Northern Ireland, while the Unionists demanded that the IRA turn in its arms. Optimists hailed the signing of a breakthrough peace plan in 1998, called the "Good Friday Accord" by Nationalists, or the "Belfast Agreement" by Unionists. This led to the release of prisoners on both sides in 2000—a highly emotional event.

Recently, additional progress has taken place on both fronts. The IRA finally "verifiably put their arms beyond use" in 2005, and backed the political peace process. In 2009, most Loyalist paramilitary groups did the same. Meanwhile, British Army surveillance towers were dismantled in 2006, and the army formally ended its 38-year-long Operation Banner campaign in 2007.

A tiny splinter group of stubborn IRA diehards (calling themselves the "Real IRA") continues to smolder. Their efforts at publicity are roundly condemned not only by hard-line Unionists, but also by former IRA leaders like government minister Martin McGuinness and his Sinn Fein party, who now prefer to pursue their Nationalist goals through the democratic process.

In 2010, the peace process was jolted forward by a surprisingly forthright apology offered by British Prime Minister David Cameron, who expressed regret for the British Army's offenses on Bloody Sunday. The apology was prompted by the Saville Report—the results of an investigation conducted by the UK government as part of the Good Friday Accord. It found that the 1972 shootings of Nationalist civil-rights marchers on Bloody Sunday by British soldiers was "unjustified" and the victims innocent (to the intense relief of the victims' families, who had fought since 1972 to clear their loved ones' names).

Major hurdles to a lasting peace persist, but the downtown checkpoints are history, and the "bomb-damage clearance sales" are over. In 2013, the G8 leaders of eight of the largest economies in the world (US President Barack Obama, Russia's President Vladimir Putin, and Germany's Chancellor Angela Merkel to name a few) chose serene, lake-splattered County Fermanagh to hold their annual summit. And today, more tourists than ever are venturing north.

Safety

A generation ago, Northern Ireland was a sadly contorted corner of the world. Today, tourists in Northern Ireland are no longer considered courageous (or reckless). You're safer in Belfast than in many other UK cities—and far safer, statistically, than in most major US cities. You have to look for trouble to find it here. Just don't seek out spit-and-sawdust pubs in working-class neighborhoods and spew simplistic and naive opinions about sensitive local topics.

Tourists notice the tension mainly during the "marching season" (Easter-

Orangeman parade

Paramilitary mural on Shankill Road

Aug, peaking in early July). July 12—"the Twelfth"—is traditionally the most confrontational day of the year in the North, when proud Protestant Unionist Orangemen march to celebrate their Britishness and their separate identity from the Republic of Ireland (often through staunchly Nationalist Catholic neighborhoods). Lie low if you stumble onto any big Orange parades.

Northern Ireland Is a Different Country

The border is almost invisible. But when you leave the Republic of Ireland and enter Northern Ireland, you *are* crossing an international border (although you don't have to flash your passport). Gas is a little cheaper in the Republic of Ireland than in Northern Ireland (so fill up before crossing the border). Meanwhile, groceries and dental procedures are cheaper in the North (put off that root canal until you hit Belfast). These price differences create a lively daily shopping trade for those living near the border.

You won't use euros here; Northern Ireland issues its own Ulster pound, which, like the Scottish pound, is interchangeable with the English pound (€1 = about £0.80; £1 = about $1.60). Some establishments near the border may take euros, but at a lousy exchange rate. So keep any euros for your return to the Republic, and get pounds from an ATM inside Northern Ireland instead. And if you're heading to Britain next, it's best to change your Ulster pounds into English ones (free at any bank in Northern Ireland, England, Wales, or Scotland).

Belfast

Seventeenth-century Belfast was just a village. The influx of English and Scottish settlers—and the subjugation of the native Irish—changed its character. Spurred on by the success of the local linen, rope-making, and especially ship-building industries, Belfast boomed. The Industrial Revolution took root with a vengeance, earning the city its nickname ("Old Smoke").

Belfast is the birthplace of the *Titanic* (and many other ships that didn't sink). In 2012, to mark the 100th anniversary of the *Titanic* disaster, a new attraction was launched in Belfast's shipyard, telling the ill-fated ship's fascinating and tragic story. Nearby, two huge, mustard-colored cranes (built in the 1970s, and once the biggest in the world, nicknamed Samson and Goliath) rise like skyscrapers. They stand idle now, but serve as a reminder of this town's former shipbuilding might...strategic enough to be the target of four Luftwaffe bombing raids in World War II.

Today, it feels like a new morning in Belfast. It's hard to believe that the bustling pedestrian center was once a subdued, traffic-free security zone. Now there's no hint of security checks, once a tiresome daily routine. Both Catholics and Protestants are rooting for the Belfast Giants ice hockey team, one of many reasons to live together peacefully.

BELFAST IN 2 DAYS

Belfast makes a pleasant overnight stop, with plenty of inexpensive accommodations, weekend hotel deals, and a relaxed neighborhood with B&Bs 30 minutes away in Bangor.

Day 1: Browse the pedestrian zones around City Hall, take the City Hall tour (11:00, none on Sun), have lunch, then ride a shared black taxi up Falls Road. Visit the Titanic Belfast after midday crowds subside. Stroll the Golden Mile.

On any evening: Make reservations for a memorable splurge meal at the Merchant Hotel, have dinner at a pub, or rub elbows with the locals in the historic Crown Liquor Saloon. See what's on at the Opera House or Lyric Theatre.

Day 2: Take the City Sightseeing bus tour or a walking tour in the morning. In the afternoon, choose among the Ulster Folk Park and Transport Museum (in nearby Cultra), Botanic Gardens, Ulster Museum, more tours (boat or bike), or Carrickfergus Castle (outside of Belfast).

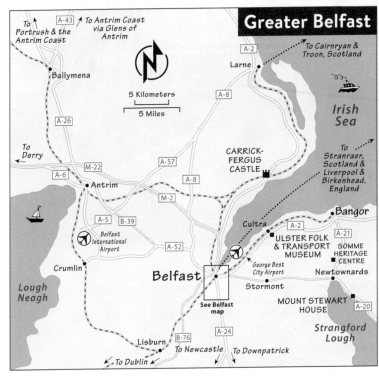

Greater Belfast

To Portrush & the Antrim Coast

A-43 To Antrim Coast via Glens of Antrim

To Cairnryan & Troon, Scotland

Larne

A-2

Ballymena

Irish Sea

5 Kilometers
5 Miles

A-8

A-26

To Derry

CARRICK-FERGUS CASTLE

To Stranraer, Scotland & Liverpool & Birkenhead, England

A-57

A-8

M-22

A-6

Antrim

M-2

Bangor

A-5   B-39

Cultra

A-2

A-21

Belfast International Airport

A-52

 ULSTER FOLK & TRANSPORT MUSEUM

SOMME HERITAGE CENTRE

Crumlin

Belfast

George Best City Airport

Newtownards

Lough Neagh

See Belfast map

Stormont

MOUNT STEWART HOUSE

A-20

Strangford Lough

Lisburn   B-76

A-24

To Newcastle   To Downpatrick

To Dublin

Yet another option is taking an all-day bus tour of the Antrim Coast.

If Day-Tripping from Dublin: Using the handy, two-hour Dublin-Belfast train (get "day return" tickets), here's a plan that works well any day but Sunday:

At 7:35, catch the early-morning train from Dublin's Connolly Station (arriving in Belfast's Central Station at 9:45). In Belfast, take the City Hall tour at 11:00, have lunch, taxi to Falls Road, and visit Titanic Belfast (or the Ulster Folk Park and Transport Museum). Return to Dublin in the evening (last train departs Belfast Mon-Sat at 20:05 and arrives in Dublin at 22:15). Confirm train times at local stations. A day trip doesn't work well on Sunday, when the trains depart later and return earlier, compressing your sightseeing time in Belfast to just six hours.

ORIENTATION

For visitors, there are four zones of interest: **northern** (Titanic Quarter—docklands with Odyssey entertainment complex and Titanic Belfast), **western** (working-class sectarian neighborhoods west of the A-12 freeway), **central** (Donegall Square, City Hall, pedestrian shopping, and TI), and **southern** (Botanic Gardens, Queen's University, and Ulster Museum).

The eastern part of Belfast is more affluent and residential, with little of interest to the average sightseer, except for Stormont (the seat of government in Northern Ireland).

The modern bookends of sightseeing interest are the Titanic Belfast attraction (in the Titanic Quarter to the north) and the Lyric Theatre (near the university district to the south). Their contemporary

BELFAST AT A GLANCE

▲▲▲**Titanic Belfast** High-tech homage to the colossal and ill-fated luxury liner on the spot where it was built and last touched dry land. **Hours:** Daily April-Sept 9:00-19:00, Oct-March 10:00-17:00. See page 285.

▲▲**Falls Road** Nationalist Catholic enclave featuring passionate murals, gardens of remembrance, a section of the Peace Wall, and assorted workaday shops and pubs. See page 288.

▲▲**City Hall** Architectural showpiece of aristocratic Victorian society built with money from the golden age of Belfast's industrial might. **Hours:** Building open Mon-Thu 8:30-17:00, Fri 8:30-16:30, closed (except for tours) Sat, closed Sun. See page 289.

▲▲**Ulster Folk Park and Transport Museum** Sprawling hillside complex split between an Old World village of original buildings and a piston-lover's fantasy of locally made vehicles of all shapes and sizes. **Hours:** March-Sept Tue-Sun 10:00-17:00; Oct-Feb Tue-Fri 10:00-16:00, Sat-Sun 11:00-16:00; closed Mon year-round. See page 294.

▲**Ulster Museum** Regional cross-section of cultural history and natural wonders offering a variety of displays from dinosaur bones to Belleek china to dueling pistols. **Hours:** Tue-Sun 10:00-17:00, closed Mon. See page 293.

▲**Botanic Gardens** A peaceful 28-acre green zone retreat surrounding the Windex-worthy Palm House and its flourishing thicket of tropical botany. **Hours:** Gardens open daily 8:00 until dusk; Palm House open Mon-Fri 10:00-12:00 & 13:00-17:00, Sat-Sun 13:00-17:00, shorter hours in winter. See page 293.

The Odyssey Modern pavilion housing kid-friendly, interactive W5 science center as well as restaurants, an ice hockey arena, and a cinema. **Hours:** Mon-Fri 10:00-17:00, Sat 10:00-18:00, Sun 12:00-18:00. See page 294.

Shankill Road and Sandy Row Unionist Protestant heartland of staunch pro-British murals, red-white-and blue banners, WWI memorials, and reverence for Ulster's industrial heritage. See page 289.

Golden Mile Retail drag connecting Queens University to City Hall, starring the Crown Liquor Saloon, Victorian Opera House, and famous Hotel Europa. See page 291.

Carrickfergus Castle Accessible citadel on Belfast Lough—witness to a French invasion, a naval raid by John Paul Jones, and landings by Scotland's Edward the Bruce and England's William of Orange. **Hours:** April-Sept daily 10:00-18:00; Oct-March Mon-Sat 10:00-16:00, Sun 14:00-16:00. See page 295.

angularities contrast sharply with the red-brick uniformity of old Belfast. The core of city navigation hinges on four central landmarks (listed from north to south): Albert Clock Tower, City Hall, Shaftesbury Square, and Queen's University. Find them on your map, and use them to navigate as you stroll the town.

Belfast's Golden Mile—stretching from Hotel Europa to the university district—connects the central and southern zones with many dinner and entertainment spots.

Tourist Information

The modern **TI** (look for *Visit Belfast* sign) has a courteous staff and inexpensive baggage storage for day-trippers (Mon-Sat 9:00-17:30, June-Sept until 19:00, Sun 11:00-16:00 year-round; a couple of doors down from the Linen Hall Library, just across Chichester Street, north of City Hall at 9 Donegall Square North, tel. 028/9024-6609, www.gotobelfast.com). City walking **tours** depart from the TI (see "Tours," later). Pick up a free copy of *Visit Belfast*, which lists all the sightseeing and evening entertainment options.

Sightseeing Pass

The **Belfast Visitor Pass** combines iLink smartcards for free bus and rail travel with sightseeing discounts for one day or two or three consecutive days within the Belfast Visitor Pass Zone (all of downtown Belfast as far out as the Ulster Folk and Transport Museum in Cultra, but not as far as Carrickfergus or Bangor). The handy one-day pass saves money for anyone visiting Titanic Belfast (10 percent discount) and the Ulster Folk and Transport Museum (30 percent discount) while connecting them by train or bus (free with pass). Buy it at the TI, any train station, either airport, Europa Bus station, or online (£6.50/1-day pass, £11/2 days, £14.50/3 days, tel. 028/9066-6630, www.translink.co.uk).

Tours

Belfast Compass Tours introduces you to the city's 300-year history on a two-hour stroll. Highlights include City Hall, St. George's Market, Albert Clock, and the opulent Merchant Hotel (£7, must book in advance, mobile 079-4425-6560 or 079-3440-7751, www.belfastcompass tours.com).

The following walking tours cover local culture and **the Troubles,** offering opposite viewpoints. Listen and learn. Or, as an Irish friend once told me, "Never give unsolicited advice...wise men don't need it and fools won't heed it."

Coiste Irish Political Tours, led by former IRA prisoners, offers the Nationalist/Republican viewpoint on extended, two-hour walks along Falls Road, visiting murals, gardens of remembrance, and peace walls. Tours meet beside the Divis Tower (the 20-story apartment house at the east end of the Divis Road near the A-12 Westlink motorway overpass) and end at the Milltown Cemetery (£10; Tue, Thu, and Sat at 11:00, Sun at 14:00; tel. 028/9020-0770, www.coiste.ie, Seamus Kelley).

Sandy Row Walking Tours provides the Unionist/Loyalist point of view during

Tour guide in Belfast

its 1.5-hour walks that center on Sandy Row, Belfast's oldest residential neighborhood. They depart from the King William Mural at the intersection of Sandy Row and Linfield Road (£7.50; daily at 10:00, 14:00, and 17:00; must book in advance, mobile 079-0925-4849, www.historic sandyrow.co.uk).

City Sightseeing's hop-on, hop-off bus tours offer the best introduction to the city's political and social history. Their open-top, double-decker buses link major sights and landmarks. Pay cash on bus or book online in advance (£12.50, 2/hour, fewer in winter, daily 10:00-16:00, tickets valid for 48 hours, 20 stops, 1.5-hour loop; departs from Castle Place on High Street, 2 blocks west of Albert Clock Tower; tel. 028/9032-1321, www.city-sightseeing. com).

City Tours offers two routes with more than 20 stops each. The red route starts on High Street (near Albert Clock) and runs more frequently (9:30-16:30), veering westward to take in Falls and Shankill roads. The black route starts at Victoria Square and departs only at 12:00 and 15:00, heading eastward to reach Stormont (parliament) and a bigger slice of the Titanic Quarter (£12.50, ticket good for both routes for 72 hours, pay cash on bus or book in advance, tel. 028/9032-1912, www.citytoursbelfast.com).

Titanic Tours Belfast is run by former TV reporter and Rick Steves' Europe guide Susie Millar. She offers a three-hour car tour (yours or hers) that picks up and drops off at your hotel. Susie's great-grandfather was a crew member who perished on that fateful cruise (£30, book in advance, mobile 078-5271-6655, www.titanictours-belfast.co.uk, info@ titanictours.com).

Lagan Boat Company shows you shipyards on a one-hour **harbor cruise**, narrated by a member of the Belfast Titanic Society. The heart of the tour is a lazy harbor cruise past rusty dry-dock gates. Tours depart from the Lagan Pedestrian Bridge

and Weir on Donegall Quay. The quay is located just past the leaning Albert Clock Tower, a 10-minute walk from the TI (£10; April-Oct daily sailings at 12:30, 14:00, and 15:30; fewer off-season, tel. 028/9024-0124, mobile 077-1891-0423, www.lagan boatcompany.com).

Belfast Bike Tours explore the countryside south of town. Departing from the front gate of Queen's University, you'll spend 2.5 hours peddling along an old canal towpath to the Giant's Ring (£15; April-Aug Mon, Wed, and Fri-Sat at 10:30 and 14:00; Sept-March Sat 10:30 and 14:00; bikes, helmets, and bottle of water provided; must reserve ahead by phone or email, mobile 078-1211-4235, www. belfastbiketours.com, info@belfastbike tours.com).

McComb's Giant's Causeway Tour visits Carrickfergus Castle, the Giant's Causeway, Dunluce Castle (photo stop only), Carrick-a-Rede Rope Bridge, and Old Bushmills Distillery (£25, doesn't include distillery admission, daily depending on demand, book through and depart from the Belfast International City Hostel, 9:00 pickup at hostel, 9:30 pickup at Hotel Europa—a block north of Central Station, back to Belfast by 19:00). Their *Game of Thrones* tour visits many of the sites where the hit fantasy TV series was filmed (£35, 8:30 pickup at Belfast International City Hostel, 9:00 pickup at Opera House stage door on the corner of Glengall Street, back to Belfast by 19:00). They also have private guides (book in advance, tel. 028/9031-5333, www.mccombscoaches. com).

Helpful Hints

Market: On Friday, Saturday, and Sunday, the Victorian confines of **St. George's Market** is a commotion of commerce and a people-watching delight. Friday is a variety market (6:00-14:00), Saturday blooms with food and garden items (9:00-15:00), and Sunday creaks with crafts and antiques (10:00-16:00). Located at the

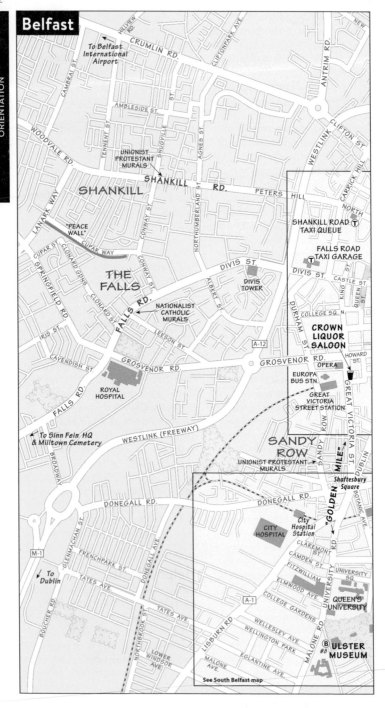

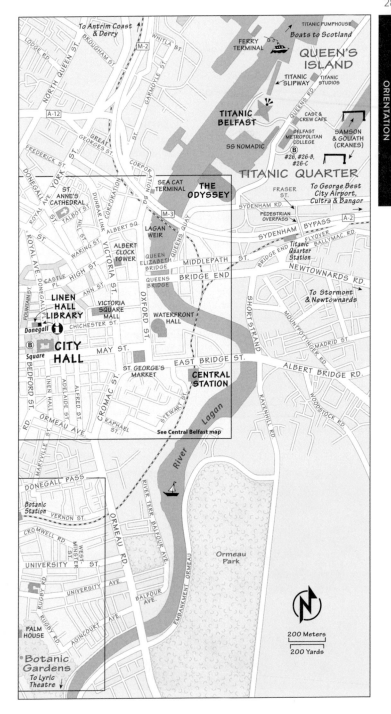

To Antrim Coast & Derry
WHITLA ST.
LODGE RD.
NORTH QUEEN ST.
BROUGHAM ST.
M-2
GARMOYLE ST.
A-12
GREAT
GEORGES ST.
FREDERICK ST.
CORPORATION ST.

TITANIC PUMPHOUSE
Boats to Scotland
FERRY TERMINAL
QUEEN'S ISLAND
TITANIC SLIPWAY
TITANIC STUDIOS
QUEENS RD.
TITANIC BELFAST
CAST & CREW CAFE
SS NOMADIC
BELFAST METROPOLITAN COLLEGE
SAMSON & GOLIATH (CRANES)
B
#26, #26-B, #26-C
TITANIC QUARTER

DONEGALL AVE.
ROYAL ST.
YORK ST.
ST. ANNE'S CATHEDRAL
TALBOT ST.
DUNBAR LINK
WARING ST.
HILL ST.
ALBERT SQ.
SEA CAT TERMINAL
THE ODYSSEY
LAGAN WEIR
M-3
QUEENS QUAY
FRASER ST.
To George Best City Airport, Cultra & Bangor
SYDENHAM RD.
PEDESTRIAN OVERPASS
A-2
SYDENHAM BYPASS
FLYOVER
BRIDGE END
BALLYMAC RD.
Titanic Quarter Station

ROYAL AVE.
DONEGALL ST.
CASTLE PL.
HIGH ST.
VICTORIA ST.
ALBERT CLOCK TOWER
QUEEN ELIZABETH BRIDGE
MIDDLEPATH
BRIDGE END
NEWTOWNARDS RD.
SHORT STRAND
MOUNTPOTTINGER RD.
MADRID ST.
To Stormont & Newtownards

LINEN HALL LIBRARY
FOUNTAIN ST.
DONEGALL PL.
ANN ST.
VICTORIA SQUARE MALL
CHICHESTER ST.
OXFORD ST.
QUEENS BRIDGE
WATERFRONT HALL

Donegall
B
Square
CITY HALL
MAY ST.
CROMAC ST.
EAST BRIDGE ST.
ALBERT BRIDGE RD.
RAVENHILL RD.
WOODSTOCK RD.

BEDFORD ST.
LINEN HALL ST.
ADELAIDE ST.
ALFRED ST.
ST. GEORGE'S MARKET
STEWART ST.
CENTRAL STATION
ORMEAU AVE.
RD.
RAPHAEL ST.
See Central Belfast map

River Lagan

MARYVILLE ST.
DONEGALL PASS
Botanic Station
VERNON ST.
ORMEAU RD.
RIVER TERR.
BALFOUR AVE.
EMBANKMENT ORMEAU

CROMWELL RD.
WEST MINSTER ST.
UNIVERSITY ST.
UNIVERSITY AVE.
RUGBY RD.
BALFOUR AVE.
AGINCOURT AVE.
Ormeau Park

PALM HOUSE
N
200 Meters
200 Yards

Botanic Gardens
To Lyric Theatre

corner of Oxford and East Bridge Streets, 5 blocks east of Donegall Square, tel. 028/9043-5704, www.belfastcity.gov.uk/markets.

Phone Tips: To call the Republic of Ireland from Northern Ireland, dial 00-353, then the area code without its initial 0, and then the local number. If calling from a Republic of Ireland number to a Northern Ireland landline (any number that begins with the prefix 028), you can simply dial 048 instead, and then the local eight-digit number. However, to call a Northern Ireland mobile phone number from the Republic, you'll need to dial as if making an international call (including the international access code, country code, and Northern Ireland's area code).

Rick's Tip: *Located directly across University Road from the red-brick university building,* **Queen's University Student Union** *is as handy for tourists as it is for students. Inside you'll find an ATM (at end of main hall, on the right), WCs, a mini-market, and Wi-Fi. Grab a quick and cheap sandwich and coffee at* **Clement's Coffee Shop** *(long hours Mon-Sat, closed Sun).*

Bike Rental: Belfast Bike Tours rents bikes only if reserved in advance (£15/day,

daily but no set hours, off Wellington Park behind Wellington Park Hotel, mobile 078-1211-4235, www.belfastbiketours.com).

SIGHTS

Titanic Quarter

Up until the mid-1990s, this district was a barren wasteland of cement slabs and rusting industrial relics. But during the Celtic Tiger boom years (which spilled over into the North), shrewd investors saw the real-estate potential and began building posh, high-rise condos.

The first landmark project to be completed was the Odyssey entertainment complex (in 2000). To draw more visitors and commemorate the proud shipbuilding industry of the Victorian and Edwardian Ages, another flagship attraction was needed. The 100th anniversary of the *Titanic* disaster in 2012 provided the perfect opportunity, and the result is a new attraction called Titanic Belfast.

THE ODYSSEY

This huge millennium-project complex offers a food pavilion, bowling alley, and W5 science center with interactive, educational exhibits for youngsters. Where else can a kid play a harp with laser-light

Modern Belfast

Titanic Trio

Most of us know the story of the *Titanic*, when the unthinkable happened to the unsinkable. Launched in Belfast in 1911, the *Titanic* was the largest and most celebrated luxury cruise liner of its time. Its sudden demise in 1912 is the most famous sea disaster of the modern era. Only 716 of the 2,260 aboard were rescued; 70 percent of the first-class passengers, with first dibs on the few lifeboats, survived.

While everyone has heard of the *Titanic*, few know that it was the middle sister of three unfortunate ships, each built in Belfast by the prestigious Harland and Wolff shipyards for the White Star Line.

In 1910, the **Olympic** was the first of the three similar vessels to be launched. It soon collided with the naval cruiser HMS *Hawke* and returned to Belfast to be repaired with parts taken from the still-under-construction **Titanic.** When World War I began, the *Olympic* served as a troop transport ship. During the war, it struck and sank a German submarine (the U-103). After the war, it returned to commercial service and later collided with the *Nantucket Lightship* (killing seven). The Olympic's last voyage was in 1935; it was demolished in 1937.

The last of the three to be built was the **Gigantic** in 1914. But after the *Titanic* sank, its name was changed (while still under construction) to **Britannic**...which was thought to be a luckier name. It was repainted white and converted to a hospital ship at the start of World War I. In 1915, it was serving in the Aegean Sea when it hit a mine—or was struck by a torpedo from a U-boat. Fortunately, it had more advanced safety features than its two older sisters—it had enough lifeboats for all onboard, and was designed to sink more slowly. Only 30 of the almost 1,100 crew and medical staff died. In 1976, French underwater explorer Jacques Cousteau found the wreck of the *Britannic* 400 feet down and brought up a few of its artifacts.

A single human thread ties all three ships together. A stewardess and nurse named Violet Jessop was aboard the *Olympic* when it collided with the HMS *Hawke*. She was also one of the lucky few to be rescued from the *Titanic*. And yes, she was again among those rescued from the sinking *Britannic*. Talk about a buoyant personality...

strings? The "W5" stands for "who, what, when, where, and why." There's also a 12-screen cinema, laser-tag gaming area, and an 8,000-seat arena where the Belfast Giants professional ice hockey team skates from September to March on Friday or Saturday nights (£15 game tickets, tel. 028/9073-9074, www.belfastgiants.com).

Cost and Hours: £8.50, kids-£6.50, Mon-Fri 10:00-17:00, Sat 10:00-18:00, Sun 12:00-18:00, 2 Queen's Quay, 10-minute walk north of Belfast's Central Station, tel. 028/9046-7790, www.w5online.co.uk.

▲▲▲TITANIC BELFAST

This £97 million attraction sits on the site of the original dry dock where the ship was built. High-tech displays tell the tale of the famous cruise liner, proudly heralded as the largest man-made moving object of its time. The sight has no actual artifacts from the underwater wreck (little has been brought up out of respect for the fact that it's a mass grave).

Cost and Hours: £15.50, daily April-Sept 9:00-19:00, Oct-March 10:00-17:00, audioguide for infoholics-£3, located where the famous ship was built on Queen's Island, tel. 028/9076-6399, www.titanicbelfast.com. Skip the £25 **White Star Premium Pass,** which covers the Titanic Belfast, Discovery Tour, and *SS Nomadic* but costs more than paying for all three individually because you get a souvenir photo.

Getting There: From Donegall Square, take bus #26 or #26B (both stop behind Belfast Metropolitan College, infrequent buses on Sun), or go by taxi (£6 ride). The Titanic Quarter train station is a 10-minute walk to the south of the Titanic Belfast.

Rick's Tip: *The **Titanic** Museum drew 800,000 visitors in its first year (double what was expected).* **Go early or late;** *big bus-tour crowds clog the exhibits from 10:00 to 14:00.* **Book ahead online** *to ensure the entry time you want.*

Tours: The Discovery Tour explains the striking architecture of the Titanic Belfast building and the adjacent slipways where the great ship was built. You also get a peek inside nearby Harland and Wolff Drawing Offices, where plans for its construction were drawn up (£7, 45 minutes, call ahead for tour times).

Eating: The ground floor includes a sandwich café as well as a carvery-style restaurant. If these options are crowded, walk one block east, through the arch in the Drawing Offices building and across Queens Road to the battleship-gray Cast & Crew café (£7-10 sandwich/soup/salad lunches, daily 12:00-18:00).

Visiting the Sight: The spacey architecture of Titanic Belfast's new building is already a landmark on the city's skyline. Six stories tall, it's clad in more than 3,000 sun-reflecting aluminum panels. Its four corners represent the bows of the many ships that were built in these yards during the golden age of Belfast.

Inside, nine galleries take you from booming 1900s Belfast, through the con-

struction and launch of the *Titanic,* and ultimately to a re-creation of its watery grave. A highlight is the Shipyard Ride, which takes you through a mock-up of the ship while it was being built. You'll learn how workers toughed out months of deafening and dangerous duty, working in five-man teams to hammer in red-hot rivets (they were paid by the rivet, and were frequently burned by chips flying off the metal). For efficiency, left- and right-handers were assigned specific hammering positions. Young boys had the hot and hazardous job of quickly catching the glowing rivets and placing them for the hammerers.

Other exhibits cover the wider story of the Harland and Wolff shipyards, including the construction of Titanic's lesser-known and also ill-fated sister ships: *Olympic* and *Britannic* (see sidebar). An upper-floor viewpoint employs innovative electronic windows to project an image of the huge, partially built *Titanic* in dry dock beside you, masking the reality of today's barren shipyard below. Another gallery surrounds you on three sides with ani-

Titanic Belfast

mated screens that glide through multiple decks, giving you a realistic feel for the ship in all its full-steam-ahead glory.

The human story of its passengers—from promenade-deck aristocrats to heroic crew members to steerage-class rabble—is also here. The passenger manifest encompassed virtually every segment of society: In today's dollars, a first-class ticket would cost $70,000, while a third-class ticket would cost $650. Unbelievably, the families of dead crew members were charged for their missing uniforms. You'll see a broad cross-section of displays from the ship's short but opulent existence.

The big-screen "Titanic Beneath" theater shows the now-famous underwater footage of the wreck nearly 12,500 feet down on the ocean floor. Only 20 percent of the dead were ever recovered. Don't miss the see-through floor panels at the foot of the movie screen, which allow you to stand on top of the watery debris field as the virtual wreck slowly passes beneath your feet.

Outside, go to the northern corner of the building (diagonally across from the eight-foot-tall, rusted-iron Titanic sign at the main southern entry). Look down at the paving stones and get oriented: Gray tiles represent land, and white ones represent ocean. As you follow the metal strip marking the fateful route (many yards) across the Atlantic, you'll find the wreck's coordinates interrupting the uncompleted route. Then look up at the parallel rows of lampposts leading away from you for 300 yards (the length of the ship). This was the slipway for initial construction of the vessel. Visualize the Titanic, partially built and crawling with workmen, rising 175 feet into the air ahead of you. It filled most of the space between the long left and center rows of lampposts. Follow the lines in the paving stones along the left row of lights, which mirrors the ship's mammoth hull, including the (too few) lifeboats. At the far end, you'll come to the water's edge,

where a curved railing simulates the stern (made famous by Kate Winslet and Leonardo DiCaprio's first and last meetings in the 1997 movie).

Nearby: Folks with a strong interest in the Titanic may want to visit the SS Nomadic tender ship that once ferried passengers between the dock and the Titanic (£3, same hours as Titanic Belfast, docked 50 yards south of Titanic Belfast and easily visible).

Sectarian Neighborhoods in West Belfast

It will be a happy day when the sectarian neighborhoods of Belfast have nothing to be sectarian about. For a look at three of the original home bases of the Troubles, explore the working-class neighborhoods of Catholic Falls Road and Protestant Shankill Road (west of the Westlink motorway), or Protestant Sandy Row (south of the Westlink motorway).

Murals (found in working-class, sectarian areas) are a memorable part of any visit to Belfast. But with more peaceful times, the character of these murals is slowly changing. The Re-Imaging Communities Program has spent £3 million in government money to replace aggressive murals with positive ones. Paramilitary themes are gradually being covered over with images of pride in each neighborhood's culture. The Titanic was built primarily by proud Protestant Ulster stock and is often seen in their neighborhood murals—reflecting their industrious work ethic. Over in the Catholic neighborhoods, you'll see more murals, depicting mythological heroes from the days before the English came.

You can get taxi tours of Falls Road or Shankill Road (see next listings), but rarely are both combined without bias in one tour. **Ken Harper** is one of a new breed of Belfast taxi drivers who will give you an insightful private tour of both neighborhoods. He's also available for custom tours (£30 minimum or £10/person, 1.25

hours, tel. 028/9074-2711, mobile 077-1175-7178, www.harpertaxitours.com, kenharper2004@hotmail.com).

▲▲FALLS ROAD (CATHOLIC)

At the intersection of Castle and King streets, you'll find the Castle Junction Car Park. On the ground floor of this nine-story parking garage, a passenger terminal (entrance on King Street) connects travelers with old black cabs—and the only Irish-language signs in downtown Belfast. These shared black cabs efficiently shuttle residents from outlying neighborhoods up and down Falls Road and to the city center. This service originated more than 40 years ago at the beginning of the Troubles, when locals would hijack city buses and use them as barricades in the street fighting. When bus service was discontinued, local paramilitary groups established the shared taxi service. Although the buses are now running again, these cab rides are still a great value for their drivers' commentary.

Falls Road

Any cab goes up Falls Road, past Sinn Fein headquarters and lots of murals, to the Milltown Cemetery (£6, sit in front and talk to the cabbie). Hop in and out. Easy-to-flag-down cabs run every minute or so in each direction on Falls Road.

Forty trained cabbies do one-hour tours (1-3 people for £30, £10/additional person, £20/additional hour, cheap for small groups, best views with 5 or fewer riders, tel. 028/9031-5777 or mobile 078-9271-6660, www.taxitrax.com).

The Sinn Fein office and bookstore are near the bottom of Falls Road. The **bookstore** is worth a look. Page through books featuring color photos of the political murals that decorated these buildings. Money raised here supports the families of deceased IRA members.

A sad, corrugated structure called the **peace wall** runs a block or so north of Falls Road (along Cupar Way), separating the Catholics from the Protestants in the Shankill Road area. The first cement wall was 20 feet high—it was later extended another 10 feet by a solid metal addition, and then another 15 feet with a metal screen. Seemingly high enough now to deter a projectile being lobbed over, this is one of many such walls erected in Belfast during the Troubles. Meant to be temporary, these barriers stay up because of old fears among the communities on both sides. But in 2013, the Northern Ireland Assembly announced its ambitious goal to remove all of these walls by 2020.

At the **Milltown Cemetery,** walk past all the Gaelic crosses down to the far right-hand corner (closest to the highway), where the IRA Roll of Honor is set apart from the thousands of other graves by little green railings. They are treated like fallen soldiers. Notice the memorial to Bobby Sands and nine other hunger strikers. They starved themselves to death in the nearby Maze Prison in 1981, protesting for political prisoner status as opposed to terrorist criminal treatment. Maze Prison closed in the fall of 2000.

SHANKILL ROAD AND SANDY ROW (PROTESTANT)

You can ride a shared black cab through the Protestant **Shankill Road** area. They depart from North Street near the intersection with Millfield Road; it's not well-marked, but watch where the cabs circle and pick up locals on the south side of the street (£30/1-2 people for one hour, £40/3-6 people, tel. 028/9032-8775).

An easier (and cheaper) way to get a dose of the Unionist side is to walk **Sandy Row**. From Hotel Europa, walk a block down Glengall Street, then turn left for a 10-minute walk along a working-class Protestant street. A stop in a Unionist memorabilia shop, a pub, or one of the many cheap eateries here may give you an opportunity to talk to a local. You'll see murals filled with Unionist symbolism. The mural of William of Orange's victory over the Catholic King James II (Battle of the Boyne, 1690) thrills Unionist hearts. You'll find it at the northern end of Sandy Row at the corner with Linfield Road.

Central Belfast

▲▲CITY HALL

This grand structure's 173-foot-tall copper dome dominates the town center. Built between 1898 and 1906, with its statue of Queen Victoria scowling down Belfast's main drag and the Neoclassical dome looming behind her, the City Hall is a stirring sight. In the garden, you'll find memorials to the *Titanic* and the landing of the

US Expeditionary Force in 1942—the first American troops to arrive in Europe en route to Berlin.

Take the worthwhile and free 45-minute tour, which gives you a rundown on city government and an explanation of the decor that makes this an Ulster political hall of fame. Queen Victoria and King Edward VII look down on city council meetings. The 1613 original charter of Belfast granted by James I is on display. Its Great Hall—bombed by the Germans in 1941—looks as great as it did the day it was made.

Cost and Hours: Free; building open Mon-Thu 8:30-17:00, Fri 8:30-16:30, closed (except for tours) Sat, closed Sun; handy Bobbin coffee shop on ground floor, tel. 028/9032-0202, www.belfastcity.gov.uk/cityhall.

Tours: Free tours run Mon-Fri at 11:00, 14:00, and 15:00—entrance on north side of building behind Queen Victoria statue; Sat at 14:00 and 15:00—entrance via south-facing back door only; no tours on Sun; call to confirm schedule and to reserve a tour.

Visiting City Hall: If you can't manage a tour, at least step into the main lobby to admire the marble-swirl staircase and the view up into the dome. In 1912, at the center of the marble floor design beneath the dome, Sir Edward Carson signed the Ulster Covenant—to be followed by 470,000 other Unionists at dozens of desks surrounding City Hall that day.

Shankill Road

City Hall

Central Belfast

Eating
1. The Morning Star Pub & Restaurant
2. Robinson & Cleaver
3. Crown Liquor Saloon & Dining Room
4. Kelly's Cellars
5. Marks & Spencer
6. Tesco Supermarket
7. Merchant Hotel & The Cloth Ear Pub
8. Taps Wine Bar
9. Wagamama & Bittles Bar

Sleeping
10. Hotel Europa
11. Jurys Inn

Some signed with their own blood. The Covenant stated Unionists would use "all means necessary" (including the might of the 100,000-strong UVF militia) to resist the Home Rule bill that had just passed in Parliament. The bill would have given the island of Ireland limited autonomy from Britain. These Protestant Unionists feared "Home Rule as Rome Rule," where they would have become the minority in an independent Catholic Ireland. World War I interrupted the implementation of Home Rule, and the partition of Ireland followed shortly after the war's end.

Rick's Tip: Victoria Square, *a glitzy American-style mall, is topped with a huge glass dome that has an observation platform offering* **fine city views.** *Take the free elevator up (Mon-Tue 9:00-19:00, Wed-Fri 9:00-21:00, Sat 9:00-18:00, Sun 13:00-18:00; 3 blocks east of City Hall—bordered by Chichester, Victoria, Ann, and Montgomery streets; www.victoriasquare.com).*

1916

This pivotal year means vastly different things to Northern Ireland's two communities.

To Nationalists (who are usually Catholic), "1916" brings to mind the Easter Uprising—which took place in Dublin in April of that year and was the beginning of the end of 750 years of British rule for most of Ireland (see page 330). Some Nationalist murals still use images of Dublin's rebel headquarters or martyred leaders like Patrick Pearse and James Connolly. To this community, 1916 emphasizes their proud Gaelic identity, their willingness to fight to preserve it, and their stubborn anti-British attitude.

To Unionists (who are usually Protestant), "1916" means the brutal WWI Battle of the Somme in France, which began that July. (For more on the Somme, visit the Somme Heritage Centre in Bangor, described on page 300.) Although both Catholic and Protestant soldiers died in this long and bloody battle, the first wave of young men who went over the top were the sons of proud Ulster Unionists. The Unionists hoped this sacrifice would prove their loyalty to the Crown—and assurance that the British would never let them be gobbled up by an Irish Nationalist state (a possible scenario just before the Great War's outbreak). You'll see Tommies heroically climbing out of their trenches in some of Belfast's Unionist murals. For the Unionists, 1916 is synonymous with devout Britishness.

LINEN HALL LIBRARY

Across the street from City Hall, the 200-year-old Linen Hall Library welcomes guests (notice the red hand above the front door facing Donegall Square North; for more on its meaning, see the sidebar on page 294). Described as "Ulster's attic," the library takes pride in being a neutral space where anyone trying to make sense of the sectarian conflict can view the Troubled Images, a historical collection of engrossing political posters. It has a fine hardbound ambience, a coffee shop, and a royal newspaper reading room.

Cost and Hours: Free; Mon-Fri 9:30-17:30, Sat until 16:00, closed Sun; 45-minute tours for £3.50 on Tue and Fri at 11:30, 17 Donegall Square North, tel. 028/9032-1707, www.linenhall.com.

GOLDEN MILE

This is the overstated nickname of Belfast's liveliest dining and entertainment district, which stretches from the Opera House (Great Victoria Street) to the university (University Road).

The **Grand Opera House,** originally built in 1895, bombed and rebuilt in 1991, and bombed and rebuilt again in

Crown Liquor Saloon

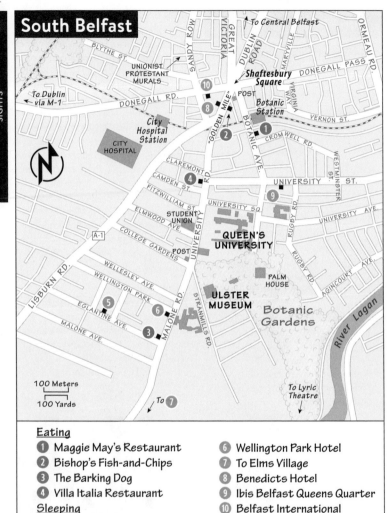

South Belfast

To Central Belfast

To Dublin via M-1

Shaftesbury Square

Botanic Station

City Hospital Station

CITY HOSPITAL

QUEEN'S UNIVERSITY

PALM HOUSE

ULSTER MUSEUM

Botanic Gardens

River Lagan

100 Meters
100 Yards

To Lyric Theatre

To ⑦

Eating

① Maggie May's Restaurant
② Bishop's Fish-and-Chips
③ The Barking Dog
④ Villa Italia Restaurant

Sleeping

⑤ Malone Lodge Hotel

⑥ Wellington Park Hotel
⑦ To Elms Village
⑧ Benedicts Hotel
⑨ Ibis Belfast Queens Quarter
⑩ Belfast International City Hostel

1993, is extravagantly Victorian and *the* place to take in a concert, play, or opera (ticket office open Mon-Sat 9:30-17:30, closed Sun; ticket office to right of main front door on Great Victoria Street, tel. 028/9024-1919, www.goh.co.uk). The **Hotel Europa,** next door, while considered to be the most-bombed hotel in the world, actually feels pretty casual (but is expensive to stay in).

Across the street is the museum-like **Crown Liquor Saloon.** Built in 1849, it's now a part of the National Trust. A wander through its mahogany, glass, and marble interior is a trip back into the days of Queen Victoria, although the privacy provided by the snugs—booths—allows for un-Victorian behavior. Upstairs, the Crown Dining Room serves pub grub and is decorated with historic photos.

South Belfast

▲ULSTER MUSEUM

While mediocre by European standards, this is Belfast's most venerable museum. It offers an earnest and occasionally thought-provoking look at a cross-section of local artifacts.

Cost and Hours: Free but £3 donation suggested; Tue-Sun 10:00-17:00, closed Mon; in Botanic Gardens on Stranmillis Road, south of downtown, tel. 028/9044-0000, www.nmni.com.

Visiting the Museum: The four-floor museum is free and pretty painless. Ride the elevator to the top floor and follow the spiraling exhibits downhill through various zones. The top floor is dedicated to rotating art exhibits, the next floor down covers local nature, and the one below that focuses on history. The ground floor covers the modern Troubles, and has a coffee shop and gift shop.

The Art Zone displays a beautifully crafted Belleek vase, as well as fine crystal and china. In the Nature Zone, audiovisuals trace how the Ice Age affected the local landscape. Dinosaur skeletons lurk, stuffed wildlife play possum, and geology rocks. Kids will enjoy the interactive Discover History room.

The delicately worded History Zone has an interesting British slant (such as the implication that most deaths in the Great Potato Famine of 1845-1849 were caused by typhus and fever epidemics—without mentioning the starvation that made peasants susceptible to these diseases in the first place). But the coverage of the modern-day Troubles is balanced and thought-provoking.

After a peek at a pretty good mummy, top things off with the *Girona* treasure. Soggy bits of gold, silver, leather, and wood were salvaged from the Spanish Armada's shipwrecked *Girona*, lost off the Antrim Coast north of Belfast in 1588.

▲BOTANIC GARDENS

This is the backyard of Queen's University, and on a sunny day, you couldn't imagine a more relaxing park setting. On a cold day, step into the Tropical Ravine for a jungle of heat and humidity. Take a quick walk through the Palm House, reminiscent of the one in London's Kew Gardens, but smaller. The Ulster Museum is on the garden's grounds.

Cost and Hours: Free, gardens open daily 8:00 until dusk; Palm House open Mon-Fri 10:00-12:00 & 13:00-17:00, Sat-Sun 13:00-17:00, shorter hours in winter; tel. 028/9031-4762, www.belfastcity.gov.uk/parks.

LYRIC THEATRE

Rebuilt in 2011, this Belfast institution represents the cultural rejuvenation of the city. The architecturally innovative theater, located on the Lagan River near Queen's University, is a good place to see quality local productions (tickets £15-25; box office open Mon-Sat 10:00-17:00, closed Sun; 55 Ridgeway Street, tel. 028/9038-1081, www.lyrictheatre.co.uk).

Ulster Museum

Palm House in Botanic Gardens

The Red Hand of Ulster

All over Belfast, you'll notice a curious symbol: a red hand facing you as if swearing a pledge or telling you to halt. It's known as the Red Hand of Ulster—and it seems to pop up everywhere. It's one of the few emblems used by both communities in Northern Ireland.

You'll spot it, faded, above the Linen Hall Library door, in the wrought-iron fences of the Merchant Hotel, on old-fashioned clothes wringers (in the Ulster Folk Park and Transport Museum at Cultra), above the front door of a bank in Bangor, in the shape of a flowerbed at Mount Stewart House, in Loyalist paramilitary murals, on shield emblems in the gates of Republican memorials, and even on the flag of Northern Ireland (the white flag with the red cross of St. George).

Nationalists display a red hand on a yellow shield as a symbol of the ancient province of Ulster. It was the official crest of the once-dominant O'Neill clan (who fought tooth and nail against English rule) and today signifies resistance to British rule in these communities.

But you'll more often see the red hand in Unionist areas. They see it as a potent symbol of the political entity of Northern Ireland. The Ulster Volunteer Force chose it for their symbol in 1913 and embedded it in the center of the Northern Irish flag upon partition of the island in 1921. You may see the red hand clenched as a fist in Loyalist murals. One Loyalist paramilitary group even named itself the Red Hand Commandos.

The origin of the red hand comes from a mythological tale of two rival clans that raced by boat to claim a far shore. The first clan leader to touch the shore would win it for his people. Everyone aboard both vessels strained mightily at their oars, near exhaustion as they approached the shore. Finally, in desperation, the chieftain leader of the slower boat whipped out his sword and lopped off his right hand...which he then flung onto the shore, thus winning the coveted land. Moral of the story? The fearless folk of Ulster will do *whatever it takes* to get the job done.

Near Belfast

▲▲ULSTER FOLK PARK AND TRANSPORT MUSEUM

This sprawling 180-acre, two-museum complex straddles the road and rail line at Cultra, midway between Bangor and Belfast (8 miles east of town).

Cost and Hours: £9 for Folk Park, £9 for Transport Museum, £11 combo-ticket covers both, £29 for families; March-Sept Tue-Sun 10:00-17:00; Oct-Feb Tue-Fri 10:00-16:00, Sat-Sun 11:00-16:00; closed Mon year-round; check the schedule for the day's special events, tel. 028/9042-8428, www.nmni.com.

Getting There: From Belfast, you can reach Cultra by taxi (£15), bus #502 (2/hour, 30 minutes, from Laganside Bus Centre), or train (£5.40 round-trip before 9:30, £3.60 after 9:30, 2/hour, 15 minutes, from any Belfast train station or from Bangor). Buses stop right in the park, but schedules are skimpy on Saturday and Sunday. Train service is more dependable (and more frequent on the weekend): Get off at the Cultra stop, which puts off between the two parks, a bit closer to the Transport Museum than to the Folk Park.

Planning Your Time: Allow three hours for your visit, and expect lots of walking. Most people will spend an hour in the Transport Museum and a couple of hours at the Folk Park. You'll arrive (by rail or car) between the two museums at a point somewhat closer to the Transport Museum. From here, you have a choice of going downhill to the Transport Museum or uphill into the Folk Park. Assess your energy level and plan accordingly. Those with a car can drive between the museum and the folk park (otherwise, it's 200 panting yards uphill). Note that the Transport Museum is all indoors. The Folk Park involves more walking between buildings spread across the upper hillside.

Visiting the Museums: The **Transport Museum** consists of three buildings. Start at the bottom and trace the evolution of transportation from 7,500 years ago—when people first decided to load an ox—to the first vertical take-off jet. In 1909, the Belfast-based Shorts Aviation Company partnered with the Wright brothers to manufacture the first commercially available aircraft. The middle building holds an intriguing section on the sinking of the Belfast-made *Titanic.* The top building covers the history of bikes, cars, and trains. The car section rumbles from the first car in Ireland (an 1898 Benz), through the "Cortina Culture" of the 1960s, to the local adventures of controversial automobile designer John DeLorean and a 1981 model of his sleek sports car.

The **Folk Park,** an open-air collection of 34 reconstructed buildings from all over the nine counties of Ulster, showcases the region's traditional lifestyles. After wandering through the old-town site (church, print shop, schoolhouse, humble Belfast row house, silent movie theater, and so on), you'll head off into the country to nip into cottages, farmhouses, and mills. Some houses are warmed by a wonderful peat fire and a friendly attendant. It can be dull or vibrant, depending upon when you visit and your ability to chat with the attendants. Drop a peat brick on the fire.

CARRICKFERGUS CASTLE
Built during the Norman invasion of the late 1100s, this historic castle stands sentry on the shore of Belfast Lough. William of Orange landed here in 1690, when he began his Irish campaign against deposed King James II. In 1778, the American privateer ship *Ranger* (the first ever to fly the Stars-and-Stripes), under the command of John Paul Jones, defeated the more heavily armed HMS *Drake* just offshore. These days the castle feels a bit sanitized and geared for kids, but it's an easy excursion if you're seeking a castle experience near the city.

Cost and Hours: £5; April-Sept daily 10:00-18:00; Oct-March Mon-Sat 10:00-16:00, Sun 14:00-16:00; tel. 028/9335-1273.

Getting There: It's a 20-minute train ride from Belfast (on the line to Larne, £6.70 round-trip before 9:30, £4.40 after 9:30). Turn left as you exit the train station and walk straight downhill for five

Ulster Folk Park and Transport Museum

Carrickfergus Castle

minutes—all the way to the waterfront—passing under the arch of the old town wall en route. You'll find the castle on your right.

EATING

Downtown

If it's £12 pub grub you want, consider these drinking holes with varied atmospheres.

The Morning Star is woody and elegant (£9-15 restaurant dinners upstairs, £6 buffet Mon-Sat 12:00-16:00; daily 12:00-22:00, down alley just off High Street at 17 Pottinger's Entry, alley entry is roughly opposite the post office, tel. 028/9023-5986).

Robinson & Cleaver has a great central location, perfect for light lunches or tasty dinners. In good weather, their balcony has terrific views of City Hall (£13 two-course early-bird dinner—before 18:30, £16 for three courses; Wed-Sat 12:00-14:30 & 17:00-21:00, Mon-Tue lunch only, closed Sun; Donegall Square North, a few doors east of the TI, tel. 028/9031-2666, www.robinsonandcleaver.com).

Crown Liquor Saloon, a stop along the Golden Mile, is small and antique. Its mesmerizing mishmash of mosaics and shareable snugs (booths) is topped with a smoky tin ceiling (Mon-Sat lunch only 11:30-15:00, Sun 12:30-15:00, 46 Great Victoria Street, across from Hotel Europa, tel. 028/9024-3187). The **Crown Dining Room** upstairs offers dependable £10-15 meals (daily 13:00-21:00, use entry on Amelia Street when the Crown Liquor Saloon is closed, tel. 028/9024-3187).

Kelly's Cellars, once a rebel hangout (see plaque above door), still has a very gritty Irish feel. It's 300 years old and hard to find, but worth it. The pub grub is basic, but the atmosphere is delicious (Mon-Sat 11:30-24:30, Sun 13:00-23:30; live traditional music Tue-Fri and Sun at 21:30, Sat at 16:30; 32 Bank Street, 100 yards behind Tesco supermarket, access via alley on left side when facing Tesco, tel. 028/9024-6058).

Supermarkets: Marks & Spencer has a coffee shop serving skinny lattes and a supermarket in its basement (Mon-Sat 8:00-18:00, Thu until 21:00, Sun 13:00-18:00, WCs on second floor, Donegall Place, a block north of Donegall Square). **Tesco,** another supermarket, is a block north of Marks & Spencer and two blocks north of Donegall Square (open slightly later than Marks & Spencer, Royal Avenue and Bank Street). Picnic on the City Hall lawn.

On Waring Street, in the Cathedral Quarter

I like the cluster of culture surrounding the Cotton Court section of Waring Street. It's about a 10-minute walk northeast of the City Hall.

Check out the lobby of **Merchant Hotel** (a grand former bank) for a glimpse of crushed-velvet Victorian splendor under an opulent dome, and consider indulging in Belfast's best afternoon tea splurge (£22.50 Mon-Fri, £29.50 Sat-Sun, Mon-Fri 12:00-16:30, Sat-Sun reserve ahead for two seatings: 12:30 or 15:00, 35 Waring Street, tel. 028/9023-4888). Don't show up in shorts and sneakers.

Taps Wine Bar is a whiff of Mediterranean warmth in this cold brick city. Try a cheerful tapas or paella meal, washed down with sangria (May-Sept daily 12:00-22:00, Oct-April closed Sun-Mon, 42 Waring Street, tel. 028/9031-1414).

The Cloth Ear is a friendly, modern, often-crowded bar serving better-than-average pub grub from the kitchen of the posh Merchant Hotel next door (Mon-Sat 12:00-20:30, Sun 13:00-19:00, 33 Waring Street, tel. 028/9026-2719).

Victoria Square Area

Although Victoria Square is a big, glitzy mall, a couple of fun options are worth considering—one inside the mall (for food) and one next door (for drinks).

Wagamama, part of a British chain, is a Japanese noodle bar located on the first floor of the Victoria Square Mall. Hearty portions of chicken ramen, *yakisoba*, and cumin beef salad are menu highlights (daily 12:00-21:30, Victoria Square, tel. 028/9023-6098).

Bittles Bar is a tiny, wedge-shaped throwback to Victorian days, hidden in the shadows on the east side of the mall next to the ornate, yellow Victorian fountain. The minuscule, terraced interior is decorated with caricatures of literary and political figures (daily 12:00-15:00, no food Sun, 70 Upper Church Lane just off Victoria Street, tel. 028/9031-1088).

South Belfast

Nearby Queen's University gives this neighborhood an energetic feel, with a mixed bag of dining options ranging from cosmopolitan to deep-fried.

Maggie May's serves hearty, simple, affordable £8-12 meals (daily 8:00-22:30, one block south of Botanic Station at 50 Botanic Avenue, tel. 028/9032-2662).

Bishop's is the locals' choice for fish-and-chips; they also serve pasta and veggie options. The classier side has table service and higher prices (daily 12:00-23:30, just south of Shaftesbury Square at Bradbury Place, tel. 028/9043-9070).

The Barking Dog is a hip grill serving tasty burgers, duck, scallops, and other filling fare. If the weather's fine, the outdoor tree-shaded front tables are ideal for people-watching (£7-10 lunches, £12-17 dinners, Mon-Sat 12:00-15:30 & 17:30-22:00, Sun 12:00-21:00, near corner of Eglantine Avenue at 33 Malone Road, tel. 028/9066-1885).

Villa Italia packs in crowds hungry for linguini and *bistecca*. With its checkered tablecloths and a wood-beamed ceiling draped with grape leaves, it's a little bit of Italy in Belfast (£10-17 meals, Mon-Sat 17:00-23:00, Sun 12:30-21:30, 3 long blocks south of Shaftesbury Square, at intersection with University Street, 39 University Road, tel. 028/9032-8356).

SLEEPING

Belfast is more of a business town than a tourist town, so business-class room rates are lower or soft on weekends (best prices booked from their websites).

In Central Belfast

$$$ Hotel Europa is Belfast's landmark hotel—fancy, comfortable, and central—with four stars and lower weekend rates. Modern yet elegant, this place is the choice of visiting diplomats (Db-£109-189 plus £16 breakfast, Great Victoria Street, tel. 028/9027-1066, www.hastingshotels.com, res@eur.hastingshotels.com).

$$ Jurys Inn, an American-style hotel that rents 190 identical modern rooms, is perfectly located two blocks from City Hall (up to 3 adults or 2 adults and 2 kids for £79-119, price varies based on season and weekend rates, breakfast-£10/person, Fisherwick Place, tel. 028/9053-3500, www.jurysinns.com, jurysinnbelfast@jurysinns.com).

South Belfast

Many of Belfast's best budget beds cluster in a comfortable, leafy neighborhood just south of Queen's University (near the Ulster Museum). Two train stations (Botanic and Adelaide) are nearby, and buses zip down Malone Road every 20 minutes. Any bus on Malone Road goes to Donegall Square East. Taxis take you downtown for about £6 (your host can call one).

$$$ Malone Lodge Hotel, by far the classiest listing in this neighborhood,

Sleep Code

Abbreviations: S=Single,
D=Double/Twin, T=Triple,
Q=Quad, b=bathroom
   **Price Rankings for Double
Rooms: $$$** Most rooms £90 or
more, **$$** £60-90, **$** £60 or less
   Notes: Room prices change;
verify rates online or by email. For
the best prices, book directly with
the hotel.

provides slick, business-class comfort in
119 spacious rooms on a quiet street (Sb-
£79-135, Db-£95-150, superior Db-£119-
169, mid-week deals, elevator, restaurant, parking, 60 Eglantine Avenue, tel.
028/9038-8000, www.malonelodgehotel.
com, info@malonelodgehotel.com).

   $$ Wellington Park Hotel is a depend-
able, if unimaginative, chain-style hotel
with 75 rooms. It's predictable but in a
good location (Db-£75-120, parking-£5/
day, 21 Malone Road, tel. 028/9038-1111,
www.wellingtonparkhotel.com, info@
wellingtonparkhotel.com).

   $ Elms Village, a huge Queen's Uni-
versity dorm complex, rents 100 basic,
institutional rooms (mostly singles, with a
few doubles) to travelers during summer
break (mid-June-late-Aug only, Sb-£39,
Db-£54, coin-op laundry, self-serve
kitchen; reception building is 50 yards
down entry street, marked *Elms Village*
on low brick wall, 78 Malone Road; tel.
028/9097-4525, www.stayatqueens.com,
accommodation@qub.ac.uk).

   $$ Benedicts Hotel has 32 rooms in
a good location at the northern fringe of
the Queen's University district. Its popular
bar is a maze of polished wood and can
be loud on weekend nights (Sb-£60-80,
Db-£79-115, elevator, 7 Bradbury Place,

tel. 028/9059-1999, www.benedictshotel.
co.uk, info@benedictshotel.co.uk).

   $$ Ibis Belfast Queens Quarter, part
of a major European hotel chain, has 56
practical rooms in a convenient location.
It's a great deal if you're not looking for
cozy character (Db-£59-89, better deals
online, breakfast-£8, elevator, a block
north of Queen's University at 75 Uni-
versity Street, tel. 028/9033-3366, www.
ibisbelfast.com).

   $ Belfast International City Hostel
is big and creatively run, and provides
the best value among Belfast's hostels. It
has 200 beds in single and double rooms
along with dorms, and is located near
Botanic Station, in the heart of the lively
university district. The hostel is the start-
ing point for McComb's minibus tours
(see page 281). Features include free lock-
ers, elevator, baggage storage, pay guest
computer, kitchen, self-serve laundry
(£4), a cheap breakfast-only cafeteria,
24-hour reception, and no curfew. Paul,
the manager of the hostel, is a veritable
TI, with a passion for his work (bed in
6-bed dorm-£11.50, bed in quad-£13.50,
S-£22.50, Db-£38-42, 22 Donegall Road,
tel. 028/9031-5435, www.hini.org.uk, info@
hini.org.uk).

TRANSPORTATION

Getting Around Belfast

If you line up your sightseeing logically,
you can do most of the town on foot.
On wheels, you have several options.
For most visitors, the Belfast Visitor Pass
saves time and money. It combines iLink
smartcards for local bus and train trips
with sightseeing discounts (see "Sightsee-
ing Pass," earlier).

By Train or Bus

Ask about **iLink smartcards,** which give
individuals one day of unlimited train
and bus travel. The **Zone 1 card** (£6.50)

covers the city center and George Best Belfast City Airport. The handy **Zone 2 card** (£10.50) includes Cultra (Ulster Folk Park and Transport Museum), Bangor, and Carrickfergus Castle. The **Zone 3 card** (£14) is really only useful for reaching Belfast's distant international airport. **Zone 4** (£16.50) gets you anywhere in Northern Ireland, including Portrush and Derry. For those lingering in the North, one-week cards offer even better deals. Buy your iLink card at any train station in the city.

If you're traveling from Belfast to only one destination—Carrickfergus Castle, Cultra, or Bangor—a "day return" ticket is cheaper than two one-way tickets.

Pink-and-white city buses go from Donegall Square East to Malone Road and my recommended accommodations. Sunday service is much less frequent (#8B or #8C, 3/hour, £2, all-day pass costs £3.40 Mon-Sat before 9:30—after 9:30 and on Sun it's £3).

For more information on iLink smartcards, trains, and buses in Belfast, contact Translink (tel. 028/9066-6630, www.translink.co.uk).

By Taxi
Taxis are reasonable and a good option. For general transport, as opposed to the taxi tours described earlier, try **Valu Cabs** (tel. 028/9080-9080). Rather than use their meters, many cabs charge a flat £5 rate for any ride up to two miles. It's £2 per mile after that. If you're going up Falls Road, ride a shared cab (see page 288) .

Arriving and Departing
For updated schedules and prices for both trains and buses in Northern Ireland, check with Translink (tel. 028/9066-6630, www.translink.co.uk). Consider a Belfast Visitor Pass (see page 280) if you're visiting just Belfast. Those going beyond Belfast can make use of the Zone 4 iLink smartcard, good for all-day train and bus use in Northern Ireland. Service is less frequent on Sundays.

By Train
Arriving by fast train, you'll go directly to Belfast's Central Station (with ATMs and free city maps in the lobby). From the station, a free Centrelink bus loops to Donegall Square, with stops near Shaftesbury Square (recommended hostel), the bus station (some recommended hotels), and the TI (free with any train or bus ticket, 4/hour, never on Sun; during morning rush hour, bus runs only between station and Donegall Square). Allow about £5 for a taxi from Central Station to Donegall Square, or £8 to my accommodation listings south of the university.

Slower trains arc through the city, stopping at several downtown stations, including Central Station, Great Victoria Station (most central, near Donegall Square and most hotels), and Botanic Station (close to the university, Botanic Gardens, and some recommended lodgings). It's easy and cheap to connect stations by train (£1.50).

From Belfast by Train to: Dublin (8/day Mon-Sat, 5/day Sun, 2 hours), **Derry** (7/day, 2.5 hours), **Larne** (hourly, 1 hour), **Portrush** (11/day Mon-Sat, 5/day Sun, 2 hours, transfer in Coleraine), **Bangor** (2/hour, 30 minutes).

By Bus
The Europa Bus Centre is behind Hotel Europa (Ulsterbus tel. 028/9033-7003 for destinations in Scotland and England).

From Belfast by Bus to: Portrush (12/day, 2 hours; scenic-coast route, 2.5 hours), **Derry** (hourly, 2 hours), **Dublin** (hourly, most via Dublin Airport, 3 hours), **Galway** (every 2 hours, 6 hours, change in Dublin), **Glasgow** (3/day, 6 hours), **Edinburgh** (3/day, 7 hours).

By Car
Driving in Belfast, although not as bad as in Dublin, is still a pain. Avoid it if possible. Street parking in the city center is geared for short shopping stops (use pay-and-

display machines, £0.30/15 minutes, one-hour maximum, Mon-Sat 9:00-18:00, free in evenings and on Sun). If you're overnighting, choose a hotel that offers parking.

By Plane
Belfast has two airports. **George Best Belfast City Airport** (airport code: BHD, tel. 028/9093-9093, www.belfastcityairport.com) is a five-minute taxi ride from town (near the docks), while **Belfast International Airport** (airport code: BFS, tel. 028/9448-4848, www.belfastairport.com) is 18 miles west of town, connected by buses from the Europa Bus Centre behind Hotel Europa.

NEAR BELFAST

BANGOR

To stay in a laid-back seaside home-town—with more comfort per pound—sleep 12 miles east of Belfast in Bangor (BANG-grr). It's a handy alternative for travelers who find Belfast booked up. Formerly a Victorian resort and seaside escape from the big city nearby, Bangor now has a sleepy residential feeling. To visit two worthwhile sights near Bangor—the Somme Heritage Centre and Mount Stewart House—consider renting a car for the day (bus service to these sights is sporadic) at nearby George Best Belfast City Airport, a 15-minute train trip from Bangor.

Orientation
Tourist Information: Bangor's TI is in a stone tower house (from 1637) on the harborfront (Mon-Fri 9:00-17:00, Sat 10:00-17:00, Sun 13:00-17:00 except closed Sun Sept-April, 34 Quay Street, tel. 028/9127-0069, www.visitardsandnorthdown.com).

Helpful Hints: The library offers free **Internet access** (30-minute limit, Mon-Thu 9:00-21:00, Fri-Sat until 17:00, closed Sun, 80 Hamilton Road, tel. 028/9127-0591). **Kare Cabs** provides local taxi service (tel. 028/9145-6777 or 028/9181-8001).

Sights near Bangor
The eastern fringe of Northern Ireland is populated mostly by people who consider themselves true-blue British citizens with a history of loyalty to the Crown that goes back more than 400 years. Two sights within reach by car from Bangor highlight this area's firm roots in British culture: the Somme Heritage Centre and Mount Stewart House.

Getting There: Patchy bus service (bus #6) can be used to reach these sights from Bangor (check schedule with Bangor TI first). I'd rent a car instead at nearby George Best Belfast City Airport, which is only 15 minutes by train from Bangor or 10 minutes from Belfast's Central Station. Because the airport is east of Belfast, your drive to these rural sights skips the headache of urban Belfast. Call ahead to confirm sight opening hours.

SOMME HERITAGE CENTRE
World War I's trench warfare was a meat grinder. More British soldiers died in the last year of the war than in all of World War II. Northern Ireland's men were not spared—especially during the bloody Battle of the Somme in France, starting in July of 1916. Among the Allied forces was the British Army's 36th Ulster Division, which drew heavily from this loyal heartland of

Northern Ireland. The 36th Ulster Division suffered brutal losses at the Battle of the Somme—of the 760 men recruited from the Shankill Road area in Belfast, only 10 percent survived.

Exhibits portray the battle experience through a mix of military artifacts, photos, historical newsreels, and life-size figures posed in trench warfare re-creations. To access the majority of the exhibits, it's essential to take the one-hour guided tour (leaving hourly, on the hour). Visiting this place is a moving experience, but it can only hint at the horrific conditions endured by these soldiers.

Cost and Hours: £6.50; Mon-Thu 10:00-16:00, Sat 11:00-16:00, closed Fri and Sun; hourly tours, 3 miles south of Bangor just off A-21 at 233 Bangor Road, tel. 028/9182-3202, www.irishsoldier.org. A coffee shop is located at the center.

MOUNT STEWART HOUSE

No manor house in Ireland better illuminates the affluent lifestyle of the Protestant ascendancy than this lush estate. After the defeat of James II (the last Catholic king of England) at the Battle of the Boyne in 1690, the Protestant monarchy was in control—and the privileged status of landowners of the same faith was assured. In the 1700s, Ireland's many Catholic rebellions seemed finally to be squashed, so Anglican landlords felt safe flaunting their wealth in manor houses surrounded by utterly perfect gardens. The Mount Stewart House in particular was designed to dazzle.

Cost and Hours: £8 for house and gardens; house open daily March-Oct 11:00-16:00, gardens from 10:00; 8 miles south of Bangor, just off A-20 beside Strangford Lough, tel. 028/4278-8387, www.nationaltrust.org.uk.

Visiting the House: Hourly tours give you a glimpse of the cushy life led by the Marquess of Londonderry and his heirs over the past three centuries. The main entry hall is a stunner, with a black-and-white checkerboard tile floor, marble columns, classical statues, and pink walls supporting a balcony with a domed ceiling and a fine chandelier. In the dining room, you'll see the original seats occupied by the rears of European heads of state, brought back from the Congress of Vienna after Napoleon's 1815 defeat. A huge painting of Hambletonian, a prize-winning racehorse, hangs above the

Gardens of Mount Stewart House

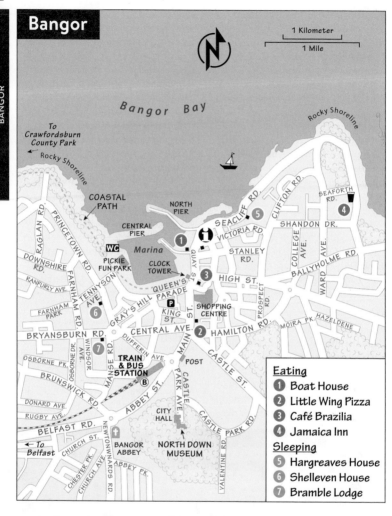

Bangor

Bangor Bay

To Crawfordsburn County Park

Rocky Shoreline

Rocky Shoreline

1 Kilometer
1 Mile

COASTAL PATH

NORTH PIER

CENTRAL PIER

Marina

WC

PICKIE FUN PARK

CLOCK TOWER

SEACLIFF RD.

CLIFTON RD.

SEAFORTH RD.

VICTORIA RD.

SHANDON DR.

STANLEY RD.

COLLEGE AVE.

WARD AVE.

BALLYHOLME RD.

HAZELDENE

MOIRA PK.

RAGLAN RD.

PRINCETOWN RD.

DOWNSHIRE RD.

RANFURLY AVE.

FARNHAM RD.

TENNYSON AVE.

FARNHAM PARK

GRAY'S HILL

QUEEN'S PARADE

QUAY ST.

HIGH ST.

PROSPECT RD.

SHOPPING CENTRE

KING ST.

CENTRAL AVE.

HAMILTON RD.

BRYANSBURN RD.

WINDSOR AVE.

MANSE RD.

DUFFERIN AVE.

MAIN ST.

CASTLE ST.

CASTLE PARK RD.

OSBORNE PK.

TRAIN & BUS STATION

POST

BRUNSWICK RD.

ABBEY ST.

CASTLE PARK AVE.

DONARD AVE.

RUGBY AVE.

BELFAST RD.

CHURCH ST.

CITY HALL

BANGOR ABBEY

NORTH DOWN MUSEUM

VALENTINE RD.

NEWTOWNARDS RD.

ABBEY PK.

CHESTER PK.

CHURCH AVE.

To Belfast

Eating
1 Boat House
2 Little Wing Pizza
3 Café Brazilia
4 Jamaica Inn

Sleeping
5 Hargreaves House
6 Shelleven House
7 Bramble Lodge

grand staircase, dwarfing a portrait of the Duke of Wellington in a hall nearby. The heroic duke (worried that his Irish birth would be seen as lower class by British blue bloods) once quipped in Parliament, "Just because one is born in a stable does not make him a horse." Irish emancipator Daniel O'Connell retorted, "Yes, but it could make you an ass."

Afterward, wander the expansive manicured **gardens**. The fantasy life of parasol-toting, upper-crust Victorian society seems to ooze from every viewpoint. Fan-

ciful sculptures of extinct dodo birds and monkeys holding vases on their heads set off predictably classic Italian and Spanish sections. An Irish harp has been trimmed out of a hedge a few feet from a flowerbed shaped like the Red Hand of Ulster. Swans glide serenely among the lily pads on a small lake.

Eating

Habitually late diners should be aware that most restaurants in town stop seating at about 20:30.

The **Boat House** is a stout stone structure hiding the finest dining experience in Bangor. It's run by two Dutch brothers who specialize in some of the freshest fish dishes in Northern Ireland (Mon-Sat 12:00-21:00, Sun until 20:00, reserve ahead, on Sea Cliff Road opposite the TI, tel. 028/9146-9253).

Little Wing Pizza is a friendly joint serving tasty pizza, pasta, and salads. Grab your food to go and munch by the marina (daily 11:00-22:00, 37 Main Street, tel. 028/9147-2777).

Café Brazilia, a popular locals' lunch hangout with a simple menu, is across from the stubby clock tower (Mon-Sat 8:30-16:30, closed Sun, 13 Bridge Street, tel. 028/9127-2763).

The **Jamaica Inn** offers pleasant pub grub with a breezy waterfront porch (food served from about 12:00-21:00, 10-minute walk east of the TI, 188 Seacliff Road, tel. 028/9147-1610).

Sleeping

Visitors arriving in Bangor (by train) come down Main Street to reach the harbor marina. You'll find my first listing to the right, along the waterfront east of the marina on Seacliff Road. The other two listings are to the left, just uphill and west of the marina. All offer a 10 percent discount if you pay cash and stay two nights (at Shelleven House, also show this book on arrival).

$$ Hargreaves House, a homey Victorian waterfront refuge with three cozy rooms, is Bangor's best value (S-£45, Sb-£50, Db-£65, large Db-£85, 15-minute walk from train station but worth it, 78 Seacliff Road, tel. 028/9146-4071, mobile 079-8058-5047, www.hargreaveshouse.com, info@hargreaveshouse.com, Pauline Mendez).

$$ Shelleven House is an old-fashioned, well-kept, stately place with 11 prim rooms on the quiet corner of Princetown Road and Tennyson Avenue (Sb-£40-45, Db-£75-90, Tb-£95-110, parking, 61 Princetown Road, tel. 028/9127-1777, www.shellevenhouse.com, shellevenhouse@aol.com, Mary and Philip Weston).

$ Bramble Lodge is closest to the train station (10-minute walk), offering three inviting and spotless rooms. Ask about their simple one-bedroom self-catering apartment around the corner (Sb-£45, Db-£70, 1 Bryansburn Road, tel. 028/9145-7924, jacquihanna_bramblelodge@yahoo.co.uk, Jacquiline Hanna).

Portrush
and the
Antrim Coast

The Antrim Coast is one of the most interesting and scenic coastlines in Ireland. Portrush, at the end of the train line, is an ideal base for exploring its highlights. Within a few miles of the train terminal, you can visit evocative castle ruins, tour the world's oldest whiskey distillery, catch a thrill on a bouncy rope bridge, and hike along the famous Giant's Causeway.

PORTRUSH AND THE ANTRIM COAST IN 1 DAY

You need a full day to explore the Antrim Coast, so allow two nights in Portrush. An ideal day could lace together all of the recommended sights, followed by nine holes on the Portrush pitch-and-putt course. In summer months, the long days this far north extend your sightseeing time (and most golf courses stay open until dusk).

By Car: A car is the best way to explore the coast. Distances are short and parking is easy.

You can visit these sights in one busy day—the Giant's Causeway, Old Bushmills Distillery, Carrick-a-Rede Rope Bridge, and Dunluce Castle. Call ahead to reserve the Old Bushmills Distillery tour, and get an early start. Arrive at the Giant's Causeway by 9:00, when crowds are sparse. Park your car in the visitors center lot (opens at 9:00; parking is included with your entry fee). Early birds will find that the trails are free and always open. Spend an hour and a half scrambling over Ireland's most unique geology.

Then catch a late-morning tour of the Old Bushmills Distillery. Grab a cheap lunch in the hospitality room afterward. A 20-minute drive east brings you to Carrick-a-Rede, where you can enjoy a scenic cliff-top trail hike all the way to the lofty rope bridge (one hour round-trip, 1.5 hours if you cross the rope bridge and explore the sea stack). Hop in your car and double back west all the way to dramatically cliff-perched Dunluce Castle for a late-afternoon tour. From here, you're only a five-minute drive from Portrush.

By Bus: In peak season, an all-day bus pass helps you get around the region economically. The **Causeway Rambler** links Portrush hourly to the Old Bushmills Distillery, Giant's Causeway, and Carrick-a-Rede Rope Bridge (£6.50/day, May-Sept only, operates roughly 10:00-18:00). The bus journey from Portrush to Carrick-a-Rede (the easternmost point of interest on the route) takes 45 minutes. Pick up a Rambler bus schedule at the TI, and buy the ticket from the driver (in Portrush, the Rambler stops at Dunluce Avenue, next to public WC, a 2-minute walk from TI; operated by Translink, tel. 028/9066-6630, www.translink.co.uk).

By Taxi: Groups (up to four) can affordably visit most sights by taxi, except the more distant Carrick-a-Rede. Rough one-way prices from Portrush: £6 (Dunluce Castle), £8 (Old Bushmills Distillery), £11 (Giant's Causeway). Try **Andy Brown's Taxi** (tel. 028/7082-2223), **Hugh's Taxi** (mobile 077-0298-6110), or **North West Taxi** (tel. 028/7082-4446).

PORTRUSH AND THE ANTRIM COAST AT A GLANCE

▲▲**Giant's Causeway** Otherworldly coastline of quirky geologic formations, breezy hikes, and mythological confrontations between Celtic giant rivals. **Hours:** Visitors center—daily 9:00-19:00; causeway—always open for hiking. See page 314.

▲▲**Old Bushmills Distillery** The oldest whiskey distillery in the world (over 400 years old) where connoisseurs tour the production process and debate the merits of triple distilling. **Hours:** April-Oct opens Mon-Sat at 9:30, Sun at 12:00, last tour at 16:00; Nov-March opens Mon-Sat at 10:00, Sun at 12:00, last tour at 15:30. See page 316.

▲▲**Carrick-a-Rede Rope Bridge** Spectacular terminus of scenic coastal hike, drawing photographers, bird-watchers, and thrill seekers. **Hours:** March-Oct daily 9:30-18:00, June-Aug until 19:00; Nov-Feb 10:00-14:30. See page 317.

▲**Dunluce Castle** Historic and haunted Irish-Scottish hybrid fortification clinging to the peak of a sea stack while daring attack from any side. **Hours:** Daily April-Sept 10:00-17:30, Oct-March 10:00-16:00. See page 318.

Portrush Victorian age working-class beach getaway and regional sightseeing base, complete with old-time arcade and world-famous Royal Portrush links golf course. See page 308.

By Bus Tour: If you're based in Belfast, you can visit most of the sights on the Antrim Coast with a **McComb's** tour (see page 281).

PORTRUSH

Homey Portrush used to be known as "the Brighton of the North." It first became a resort in the late 1800s, as railroads expanded to offer the new middle class a weekend by the shore. Victorian society believed that swimming in salt water would cure many common ailments.

While it's already seen its best days, Portrush retains the atmosphere and architecture of a genteel seaside resort. Its peninsula is filled with lowbrow, family-oriented amusements, fun eateries, and B&Bs. Summertime fun-seekers promenade along the tiny harbor and tumble down to the sandy beaches, which extend in sweeping white crescents on either side.

Students from nearby University of Ulster at Coleraine give the town a little more personality. Along with the usual arcade amusements, there are nightclubs, restaurants, summer theater productions (July-Aug) in the Town Hall, and convivial pubs that attract customers all the way from Belfast.

July and August are beach-resort boom time. June and September are laid-back and lazy. Families pack Portrush on Saturdays, and revelers from Belfast crowd its hotels on Saturday nights.

Orientation

Portrush's easily walkable town center features sea views in every direction. On one side are the harbor and most of the restaurants, and on the other are Victorian townhouses and vast, salty vistas. The tip of the peninsula is filled with tennis courts, lawn-bowling greens, putting greens, and a park.

Tourist Information: The TI is located underneath the very central, red-brick Town Hall (April-Sept 9:30-17:00, Sat-Sun 12:00-17:00; closed Oct-March; Kerr Street, tel. 028/7082-3333). Get the Collins Northern Ireland Visitors Map (£5), the free *Visitor Attractions* brochure, and, if needed, a free Belfast map.

Internet Access: Ground Espresso Bar has one coin-op public computer (daily 8:30-18:00, until 22:00 July-Aug, 52 Main Street, tel. 028/7082-5979).

Bike Rental: The **Harbour Heights B&B** rents sturdy mountain bikes for £12/day, a great way to experience the gorgeous Antrim Coast.

Rick's Tip: *Over a four-day weekend in mid-May, thousands of* **motorcycle fans crowd Portrush** *to watch the* **Northwest 200 Race.** *Accommodations fill up a year ahead, and traffic is the pits (dates and details at www.northwest200.org).*

Sights

BARRY'S OLD-TIME AMUSEMENT ARCADE

This is a fun chance to see Northern Ireland at play (open weekends and summer only). Located just below the train station on the harbor, it's filled with "candy floss" (cotton candy) stands and kids learning the art of one-armed bandits, 10p at a time. Get £1 worth of 10p coins from the machine and go wild, or brave the tiny roller coaster and bumper cars (July-mid-Sept daily 12:30-22:30, shorter hours

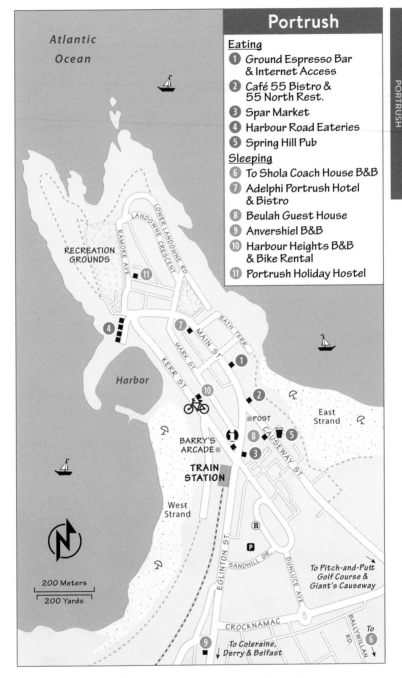

Portrush

Eating

1. Ground Espresso Bar & Internet Access
2. Café 55 Bistro & 55 North Rest.
3. Spar Market
4. Harbour Road Eateries
5. Spring Hill Pub

Sleeping

6. To Shola Coach House B&B
7. Adelphi Portrush Hotel & Bistro
8. Beulah Guest House
9. Anvershiel B&B
10. Harbour Heights B&B & Bike Rental
11. Portrush Holiday Hostel

Atlantic Ocean

RECREATION GROUNDS

LANDOWNE AVE

LOWER LANDOWNE RD

LANDOWNE CRESCENT

RAMORE AVE

BATH TERR.

MAIN ST

MARK ST

KERR ST

Harbor

POST

East Strand

BARRY'S ARCADE

TRAIN STATION

CAUSEWAY ST

West Strand

EGLINTON ST

SANDHILL DR.

DUNLUCE AVE

To Pitch-and-Putt Golf Course & Giant's Causeway

CROCKNAMAC

BALLYWILLAN RD

To Coleraine, Derry & Belfast

To

200 Meters
200 Yards

May-June, closed mid-Sept-April; tel. 028/7082-2340, www.barrysamusements. com).

PITCH-AND-PUTT AT THE ROYAL PORTRUSH GOLF CLUB

Irish courses, like those in Scotland, are highly sought after for their lush greens in glorious settings. Serious golfers can get a tee time at the Royal Portrush, which hosted the British Open in 1951 and is set to host it again in 2019 (green fees Mon-Fri-£160, Sat-Sun-£180). Those on a budget can play the adjacent, slightly shorter Valley Course (green fees Mon-Fri-£42.50, Sat-Sun-£55). Meanwhile, rookies can get a wee dose of this wonderful golf setting at the neighboring Skerries 9 Hole Links pitch-and-putt range. You get two clubs and balls for £8 (daily 8:30-19:00, 10-minute walk from station, tel. 028/7082-2311, www.royalportrush golfclub.com).

Eating

Being both a get-away-from-Belfast and close-to-a-university (at Coleraine) beach town, Portrush has more than enough chips joints. Eglinton Street is lined with cheap and cheery eateries.

Lunch Spots

Ground Espresso Bar makes fresh £5 sandwiches and *panini*, soup, and great coffee (daily July-Aug 9:00-22:00, Sept-June 9:00-17:00, 52 Main Street, tel. 028/7082-5979). They also offer coin-op Internet access.

Café 55 Bistro serves basic sandwiches with a great patio view (May-Sept Mon-Fri 9:00-17:00, Sat-Sun 9:00-21:30, shorter hours off-season, 1 Causeway Street, beneath fancier 55 North restaurant run by same owners—listed below, tel. 028/7082-2811).

The **Spar Market** has what you'll need for your Antrim Coast picnic (daily 7:00-20:00, across from Barry's Arcade on Main Street, tel. 028/7082-5447).

Fine Dining

55 North (named for the local latitude) has the best sea views in town, with windows on three sides. The filling pasta-and-fish plates are a joy (£10-17 plates, daily 12:30-14:00 & 17:00-21:00 except closed Mon Sept-June, 1 Causeway Street, tel. 028/7082-2811).

Adelphi Bistro is a good bet for its relaxed, family-friendly atmosphere and

Dining in Portrush

hearty meals (daily 12:00-15:00 & 17:00-21:00, 67 Main Street, tel. 028/7082-5544).

Harbour Road Eateries

The following four restaurants, located within 50 yards of each other (all under the same ownership and overlooking the harbor on Harbour Road), offer some of the best food values in town.

Ramore Wine Bar—salty, modern, and much-loved—bursts with happy eaters. They have the most inviting menu that I've seen in Ireland, featuring huge meals ranging from steaks to vegetarian food. Share a piece of the decadent banoffee (banana toffee) pie with a friend (£9-15 plates, daily 12:15-14:15 & 17:00-21:30, tel. 028/7082-4313).

Downstairs, sharing the same building as the Ramore Wine Bar, is the energetic **Coast Pizzeria,** with great Italian dishes. Come early for a table, or sit at the bar (daily 17:00-21:30, Sept-June closed Mon-Tue, tel. 028/7082-3311).

The **Harbour Bistro** offers a more subdued, darker bistro ambience than the previous two eateries, with meals for a few pounds more (£9-16 dinners, daily 17:00-21:30, tel. 028/7082-2430).

The **Mermaid Kitchen & Bar** is all about fresh fish dishes with a Spanish twist and great harbor views. Those sitting at the bar get a bird's-eye view of the fun banter and precision teamwork of the kitchen staff (Wed-Sun 17:30-22:00, closed Mon-Tue, tel. 028/7082-6969).

Pubs

The **Harbour Bar** has an old-fashioned pub downstairs and a plush, overstuffed, dark lounge upstairs (next to Harbour Bistro). Or try **Spring Hill Pub,** with a friendly vibe and occasional music session nights (17 Causeway Street, tel. 028/7082-3361).

Sleeping

August and Saturday nights can be tight (and loud) with young party groups. Rates vary with the view and season—probe

for softness. Many listings face the sea, though sea views are worth paying for only if you get a bay window. Ask for a big room (some doubles can be very small; twins are bigger). Lounges are invariably grand and have bay-window views. Most places listed have lots of stairs. All but Shola Coach House are perfectly central and within a few minutes' walk of the train station. Parking is easy.

$$ Shola Coach House is a memorable treat that exceeds other B&B experiences in Northern Ireland. About 1.5 miles south of town, it's easiest for drivers (otherwise it's a 30-minute uphill walk or £4 taxi ride). The secluded, 165-year-old, renovated stone structure once housed the coaches and horses for a local landlord. The decor of the four rooms is tasteful, the garden patio is delightful, and Sharon and David Schindler keep it spotless (Db-£90-110, Tb-£135-150, parking, Gateside Road at top of Ballywillan Road, tel. 028/7082-5925, mobile 075-6542-7738, www.sholabandb.com, sholabandb@gmail.com).

$$ Adelphi Portrush is a breath of fresh air, with 28 tastefully furnished modern rooms, friendly staff, and a hearty bistro downstairs (Sb-£55-109, Db-£69-109, Tb-£99-139, Qb-£129-169, 67 Main Street, tel. 028/7082-5544, www.adelphiportrush.com, stay@adelphiportrush.com).

The Scottish Connection

The Romans called the Irish the "Scoti" (meaning pirates). When the Scoti crossed the narrow Irish Sea and invaded the land of the Picts 1,500 years ago, that region became known as Scoti-land. Ireland and Scotland were never conquered by the Romans, and they retained similar clannish Celtic traits. Both share the same Gaelic branch of the linguistic tree.

On clear summer days from Carrick-a-Rede, the island of Mull in Scotland—only 17 miles away—is visible. Much closer on the horizon is the boomerang-shaped Rathlin Island, part of Northern Ireland. Rathlin is where Scottish leader Robert the Bruce (a compatriot of William "Braveheart" Wallace) retreated in 1307 after defeat at the hands of the English. Legend has it that he hid in a cave on the island, where he observed a spider patiently rebuilding its web each time a breeze knocked it down. Inspired by the spider's perseverance, Robert gathered his Scottish forces once more and finally defeated the English at the decisive battle of Bannockburn.

Flush with confidence from his victory, Robert the Bruce decided to open a second front against the English...in Ireland. In 1315, he sent his brother Edward to enlist their Celtic Irish cousins in an effort to thwart the English. After securing Ireland, Edward hoped to move on and enlist the Welsh, thus cornering England with their pan-Celtic nation. But Edward's timing was bad—Ireland was in the midst of famine. His Scottish troops had to live off the land and began to take food and supplies from the starving Irish. He might also have been trying to destroy Ireland's crops to keep them from being used as a colonial "breadbasket" to feed English troops. The Scots quickly wore out their welcome, and Edward the Bruce was eventually killed in battle near Dundalk in 1318.

It's interesting to imagine how things might be different today if Ireland and Scotland had been permanently welded together as a nation 700 years ago. You'll notice the strong Scottish influence in this part of Ireland when you ask a local a question and he answers, "Aye, a wee bit." The Irish joke that the Scots are just Irish people who couldn't swim home.

$ Beulah Guest House, with 11 prim rooms, is a traditional, good-value place, run by cheerful Helen and Charlene McLaughlin (S with shower in room and toilet down the hall–£33, Sb–£45-60, Db–£60-75, Tb–£85-105, parking at rear, 16 Causeway Street, tel. 028/7082-2413, www.beulahguesthouse.com, stay@beulahguesthouse.com).

$ Anvershiel B&B, with six rooms, is a 10-minute walk south of the train station. Jovial Victor Bow, who runs the show with his wife Erna, really knows local golf options (Sb–£45, Db–£65, Tb–£95,

Qb–£125, cash only, parking, 16 Coleraine Road, tel. 028/7082-3861, www.anvershiel.com, enquiries@anvershiel.com).

$ Harbour Heights B&B rents nine homey rooms, each named after a different town in County Antrim. It has an inviting guest lounge, supervised by two tabby cats, overlooking the harbor. Friendly South African hosts Sam and Tim Swart—a photographer—manage the place with a light hand (Sb–£40-45, Db–£65-85, family rooms, bike rentals, 17 Kerr Street, tel. 028/7082-2765, mobile 078-9586-6534, www.harbourheights

portrush.com, info@harbourheights portrush.com).

$ Portrush Holiday Hostel offers 41 beds and clean, well-organized, economical lodging (£12.50-15/bed in 10-bed dorm room, £17/bed in 4-bed dorm room, S-£20, Sb-£25, D-£34, Db-£38-40, Qb-£45-55, wash-and-dry laundry service-£6, mobile 078-8178-2181 or 078/5037-7367, 24 Princess Street, www.portrushholidayhostel.com, info@portrushholidayhostel.com).

Transportation
Arriving and Departing
BY TRAIN OR BUS

The train tracks stop at the base of the tiny peninsula that Portrush fills (no baggage storage at station). Most of my listed B&Bs are within a 10-minute walk of the train station. The bus stop is two blocks from the train station.

Day Pass: Consider a £16.50 Zone 4 iLink smartcard, good for all-day train and bus use in Northern Ireland year-round (£15 top-up for each additional day; for more on iLink cards, see page 298). Translink has useful updated schedules and prices for both trains and buses in

Northern Ireland (tel. 028/9066-6630, www.translink.co.uk).

From Portrush by Train to: Coleraine (hourly, 12 minutes, sparse on Sun morning), **Belfast** (11/day Mon-Sat, 5/day Sun, 2 hours, transfer in Coleraine), **Dublin** (7/day Mon-Sat, 2/day Sun, 5 hours, transfer in Coleraine or Belfast).

From Portrush by Bus to: Belfast (12/day, 2 hours; scenic coastal route, 2.5 hours), **Dublin** (4/day, 5.5 hours).

BY CAR

If driving between Portrush and Belfast, don't miss the slower-but-scenic coastal route via the Glens of Antrim, if time allows.

ANTRIM COAST

The craggy 20-mile stretch of the Antrim Coast extending eastward from Portrush to Ballycastle rates second only to the tip of the Dingle Peninsula as the prettiest chunk of coastal Ireland.

With a car, it's easy to tour the coast in one busy, memorable day. Without a car, you can take buses (May-Sept only) or a taxi from Portrush to get to the sights. For specifics, see page 306.

Giant's Causeway, along the Antrim Coast

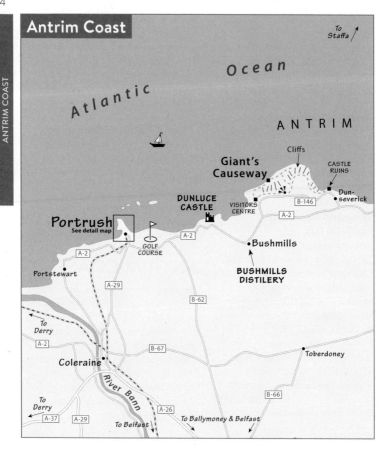

Antrim Coast

To Staffa

Atlantic

Ocean

ANTRIM

Cliffs

CASTLE RUINS

Giant's Causeway

DUNLUCE CASTLE

VISITORS CENTRE

B-146

Dun-severick

A-2

Portrush
See detail map

GOLF COURSE

A-2

•Bushmills

BUSHMILLS DISTILERY

A-2

Portstewart

A-29

B-62

To Derry

A-2

B-67

Toberdoney

Coleraine

River Bann

B-66

To Derry

A-37   A-29   To Belfast   A-26   To Ballymoney & Belfast

Sights

▲▲GIANT'S CAUSEWAY

This five-mile-long stretch of coast-line, a World Heritage Site, is famous for its bizarre basalt columns. The shore is covered with largely hexagonal pillars that stick up at various heights. It's as if the earth were offering God his choice of 37,000 six-sided cigarettes.

Geologists claim the Giant's Cause-way was formed by volcanic eruptions more than 60 million years ago. As the surface of the lava flow quickly cooled, it contracted and crystallized into columns (resembling the caked mud at the bottom of a dried-up lakebed, but with deeper cracks). As the rock later settled and eroded, the columns broke off into the

many stair-like steps that now honey-comb the Antrim Coast.

Of course, in actuality, the Giant's Causeway was made by a giant Ulster warrior named Finn MacCool who knew of a rival giant living on the Scottish island of Staffa. Finn built a stone bridge over to Staffa to spy on his rival, and found out that the Scottish giant was much bigger. Finn retreated back to Ireland and had his wife dress him as a sleeping infant, just in time for the rival giant to come across the causeway to spy on Finn. The rival, shocked at the infant's size, fled back to Scotland in terror of whomever had sired this giant baby. Breathing a sigh of relief, Finn tore off the baby clothes and pru-dently knocked down the bridge. Today,

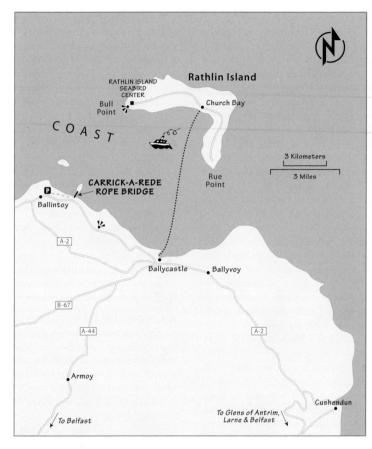

proof of this encounter exists in the geologic formation that still extends undersea and surfaces at Staffa.

Cost and Hours: The visitors center costs £9, which includes parking, and is open daily 9:00-19:00 (also has gift shop and café). The causeway is free and always open, and hiking trails are open from dawn to dusk. If you pay to enter the visitors center, you can borrow a great audioguide to take along on your hike. Tel. 028/2073-1855, www.nationaltrust.org.uk/giantscauseway.

Visiting the Causeway: For cute variations on the Finn story, as well as details on the ridiculous theories of modern geologists, start in the **Giant's Causeway Visitors Centre**. It's filled with interac-tive exhibits giving a worthwhile history of the Giant's Causeway, with a regional overview. On the far wall opposite the entrance, check out the interesting three-minute film showing the evolution of the causeway from molten lava to the geometric, geologic wonderland of today. The large 3-D model of the causeway offers a bird's-eye view of the region. Some of the exhibits are geared to kids who get a kick out of all things giant-related.

The causeway itself is the highlight of the entire coast. The audioguide (included with the visitors center ticket) highlights 15 stops along the causeway, each with a photo of the formation being described; all stops are shown on the map you'll receive with your ticket.

From the visitors center, you have several options for visiting the causeway:

By Minibus: A minibus (4/hour from 9:00, £1 each way) zips tired tourists a half-mile from the visitors center down a paved road and along the tidal zone to the causeway. This standard route (the blue dashed line on your map) offers the easiest access and follows the stops on your audioguide. Some choose to walk down this route to the causeway, and then take the shuttle back up.

By Foot: For a more varied dose of causeway views, consider the cliff-top trail (the red dashed line on your map). Take the easy-to-follow trail uphill from the visitors center 10 minutes and catch your breath at Weir's Snout, the great fence-protected precipice viewpoint. It's only 15 level minutes farther to reach the Shepherd's Steps. Then grab the banister on the steep (and slippery on wet days) stairs that zigzag down the switchbacks toward the water. At the T-junction, go 100 yards right, to the towering rock pipes of "the Organ." (You can walk another 500 yards east around the headland, but the trail dead-ends there.) Now retrace your steps west on the trail (don't go up the steps again), continuing down to the tidal zone, where the "Giant's Boot" (6 feet tall, on the right) provides some photo fun. Another 100 yards farther is the dramatic point where the causeway meets the sea. Just beyond that, at the asphalt turnaround, is the bus stop where you can catch a shuttle bus back to the visitors center.

Explore the uneven, wave-splashed rock terraces, watching your every easy-to-trip step. Look for "wishing coins"—rusted and bent—that have been jammed into the cracks of rock just behind the turnaround (where the trail passes through a notch in the 20-foot-high rock wall). With time and energy, you can skip the bus and walk back up to the visitors center, listening to the audioguide at the highlighted stops.

The Full Monty: Hardy hikers can spend a couple of hours exploring the trail that runs along a five-mile section of the Causeway Coast (yellow dashed line on your map). However, occasional rock falls and slides can close this route (ask first at Portrush TI, or call ahead to visitors center). A £1 hiking guide, sold at the TI, points out the highlights named by 18th-century guides (Camel's Back, Giant's Eye, and so on).

A good plan is to take the Causeway Rambler bus or a taxi from Portrush to the meager ruins of Dunseverick Castle (east of Giant's Causeway on B-146). Get off there and hike west, following the cliff-hugging contours of Benbane Head back to the visitors center. Then travel back to Portrush by taxi or Rambler bus (check bus schedules ahead of time at Portrush TI or at www.translink.co.uk).

▲▲OLD BUSHMILLS DISTILLERY

Bushmills claims to be the world's oldest distillery. Though King James I (of Bible fame) only granted Bushmills its license to distill "Aqua Vitae" in 1608, whiskey has been made here since the 13th century. Distillery tours waft you through the process, making it clear that Irish whiskey is triple distilled—and therefore smoother than Scotch whisky (distilled merely twice and minus the "e").

Cost and Hours: £7.50; April-Oct tours on the half-hour Mon-Sat from 9:30, Sun from 12:00, last tour at 16:00; Nov-March tours Mon-Sat at 10:00, 11:00, 12:00, 13:30,

Old Bushmills Distillery

14:30, and 15:30, Sun from 12:00. To find Bushmills, look for the distillery sign a quarter-mile from Bushmills town center. Tel. 028/2073-3218, www.bushmills.com.

Visiting the Distillery: The 45-minute tour starts with the mash pit, which is filled with a porridge that eventually becomes whiskey. (The leftovers of that porridge are fed to the county's particularly happy cows.) You'll see thousands of oak casks—the kind used for Spanish sherry—filled with aging whiskey.

The finale, of course, is the opportunity for a sip in the 1608 Bar—the former malt barn. Visitors get a single glass of their choice. Hot-drink enthusiasts might enjoy a cinnamon-and-cloves hot toddy. Teetotalers can just order tea, totally.

To see the distillery at its lively best, visit when the 100 workers are staffing the machinery—Monday morning through Friday noon (weekend tours see a still still). Stick close to the guide to hear the commentary in this loud environment. Tours are limited to 35 people and book up. In summer, call ahead to put in your name and get a tour time. After the tour, you can get a decent lunch in the tasting room.

▲▲CARRICK-A-REDE ROPE BRIDGE

For 200 years, fishermen hung a narrow, 90-foot-high bridge (planks strung between wires) across a 65-foot-wide chasm between the mainland and a tiny island. Today, the bridge (while not the original version) gives access to the sea stack where salmon nets were set (until 2002) during summer months to catch the fish turning and hugging the coast's corner. (The complicated system is described at the gateway.) A pleasant, 30-minute, one-mile walk from the parking lot takes you to the rope bridge. Cross over to the island for fine views and great seabird-watching, especially during nesting season.

Cost and Hours: £5.90 trail and bridge fee, pay at hut beside parking lot; daily March-Oct 9:30-18:00, June-Aug until 19:00; Nov-Feb 10:00-14:30; tel. 028/2076-9839, www.nationaltrust.org. uk. A coffee shop and WCs are near the parking lot.

Nearby: If you have a car and a picnic lunch, don't miss the terrific coastal **viewpoint** rest area one mile steeply uphill and east of Carrick-a-Rede (on B-15 to Ballycastle). This grassy area offers one

Carrick-a-Rede Rope Bridge

of the best picnic views in Northern Ireland (picnic tables but no WCs). Feast on bird's-eye views of the rope bridge, nearby Rathlin Island, and the not-so-distant Island of Mull in Scotland.

▲DUNLUCE CASTLE

These romantic ruins, perched dramatically on the edge of a rocky headland, are a testimony to this region's turbulent past. During the Middle Ages, the castle resisted several sieges. But on a stormy night in 1639, dinner was interrupted as half of the kitchen fell into the sea (Ireland's first fast food?). That was the last straw for the lady of the castle. The countess of Antrim packed up and moved inland, and the castle "began its slow submission to the forces of nature."

Cost and Hours: £5, daily April-Sept 10:00-17:30, Oct-March 10:00-16:00, no tours but free audioguide, tel. 028/2073-1938.

Visiting the Castle: While it's one of the largest castles in Northern Ireland and is beautifully situated, there's precious little left to see among Dunlace's broken walls.

Before entering, catch the great seven-minute film about the history of the castle (across from the ticket desk). The ruins themselves are dotted with anchored plaques that show interesting artists' renditions of how the place would have looked 400 years ago. The six-stop audioguide is free and fleshes out the story.

The 16th-century expansion of the castle was financed by the salvaging of a shipwreck. In 1588, the Spanish Armada's *Girona*—overloaded with sailors and the valuables of three abandoned sister ships—sank on her way home after the aborted mission against England. More than 1,300 drowned, and only five survivors washed ashore. The shipwreck was excavated in 1967, and a bounty of golden odds and silver ends wound up in Belfast's Ulster Museum. The Tower Museum in Derry has a similar collection of Armada artifacts from a different shipwreck farther west.

Dunluce Castle

BEST OF THE REST

DERRY

No city in Ireland connects the kaleidoscope of historical dots more colorfully than Derry. From a Viking-pillaged port to a cannonball-battered siege survivor; from a WWII naval base to a flashpoint of sectarian Troubles...Derry has seen it all.

When Ireland was being divvied up, the River Foyle was the logical border between the North and the Republic. But, for sentimental and economic reasons, the North kept Derry, which is otherwise on the Republic's side of the river. Consequently, this predominantly Catholic-Nationalist city was much contested throughout the Troubles.

Even its name is disputed. While most of its population and its city council call it "Derry," some maps, road signs, and all train schedules in the UK use "Londonderry," the name on its 1662 royal charter and the one favored by Unionists.

Still, the conflict is only one dimension of Derry; this pivotal city has a more diverse history, a prettier setting, and a more welcoming vibe than bigger Belfast.

The past decade has brought some refreshing changes. Most British troops departed in mid-2007, after 38 years in Northern Ireland. In 2011, a pedestrian bridge across the River Foyle was completed—and dubbed the "Peace Bridge" because it links the predominantly Protestant east bank with the predominantly Catholic west bank. Today, you can feel comfortable wandering the streets and enjoying this "legend-Derry" Irish city.

Orientation

The River Foyle flows north, slicing Derry into eastern and western chunks. The old town walls and almost all worthwhile sights are on the west side. (The tiny train station and Ebrington Square—at the end of the Peace Bridge—are on the east side.) Waterloo Place and the adjacent Guildhall Square, just outside the north corner of the old city walls, are the pedestrian hubs.

Derry

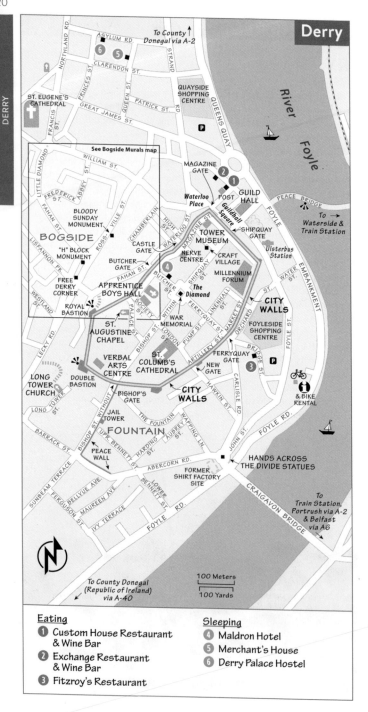

Derry

To County
Donegal via A-2

QUAYSIDE
SHOPPING
CENTRE

River

Foyle

MAGAZINE
GATE

Waterloo
Place

POST

GUILD
HALL

PEACE BRIDGE

To →
Waterside &
Train Station

Guildhall Square

SHIPQUAY
GATE

TOWER
MUSEUM

Ulsterbus
Station

See Bogside Murals map

BOGSIDE

Bloody
Sunday
Monument

CASTLE
GATE

NERVE
CENTRE

CRAFT
VILLAGE

"H" BLOCK
MONUMENT

BUTCHER
GATE

MILLENNIUM
FORUM

CITY
WALLS

FREE
DERRY
CORNER

APPRENTICE
BOYS HALL

The
Diamond

FOYLESIDE
SHOPPING
CENTRE

ROYAL
BASTION

WAR
MEMORIAL

ST.
AUGUSTINE'S
CHAPEL

FERRYQUAY
GATE

VERBAL
ARTS
CENTRE

ST.
COLUMB'S
CATHEDRAL

NEW
GATE

& BIKE
RENTAL

LONG
TOWER
CHURCH

DOUBLE
BASTION

BISHOP'S
GATE

CITY
WALLS

JAIL
TOWER

FOUNTAIN

PEACE
WALL

HANDS ACROSS
THE DIVIDE STATUES

FORMER
SHIRT FACTORY
SITE

To
Train Station,
Portrush via A-2
& Belfast
via A6

N

To County Donegal
(Republic of Ireland)
via A-40

100 Meters

100 Yards

Eating

1 Custom House Restaurant
& Wine Bar

2 Exchange Restaurant
& Wine Bar

3 Fitzroy's Restaurant

Sleeping

4 Maldron Hotel

5 Merchant's House

6 Derry Palace Hostel

Day Plan: Visit the Tower Museum and follow my self-guided walk along the town walls. Then see the powerful Bogside murals, following my self-guided tour. If you have extra time, an overnight in Derry would help you appreciate this underrated city even more.

Drivers heading north from Westport or Galway to Portrush should get an early start. (Donegal town is conveniently located for lunch.) For a short stop in Derry, park at the garage across from the TI and spend a couple of hours seeing the essentials: Visit the Tower Museum and catch some views from the town wall, before continuing on to Portrush (one hour away) for the night.

Getting to Derry: Next to the river on the east side of town, the **train station** has service to **Portrush** (8/day, 1.5 hours, change in Coleraine), **Belfast** (8/day, 2.5 hours), and **Dublin** (6/day, 5 hours). The **Ulsterbus station,** next to the river on the west side of town, connects the same towns with similar frequency and times as the trains, but offers quicker, better service to **Galway** (6/day, 5.5 hours). Keep in mind that some bus and train schedules may say "Londonderry" or "L'Derry" instead of "Derry."

Tourist Information: The TI sits on the riverfront and offers a room-finding service, rents bikes, and books tours (July-Sept Mon-Sat 9:00-19:00, Sun 10:00-17:00; Oct-June Mon-Fri 9:00-18:00, Sat 10:00-17:00, closed Sun; 44 Foyle Street, tel. 028/7126-7284, www.derryvisitor.com).

Tours: For walking tours, consider **McCrossan's City Tours** (£4, tel. 028/7127-1996, mobile 077-1293-7997, www.derrycitytours.com) and **Bogside History Tours** (£6, mobile 077-3145-0088, www.bogside-history-tours.com). **City** Sightseeing's bus tours offer a good overview (£12.50, mobile 075-4301-2577, www.citysightseeingderry.com).

⊙ Walk the Walls

The ▲▲old city walls, built from 1613 to 1618 and still intact, hold an almost mythic place in Irish history.

It was here in 1688 that a group of brave apprentice boys made their stand, slamming the gates shut in the face of the approaching Catholic forces of deposed King James II. This act galvanized the indecisive Protestant defenders inside the walls. A grinding 105-day siege followed, during which 20,000 perished. The siege was finally broken in 1689, when supply ships broke through a boom stretched across the River Foyle. The sacrifice of the city turned the tide in favor of newly crowned Protestant King William of Orange, who arrived in Ireland soon after to defeat James at the pivotal Battle of the Boyne.

Almost 20 feet high and at least as thick, the walls form a mile-long oval loop that you can cover in less than an hour. The most interesting section is the half-circuit facing the Bogside, starting at Magazine Gate (stairs face the Tower Museum Derry inside the walls) and finishing at Bishop's Gate.

• *Enter the walls at Magazine Gate and find the stairs opposite the Tower Museum. Once atop the walls, head left.*

Walk the wall as it heads uphill. In the row of buildings on the left (just before crossing over Castle Gate), you'll see an arch entry into the **Craft Village,** an alley lined with shops and cafés that showcase the city's economic rejuvenation (Mon-Sat 9:30-17:30, closed Sun).

• *After crossing over Butcher Gate, stop in front of the grand building with the four columns to view the...*

First Derry Presbyterian Church: This stately Neoclassical, red-sandstone church was finished in 1780. Over the next 200 years, time took its toll on the structure, which was eventually closed due to dry rot and Republican fire-bombings. In 2011, the renovated church reopened to cross-community approval (another sign of the slow reconciliation in Derry). The **Blue Coat School** exhibit behind the church highlights the important role of Presbyterians in local history (free but donation expected, closed Sat-Tue in summer and all of Oct-April, tel. 028/7126-1550).

• *Just up the block is the...*

Apprentice Boys Memorial Hall: Built in 1873, this hall houses the private lodge of an all-male Protestant organization dedicated to the memory of the original 13 apprentice boys who saved the day during the 1688 siege. Each year, on the Saturday closest to the August 12 anniversary date, the modern-day Apprentice Boys Society commemorates the end of the siege with a controversial march atop the walls, considered sacred ground for Unionists. The **Siege Museum** stands behind the hall (due to open in 2016).

Next, you'll pass a large, square pedestal that once supported a column in honor of Governor George Walker, the commander of the defenders during the siege. In 1972, the IRA blew up the column, which had 105 steps to the top (one for each day of the siege).

• *Opposite the empty pedestal is the small Anglican...*

St. Augustine Chapel: This Anglican chapel is where some believe the original sixth-century monastery of St. Columba (St. Colmcille in Irish) stood. The grounds are open to visitors (Mon-Sat 10:30-16:30, closed Sun except for worship).

As you walk, you'll pass a long wall (on the left)—all that remains of a former **British Army base,** which stood here until 2006. The dismantling of its towers—as well as the removal of most of the British Army from Northern Ireland—is a positive sign in cautiously optimistic Derry.

Stop at the **Double Bastion** fortified platform that occupies this corner of the city walls. Its cannon is nicknamed "Roaring Meg" for its fury during the siege. From here, you can see across the Bogside to the hills of County Donegal in the Republic.

Directly below and to the right are **Free Derry Corner** and **Rossville Street,** where the tragic events of Bloody Sunday took place in 1972. Down on the left is the 18th-century **Long Tower** Catholic church, named after the monk-built round tower that once stood in the area.

• *Head to the grand brick building behind you. This is the...*

Verbal Arts Centre: This center promotes the development of poetry, drama, writing, and storytelling. Drop by Bloom's Cafe to see the schedule of performances (closed Sat-Sun, tel. 028/7126-6946, www.verbalartscentre.co.uk).

• *Go left another 50 yards around the corner to reach...*

Bishop's Gate: From here, look up Bishop Street Within (inside the walls). This was the site of a British Army surveillance tower, which overlooked the neighborhood until 2006. Now look in the other direction to see Bishop Street Without (outside the walls). You'll spot a modern

Siege-defending cannons atop walls

Bishop's Gate

wall topped by a high mesh fence, running along the left side of Bishop Street Without. This so-called **"peace wall"** was built for the security of the Protestant enclave living behind it in the Fountain neighborhood. When the Troubles reignited 45 years ago, 20,000 Protestants lived on this side of the river. Sadly, this small housing development of 1,000 people is all that remains today. The rest have moved across the river to the mostly Protestant Waterside district. The stone tower halfway down the "peace wall" is all that remains of the jail that briefly held doomed rebel Wolfe Tone after the 1798 revolt.

• From Bishop's Gate, those short on time can descend from the walls and walk 15 minutes directly back through the heart of the old city, along Bishop Street Within and Shipquay Street to Guildhall Square.

◑ Bogside Murals Walk

The Catholic Bogside area was the tinderbox of the modern Troubles in Northern Ireland. Bloody Sunday, a terrible confrontation during a march that occurred more than 40 years ago, sparked a sectarian inferno; the ashes have not yet fully cooled. Today, the ▲▲murals of the Bogside give visitors a glimpse of this community's perception of those events.

Getting There: The events are memorialized in 12 murals painted on the ends of residential flats along a 300-yard stretch of Rossville Street and Lecky Road, where the march took place. You can reach them from Waterloo Place via William Street, from the old city walls at Butcher Gate via the long set of stairs extending below Fahan Street on the grassy hillside, or by the stairs leading down from the Long Tower Church. Today, this neighborhood is gritty but safe.

The Artists: Two brothers, Tom and William Kelly, and their childhood friend Kevin Hasson are known as the Bogside Artists. They grew up in the Bogside and witnessed the tragic events that took

place there, which led them to begin painting the murals in 1994. In a surprising and hopeful development, Tom was later invited into Derry's Protestant Fountain neighborhood to work with a youth club there on three proud heritage murals that were painted over paramilitary graffiti. For more about this unique trio, visit their website—www.bogsideartists.com.

The Murals: Start out at the corner of Rossville and William streets.

The Bogside murals face different directions (and some are partially hidden by buildings), so they're not all visible from a single viewpoint. Plan on walking three long blocks along Rossville Street (which becomes Lecky Road) to see them all. Residents are used to visitors and don't mind if you photograph the murals.

From William Street, walk south along the right side of Rossville Street toward Free Derry Corner. The murals will all be on your right.

The first mural you'll walk past is the colorful ❶ *Peace,* showing the silhouette of a dove in flight (left side of mural) and an oak leaf (right side of mural), both created from a single ribbon.

❷ *The Hunger Strikers* features participants of the 1981 Maze Prison hunger

Peace *mural in Bogside*

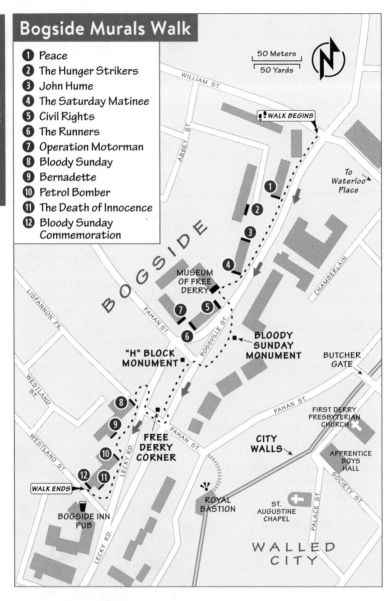

Bogside Murals Walk

1. Peace
2. The Hunger Strikers
3. John Hume
4. The Saturday Matinee
5. Civil Rights
6. The Runners
7. Operation Motorman
8. Bloody Sunday
9. Bernadette
10. Petrol Bomber
11. The Death of Innocence
12. Bloody Sunday Commemoration

50 Meters
50 Yards

WILLIAM ST.

WALK BEGINS

ABBEY ST.

To Waterloo Place

BOGSIDE

CHAMBERLAIN

LISFANNON PK.

FAHAN ST.

MUSEUM OF FREE DERRY

ROSSVILLE ST.

BLOODY SUNDAY MONUMENT

BUTCHER GATE

"H" BLOCK MONUMENT

WESTLAND ST.

FAHAN ST.

FIRST DERRY PRESBYTERIAN CHURCH

WESTLAND ST.

LECKY RD.

FAHAN ST.

FREE DERRY CORNER

CITY WALLS

APPRENTICE BOYS HALL

WALK ENDS

SOCIETY ST.

BOGSIDE INN PUB

ROYAL BASTION

ST. AUGUSTINE CHAPEL

PALACE ST.

LECKY RD.

WALLED CITY

strike, as well as their mothers, wives, and sisters, who sacrificed and supported them in their fatal decision (10 strikers died).

Smaller and easy to miss (above a ramp with banisters) is ❸ *John Hume*. It's actually a collection of four faces (clockwise from upper left): Nationalist leader John Hume, Martin Luther King Jr., Nelson Mandela, and Mother Teresa. The Brooklyn Bridge in the middle symbolizes the bridges of understanding that the work of these four Nobel Peace Prize winners created. Born in the Bogside, Hume still maintains a home here.

Bloody Sunday

Civil rights groups began to protest in Northern Ireland in the mid-1960s, inspired by marches in America. Initially, their goals were to gain better housing, secure fair voting rights, and end employment discrimination. Tensions mounted and clashes with the predominantly Protestant Royal Ulster Constabulary police force became frequent. The British Army was called in to keep the peace.

On January 30, 1972, about 10,000 people protesting internment without trial held an illegal march sponsored by the Northern Ireland Civil Rights Association. British Army barricades kept them from the center of Derry, so they marched through the Bogside neighborhood.

That afternoon, some youths rioted on the fringe of the march. An elite parachute regiment had orders to move in and make arrests in the Rossville Street area. Shooting broke out, and after 25 minutes, 13 marchers were dead and 13 were wounded (one of the wounded later died). The soldiers claimed they came under attack from gunfire and nail-bombs. The marchers said the army shot indiscriminately at unarmed civilians.

The clash, called "Bloody Sunday," uncorked pent-up frustration. Moderate Nationalists morphed into staunch Republicans overnight and released a flood of fresh IRA volunteers. An investigation at the time exonerated the soldiers, but the relatives of the victims insisted on their innocence.

In 1998, then-British Prime Minister Tony Blair promised a new inquiry, which became the longest and most expensive in British legal history. In 2010, a 12-year investigation—the Saville Report—determined that the Bloody Sunday civil rights protesters were innocent and called the deaths of 14 protesters unjustified.

In a dramatic 2010 speech in the House of Commons, British Prime Minister David Cameron apologized to the people of Derry. "What happened on Bloody Sunday was both unjustified and unjustifiable. It was wrong," he declared. Cheers rang out in Derry's Guildhall Square, where thousands had gathered to watch the speech. After 38 years of struggle, Northern Ireland's bloodiest wound began healing.

❹ **The Saturday Matinee** depicts an outgunned but undaunted local youth behind a screen shield. He holds a stone, ready to throw, while a British armored vehicle approaches. Why *Saturday Matinee*? The weekend was the best time for locals to "have a go at" the army; people were off work and out of school.

Nearby is ❺ *Civil Rights,* showing a marching Derry crowd carrying an anti-sectarian banner. In the building behind this mural, you'll find the small but intense **Museum of Free Derry** (may be closed for renovation; otherwise, £3, open Mon-Fri 9:30-16:30 year-round, also open Sat-Sun 13:00-16:00 in summer, 55 Glenfada Park, tel. 028/7136-0880, www. museumoffreederry.org).

Cross over to the other side of Rossville Street to see the **Bloody Sunday Monument.** This small, fenced-off stone obelisk lists the names of those who died that day. Take a look at the map pedestal by the monument, which shows how a rubble barricade was erected to block the street.

Cross back again, this time over to the

grassy median strip that runs down the middle of Rossville Street. At this end stands a granite letter **H** inscribed with the names of the 10 IRA hunger strikers who died in the H-block of Maze Prison in 1981.

From here, as you look across at the corner of Fahan Street, you get a good view of two murals. In ❻ *The Runners* (right), rioting youths flee tear gas used by the British Army to disperse crowds. Meanwhile, in ❼ *Operation Motorman* (left), a soldier wields a sledgehammer to break through a house door, depicting the British Army's efforts to open up the Bogside's areas controlled by the IRA from 1969-1972.

Walk down to the other end of the median strip where the white wall of **Free Derry Corner** announces "You are now entering Free Derry." This was the gabled end of a string of houses that stood here more than 40 years ago—a traditional meeting place for speakers to address crowds during the Troubles.

Cross back to the right side of the street (now Lecky Road) to see ❽ *Bloody Sunday,* in which a small group of men carry a body from that ill-fated march.

Near it is a mural called ❾ *Berna-dette.* The woman with the megaphone is outspoken civil-rights leader Bernadette Devlin McAliskey, who at age 21 became the youngest elected member of British Parliament. Behind her a supporter bangs a trash-can lid, a traditional expression of protest.

❿ *Petrol Bomber,* showing a teen wearing a gas mask, captures the Battle of the Bogside, when locals barricaded their community, shutting out British rule.

In ⓫ *The Death of Innocence,* a young girl stands in front of bomb wreckage. She is Annette McGavigan, a 14-year-old who was killed on this corner by crossfire in 1971. She was the 100th fatality of the Troubles, which eventually took more than 3,000 lives. The butterfly above her symbolizes the hope for peace. For years, the artists left the butterfly an empty silhouette; They finally filled in the butterfly with optimistic colors in the summer of 2006.

Finally, around the corner, you'll see a circle of male faces: ⓬ *Bloody Sunday Commemoration,* painted in 1997 to observe the 25th anniversary of the tragedy, shows the 14 victims.

Across the street, drop into the **Bogside Inn** for a beverage and check out the

Bernadette Devlin mural in Bogside

black-and-white photos of events in the area during the Troubles. This pub has been here through it all, and lives on to tell the tale.

While these murals preserve the struggles of the late 20th century, today violence has given way to negotiations. Nationalist leader John Hume (who shared the 1998 Nobel Peace Prize with Unionist leader David Trimble) once borrowed a quote from Gandhi to explain his nonviolent approach: "An eye for an eye leaves everyone blind."

Sights

▲▲TOWER MUSEUM DERRY

Occupying a reconstructed medieval tower, this museum provides an excellent introduction to the city. Combining modern audiovisual displays with historical artifacts, the exhibits tell the story of the city with an unbiased viewpoint, sorting out the roots of the Troubles. The museum is divided into two sections: the Story of Derry (on the ground floor) and the Spanish Armada (on the four floors of the tower).

Cost and Hours: £4, daily 10:00-16:30, free audioguide for Armada exhibits, Union Hall Place, tel. 028/7137-2411, www.derrycity.gov.uk/museums/tower-museum.

Eating and Sleeping

The **Custom House Restaurant & Wine Bar** is the classiest place in town (£14-19, Mon-Sat 12:00-14:30 & 17:30-21:30, Sun 13:00-21:00, Queens Quay). **Exchange Restaurant and Wine Bar,** near the river behind Waterloo Place, is hip and trendy (Mon-Sat 12:00-14:30 & 17:30-22:00, Sun 16:00-21:00, Queen's Quay, tel. 028/7127-3990). Busy **Fitzroy's** is the local favorite (Mon-Sat 12:00-22:00, Sun 13:00-20:00, 2 Bridge Street).

$$$ Maldron Hotel is actually inside Derry's historic walls (www.maldronhotelderry.com). **$$ Merchant's House** is a fine Georgian townhouse (www.thesaddlershouse.com). **$ Derry Palace Hostel** is a 10-minute walk north of Waterloo Place (www.derrycentralhostel.com).

Operation Motorman *mural*

Irish History and Culture

Ireland is rich with history, art, music, and language.

IRISH HISTORY

Prehistory
Ireland became an island when rising seas covered the last land bridge (7000 B.C.), a separation from Britain that the Irish would fight to maintain for the next 9,000 years. (Snakes were too slow to migrate before the seas cut Ireland off, despite later legends about St. Patrick banishing them.) By 6000 B.C., Stone Age hunter-fishers had settled on the east coast, followed by Neolithic farmers from the island of Britain. These early inhabitants left behind impressive but mysterious funeral mounds (passage graves) and large Stonehenge-type stone circles.

The Celts
(500 B.C.- A.D. 450)
More an invasion of ideas than of armies, the Celtic culture from Central Europe settled in Ireland, where it would dom-inate for a thousand years. There were more than 300 *tuatha* (clans) in Ireland, each with its own *rí* (king), who would've happily chopped the legs off anyone who called him "petty." The island was nomi-nally ruled by a single *Ard Rí* (high king) at the **Hill of Tara** (north of Dublin), though there was no centralized nation.

In 55 B.C., the Romans conquered the Celts in England, but they never invaded Ireland. Irish history forever skewed in a different direction—Gaelic, not Latin. The Romans called Ireland **Hibernia,** meaning Land of Winter; it was apparently too cold and bleak to merit an attempt at colonization.

The Age of Saints and Scholars
(A.D. 450-800)
When Ancient Rome fell, Gaelic Ireland was unaffected. There was no Dark Age here, and the island was a beacon of cul-ture for the rest of Europe. Ireland (popu-lation c. 750,000) was still a land of many feuding kings, but the culture was stable.

Christianity and Latin culture arrived first as a trickle from trading contacts with Christian Gaul (France), then more emphatically in A.D. 432 with **St. Patrick,** who persuasively converted the sun- and nature-worshipping Celts. Legends say he drove Ireland's snakes (symbolic of pagan beliefs) into the sea and explained the Trinity with a shamrock—three leaves on one stem.

Later monks continued Christianizing the island. They flocked to scattered, isolated monasteries, living in stone igloo beehive huts, translating and illustrating manuscripts. Perhaps the greatest works of art from all of Dark Age Europe are these manuscripts, particularly the ninth-century Book of Kells (in Dublin).

By 800, **Charlemagne** was importing Irish monks to help run his Frankish kingdom. Meanwhile, Ireland remained a relatively cohesive society based on monastic settlements rather than cities. Impressive round towers from those settlements still dot the Irish landscape—silent reminders of this exalted age.

Viking Invasion
(800-1100)

In 795, Viking pirates from Norway invaded, first testing isolated island monasteries, then boldly sailing up Irish rivers into the interior. The many raids wreaked havoc on the monasteries and continued to shake Irish civilization for two chaotic centuries. In 841, a conquering Viking band decided to winter in Ireland, eventually building the island's first permanent walled cities, Dublin and Waterford. The Viking raiders slowly evolved into Viking traders. They were the first to introduce urban life and commerce to Ireland. Over the centuries, Viking settlers married Gaelic gals and slowly blended in.

Anglo-Norman Arrival
(1100-1500)

The Normans were Ireland's next aggressive guests. In 1169, a small army of well-armed soldiers of fortune invaded Ireland under the pretense of helping a deposed Irish king regain his lands. This was the spearhead of a century-long invasion by the so-called Anglo-Normans— the French-speaking rulers of England, descended from William the Conqueror and his troops.

By 1250, the Anglo-Normans occupied two-thirds of the island. But when the **Black Death** came in 1348, it spread rapidly and fatally in the tightly packed Norman settlements. The plague, along with Normans intermarrying with Gaels, eventually diluted Norman identity and shrank English control. But even as Anglo-Norman power eroded, the English kings considered Ireland theirs.

The End of Gaelic Rule
(1500s)

Martin Luther's **Reformation** split the Christian churches into Catholic and Protestant, making Catholic Ireland a hot potato for newly Protestant England to handle. In 1534, angered by **Henry VIII** and his break with Catholicism, the **Earls of Kildare** (father, then son) led a rebellion. Henry crushed the revolt, executed the earls, and confiscated their land. Henry's daughter, **Elizabeth I,** gave the land to English Protestant colonists (called "planters"). The next four centuries would see a series of rebellions by Gaelic-speaking Irish-Catholic farmers fighting to free themselves from rule by English-speaking Protestant landowners.

Hugh O'Neill (1540-1616), a Gaelic chieftain angered by planters and English abuses, led a Gaelic revolt in 1595. At the Battle of Yellow Ford (1598), guerrilla tactics brought about an initial Irish victory. But after the disastrous **Battle of Kinsale** (1601), O'Neill ceded a half-million acres to England, signaling the end of Gaelic Irish rule.

English Colonization and Irish Rebellion
(1600s)

By 1641, 25,000 Protestant English and Scottish planters had settled into the confiscated land, making Ulster (in the northeast) the most English area of the island.

Then, **Oliver Cromwell**—who had pulled off a *coup d'état* in England—invaded and conquered Ireland (1649-1650) with a Puritanical, anti-Catholic zeal. Cromwell confiscated 11 more million acres of land from Catholic Irish landowners to give to English Protestants.

In 1688-1689, Irish rebels rallied around Catholic **King James II,** who had been deposed by the English Parliament. He wound up in Ireland, where he formed an army to retake the crown. The showdown came at the massive **Battle of the Boyne** (1690), north of Dublin. James and his 25,000 men were defeated by the troops of Protestant **King William III** of Orange. From this point on, the color orange became a symbol in Ireland for pro-English, pro-Protestant forces.

Protestant Rule
(1700s)

During the 18th century, urban Ireland thrived economically, and even culturally, under the English. Dublin in the 1700s (pop. 50,000) was Britain's second city, and one of Europe's wealthiest and most sophisticated.

But beyond Dublin, rebellion continued to brew. Irish nationalists were inspired by budding democratic revolutions in America (1776) and France (1789). Increasingly, the issue of Irish independence was less a religious question than a political one.

England tried to solve the Irish problem politically by forcing Ireland into a "Union" with England as part of a "United Kingdom" (**Act of Union,** 1801). The 500-year-old Irish Parliament was dissolved, with its members becoming part of England's Parliament in London. From then on, "Unionists" have been those who oppose Irish independence, wanting to preserve the country's union with England.

Votes, Violence, and the Famine
(1800s)

Irish politicians lobbied in the British Parliament for Catholic rights, reform of absentee-landlordism, and for **Home Rule.** But any hope of an Irish revival was soon snuffed out by the biggest catastrophe in Irish history: the **Great Potato Famine** (1845-1849). Legions of people (between 500,000 and 1.1 million) starved to death or died of related diseases. Another 1-2 million emigrated.

Ireland was ruined. Many of the best and brightest fled, and the island's economy—and spirit—took generations to recover. And culturally, old Gaelic, rural Ireland was being crushed under the Industrial Revolution and the political control wielded by Protestant England.

Easter Uprising and War of Independence
(1900-1920)

As the century turned, Ireland prepared for the inevitable showdown with Britain. On Easter Monday, April 24, 1916, Irish nationalists marched on Dublin and proclaimed Ireland an independent republic. British troops struck back and in a week suppressed the insurrection. When the British government swiftly executed the ringleaders, Ireland resolved to win its independence at all costs.

In the 1918 elections, the separatist Sinn Fein party (meaning "Ourselves") won big, but these new members of Parliament refused to go to London. Instead, they formed their own independent Irish Parliament in Dublin. Then Irish rebels began ambushing policemen—seen as the eyes and ears of British control—sparking the **War of Independence** in 1919. The fledgling Irish Republican Army faced 40,000

British troops. A thousand people died in this multiyear guerrilla war of street fighting, sniper fire, jailhouse beatings, terrorist bombs, and reprisals.

Partition and Civil War
(1920-1950)

Finally, Britain agreed to Irish independence. But Ireland itself was a divided nation—the southern three-quarters of the island was mostly Catholic, Gaelic, rural, and for Home Rule; the northern quarter was Protestant, English, industrial, and Unionist. The solution? In 1921, the British Parliament partitioned the island into two independent, self-governing countries within the British Commonwealth: **Northern Ireland** and the **Irish Free State.**

Ireland's various political factions wrestled with this compromise solution, and the island plunged into a **Civil War** (1922-1923). The hard-line IRA opposed the partition. Dublin and the southeast were ravaged in a year of bitter fighting before the Irish Free State emerged victorious. The IRA went underground, moving its fight north and trying for the rest of the century to topple the government of Northern Ireland.

In 1949, the Irish Free State left the Commonwealth and officially became the **Republic of Ireland.**

Troubles in the North
(1950-2000)

The Republic moved toward prosperity in the second half of the century, but Northern Ireland—with a slight Protestant majority and a large, disaffected Catholic minority—was plagued by the **Troubles.** In 1967, organized marches and demonstrations demanded equal treatment for Catholics. Protestant **Unionist Orangemen** countered by marching through Catholic neighborhoods, provoking riots. In 1969, Britain sent troops to help Northern Ireland keep the peace.

From the 1970s to the 1990s, the North was a low-level battlefield, with the IRA using terrorist tactics to achieve their political ends. The Troubles, which claimed some 3,000 lives, continued with bombings, marches, hunger strikes, rock-throwing, and riots (notably Derry's **Bloody Sunday** in 1972).

Finally, after a string of failed peace agreements, came the watershed 1998 settlement known as the **Good Friday Peace Accord** (to pro-Irish Nationalists) or the **Belfast Agreement** (to pro-British Unionists).

Global Nations
(2000 and Beyond)

After years of negotiation, in 2005 the IRA formally announced an end to its armed campaign, promising to pursue peaceful, democratic means. In 2007, London returned control of Northern Ireland to the popularly elected Northern Ireland Assembly. Perhaps most important, after almost 40 years, the British Army withdrew 90 percent of its forces from Northern Ireland that summer.

Now it's up to Northern Ireland to keep the peace. The 1998 peace accord gives Northern Ireland the freedom to leave the UK if ever the majority of the population approves a referendum to do so. At the same time, the Republic of Ireland withdrew its constitutional claim to the entire island of Ireland. Northern Ireland now has limited autonomy from London, with its own democratically elected, power-sharing government.

IRISH CULTURE

Irish Art

Megalithic tombs, ancient gold- and metalwork, illuminated manuscripts, high crosses carved in stone, paintings of rural Ireland, and provocative political murals—Ireland comes with some fascinating art. Here are a few highlights.

Megalithic Period: During the Stone Age, 5,000 years ago, farmers living in the **Valley of the Boyne,** north of Dublin, built a "cemetery" of approximately 40 **burial mounds.** The most famous of these mound tombs is the passage tomb at Newgrange, part of Brú na Bóinne, which also features some of Europe's best examples of megalithic (big rock) art.

The Age of Saints and Scholars: Christianity grew in Ireland from St. Patrick's first efforts in the fifth century A.D. During this "Golden Age" of Irish civilization, monks, along with metalworkers and stonemasons, created imaginative designs and distinctive stylistic motifs for **manuscripts**, **metal objects,** and **crosses.**

Monks wrote out and richly decorated manuscripts of the Gospels. The most beautiful and imaginative of these illuminated manuscripts is the **Book of Kells** (c. A.D. 800). Crafted by Irish monks at a monastery on the Scottish island of Iona, the book was brought to Ireland for safekeeping from rampaging Vikings. Many consider this book the finest piece of art from Europe's Dark Ages (now at Dublin's Trinity College Library).

The monks used Irish high crosses to celebrate the triumph of Christianity and to educate the illiterate masses through simple stone carvings on biblical themes. The **Cross of Murdock** (Muiredach's Cross, A.D. 923) is 18 feet tall, towering over the remains of the monastic settlement at Monasterboice. It is but one of many monumental crosses in Ireland.

Native Irish Art: The English suppressed Celtic Irish culture, replacing native styles with English traditions in architecture, painting, and literature. But in the late 19th century, revivals in Irish language, folklore, music, and art began to surface. **Jack B. Yeats** (1871-1957, brother of the poet W. B. Yeats), Belfast-born painter **Paul Henry** (1876-1958), and **Sean Keating** (1889-1977) were among the painters who looked to traditional Irish subjects for inspiration, focusing on Ireland's people, the country's rugged beauty, and its struggle for independence.

Traditional Irish Music

Traditional music is alive and popular in pubs throughout Ireland. "Sessions" (musical evenings) may be planned and advertised or impromptu. Traditionally, musicians just congregate and play for the love of it. There will generally be a fiddle, a flute or tin whistle, a guitar, a *bodhrán* (goatskin drum), and maybe an accordion or mandolin.

The music often comes in sets of three songs. The wind and string instruments embellish melody lines with lots of tight ornamentation. Whoever happens to be leading determines the next song only as the current tune is about to be finished.

Percussion generally stays in the background. The *bodhrán* (BO-run) is played with a small, two-headed club. The performer's hand stretches the skin to change the tone and pitch. You'll sometimes be lucky enough to hear a set of bones crisply played. These are two cow ribs (boiled and dried) that are rattled in one hand like spoons or castanets.

Watch closely if a piper is playing. The Irish version of bagpipes, the *uilleann* (ILL-in) pipes are played by inflating the airbag with a bellows (under the elbow) rather than with a mouthpiece. The sound is more melodic, with a wider range than the Highland pipes. It takes amazing coordination to play this instrument well, and the sound can be haunting.

Occasionally, the fast-paced music will stop and one person will sing a lament. Called *sean nos* (Irish Gaelic for "old style"), this slightly nasal vocal style may be a remnant of the ancient tradition whose stories—often of love lost, emigration to a faraway land, or a heroic rebel death struggling against English rule—are always heartfelt.

Irish Literature

Since the Book of Kells, Ireland's greatest contributions to the world of art have been through words. After Christianity transformed Ireland into a refuge of literacy (while the rest of Europe crumbled into the Dark Ages), Charlemagne's imported Irish monks invented "minuscule," which became the basis of the lowercase letters we use in our alphabet today. The cultural importance placed on the word (spoken, and, for the past 1,500 years, written) is today reflected in the rich output of modern Irish writers.

William Butler Yeats' early poems and plays are filled with fairies and idyllic rural innocence, while his later poems reflect Ireland's painful transition to independence. Yeats' Nobel Prize for literature (1923) was eventually matched by three later, Nobel-winning Irish authors: **George Bernard Shaw** (1925), **Samuel Beckett** (1969), and **Seamus Heaney** (1995).

Dublin-born **Oscar Wilde** wowed London with his quick wit, outrageous clothes, and flamboyant personality. Wilde wrote the darkly fascinating *Picture of Dorian Gray* (1890) and skewered upper-class Victorian society in witty comedic plays such as *The Importance of Being Earnest* (1895). Meanwhile, **Bram Stoker** was conjuring up a Gothic thriller called *Dracula* (1897). Most inventive of all, perhaps, was **James Joyce,** who captured literary lightning in a bottle with his modern, stream-of-consciousness *Ulysses*, set on a single day in Dublin (June 16, 1904).

In recent decades, the bittersweet Irish literary parade has been inhabited by tragically volcanic characters like **Brendan Behan,** who exclaimed, "I'm a drinker with a writing problem." Bleak poverty

experienced in childhood was the catalyst for **Frank McCourt**'s memorable *Angela's Ashes*. Among the most celebrated of today's Irish writers is **Roddy Doyle,** whose feel for working-class Dublin resonates in his novels of contemporary life (such as *The Commitments*).

Irish Language

The Irish have a rich oral tradition that goes back to their ancient fireside storytelling days. Part of the fun of traveling here is getting an ear for the way locals express themselves.

Irish Gaelic is one of four surviving Celtic languages, along with Scottish Gaelic, Welsh, and Breton. Some proud Irish choose to call their native tongue "Irish" instead of "Gaelic" to ensure that there is no confusion with the language spoken in parts of Scotland.

Only 165 years ago, the majority of the Irish population spoke Irish Gaelic. But most of the speakers were of the poor laborer class that either died or emigrated during the Famine. After the Famine, parents and teachers understood that their children would be better off speaking English if they emigrated to the US, Canada, Australia, or England. Children in schools wore a tally stick around their necks, and a notch was cut by teachers

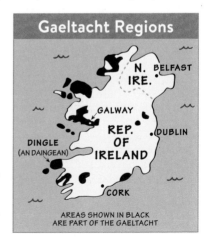

Gaeltacht Regions

AREAS SHOWN IN BLACK ARE PART OF THE GAELTACHT

Irish Place Names

Here are a few words that appear in Irish place names. You'll see these on road signs or at tourist sights.

Irish	Phonetics	English
alt	*ahlt*	cliff
an lár	*ahn lar*	city center
ard	*ard*	high, height, hillock
baile	*BALL-yah*	town, town land
beag	*beg*	little
bearna	*bar-na*	gap
boireann	*burr-en*	large rock, rocky area
bóthar	*boh-er*	road
bun	*bun*	end, bottom
caiseal	*CASH-el*	circular stone fort
caislean	*cash-LOIN*	castle
cathair	*caht-HAR*	circular stone fort, city
cill	*kill*	church
cloch	*clockh*	stone
doire	*dih-ruh*	oak
droichead	*DROCKH-ed*	bridge
drumlin	*DRUM-lin*	small hill
dun	*doon*	fort
gaeltacht	*GAIL-tekt*	Irish language district
gall	*gaul*	foreigner
garda	*gar-dah*	police
gort	*gort*	field
inis	*in-ish*	island
mileac	*mee-luch*	low marshy ground
mór	*mor*	large
muck	*muck*	pig
oifig an phoist	*UFF-ig un fwisht*	post office
poll	*poll*	hole, cave
rath	*rath*	ancient earthen fort
ross	*ross*	peninsula
sí	*shee*	fairy mound, bewitching
slí	*slee*	route, way
sliabh	*sleeve*	mountain
sraid	*shrawd*	street
teach	*chockh*	house
trá	*traw*	beach, strand
tur	*toor*	tower

each time a child was caught speaking Irish. At the end of the day, the child received a whack for each notch in the stick. It wasn't until a resurgence of cultural pride in the late 19th century that an attempt was made to promote the language again.

These days, less than 5 percent of the Irish population is fluent in their native tongue. However, it's taken seriously enough that all national laws must first be written in Irish, then translated into English. Irish Gaelic can be heard most often in the western counties of Kerry, Galway, Mayo, and Donegal. You'll know you're entering an Irish Gaelic-speaking area when you see a sign saying Gaeltacht (GAIL-tekt).

Irish Gaelic has no "th" sound—which you can hear today when an Irish person says something like "turdy-tree" (thirty-three). There are also no equivalents of the simple words "yes" and "no." Instead, answers are given in an affirmative or negative rephrasing of the question. For example, a question like "Did you mail the letter today?" would be answered with "I did (mail the letter)," rather than a simple "yes." Or "It's a nice day today, isn't it?" would be answered with "It is," or "'Tis."

Practicalities

TOURIST INFORMATION

Ireland's national tourist office is called **Tourism Ireland** (in the US), **Fáilte Ireland** (in Ireland), and **Discover Ireland** (in cyberspace). It offers a wealth of information on both the Republic of Ireland and Northern Ireland. Before your trip, scan their website (www.discoverireland.com) and download brochures and maps.

In Ireland, your best first stop in every town is the tourist information office—abbreviated **TI** in this book. (The nationwide tourist-information number for travelers calling from within Ireland is 1-850-230-330.) Prepare a list of questions and a proposed plan to double-check. Pick up a city map, confirm opening hours of sights, and get information on public transit (including bus and train schedules), walking tours, special events, and nightlife.

TRAVEL TIPS

Time Zones: Ireland, which is one hour earlier than most of continental Europe, is five/eight hours ahead of the East/West coasts of the US. The exceptions are the beginning and end of Daylight Saving Time: Ireland and Europe "spring forward" the last Sunday in March (two weeks after most of North America) and "fall

Finding Your Irish Roots

Many come to the Emerald Isle to trace their Irish ancestry. But too few give it enough thought before they set foot on the old sod, and instead show up and start "asking around." While this approach may give you an opportunity to meet nice Irish people, preparation can save time and increase your chances of making a real connection to your Celtic roots.

Many think their Irish ancestors were from County Cork, because Cobh is listed as their emigration departure port. But Cobh was the primary departure port for the vast majority of Irish emigrants—regardless of where they had resided in Ireland. An even earlier wave of Irish emigrants (mostly Scots-Irish from Ulster) sailed from the port of Derry (the second busiest emigration port).

If you have an idea of what town your ancestors hailed from, go online and search for its location (www.google.com/maps is a good starting point). Correct spelling is essential: Ballyalloly is up north in County Down while Ballyally is down south in County Cork. There's a town named Kells in four different Irish counties.

Fáilte Ireland, the official government-sponsored Irish tourist board, is a safe bet for reputable genealogy sources (www.discoverireland.ie). Browse www.irishgenealogy.ie or www.ancestry.com. The recently enabled online access to both the 1901 and 1911 Irish censuses has been a boon (www.census.nationalarchives.ie). However, it's not a perfect science: Many precious birth records (some dating back to the 1200s) went up in smoke when offices in the Four Courts building in Dublin burned in 1922 during the Irish Civil War.

Before you get to Ireland, contact the **Genealogy Advisory Service** at the **National Library** in Dublin (tel. 01/603-0213, www.nli.ie, genealogy@nli.ie) or the helpful genealogy search service in Cobh (tel. 021/481-3591, www.cobhheritage.com/genealogy, genealogy@cobhheritage.com). If you think your heritage might be Scots-Irish, contact the **Mellon Centre for Migration Studies,** near Omagh in Northern Ireland (tel. 028/8225-6315, www.qub.ac.uk/cms, mcms@librariesni.org.uk).

Another option is to hire a qualified expert for assistance; Fáilte Ireland may have a recommendation. If you're willing to invest in an experienced researcher, you may get better results. Consider Sean Quinn of **My Ireland Heritage,** who is based near Dublin in Trim, County Meath, but is able to work across Ireland (tel. 01/689-0213, www.myirelandheritage.com, sean@myirelandheritage.com).

With a few emails, phone calls, and Internet searches, you may be rewarded with a pint shared with some Irish guy or gal who looks a lot like you.

back" the last Sunday in October (one week before North America). For a handy online time converter, see www.timeanddate.com/worldclock.

Business Hours: In Ireland, most stores are open Monday through Saturday from roughly 10:00 to 17:30, with a late night on Wednesday or Thursday (until 19:00 or 20:00). On Sundays, many shops are closed and public transportation options are fewer (for example, no bus service to or from smaller towns).

Discounts: Discounts (called "concessions" in Ireland) aren't listed in this book.

However, many sights offer discounts for youths (up to age 18), students (with proper identification cards, www.isic.org), families, and seniors (loosely defined as retirees or those willing to call themselves a senior). Always ask. Some discounts are available only for citizens of the European Union (EU).

HELP!

Emergency and Medical Help

Dial 999 for police or a medical emergency. Or ask at your hotel for help—they'll know the nearest medical and emergency services. If you get a minor ailment, do as the locals do, and go to a pharmacist for advice.

Theft or Loss

To replace a passport, you'll need to go in person to an embassy or consulate office (listed below). If your credit and debit cards disappear, cancel and replace them. If your things are lost or stolen, file a police report, either on the spot or within a day or two; you'll need it to submit an insurance claim for rail passes or travel gear, and it can help with replacing your passport or credit and debit cards. For more information, see www.ricksteves.com/help.

Damage Control for Lost Cards

If you lose your credit, debit, or ATM card, you can stop people from using your card by reporting the loss immediately to your card company. Call these 24-hour US numbers collect: Visa (tel. 303/967-1096), MasterCard (tel. 636/722-7111), and American Express (tel. 336/393-1111). In the Republic of Ireland, to make a collect call to the US, dial 1-800-550-000. In Northern Ireland, dial 0-800-89-0011. Press zero or stay on the line for an operator. Visa's and MasterCard's websites list

European toll-free numbers by country.

If you report your loss within two days, you typically won't be responsible for any unauthorized transactions on your account, although many banks charge a liability fee of $50. You can generally receive a temporary replacement card within two or three business days in Europe.

Embassies and Consulates

US Embassy in Dublin: Tel. 01/630-6200 (42 Elgin Road, http://dublin.usembassy.gov)

US Consulate in Belfast: Tel. 028/9038-6100, after-hours emergency mobile 012-5350-1106 (223 Stranmillis Road, http://belfast.usconsulate.gov)

MONEY

This section offers advice on how to pay for purchases on your trip (including getting cash from ATMs and paying with plastic), VAT (sales tax) refunds, and tipping.

What to Bring

Bring both a credit card and a debit card. You'll use the debit card at cash machines (ATMs) to withdraw local currency for most purchases, and the credit card to pay for larger items. Some travelers carry a third card, in case one gets demagnetized or eaten by a rogue machine.

For an emergency stash, bring several hundred dollars in hard cash in $20 bills. If you need to exchange the bills, go to a bank; avoid using currency-exchange booths because of their lousy rates and/or outrageous (and often hard-to-spot) fees.

Cash

Cash is just as desirable in Europe as it is at home. Small businesses (B&Bs, mom-and-pop cafés, shops, etc.) prefer that you pay your bills with cash. Some vendors will charge you extra for using a credit card, some won't accept foreign credit

Exchange Rates

Check www.oanda.com for the latest exchange rates.

1 euro (€1) = about $1.10

1 British pound (£1) = about $1.60

The **Republic of Ireland** uses the euro. To convert prices in euros to dollars, add about 10 percent: €20 = about $22, €50 = about $55. Just like the dollar, one euro (€) is broken down into 100 cents. Coins range from €0.01 to €2, and bills from €5 to €500.

Northern Ireland uses the British pound sterling. To convert prices in pounds to dollars, add 60 percent: £20 = about $32, £50 = about $80. Coins range from 1 pence to £2, and bills from £5 to £50.

cards, and some won't take any credit cards at all. Cash is the best—and sometimes only—way to pay for cheap food, bus fare, taxis, and local guides.

Throughout Europe, ATMs are the standard way for travelers to get cash. They work just like they do at home. To withdraw money from an ATM, you'll need a debit card (ideally with a Visa or MasterCard logo for maximum usability), plus a PIN code (numeric and four digits). For increased security, shield the keypad when entering your PIN code. Try to withdraw large sums of money to reduce the number of per-transaction bank fees you'll pay.

Whenever possible, use ATMs located outside banks—a thief is less likely to target a cash machine near surveillance cameras, and if your card is munched by a machine, you can go inside for help.

Don't use an ATM if anything on the front of the machine looks loose or damaged (a sign that someone may

have attached a "skimming" device to capture account information). If a cash machine eats your ATM card, check for a thin plastic insert with a tongue hanging out (thieves use these devices to extract cards).

Stay away from "independent" ATMs such as Travelex, Euronet, YourCash, Cardpoint, and Cashzone, which charge huge commissions, have terrible exchange rates, and may try to trick users with "dynamic currency conversion" (described at the end of "Credit and Debit Cards," next).

If you want to monitor your accounts online during your trip to detect any unauthorized transactions, be sure to use a secure connection (see page 352).

Although you can use a credit card to withdraw cash at an ATM, this comes with high bank fees and only makes sense in an emergency.

Credit and Debit Cards

For purchases, Visa and MasterCard are more commonly accepted than American Express. Just like at home, credit and debit cards work easily at larger hotels, restaurants, and shops. I typically use my debit

ATMs are easy to find.

card to withdraw cash to pay for most purchases.

I use my credit card sparingly: to book hotel reservations, to buy advance tickets for events or sights, to cover major expenses (such as car rentals or plane tickets), and to pay for things online or near the end of my trip (to avoid another visit to the ATM). While you could instead use a debit card for these purchases, a credit card offers a greater degree of fraud protection.

Ask Your Credit- or Debit-Card Company: Before your trip, contact the company that issued your debit or credit cards.

• Confirm that your **card will work overseas,** and alert them that you'll be using it in Europe; otherwise, they may deny transactions if they perceive unusual spending patterns.

• Ask for the specifics on transaction **fees.** When you use your credit or debit card—either for purchases or ATM withdrawals—you'll typically be charged additional "international transaction" fees of up to 3 percent (1 percent is normal) plus $5 per transaction. If your fees seem high, consider getting a different card just for your trip: Capital One (www.capitalone.com) and most credit unions have low-to-no international fees.

• Verify your daily ATM **withdrawal limit,** and if necessary, ask your bank to adjust it. I prefer a high limit that allows me to take out more cash at each ATM stop and save on bank fees; some travelers prefer to set a lower limit in case their card is stolen. Note that foreign banks also set maximum withdrawal amounts for their ATMs.

• Get your bank's emergency **phone number** in the US (but not its 800 number, which isn't accessible from overseas) to call collect if you have a problem.

• Ask for your credit card's **PIN** in case you need to make an emergency cash withdrawal or encounter Europe's chip-and-PIN system; the bank won't tell you your PIN over the phone, so allow time for it to be mailed to you.

Magnetic-Stripe versus Chip-and-PIN Credit Cards: Europeans are increasingly using chip-and-PIN credit cards embedded with an electronic security chip and requiring a four-digit PIN. Your American-style card (with just the old-fashioned magnetic stripe) will work fine in most places. But there could be minor inconveniences; it might not work at unattended payment machines, such as those at train and subway stations, toll plazas, parking garages, bike-rental kiosks, and gas pumps. If you have problems, try entering your card's PIN, look for a machine that takes cash, or find a clerk who can process the transaction manually.

No matter what kind of card you have, it pays to carry euros and/or pounds; remember, you can always use an ATM to withdraw cash with your magnetic-stripe debit card.

Dynamic Currency Conversion: If merchants or hoteliers offer to convert your purchase price into dollars (called dynamic currency conversion, or DCC), refuse this "service." You'll pay even more in fees for the expensive convenience of seeing your charge in dollars. If your receipt shows the total in dollars only, ask for the transaction to be processed in the local currency. If the clerk refuses, pay in cash. Similarly, if an ATM offers to "lock in" or "guarantee" your conversion rate, choose "proceed without conversion" and opt for euros or pounds over dollars.

Tipping

Tipping in Ireland isn't as automatic and generous as it is in the US. For special service, tips are appreciated, but not required. As in the US, the proper amount depends on your resources, tipping philosophy, and the circumstances, but some general guidelines apply.

Restaurants: At a pub or restaurant with waitstaff, check the menu or your bill to see if the service is included; if not, tip about 10 percent. At pubs where you order at the counter, there's no need to tip.

Taxis: For a typical ride, round up your fare a bit (for instance, if the fare is €9, give €10). If the cabbie hauls your bags and zips you to the airport to help you catch your flight, you might want to toss in a little more. But if you feel like you're being driven in circles or otherwise ripped off, skip the tip.

Services: In general, if someone in the service industry does a super job for you, a small tip of a euro or two is appropriate...but not required. If you're not sure whether (or how much) to tip for a service, ask a local for advice.

Getting a VAT Refund

Wrapped into the purchase price of your Irish souvenirs is a Value-Added Tax (VAT); it's 23 percent in the Republic and 20 percent in Northern Ireland. You're entitled to get most of that tax back if you purchase your goods at a store that participates in the VAT-refund scheme. In Ireland, you do not have to meet a minimum purchase amount in order to qualify for a refund.

Getting your refund is straightforward and, if you buy a substantial amount of souvenirs, well worth the hassle. (Note that if the store ships the goods to your US home, VAT is not assessed on your purchase.) You'll need to:

Get the paperwork. Have the merchant completely fill out the necessary refund document, called a "Tax-Free Shopping Cheque." You'll have to present your passport. Get the paperwork done before you leave the store to ensure you'll have everything you need (including your original sales receipt).

Get your stamp at the border or airport. Process your VAT document at your last stop in the European Union (such as at the airport) with the customs agent who deals with VAT refunds. Arrive an additional hour before you need to check

in for your flight to allow time to find the local customs office—and to stand in line. It's best to keep your purchases in your carry-on. If they're too large or dangerous to carry on (such as knives), pack them in your checked bags and alert the check-in agent. You'll be sent (with your tagged bag) to a customs desk outside security; someone will examine your bag, stamp your paperwork, and put your bag on the belt. You're not supposed to use your purchased goods before you leave. If you show up at customs wearing your new Irish sweater, officials might look the other way—or deny you a refund.

Collect your refund. You'll need to return your stamped document to the retailer or its representative. Many merchants work with services, such as Global Blue or Premier Tax Free, that have offices at major airports, ports, or border crossings (either before or after security, probably strategically located near a duty-free shop). These services, which extract a 4 percent fee, can refund your money immediately in cash or credit your card (within two billing cycles). If the retailer handles VAT refunds directly, it's up to you to contact the merchant for your refund. You can mail the documents from home, or more quickly, from your point of departure. You'll then have to wait—it can take months.

Customs for American Shoppers

You are allowed to take home $800 worth of items per person duty-free, once every 31 days. You can take home many processed and packaged foods: vacuum-packed cheeses, dried herbs, jams, baked goods, candy, chocolate, oil, vinegar, mustard, and honey. Fresh fruits and vegetables and most meats are not allowed, with exceptions for some canned items.

You can bring home one liter of alcohol duty-free. It can be packed securely in your checked luggage, along with any other liquid-containing items. But if you want to pack the alcohol (or any liquid-packed food) in your carry-on bag for your flight home, buy it at a duty-free shop at the airport.

For details on allowable goods, customs rules, and duty rates, visit http://help.cbp.gov.

SIGHTSEEING

Sightseeing can be hard work. Use these tips to make your visits to Ireland's finest sights meaningful, fun, efficient, and painless.

Plan Ahead

Set up an itinerary that allows you to fit in all your must-see sights. For a one-stop look at opening hours, see the "At a Glance" sidebars for major destinations. Most sights keep stable hours, but you can easily confirm the latest by checking with the TI or visiting museum websites.

Many museums are closed or have reduced hours at least a few days a year, especially major holidays. In summer, some sights may stay open late. Off-season, many museums have shorter hours. Whenever you go, don't put off visiting a must-see sight—you never know if a place will close unexpectedly for a holiday, strike, or restoration.

Going at the right time helps avoid crowds. This book offers tips on the best times to see specific sights. Try visiting popular sights very early or very late. Evening visits are usually peaceful, with fewer crowds.

At Sights

Here's what you can typically expect:

Entering: Be warned that you may not be allowed to enter if you arrive 30 to 60 minutes before closing time. And guards start ushering people out well before the actual closing time, so don't save the best for last.

Some important sights have a security check, where you must open your bag or send it through a metal detector. Some sights require you to check daypacks and coats. (If you'd rather not check your day-pack, try carrying it tucked under your arm like a purse as you enter.)

Photography: If the museum's photo policy isn't clearly posted, ask a guard. Generally, taking photos without a flash or tripod is allowed. Some sights ban photos altogether.

Temporary Exhibits: Museums may show special exhibits in addition to their permanent collection. Some exhibits are included in the entry price, while others come at an extra cost (which you may have to pay even if you don't want to see the exhibit).

Expect Changes: Artwork can be on tour, on loan, out sick, or shifted at the whim of the curator. Pick up a floor plan as you enter, and ask museum staff if you can't find a particular item.

Audioguides and Apps: Many sights rent audioguides, which generally offer dry-but-useful recorded descriptions (sometimes included with admission). If you bring your own earbuds, you can enjoy better sound. Increasingly, sights offer apps—often free—that you can download to your mobile device (check their websites).

Services: Important sights may have an on-site café or cafeteria (usually a handy place to rejuvenate during a long visit). The WCs at sights are free and generally clean.

Before Leaving: At the gift shop, scan the postcard rack or thumb through a guidebook to be sure that you haven't overlooked something that you'd like to see.

Sightseeing Passes

Ireland offers two passes (each covering a different set of sights) that can save you money. The first is smart for anyone, and the second works best for two people traveling together. Twosomes who love to sightsee should get both passes.

Heritage Card: This pass gets you into nearly 100 historical monuments, gardens, and parks maintained by the OPW (Office of Public Works) in the Republic of Ireland. It will pay off if you plan on visiting half a dozen or more included sights over the course of your trip. People traveling by car are most likely to get their money's worth out of the card (€25, seniors age 60 and older-€20, students-€10, families-€60, covers entry to all Heritage sights for one year, comes with handy map and list of sights' hours and prices, purchase at the first Heritage sight you visit, cash only, tel. 01/647-6592, www.heritage ireland.ie, heritagecard@opw.ie).

Heritage Island Visitor Attractions Guide: Ambitious travelers covering more ground should seriously consider this €7 essential attractions guide and discount book, which is best bought online; allow two weeks for free delivery to North America. It's also sold at some—but not all—of the sites it covers. It gives a variety of discounts (usually 2-for-1 discounts, but occasionally 10-20 percent off) at more than 80 sights in the Republic of Ire-

land and Northern Ireland. This is a great no-brainer deal for two people traveling together (tel. 01/775-3870, www.heritage island.com).

SLEEPING

I favor hotels and restaurants that are handy to your sightseeing activities. Rather than list hotels scattered throughout a city, I choose hotels in my favorite neighborhoods.

Book your accommodations well in advance, especially if you'll be traveling during busy times (such as July and August in Dingle). See page 366 for a list of major holidays and festivals throughout Ireland; for tips on making reservations, see page 346.

The Republic of Ireland and Northern Ireland have banned smoking in the workplace (pubs, offices, taxicabs, etc.), but some hotels still have a floor or two of rooms where guests are allowed to smoke. If you don't want a room that a smoker might have occupied before you, let the hotelier know when you make your reservation. All my recommended B&Bs pro-

Sleep Code

Price Rankings

To help you easily sort through my listings, I've divided the accommodations into three categories, based on the highest price for a basic double room with bath during high season:

$$$	Higher Priced
$$	Moderately Priced
$	Lower Priced

Prices can change without notice; verify the hotel's current rates online or by email. For the best prices, always book directly with the hotel.

Abbreviations

I use the following code to describe accommodations in this book. Prices are listed per room, not per person. When a price range is given for a type of room (such as double rooms listing for €100-150), it means the price fluctuates with the season, size of room, or length of stay; expect to pay the upper end for peak-season stays.

S = Single room (or price for one person in a double)

D = Double or twin room. "Double beds" can be two twins sheeted together and are usually big enough for nonromantic couples.

T = Triple (generally a double bed with a single)

Q = Quad (usually two double beds; adding an extra child's bed to a T is usually cheaper)

b = Private bathroom with toilet and shower or tub

According to this code, a couple staying at a "Db-€100" hotel would pay a total of €100 (about $110) for a double room with a private bathroom. Unless otherwise noted, breakfast is included and credit cards are accepted. There's almost always free Wi-Fi and/or a guest computer available.

hibit smoking. Even in places that allow smoking in the sleeping rooms, breakfast rooms are nearly always smoke-free.

Rates and Deals

I've described my recommended accommodations using a Sleep Code (see sidebar). The prices I list are for one-night stays in peak season, and assume you're booking directly with the hotel or B&B (not through an online hotel-booking engine or TI). Booking services extract a commission from the hotel, which logically closes the door on special deals. Book direct.

My recommended accommodations generally have a website (often with a built-in booking form) and an email address; you can expect a response within a couple of days (and often sooner).

If you're on a budget, it's smart to contact several hotels to ask for their best price. Comparison-shop and make your choice. In general, prices can soften if you do any of the following: offer to pay cash, stay at least three nights, or mention this book. You can also try asking for a cheaper room or a discount.

Types of Accommodations

Ireland has a rating system for hotels and B&Bs. These stars and shamrocks are supposed to imply quality, but I find that they mean only that the place sporting symbols is paying dues to the tourist board. These rating systems often have little to do with value.

Hotels

Many of my recommended hotels have three floors of rooms and steep stairs; expect good exercise. Older properties often do not have elevators. If stairs are an issue, ask about ground-floor rooms or choose a hotel with a lift (elevator).

An "en suite" room has a bathroom (toilet and shower/tub) attached to the room; a room with a "private bathroom" can mean that the bathroom is all yours, but it's across the hall. If you want your own bathroom inside the room, request "en suite."

Hoteliers can be a great help and source of advice. Most know their city well, and can assist you with everything from public transit and airport connections to finding a good restaurant, the nearest launderette, or a Wi-Fi hotspot.

Even at the best places, mechanical breakdowns occur: Air-conditioning malfunctions, sinks leak, hot water turns cold, and toilets gurgle and smell. Report your concerns clearly and calmly at the front desk. For more complicated problems, don't expect instant results.

To guard against theft in your room, keep valuables out of sight. Some rooms come with a safe, and other hotels have safes at the front desk. I've never bothered using one.

Checkout can pose problems if surprise charges pop up on your bill. If you settle your bill the afternoon before you leave, you'll have time to discuss and address any points of contention (before 19:00, when the night shift usually arrives).

Above all, keep a positive attitude. Remember, you're on vacation. If your hotel or B&B is a disappointment, spend more time out enjoying the city you came to see.

Big Modern Hotel Chains: Common in bigger cities all over Ireland, these hotels can be a great value. They're as cozy as a Motel 6, but they come with private showers/WCs, elevators, good security, and often an attached restaurant.

While most chain hotels have 24-hour reception, the service lacks a personal touch (at some, you'll check in at a self-service kiosk). Breakfast and Wi-Fi generally cost extra. But the chain hotel option is especially worth considering for families, as kids often stay for free. The best deals generally must be prepaid a few weeks ahead and may not be refundable—read the fine print carefully.

The biggies are Jurys Inn (book online at www.jurysinns.com), Comfort/Quality Inns (Republic of Ireland tel. 1-800-500-600, Northern Ireland tel. 0800-444-444, US tel. 877-424-6423, www.choicehotels.com), and Travelodge (also has freeway locations for tired drivers, reservation center in Britain tel. 08700-850-950, www.travelodge.co.uk).

B&Bs

Compared to hotels, bed-and-breakfast places give you double the cultural intimacy for half the price. If you have a reasonable but limited budget, skip hotels and go the B&B way.

B&Bs range from large guesthouses with 10-15 rooms to small homes renting out a couple of spare bedrooms, but typically have six rooms or fewer. My top listings are run by people who enjoy welcoming the world to their breakfast table.

Many B&Bs take credit cards, but may add the card service fee to your bill (about 3 percent). If you do need to pay cash for your room, plan ahead to have enough on hand when you check out.

Many B&B owners are also pet owners. If you're allergic, ask about pets when you reserve.

Making Hotel Reservations

Reserve your rooms several weeks in advance—or as soon as you've pinned down your travel dates. Note that some national holidays merit your making reservations far in advance (see page 366).

Requesting a Reservation: It's easiest to book your room through the hotel's website. (For the best rates, always use the hotel's official site and not a booking agency's site.) If there's no reservation form, or for complicated requests, send an email (see below for a sample request).

The hotelier wants to know:
- the number and type of rooms you need
- the number of nights you'll stay
- your date of arrival (use the European style for dates: day/month/year)
- your date of departure
- any special needs (such as bathroom in the room or down the hall, cheapest room, twin beds vs. double bed)

Confirming a Reservation: Most places will request a credit-card number to hold your room. If they don't have a secure online reservation form—look for the *https*—you can email it (I do), but it's safer to share that confidential info via a phone call or two emails (splitting your number between them).

Canceling a Reservation: If you must cancel, it's courteous—and smart—to do so with as much notice as possible, especially for smaller family-run places. Be warned that cancellation policies can be strict; read the fine print or ask about these before you book. Internet deals may require prepayment, with no refunds for cancellations.

Reconfirming a Reservation: Always call or email to reconfirm your room reservation a few days in advance. For B&Bs or small hotels, I call again on my day of arrival to tell my host what time I expect to get there (especially important if arriving late—after 17:00).

Phoning: For tips on calling hotels overseas, see page 353.

From: rick@ricksteves.com
Sent: Today
To: info@hotelcentral.com
Subject: Reservation request for 19-22 July

Dear Hotel Central,
I would like to reserve a room for 2 people for 3 nights, arriving 19 July and departing 22 July. If possible, I would like a quiet room with a double bed and private bathroom inside the room.

Please let me know if you have a room available and the price.

Thank you!
Rick Steves

Keep in mind that B&B owners are at the whim of their guests—if you're getting up early, so are they; and if you check in late, they'll wait up for you. It's polite to call ahead to confirm your reservation the day before and give them a rough estimate of your arrival time.

B&Bs serve a hearty "Irish fry" breakfast (for more about B&B breakfasts, see "Eating," later in this chapter). Because your B&B owner is also the cook, breakfast hours are usually abbreviated (typically about an hour, starting at about 8:00—make sure you know the exact time before you turn in for the night). It's an unwritten rule that guests shouldn't show up at the very end of the breakfast period and expect a full cooked breakfast. If you do arrive at the last minute (or if you need to leave before breakfast is served), most B&B hosts are happy to let you help yourself to cereal, fruit or juice, and coffee.

In the Room: Most B&Bs have a "tea service" in the room: an electric kettle, cups, tea bags, coffee packets, and a pack of biscuits.

Your bedroom probably won't include a phone, but nearly every B&B has free Wi-Fi (if they don't, I'll note it in the listing).

Electrical outlets sometimes have switches that turn the current on or off; if your electrical appliance isn't working, flip the switch at the outlet.

You'll likely encounter unusual bathroom fixtures. The "pump toilet" has a flushing handle that doesn't kick in unless you push it just right: too hard or too soft, and it won't go. (Be decisive but not ruthless.)

Most B&B baths have an instant water heater. This looks like an electronic box under the shower head with dials and buttons: One control adjusts the heat, while another turns the flow off and on (let the water run for a few seconds to moderate the temperature before you hop in). If the hot water doesn't work, you may need to flip a red switch (often located just outside the bathroom). If the shower looks mysterious, ask your B&B host for help... before you take your clothes off.

Americans often assume they'll get new towels each day. The Irish don't. Hang them up to dry and reuse.

Hostels

A hostel provides cheap beds where you sleep in a room with strangers for about €25 per night. Travelers of any age are welcome if they don't mind dorm-style accommodations and meeting other travelers. Most hostels offer kitchen facilities, guest computers, Wi-Fi, and a self-service laundry. Bedding is usually provided, including sheets.

There are two kinds of hostels: Independent hostels tend to be easygoing, colorful, and informal (no membership required); try www.hostelworld.com, www.hostelz.com, or www.hostels.com. Ireland's Independent Holiday Hostels (www.hostels-ireland.com) is a network of independent hostels, requiring no

Friendly hotel staff

Cozy B&B bedroom

membership and welcoming all ages.

Official hostels are part of Hostelling International (HI), share an online booking site (www.hihostels.com), and typically require that you either have a membership card or pay extra per night.

Other Accommodation Options

Renting an apartment, house, or villa can be a fun and cost-effective way to go local. Websites such as Booking.com, Airbnb, VRBO, and FlipKey let you browse properties and correspond directly with European property owners or managers.

Airbnb and Roomorama also list rooms in private homes. Beds range from air-mattress-in-living-room basic to plush-B&B-suite posh. If you want a place to sleep that's free, Couchsurfing.org is a vagabond's alternative to Airbnb. It lists millions of outgoing members who host fellow "surfers" in their homes.

EATING

For years, Irish food was just something you ate to survive rather than to savor. In this country, long known as the "land of potatoes," the diet reflected the economic circumstances. But times have changed. You'll find modern-day Irish cuisine delicious and varied, from vegetables, meat, and dairy products to fresh- and saltwater fish. Try the local specialties wherever you happen to be eating.

When restaurant-hunting, choose a spot filled with locals, not tourists. Venturing even a block or two off the main drag leads to higher-quality food for less than half the price of the tourist-oriented places. Locals eat better at lower-rent locales.

At classier restaurants, look for "early-bird specials," which allow you to eat well and affordably, but early (about 17:30-19:00).

Tipping: As I mentioned earlier, if you're at a restaurant with waitstaff, check your bill; if a service charge is listed, there's

The Good and Bad of Online Reviews

User-generated travel review websites—such as TripAdvisor, Booking.com, and Yelp—give you access to actual reports—good and bad—from travelers who have experienced the hotel, restaurant, tour, or attraction.

While these sites try hard to weed out bogus users, I've seen hotels "bribe" guests (for example, offer a free breakfast) in exchange for a positive review. Nor can you always give credence to negative reviews: Different people have different expectations.

A user-generated review is based on the experience of one person, who likely stayed at one hotel and ate at a few restaurants, and doesn't have much of a basis for comparison. A guidebook is the work of a trained researcher who visited many alternatives to assess their relative value. When I've checked out top-rated TripAdvisor listings in various towns, I've found that some are gems but just as many are duds.

Guidebooks and review websites both have their place, and in many ways, they're complementary. If a hotel or restaurant is well-reviewed in a guidebook, and also gets good ratings on one of these sites, it's likely a winner.

no need to tip more. If not, tip about 10 percent. But if you order your food at a counter (as is often the case in pubs), you're not expected to tip.

Breakfast

The traditional breakfast, the "Irish Fry" (known in the North as the "Ulster Fry"), is a hearty way to start the day—with juice, tea or coffee, cereal, eggs, bacon, sausage, a grilled tomato, sautéed mushrooms, and optional black pudding (made with blood sausage). Toast is served with butter and marmalade. Home-baked Irish soda bread can be an ambrosial eye-opener for those of us raised on Wonder bread. This meal tides many travelers over until dinner. But there's nothing un-Irish about skipping the "fry"—few locals actually start their day with this heavy traditional breakfast. You can simply skip the heavier fare and enjoy the cereal, juice, toast, and tea (surprisingly, the Irish drink more tea per capita than the British).

Budget Eating

Picnicking saves time and money. Try boxes of orange juice (pure, by the liter), fresh bread (especially Irish soda bread), tasty Cashel blue cheese, meat, a tube of mustard, local-eatin' apples, bananas, small tomatoes, a small tub of yogurt (it's drinkable), rice crackers, trail mix or nuts, plain digestive biscuits (the chocolate-covered ones melt), and any local specialties. At open-air markets and supermarkets, you can get produce in small quantities. Supermarkets often have good deli sections, packaged sandwiches, and sometimes salad bars. Hang on to the half-liter mineral-water bottles (sold everywhere for about €1.50); buy juice in cheap liter boxes, then drink some and store the extra in your water bottle. I often munch a relaxed "meal on wheels" in a car, train, or bus to save 30 precious minutes for sightseeing.

Pub Grub and Beer

If beer is not your cup of tea, don't wine about it. Pubs are a basic part of the Irish social scene, and whether you're a teetotaler or a beer-guzzler, they should be a part of your travel here. Whether in rural villages or busy Dublin, a pub (short for "public house") is an extended living room where, if you don't mind the stickiness, you can feel the pulse of Ireland.

Smart travelers use pubs to eat, drink, get out of the rain, watch the latest sporting event, and make new friends. Unfortunately, many city pubs have been afflicted with an excess of brass, ferns, and video games. Today the most traditional atmospheric pubs are in Ireland's countryside and smaller towns.

Pubs are generally open daily from 11:00 to 23:30 and Sunday from noon to 22:30. Pubs that serve meals generally offer lunch from about 12:30 to 15:00, and dinner from 17:00 to 21:00. Outside of mealtimes, usually only snacks and simple sandwiches are available. And some pubs don't serve hot meals at all, and only have snacks.

Children can be served soft drinks and food in pubs (but may be seated in the restaurant section or a courtyard). You'll often see signs behind the bar asking that children vacate the premises by 20:00. You must be 18 to order a beer, and the Gardí (police) are cracking down hard on pubs that don't enforce this law.

Food: Pub grub gets better every year—it's Ireland's best eating value. But don't expect high cuisine; this is, after all, comfort food. For about $15-20, you'll get a basic hot lunch or dinner in friendly

A new generation of Irish food

surroundings. Pubs that are attached to restaurants, advertise their food, are crowded with locals, and are more likely to have fresh food and a chef than sell lousy microwaved snacks.

Pub menus consist of a hearty assortment of traditional dishes, such as Irish stew (mutton with mashed potatoes, onions, carrots, and herbs), soups and chowders, coddle (bacon, pork sausages, potatoes, and onions stewed in layers), fish-and-chips, collar and cabbage (boiled bacon coated in bread crumbs and brown sugar, then baked and served with cabbage), boxty (potato pancake filled with fish, meat, or vegetables), and champ (potato mashed with milk and onions). Irish soda bread nicely rounds out a meal. In coastal areas, a lot of seafood is available, such as mackerel, mussels, and Atlantic salmon. There's seldom table service in Irish pubs. Order drinks and meals at the bar. Pay as you order, and only tip (by rounding up) if you like the service.

I recommend certain pubs to eat in, and your B&B host is usually up-to-date on the best neighborhood pub grub. Ask for advice (but adjust for nepotism and cronyism, which run rampant).

Drink: When you say "a beer, please" in an Irish pub, you'll get a pint of Guinness (the tall blonde in a black dress). If you want a small beer, ask for a glass, which is a half-pint. Never rush your bartender when he's pouring a Guinness. It's an almost-sacred two-step process that requires time for the beer to settle.

The Irish take great pride in their beer. At pubs, long hand pulls are used to draw the traditional, rich-flavored "real ales" up from the cellar. These are the connoisseur's favorites: They're fermented naturally, vary from sweet to bitter, and often have a hoppy or nutty flavor. Experiment with obscure local microbrews (a small but growing presence on the Irish beer scene). Short hand pulls at the bar mean colder, fizzier, mass-produced, and less interesting keg beers. Stout is dark and more bitter, like Guinness. If you think you don't like Guinness, try it in Ireland. It doesn't travel well and is better in its homeland. Murphy's is a very good Guinness-like stout, but a bit smoother and milder. For a cold, refreshing, basic, American-style beer, ask for a lager, such as Harp. Ale drinkers swear by Smithwick's (I know I do). Caffrey's is a satisfying cross between stout and ale. Try the draft cider (sweet or dry)...carefully. Teetotalers can order a soft drink.

You're a guest on your first night; after that, you're a regular. A wise Irishman once said, "It never rains in a pub." The relaxed, informal atmosphere feels like a refuge from daily cares. Women traveling alone need not worry—you'll become part of the pub family in no time.

Craic (pronounced "crack"), Irish for "fun" or "a good laugh," is the sport that accompanies drinking in a pub. People are there to talk. To encourage conversation, stand or sit at the bar, not at a table.

In 2004, the Irish government passed a law making all pubs in the Republic smoke-free. Smokers now take their

A hearty Irish dinner

pints outside, turning alleys into covered smoking patios. An incredulous Irishman responded to the law by saying, "What will they do next? Ban drinking in pubs? We'll never get to heaven if we don't die."

It's a tradition to buy your table a round, and then for each person to reciprocate. If an Irishman buys you a drink, thank him by saying, "*Go raibh maith agat*" (guh rov mah UG-ut). Offer him a toast in Irish—"*Slainte*" (SLAWN-chuh), the equivalent of "cheers." A good excuse for a conversation is to ask to be taught a few words of Irish Gaelic.

STAYING CONNECTED

Staying connected in Europe gets easier and cheaper every year. The simplest solution is to bring your own device— mobile phone, tablet, or laptop—and use it just as you would at home (following the tips below, such as connecting to free Wi-Fi whenever possible). Another option is to buy a European SIM card for your mobile phone—either your US phone or one you buy in Europe. Or you can travel without a mobile device and use European landlines and computers to connect. Each of these options is described below.

You'll find even more details about staying connected at www.ricksteves.com/phoning.

Using Your Mobile Device in Europe

Roaming with your mobile device in Europe doesn't have to be expensive. These budget tips and options will keep your costs in check.

Use free Wi-Fi whenever possible. Unless you have an unlimited-data plan, you're best off saving most of your online tasks for Wi-Fi. You can access the Internet, send texts, and even make voice calls over Wi-Fi.

Many cafés (including Starbucks and McDonald's) have hotspots for custom-

ers; look for signs offering it and ask for the Wi-Fi password when you buy something. You'll also often find Wi-Fi at TIs, city squares, major museums, public-transit hubs, and airports, and aboard trains and buses.

Sign up for an international plan. Most providers offer a global calling plan that cuts the per-minute cost of phone calls and texts, and a flat-fee data plan that includes a certain number of megabytes. Your normal plan may already include international coverage (T-Mobile's does).

Before your trip, call your provider or check online to confirm that your phone will work in Europe, and research your provider's international rates. A day or two before you leave, activate the plan by calling your provider or logging on to your mobile phone account. Remember to cancel your plan (if necessary) when your trip's over.

Minimize the use of your cellular network. When you can't find Wi-Fi, you can use your cellular network—convenient but slower and potentially expensive—to connect to the Internet, text, or make voice calls. When you're done, avoid further charges by manually switching off "data roaming" or "cellular data" (in your device's Settings menu; if you don't know how to switch it off, ask your service provider or Google it). Another way to make sure you're not accidentally using data roaming is to put your device in "airplane" or "flight" mode (which also disables phone calls and texts, as well as data), and then turn on Wi-Fi as needed.

Don't use your cellular network for bandwidth-gobbling tasks, such as Skyping, downloading apps, and watching YouTube—save these for when you're on Wi-Fi. Using a navigation app such as Google Maps can take lots of data, so use this sparingly.

Limit automatic updates. By default, your device is constantly checking for a data connection and updating apps. It's

Tips on Internet Security

Using the Internet while traveling brings added security risks, whether you're getting online with your own device or at a public terminal using a shared network.

First, make sure that your device is running the latest version of its operating system and security software. Next, ensure that your device is password- or passcode-protected so thieves can't access your information if your device is stolen. For extra security, set passwords on apps that access key info (such as email or Facebook).

On the road, use only legitimate Wi-Fi hotspots. Ask the hotel or café staff for the specific name of their Wi-Fi network, and make sure you log on to that exact one. Hackers sometimes create a bogus hotspot with a similar or vague name (such as "Hotel Europa Free Wi-Fi"). The best Wi-Fi networks require entering a password.

Be especially cautious when checking your online banking, credit-card statements, or other personal-finance accounts. Internet security experts advise against accessing these sites while traveling. Even if you're using your own mobile device at a password-protected hotspot, any hacker who's logged on to the same network may be able see what you're doing. If you do need to log on to a banking website, use a hard-wired connection (such as an Ethernet cable in your hotel room) or a cellular network, which is safer than Wi-Fi.

Never share your credit-card number (or any other sensitive information) online unless you know that the site is secure. A secure site displays a little padlock icon, and the URL begins with *https* (instead of the usual *http*).

smart to disable these features so they'll only update when you're on Wi-Fi, and to change your device's email settings from "auto-retrieve" to "manual" (or from "push" to "fetch").

It's also a good idea to keep track of your data usage. On your device's menu, look for "cellular data usage" or "mobile data" and reset the counter at the start of your trip.

Use Skype or other calling/messaging apps for cheaper calls and texts. Certain apps let you make voice or video calls or send texts over the Internet for free or cheap. If you're bringing a tablet or laptop, you can also use them for voice calls and texts. All you have to do is log on to a Wi-Fi network, then contact any of your friends or family members who are also online and signed into the same service.

You can make voice and video calls using Skype, Viber, FaceTime, and Google+ Hangouts. If the connection is bad, try making an audio-only call.

You can also make voice calls from your device to telephones worldwide for just a few cents per minute using Skype, Viber, or Hangouts if you prebuy credit.

To text for free over Wi-Fi, try apps like Google+ Hangouts, What's App, Viber, and Facebook Messenger. Apple's iMessage connects with other Apple users, but make sure you're on Wi-Fi to avoid data charges.

Using a European SIM Card

This option works well for those who want to make a lot of voice calls at cheap local rates. Either buy a phone in Europe (as lit-

Phoning Cheat Sheet

Here are the instructions for dialing, along with examples of how to call one of my recommended hotels in Dublin (tel. 01/679-6500) and in Belfast (tel. 028/9027-1066).

Calling from the US to Europe: Dial 011 (US access code), country code (353 for the Republic of Ireland, 44 for Northern Ireland), and phone number.* To call the hotel in Dublin, I dial 011-353-1-679-6500. To call the Belfast hotel, I dial 011-44-28-9027-1066.

Calling from Europe to the US: Dial 00 (Europe access code), country code (1 for US), area code, and phone number. To call my office in Edmonds, Washington, I dial 00-1-425-771-8303.

Calling country to country within Europe: Dial 00, country code, and phone number.* To call the Dublin hotel, whether from France or from Northern Ireland, I dial 00-353-1-679-6500; to call the Belfast hotel from France or the Republic, I dial 00-44-28-9027-1066.

Calling within the Republic or Northern Ireland: Dial the entire phone number, including the area code with its zero. To call the Dublin hotel from Dingle, I dial 01/679-6500. To call the Belfast hotel from Derry, I dial 028/9027-1066.

Calling with a mobile phone: The "+" sign on your mobile phone automatically selects the access code you need (for a "+" sign, press and hold "0").* To call the Dublin hotel from the US or Europe, I dial +353-1-679-6500.

For more dialing help, see www.howtocallabroad.com.

*If the phone number starts with zero, drop it for all countries except Italy.

Country	Country Code	Country	Country Code
Austria	43	Hungary	36
Belgium	32	Ireland/N Ireland	353/44
Czech Republic	420	Italy	39
Denmark	45	Netherlands	31
England	44	Norway	47
France	33	Portugal	351
Germany	49	Scotland	44
Gibraltar	350	Spain	34
Greece	30	Switzerland	41

tle as $40 from mobile-phone shops anywhere), or bring an "unlocked" US phone (check with your carrier about unlocking it). With an unlocked phone, you can replace the original SIM card (the microchip that stores info about the phone) with one that will work with a European provider.

In Europe, buy a European SIM card. Inserted into your phone, this card gives you a European phone number—and European rates. SIM cards are sold at mobile-phone shops, department-store electronics counters, some newsstands, and even at vending machines. Costing about $5-10, they usually include about that much prepaid calling credit, with no contract and no commitment. You can still use your phone's Wi-Fi function to get online. To get a SIM card that also includes data costs (including roaming), figure on paying $15-30 for one month of data within the country you bought it. This can be cheaper than data roaming through your home provider. To get the best rates, buy a new SIM card whenever you arrive in a new country.

I like to buy SIM cards at a mobile-phone shop where there's a clerk to help explain the options and brands. Certain brands—including Lebara and Lycamobile, both of which operate in multiple European countries—are reliable and economical. Ask the clerk to help you insert your SIM card, set it up, and show you how to use it. In some countries you'll be required to register the SIM card with your passport as an antiterrorism measure (which may mean you can't use the phone for the first hour or two).

When you run out of credit, you can top it up at newsstands, tobacco shops, mobile-phone stores, or many other businesses (look for your SIM card's logo in the window), or online.

Using Landlines and Computers in Europe

It's easy to travel in Europe without a mobile device. You can check email or browse websites using public computers and Internet cafés, and make calls from your hotel room and/or public phones.

Phones in your **hotel room** can be inexpensive for local calls and calls made with cheap international phone cards (sold at newsstands, street kiosks, and train stations). Some cards work in both the Republic of Ireland and the UK—confirm before buying a card by checking for both an 1800 access number (used in the Republic of Ireland) and an 0800 access number (for the UK—don't use the 0845, 0870, or 0871 numbers, which cost about 10p per minute).

Public pay phones are getting harder to find, and they're expensive. In the Republic, you'll need a Telecom Éireann phone card (buy at newsstands, TIs, and some post offices). At pay phones in Northern Ireland (and the rest of Britain), you'll pay with a major credit card (minimum charge of £1.20) or coins (minimum fee of £0.60). Only unused coins will be returned, so put in biggies with caution.

It's always possible to find **public computers:** at your hotel (many have one in their lobby for guests to use), or at an Internet café or library (ask your hotelier or the TI for the nearest location). If typing on a European keyboard, use the "Alt Gr" key to the right of the space bar to insert the extra symbol that appears on some keys. If you can't locate a special character (such as @), simply copy it from a Web page and paste it into your email message.

Mail

You can mail one package per day to yourself worth up to $200 duty-free from Europe to the US (mark it "personal purchases"). If you're sending a gift to someone, mark it "unsolicited gift." For details, visit www.cbp.gov and search for "Know Before You Go."

The Irish postal service works fine, but for quick transatlantic delivery (in either direction), consider services such as DHL (www.dhl.com).

TRANSPORTATION

This section covers the basics on trains, buses, long-distance taxis, rental cars, and flights.

To see all of Ireland, especially the sights with far-flung rural charm, I prefer the freedom of a rental car. Connemara, the Ring of Kerry, the Antrim Coast, and the Valley of the Boyne are really only worth it if you have wheels. To help you plan your trip, see my recommended two-week itinerary on page 24; you can adjust it to accommodate your interests and available time frame.

The best overall source of schedules for public transportation in the Republic of Ireland as well as Northern Ireland—including rail, cross-country and city buses, and Dublin's LUAS transit—is the Tourism Ireland domestic website: www.discoverireland.ie (select "Getting Around" near the bottom of the page).

Trains

To research Irish rail connections online, you need to access two sites. For the Republic of Ireland use www.irishrail.ie. For Northern Ireland use www.translink.co.uk. For train schedules on the rest of the European continent, check www.bahn.com (Germany's excellent Europe-wide timetable).

It really pays to buy your train tickets online ahead of time. Fifty-percent online discounts are not unheard of, but online fares fluctuate widely and unpredictably.

It's easy to purchase Irish rail passes in Ireland at major stations (Dublin info tel. 01/836-6222). But most tourists don't travel enough in Ireland to make a rail or bus pass pay off. Chances are that you'll save money by buying point-to-point tickets as you go. Fares are often higher for peak travel on Fridays and Sundays. To avoid long station lines in Dublin, you

can book train tickets in advance online (usually with a hefty discount on the fare). Otherwise, you can book by phone with your credit card or in person at the Iarnrod Éireann Travel Centre (Mon-Fri 9:00-17:00, closed Sat-Sun, 35 Lower Abbey Street, tel. 01/703-4070). Be aware that very few Irish train stations have storage lockers.

For more train tips, visit www.ricksteves.com/rail.

Buses

If you opt for public transportation, you'll probably spend more time on Irish buses than Irish trains. But be aware: Public transportation (especially cross-country Irish buses) will likely put your travels into slow motion.

For example, driving across County Kerry from Kenmare to Dingle takes two hours. If you go by bus, the same trip takes four hours—twice as long. The trip by bus requires two transfers (in Killarney and Tralee, each involving a wait for the next bus), and the buses often take a rural milk-run route, making multiple stops along the way. Not every Irish coach trip will involve this kind of delay. But if you opt to go by coach, be realistic about your itinerary and study the schedules ahead of time. The Bus Éireann Expressway Bus Timetable comes in handy (free, available at some bus stations or online at www.buseireann.ie, bus info tel. 01/836-6111).

Buses are usually slower than trains (by about a third), but they're also much cheaper. Round-trip bus tickets usually cost less than two one-way fares. The Irish distinguish between "buses" (for in-city travel with lots of stops) and "coaches" (long-distance cross-country runs).

You may need to do some trips partly by train. For instance, if you're going from Dublin to Dingle without a car, you'll need to take a train to Tralee and catch a bus from there. Similarly, to go from Dublin to Kinsale without a car, take a train to Cork and then a bus; and from Dublin to

Ireland Public Transportation

Rail
Bus (not all lines shown)
Boat

25 Kilometers
25 Miles

Dunfanaghy
Bunbeg
Burtonport
Letterkenny
Donegal
Enniskillen
Belmullet
Sligo
Ballina
Ballymote
Foxford
Carrick-on-Shannon
Castlebar
Boyle
Westport
Knock
Strokestown
Dromod
Claremorris
Longford
Letterfrack
Roscommon
Clifden
Cong
Galway
Ballinasloe
Athlone
Rossaveel
Athenry
Kilronan
REPUBLIC
Aran Islands
OF
Doolin
IRELAND
Cliffs of Moher
Ennis
Nenagh
Killimer
Thurles
Shannon
Limerick
Tarbert
Limerick Junction
Cashel
Charleville
Tipperary
Tralee
Cahir
Clonmel
Dingle
Kerry
Farranfore
Mallow
Killarney
Midleton
Cahersiveen
Youghal
Kenmare
Blarney
Cork
Cobh
Waterville
Ringaskiddy
Ardgroom
Bantry
Kinsale
Skibbereen

Atlantic
Ocean

To Roscoff & Cherbourg, France

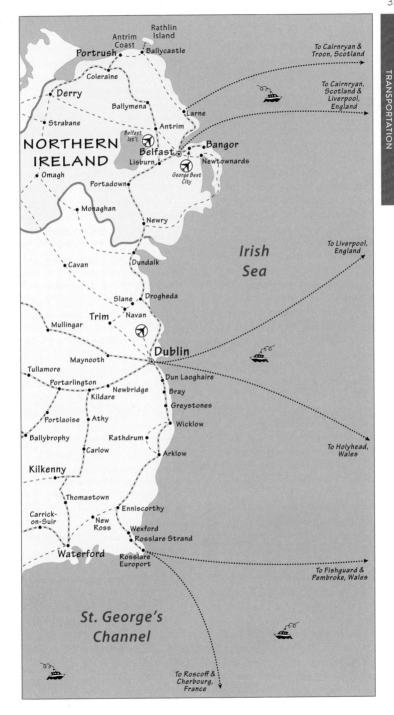

Doolin, take a train to Galway or Ennis and then a bus.

If you're traveling up and down Ireland's west coast, buses are best (or a combination of buses and trains); relying on rail only here is too time-consuming. Note that some rural coach stops are by "request only." This means the coach will drive right on by unless you flag it down by extending your arm straight out, with your palm open.

Bus stations are normally at or near train stations. Before you board the coach, you'll be asked to stow your bag in the large compartment beneath the passenger cabin. Try to get a window seat on the side of the coach where the luggage is unloaded, and be alert whenever the bus stops to take on or let off passengers. Otherwise, someone may—likely accidentally—take your bag. Many bags look alike; decorate yours distinctively. On some Irish buses, sports games are piped throughout the bus; have earplugs handy if you prefer a quieter ride.

Some companies offer **backpacker's bus circuits.** These hop-on, hop-off bus circuits take mostly youth hostelers around the country cheaply and easily, with the assumption that they'll be sleeping in hostels along the way. For example, Paddy Wagon offers three- to six-day tours that can be combined into a longer tour covering Ireland (May-Oct, 5 Beresford Palace, Dublin, tel. 01/823-0822, www.paddywagontours.com). They also offer day tours to the Giant's Causeway, Belfast, Cliffs of Moher, Glendalough, or Kilkenny.

Renting a Car

Travelers from North America are understandably hesitant when they consider driving in Ireland, where you must drive on the left side of the road. The Irish government statistics say that 10 percent of all car accidents on Irish soil involve a foreign tourist. But careful drivers—with the patient support of an alert navigator—

usually get the hang of it by the end of the first day.

Rental companies require you to be at least 21 years old and to have held your license for two years. Drivers under 25 may incur a young-driver surcharge. In the Republic of Ireland, you generally can't rent a car if you're 75 or older (unless you have a note from your doctor), and you'll usually pay extra if you're 70-74. Some companies in Northern Ireland won't rent to anyone over 69. (Note that you can't lease a car in Ireland.)

Research car rentals before you go. It's cheaper to arrange most car rentals from the US. Compare rates among several companies. Most of the major US rental agencies (including Avis, Budget, Enterprise, Hertz, and Thrifty) have offices throughout Ireland. Also consider the two major Europe-based agencies, Europcar and Sixt. It can be cheaper to use a consolidator, such as Auto Europe/Kemwel (www.autoeurope.com) or Europe by Car (www.europebycar.com), which compares rates at several companies to get you the best deal—but because you're working with a middleman, it's especially important to ask in advance about add-on fees and restrictions.

Always read the fine print carefully for add-on charges—such as one-way dropoff fees, airport surcharges, or mandatory insurance policies—that aren't included in the "total price." You may need to query rental agents pointedly to find out your actual cost.

For the best deal, rent by the week with unlimited mileage. To save money on fuel, ask for a diesel car. In midsummer expect to pay at least $300 per week (more for an automatic), not including fuel and minimum insurance, for a basic compact-size car (like a Ford Escort 1.3-liter). With full insurance, the price of the same car goes up about $180 per week ($575 for an automatic).

Almost all rentals are manual by default, so if you need an automatic, you must request one in advance. Be aware that cars with automatic transmission not only cost more to rent but also tend to be larger models, which aren't as maneuverable on narrow, winding roads. Weigh these considerations against the fact that in Ireland you'll be sitting on the right side of the car and shifting with your left hand... while driving on the left side of the road. The floor pedals are in the same locations as in the US, and the gears are still found in the same basic "H" pattern as at home (i.e., first gear, second, etc.).

Big companies have offices in most cities, but small local rental companies can be cheaper. Some companies, such as Auto Europe (www.autoeurope.com) or Dan Dooley (www.dan-dooley.ie), will do longer-term rentals at a slight discount.

Compare pickup costs (downtown can be less expensive than the airport—but isn't recommended in congested urban Dublin), and explore drop-off options. Always check the hours of the location you choose: Many rental offices close from midday Saturday until Monday morning and, in smaller towns, at lunchtime.

When you pick up the rental car, check it thoroughly and make sure any damage is noted on your rental agreement. Find out how your car's lights, turn signals, wipers, radio, and fuel cap function, and know what kind of fuel the car takes (diesel vs. unleaded).

If your trip covers both Ireland and Great Britain (Scotland, England, and Wales), you're better off with two separate car rentals, rather than paying for your car to ride the ferry between the two islands. On an all-Ireland trip, you can drive your rental car from the Republic of Ireland into Northern Ireland, but be aware of drop-off charges (as much as $150-200) if you return it in the North. You'll pay a smaller drop-off charge (as much as $50-100) for picking up the car at one place and dropping it off at another within the same country (even picking up in downtown Dublin and dropping off at Dublin Airport). If you pick up the car in a smaller city, you'll more likely survive your first day on the Irish roads. If you drop the car off early or keep it longer, you'll be credited or charged at a fair, prorated price.

Car Insurance Options

When you rent a car, you're liable for a very high deductible, sometimes equal to the entire value of the car. Limit your financial risk with one of these two options: Buy Collision Damage Waiver (CDW) coverage with a low or zero deductible from the car-rental company, or get coverage through your credit card (more complicated, and few credit cards now offer free coverage in Ireland).

Basic **CDW** includes a very high deductible (typically $1,000-1,500). Though each rental company has its own variation, basic **CDW** costs $10-30 a day (figure roughly 30 percent extra) and reduces your liability, but does not eliminate it. When you reserve or pick up the car, you'll be offered the chance to "buy down" the basic deductible to zero (for an additional $10-30/day; this is sometimes called "super CDW" or "zero-deductible coverage").

If you opt for **credit-card coverage** (and your credit card is one of the few accepted for this type of coverage in Ireland), there's a catch. You'll technically have to decline all coverage offered by the car-rental company, which means they can place a hold on your card (which can be up to the full value of the car). In case of damage, it can be time-consuming to resolve the charges with your credit-card company. Before you decide on this option, quiz your credit-card company about how it works.

For more on car-rental insurance, see www.ricksteves.com/cdw.

Driving

Ireland's new motorways have vastly improved the cross-country driving experience and now link most major cities (Dublin, Belfast, Cork, Waterford, Limerick, and Galway). But the best intimate sites still require you to drive on narrow country lanes.

Note that your US credit and debit cards are unlikely to work at self-service gas pumps and automated parking garages, which use chip-and-PIN credit cards that are not yet the norm in the US. Luckily, the vast majority of Irish gas stations have a live attendant inside who can process your gas purchase (as long as it's not too late at night). The easiest solution is carrying sufficient cash in euros (pounds in the North).

An Irish Automobile Association membership comes with most rentals (www.aaireland.ie). Understand its towing and emergency road-service benefits.

Driving in Ireland is basically wonderful—once you remember to stay on the left and after you've mastered the roundabouts. Don't let a roundabout spook you. After all, you routinely merge into much faster traffic with cars slipping into your blind spot on American highways back home. The traffic in a roundabout has the right-of-way; entering traffic yields (look to your right as you merge). It helps to remember that the driver is always in the center of the road.

Be warned: Every year I get a few emails from traveling readers advising me that, for them, driving in Ireland was a nerve-racking and regrettable mistake. If you want to get a little slack on the roads, try to time your car rental to begin on a Sunday morning when you can acclimate to driving at a mellower pace.

Car travel in Ireland isn't fast. Plan your itinerary estimating an average speed of 40 mph (1 km per minute). Give your itinerary a reality check by finding distances and driving times between towns online (www.google.com/maps or www.viamichelin.com).

Road Rules: Don't drink and drive. The Gardí (police) set up random checkpoints. If you've had more than one pint, you're legally drunk in Ireland.

Be aware of typical European road rules; for example, you may not use a mobile phone while driving (unless you have a hands-free headset), and headlights must be on in poor day lighting. In Ireland, you're not allowed to turn left on a red light unless a sign or signal specifically authorizes it, and on motorways it's illegal to pass drivers on the left. Seat belts are mandatory for all, and kids under 12 or under 1.5 meters tall (about 4 feet, 9 inches) must ride in a child-safety seat.

Ask your car-rental company about these rules, or check the US State Department website (www.travel.state.gov, search for your country in the "Learn about your destination" box, then click on "Travel and Transportation").

Speed Limits: Speed limits are 50 kilometers per hour (roughly 30 miles per hour) in towns, 80 kph (approximately 50 mph) on rural roads (such as R-257,

STOP **AND LEARN THESE ROAD SIGNS**

Speed Limit (km/hr)	Yield	No Passing	End of No Passing Zone
Danger	Intersection	Roundabout Ahead	Expressway
No Through Road	No Entry	Restrictions No Longer Apply	No Stopping
Parking	No Parking	Road Narrows	Peace

Driving in Ireland

Detail map (Aran Islands / Cliffs of Moher area):

Kilronan • Aran Islands • Doolin

Cliffs of Moher — 7m .25h ... Doolin

Doolin — 25m .75h — Ennis

Cliffs of Moher — 30m 1h — Kilrush

Kilrush • Killimer

Killimer — 30m .75h — Tarbert

Tralee

Main map labels:

Bunbeg • Loop: 7.5m • 4h — Derry

Portrush — 40m .75h

Giant's Causeway

Derry — 10m .25h — Portrush

Derry — 60m 1.25h — Bangor

Donegal — 45m 1.25h — Derry

Derry — 35m .75h — Omagh

Omagh — 60m • 1.75h

Bangor — 15m .25h — Belfast

Donegal — 40m 1h — Sligo

Sligo

NORTHERN IRELAND

100m • 2.5h

105m • 2.5h

Westport — 65m • 1.5h — Sligo

Sligo — 130m • 3.25h — Belfast

Belfast

Brú na Bóinne (Newgrange)

Westport — 45m • 1.75h — Letterfrack

Westport — 30m 1h — Cong

Letterfrack — 50m 1.25h — Cong

Cong — 30m 1h — Galway

Rossaveel — 30m 1h — Galway

Aran Islands

IRELAND

Trim — 20m .5h — Brú na Bóinne

Trim — 35m • .75h

Trim — 30m • .5h — Dublin

Galway — 125m • 2.5h — Dublin

See detail map above

Doolin

Galway — 45m • 1.25h

Galway — 50m 1.25h — Shannon

Shannon — 15m .25h — Limerick

Dingle

Loop: 30m 2h

Doolin — 40m 1h — Shannon

Shannon — 30m 1.25h

Shannon — 60m • 1.5h — Limerick

Galway — 125m • 2.75h — Dublin

Limerick — 75m • 1.5h — Dublin

Dublin — 30m • 1h — Glendalough

Kilkenny — 95m 2.25h — Glendalough

Glendalough

Kilkenny — 65m • 1.25h — Waterford

m = miles
h = hours
...... = ferry

Tralee — 130m • 3h — Cashel

Limerick — 40m • 1h — Cashel

Cashel — 30m .75h — Kilkenny

Cashel — 45m 1.25h — Waterford

Waterford — 75m • 2h — Wexford

Waterford — 35m • 1h — Wexford

Killarney — 40m 1.5h — Tralee

Killarney — 20m .5h — Kenmare

Killarney — 20m 1h — Kenmare

Kenmare — 60m • 1.25h — Blarney

Blarney

Loop: 100m • 4.5h

Cork

Cork — 90m • 2.5h — Kinsale

Kinsale — 15m .5h

Waterford — 10m .25h — Rosslare

Wexford • Rosslare

Cobh

Note: Your times may vary based on traffic, construction, and sheep on road.

R-600, etc.), 100 kph (about 60 mph) on national roads (N-8, N-30, etc.), and 120 kph (roughly 75 mph) on motorways (M-1, M-50, etc.). Note that road-surveillance cameras strictly enforce speed limits. Any driver (including foreigners renting cars) photographed speeding will get a nasty bill in the mail. (Cameras—you'll see the foreboding gray boxes—flash on your rear license plate in order not to invade the privacy of anyone sharing the front seat with someone they shouldn't be with.)

Signage: Road signs can be confusing, too little, and too late. There are three main kinds of directional signs: (1) Green signs are found on major national routes and give distances in kilometers; (2) white signs with black lettering are posted on regional roads; and (3) blue signs are used on motorways (freeways). Brown informational signs alert drivers to sights, lodging, and tourist offices.

Navigation Maps and Apps: Plan to buy a good map. The Complete Road Atlas of Ireland by Ordnance Survey (€10, handy ring-binder style) is the best Irish road map. The tourist-oriented Collins Touring maps do a good job of highlighting the many roadside attractions you might otherwise drive right past.

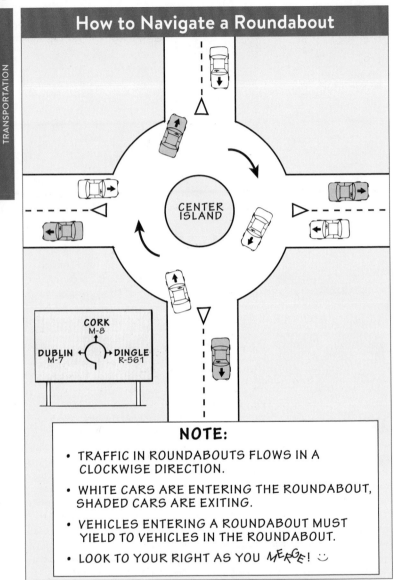

When driving in Europe, you can use the mapping app on your phone as long as you have an international data plan. Without a data plan (or to conserve data), you can rely on offline maps (via a mapping app or by downloading Google maps). As an alternative, you could rent a GPS device or bring your own GPS device from home (but you'll need to buy and download European maps before your trip).

A number of well-designed offline mapping apps allow you much of the convenience of online maps without any costly data demands. City Maps 2Go is popular; OffMaps and Navfree also offer good, zoomable offline maps—similar to Google Maps—for much of Europe.

Even if you have a full complement of maps and apps, be sure to try this at least once: Ask locals for directions—it's almost always a rich experience and a fast way to meet the Irish.

Countryside Driving: When it comes to narrow rural roads, adjust your perceptions of personal space. It's not "my side of the road" or "your side of the road." It's just "the road"—and it's shared as a cooperative adventure.

Locals are usually courteous, pulling over against a hedgerow and blinking their headlights for you to pass while they wait. Return the favor when you are closer to a wide spot in the road than they are. Buses always have the right of way on narrow rural roads, so you'll need to back up to give way.

Motorways (Freeways) and Tolls: The shortest distance between any two points is usually the motorway (freeway). Miss a motorway exit and you can lose 30 minutes.

Tolls on the M-50 ring road surrounding Dublin are paid electronically with an eFlow pass; confirm that your rental car has a pass installed if you'll be driving near Dublin. Other Irish motorways, linking smaller cities farther from Dublin, may carry tolls (under €3), which must be paid as you pass through (easiest with cash).

Fuel: In Northern Ireland, unleaded costs about £1.35 per liter; in the Republic, unleaded is about €1.55 per liter. Diesel fuel pumps are black in Ireland.

Parking: Parking is confusing. One yellow line marked on the pavement means no parking Monday through Saturday during business hours. Double yellow lines mean no parking at any time. Broken yellow lines mean short stops are OK, but you should always look for explicit signs or ask a passerby.

Even in small towns, rather than fight it, I just pull into the most central parking

lot I can find. As for street parking, signs along the street will state whether pay-and-display or parking disk laws are in effect for that area. The modern pay-and-display machines are solar-powered and placed regularly along the street (about six feet tall, look for blue circle with white letter P). I keep some extra coins in the ashtray for these machines (no change given for large coins). The use of parking disks is less common these days, but if you need disks, they're sold at nearby shops. You buy one disk for each hour you want to stay. Scratch off the time you arrived on the disk and put it on your dashboard.

Flights

The best comparison search engine for both international and intra-European flights is www.kayak.com. For inexpensive flights within Europe, try www.skyscanner.com or www.hipmunk.com; for inexpensive international flights, try www.vayama.com.

Flying to Europe: Start looking for international flights 4-5 months before your trip, especially for peak-season travel. Off-season tickets can be purchased a month or so in advance. Depending on your itinerary, it can be efficient to fly into one city and out of another.

Flying Within Europe: If you're considering a train ride that's more than five hours long, a flight may save you both time and money. When comparing your options, factor in the time it takes to get to the airport and how early you'll need to arrive to check in.

These days you can fly within Europe on major airlines affordably for around $100 a flight. If you go instead with a budget airline such as easyJet or Ryanair, be aware of the potential drawbacks and restrictions: nonrefundable and non-changeable tickets, minimal or non-existent customer service, pricey and time-consuming treks to secondary airports, and stingy baggage allowances

Begin Your Trip at www.RickSteves.com

My mobile-friendly **website** is *the* place to explore Europe. You'll find thousands of fun articles, videos, photos, and radio interviews organized by country; a wealth of money-saving tips for planning your dream trip; monthly travel news dispatches; my travel talks and travel blog; my latest guidebook updates (www.ricksteves.com/update); and my free Rick Steves Audio Europe app. You can also follow me on Facebook and Twitter.

Our **Travel Forum** is an immense, yet well-groomed collection of message boards, where our travel-savvy community answers questions and shares their personal travel experiences—and our well-traveled staff chimes in when they can be helpful (www.ricksteves.com/forums).

Our **online Travel Store** offers travel bags and accessories that I've designed specifically to help you travel smarter and lighter. These include my popular bags (rolling carry-on and backpack versions, which I helped design...and live out of four months a year), money belts, totes, toiletries kits, adapters, other accessories, and a wide selection of guidebooks and planning maps.

Choosing the right **rail pass** for your trip—amid hundreds of options—can drive you nutty. Our website will help you find the perfect fit for your itinerary and your budget: We offer easy, one-stop shopping for rail passes, seat reservations, and point-to-point tickets.

Want to travel with greater efficiency and less stress? We organize **tours** with more than three dozen itineraries and more than 1,000 departures, reaching the best destinations in this book...and beyond. We offer 8- and 14-day Ireland tours, as well as multiple tours in nearby England, Wales, and Scotland. You'll enjoy great guides, a fun bunch of travel partners (with small groups of 24 to 28 travelers), and plenty of room to spread out in a big, comfy bus when touring between towns. You'll find European adventures to fit every vacation length. For all the details, and to get our Tour Catalog and a free Rick Steves Tour Experience DVD (filmed on location during an actual tour), visit www.ricksteves.com or call us at 425/608-4217.

with steep overage fees. If you've got lots of luggage, a cheap flight can quickly become a bad deal. To avoid unpleasant surprises, read the small print before you book.

Flying to the US: Because security is extra tight for flights to the US, be sure to give yourself plenty of time at the airport. It's also important to charge your electronic devices before you board because security checks may require you to turn them on (see www.tsa.gov for the latest rules).

RESOURCES FROM RICK STEVES

Rick Steves Best of Ireland is one of many books in my series on European travel, which includes country guidebooks, city guidebooks (London, Rome, Florence, Paris, etc.), Snapshot guides (excerpted chapters from my country guides), Pocket Guides (full-color little books on big cities), and my budget-travel skills handbook, *Rick Steves Europe Through the Back Door*. Most of my titles are available as ebooks. My foreign phrase books are practical and budget-oriented. A more

Vide *Steves' Eur* bottom with To watch full ep the see www.ricksteves your travel I.Q. with vi popular classes (includin travel skills, packing smart, for travelers, travel as a politica individual talks covering most Eur countries), see www.ricksteves.com/travel-talks.

Audio: My weekly public radio show, *Travel with Rick Steves*, features interviews with travel experts from around the world. A com-

plete archive of 10 years of programs (over 400 in all) is available in the radio section of www.ricksteves.com/radio. Most of this audio content is available for free through my **Rick Steves Audio Europe** app (see page 22).

...ALS

...us national holidays (when banks
...d a festival, verify its dates by
...overireland.com).

HOLIDAYS

This list includes ...d, Dublin (Irish music and culture festival,
and many sight... siebartrad.com)
checking the ...ick's Day (parades, drunkenness, 4-day festival in
...blin, www.stpatricksday.ie)

	Good Friday
...28	Easter Sunday and Monday
...n–early April	International Pan Celtic Festival, Carlow (www.panceltic.ie)
May 2	Labor Day; Early May Bank Holiday, Ireland and UK
May 30	Spring Bank Holiday, UK
June 6	June Holiday, Ireland
Mid–June	Bloomsday, Dublin (James Joyce festival, www.jamesjoyce.ie)
Late June	Patrún Festival, Kilronan (currach boat races)
Late June	St. John's Eve Bonfire Night, Kilronan
July 12	Battle of the Boyne anniversary, Northern Ireland (Protestant marches, protests)
Mid- to late July	Galway Arts Festival
Late July–early Aug	Galway Horse Races (www.galwayraces.com)
Aug 1	August Bank Holiday, Ireland
Early Aug	Dingle Horse Races (www.dingleraces.ie)
Early–mid-Aug	Dingle Regatta (boat races)
Early–mid-Aug	Puck Fair, Killorglin, Kerry ("Ireland's Oldest Fair" and drink-fest, www.puckfair.ie)
Early–mid-Aug	Féile an Phobail, West Belfast (Irish cultural festival, www.feilebelfast.com)
Mid-Aug	Kenmare Fair (www.kenmare.com)
Aug 29	Late Summer Bank Holiday, UK only
Late Aug	Rose of Tralee International Festival (http://roseoftralee.ie)
Late Aug–early Sept	Blessing of the Boats, Dingle (maritime festival)
Mid-Sept	Galway Races (www.galwayraces.com)
Late Sept	Galway Oyster Festival (www.galwayoysterfest.com)
Oct 31	October Bank Holiday, Ireland
Late Oct	Galway Races (www.galwayraces.com)
Dec 25	Christmas holiday, Ireland and UK
Dec 26	St. Stephen's Day, Ireland; Boxing Day, UK
Dec 31	New Year's Eve

CONVERSIONS AND CLIMATE

Numbers and Stumblers

- Europeans write a few of their numbers differently than we do. 1= 1, 4 = 4, 7 = 7.
- In Europe, dates appear as day/month/year. Christmas is always 25/12.
- Commas are decimal points and decimals are commas. A dollar and a half is $1,50, and one thousand is 1.000.
- When counting with fingers, start with your thumb. If you hold up your first finger to request one item, you'll probably get two.
- What Americans call the second floor of a building is the first floor in Europe.
- On escalators and moving sidewalks, Europeans keep the left "lane" open for passing. Keep to the right.

Clothing and Shoe Sizes

Shoppers can use these US-to-European comparisons as guidelines.

Women: For clothing or shoe sizes, add 30 (US shirt size 10 = European size 40; US shoe size 8 = European size 38-39).

Men: For shirts, multiply by 2 and add about 8 (US size 15 = European size 38). For jackets and suits, add 10. For shoes, add 32-34.

Children: For clothing, subtract 1-2 sizes for small children and subtract 4 for juniors. For shoes up to size 13, add 16-18, and for sizes 1 and up, add 30-32.

Metric Conversions

A **kilogram** equals 1,000 grams and about 2.2 pounds. One hundred **grams** (a common unit of sale at markets) is about a quarter-pound.

One **liter** is about a quart, or almost four to a gallon.

A **kilometer** is six-tenths of a mile. To convert kilometers to miles, cut the kilometers in half and add back 10 percent of the original (120 km: 60 + 12 = 72 miles). One **meter** is 39 inches.

Using the **Celsius** scale, 0°C equals 32°F. To roughly convert Celsius to Fahrenheit, double the number and add 30. For weather, 28°C is 82°F—perfect. For health, 37°C is just right. At a launderette, 30°C is cold, 40°C is warm (default setting), and 60°C is hot.

Ireland's Climate

First line, average daily high; second line, average daily low; third line, average days without rain. For worldwide weather statistics, check www.wunderground.com.

Dublin

J	F	M	A	M	J	J	A	S	O	N	D
46°	47°	51°	55°	60°	65°	67°	67°	63°	57°	51°	47°
34°	35°	37°	39°	43°	48°	52°	51°	48°	43°	39°	37°
18	18	21	19	21	19	18	19	18	20	18	17

Packing Checklist

Clothing

- ❑ 5 shirts: long- & short-sleeve
- ❑ 2 pairs pants or skirt
- ❑ 1 pair shorts or capris
- ❑ 5 pairs underwear & socks
- ❑ 1 pair walking shoes
- ❑ Sweater or fleece top
- ❑ Rainproof jacket with hood
- ❑ Tie or scarf
- ❑ Swimsuit
- ❑ Sleepwear

Money

- ❑ Debit card
- ❑ Credit card(s)
- ❑ Hard cash ($20 bills)
- ❑ Money belt or neck wallet

Documents & Travel Info

- ❑ Passport
- ❑ Airline reservations
- ❑ Rail pass/train reservations
- ❑ Car-rental voucher
- ❑ Driver's license
- ❑ Student ID, hostel card, etc.
- ❑ Photocopies of all the above
- ❑ Hotel confirmations
- ❑ Insurance details
- ❑ Guidebooks & maps
- ❑ Notepad & pen
- ❑ Journal

Toiletries Kit

- ❑ Toiletries
- ❑ Medicines & vitamins
- ❑ First-aid kit
- ❑ Glasses/contacts/sunglasses (with prescriptions)
- ❑ Earplugs
- ❑ Packet of tissues (for WC)

Miscellaneous

- ❑ Daypack
- ❑ Sealable plastic baggies
- ❑ Laundry soap
- ❑ Clothesline
- ❑ Sewing kit
- ❑ Travel alarm/watch

Electronics

- ❑ Smartphone or mobile phone
- ❑ Camera & related gear
- ❑ Tablet/ereader/media player
- ❑ Laptop & flash drive
- ❑ Earbuds or headphones
- ❑ Chargers
- ❑ Plug adapters

Optional Extras

- ❑ Flipflops or slippers
- ❑ Mini-umbrella or poncho
- ❑ Travel hairdryer
- ❑ Belt
- ❑ Hat (for sun or cold)
- ❑ Picnic supplies
- ❑ Water bottle
- ❑ Fold-up tote bag
- ❑ Small flashlight
- ❑ Small binoculars
- ❑ Small towel or washcloth
- ❑ Inflatable pillow
- ❑ Tiny lock
- ❑ Address list (to mail postcards)
- ❑ Postcards/photos from home
- ❑ Extra passport photos
- ❑ Good book

INDEX

MAP INDEX

Start your trip at

Our website enhances this book and turns

Explore Europe

At ricksteves.com you can browse through thousands of articles, videos, photos and radio interviews, plus find a wealth of money-saving travel tips for planning your dream trip. And with our mobile-friendly website, you can easily access all this great travel information anywhere you go.

TV Shows

Preview the places you'll visit by watching entire half-hour episodes of Rick Steves' Europe (choose from all 100 shows) on-demand, for free.

ricksteves.com

your travel dreams into affordable reality

Radio Interviews

Enjoy ready access to Rick's vast library of radio interviews covering travel tips and cultural insights that relate specifically to your Europe travel plans.

Travel Forums

Learn, ask, share! Our online community of savvy travelers is a great resource for first-time travelers to Europe, as well as seasoned pros. You'll find forums on each country, plus travel tips and restaurant/hotel reviews. You can even ask one of our well-traveled staff to chime in with an opinion.

Travel News

Subscribe to our free Travel News e-newsletter, and get monthly updates from Rick on what's happening in Europe.

Audio Europe™

Rick's Free Travel App

Get your FREE Rick Steves Audio Europe™ app to enjoy…

- Dozens of self-guided tours of Europe's top museums, sights and historic walks
- Hundreds of tracks filled with cultural insights and sightseeing tips from Rick's radio interviews
- All organized into handy geographic playlists
- For Apple and Android

With Rick whispering in your ear, Europe gets even better.

Find out more at ricksteves.com

Pack Light and Right

Gear up for your next adventure at ricksteves.com

Light Luggage

Pack light and right with Rick Steves' affordable, custom-designed rolling carry-on bags, backpacks, day packs and shoulder bags.

Accessories

From packing cubes to moneybelts and beyond, Rick has personally selected the travel goodies that will help your trip go smoother.

Rick Steves has

Save time and energy

This guidebook is your independent-travel toolkit. But for all it delivers, it's still up to you to devote the time and energy it takes to manage the preparation and logistics that are essential for a happy trip. If that's a hassle, there's a solution.

Rick Steves Tours

A Rick Steves tour takes you to Europe's most

great tours, too!

with minimum stress

interesting places with great guides and small groups of 28 or less. We follow Rick's favorite itineraries, ride in comfy buses, stay in family-run hotels, and bring you intimately close to the Europe you've traveled so far to see. Most importantly, we take away the logistical headaches so you can focus on the fun.

nearly half of them repeat customers—along with us on four dozen different itineraries, from Ireland to Italy to Istanbul. Is a Rick Steves tour the right fit for your travel dreams? Find out at ricksteves.com, where you can also get Rick's latest tour catalog and free Tour Experience DVD.

Europe is best experienced with happy travel partners. We hope you can join us.

Join the fun

This year we'll take 25,000 free-spirited travelers—

See our itineraries at ricksteves.com

Rick Steves

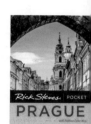

BEST OF GUIDES

Best of France
Best of Germany
Best of Ireland
Best of Italy
Best of Spain

EUROPE GUIDES

Best of Europe
Eastern Europe
Europe Through the Back Door
Mediterranean Cruise Ports
Northern European Cruise Ports

COUNTRY GUIDES

Croatia & Slovenia
England
France
Germany
Great Britain
Ireland
Italy
Portugal
Scandinavia
Scotland
Spain
Switzerland

CITY & REGIONAL GUIDES

Amsterdam & the Netherlands
Belgium: Bruges, Brussels, Antwerp & Ghent
Barcelona
Budapest
Florence & Tuscany
Greece: Athens & the Peloponnese
Istanbul
London
Paris
Prague & the Czech Republic
Provence & the French Riviera
Rome
Venice
Vienna, Salzburg & Tirol

SNAPSHOT GUIDES

Basque Country: Spain & France
Berlin
Copenhagen & the Best of Denmark
Dublin
Dubrovnik
Edinburgh
Hill Towns of Central Italy
Italy's Cinque Terre
Krakow, Warsaw & Gdansk
Lisbon

Maximize your travel skills with a good guidebook.

RickSteves.com ● ● @RickSteves

PHOTO CREDITS

Avalon Travel
An imprint of Perseus Books
A division of Hachette Book Group
1700 Fourth Street
Berkeley, CA 94710

Text © 2016 by Rick Steves' Europe, Inc.

Maps © 2016 by Rick Steves' Europe, Inc. All rights reserved.

Printed in Canada by Friesens

First printing June 2016

ISBN 978-1-63121-319-9
ISSN 2471-0954

For the latest on Rick's lectures, guidebooks, tours, public radio show, and public television series, contact Rick Steves' Europe, 130 Fourth Avenue North, Edmonds, WA 98020, 425/771-8303, www.ricksteves.com, rick@ricksteves.com.

RICK STEVES' EUROPE
Special Publications Manager: Risa Laib
Managing Editor: Jennifer Madison Davis
Project Editor: Suzanne Kotz
Editorial & Production Assistant: Jessica Shaw
Graphic Content Director: Sandra Hundacker
Maps & Graphics: David C. Hoerlein, Mary Rostad

AVALON TRAVEL
Editorial Director: Kevin McLain
Senior Editor and Series Manager: Madhu Prasher
Editor: Jamie Andrade
Associate Editor: Sierra Machado
Copy Editor: Naomi Adler Dancis
Proofreader: Kelly Lydick
Indexer: Stephen Callahan
Interior Design & Layout: McGuire Barber Design
Cover Design: Kimberly Glyder Design
Maps & Graphics: Kat Bennett, Kathryn Osgood

PHOTO CREDITS
Front Cover: Top left: Dublin Castle © Matthew Ragen/123rf.com; middle: Temple Bar in Dublin © Pijvv/Dreamstime.com; right: sheep © Andreas Ludwig/123rf.com. Bottom: Carrick-a-Rede Rope Bridge, County Antrim, Northern Ireland © Richard Semik/123rf.com
Back Cover: Left: Blarney Castle in County Cork © SomethingIrish/Dreamstime.com; middle: Ha' Penny Bridge, Liffey River in Dublin © Pavel Losevsky/123rf.com; right: Cliffs of Moher in County Clare © Lukasz Janyst/123rf.com

More for your trip!
Maximize the experience with Rick Steves as your guide

Guidebooks
London and Britain guides make side-trips smooth and affordable

Planning Maps
Use the map that's in sync with your guidebook

Rick's TV Shows
Preview where you're going with 4 shows on Ireland

Free! Rick's Audio Europe™ App
Hear Ireland travel tips from Rick's radio shows

Small Group Tours
Take a lively Rick Steves tour through Ireland

For all the details, visit ricksteves.com